RACING & FOOTB
FOOTBALL
Guide 2005–2006

Edited by Sean Gollogly and Paul Charlton

Contributors: Stuart Carruthers, Paul Charlton, Steve Cook, Alex Deacon, James Goldman, Chris Mann, Mirio Mella, Max Oram, Andy Smith, James Smith, Nigel Speight.

Published in 2005 by Raceform,
Compton, Newbury, Berkshire RG20 6NL
Raceform Ltd is a wholly-owned subsidiary of Trinity Mirror plc

A catalogue record for this book is available from the
British Library.

ISBN 1-904317-89-8

Printed by in Great Britain by William Clowes Ltd, Beccles, Suffolk

Cover photo: Chelsea's John Terry of Chelsea battles it out with
Stan Lazaridis of Birmingham City in the 1-1 draw
at Stamford Bridge in April 2005

Sponsored by Stan James

Contents

Sponsored by Stan James

Editor's introduction

WOW! Liverpool certainly gave us a season to remember!

They might have been one of the most frustrating sides around from a betting point of view, punching above their weight in Europe whie faltering at every turn in the Premiership, but only the most die-hard Evertonian would begrudge them their stunning Champions League win.

But the fact they were such big underdogs, having spent tens of millions of pounds in recent years shows how far the financial aspect of the game has spiralled out of control.

As clubs like Wrexham are forced into administration, the gulf between rich and poor has never been wider.

In the Premiership, there are only three serious contenders for the title and none of them are short of a bob or two.

Of course, Chelsea are the poster boys for football's brand of global capitalism and having already become the team to beat, are in the process of assuming the mantle of the team everybody loves to hate - perhaps even more so than when Ken Bates was in charge.

But that doesn't mean that as punters, we can't be friends with Chelsea. Alex Deacon and Figaro both rate the Blues good things for the title at around evens or better, while Figaro's brilliant analysis of the half-time/full-time markets (see page 12) describes a way to back the Blues week in, week out at fancy prices.

And that's not to say the top flight is totally predictable. The *Outlook Index*, our unique and exclusive ratings system, shows that there is little to choose between the Premiership's also-rans - Everton were last season's exemplars, starting as one of the favourites for relegation but finishing in a Champions League spot.

That said, the financial hardship faced by virtually every lower division club has levelled the playing field outside the top flight, and meant that big-priced winners were a feature of last season.

The general failure of the relegated clubs in the Championship highlighted the fact that you need more than a few puffed-up ex-Premiership 'names' to make the grade in this division.

Likewise, the big-priced victories of Luton and Yeovil in the two divisions below suggest that a more in-depth approach to football betting is required in this sphere.

As the saying goes, 'knowledge is power' and in betting terms it's never been more important for football punters to arm themselves with as much information as they can about the markets they play in.

This Annual is jam-packed with comprehensive analysis and data. Whatever you fancy on the punting menu you'll find it's catered for here, from the Wessex Stadium to the San Siro.

We give you our unique high-low *Outlook Form* ratings as well as our *Outlook Index* ratings for England, the SPL and the four major European leagues, allowing comparisons across divisions and national leagues.

Our unique *Index*-based features provide the optimum back or lay exchange prices that allow readers to exploit the hysterical, foolhardy and often just plain wrong odds that are a daily feature of this burgeoning football betting medium.

As in Figaro's Analysis, the *Racing & Football Outlook's* year was unquestionably a game of two halves, with our slick new redesign hitting the shelves in February. But this was certainly not a question of style over substance.

The new-look RFO saw us not only increase the size of the paper, but also introduce a number of new features and expand on some old favourites to bring our readers an unrivalled weekly football betting service.

It seems that you also recognised this, as four record-breaking editions proved.

With unbeatable match stats, comprehensive fixtures and form and expert analyisis every week, you - the reader - could not be better equipped to survive in the punting jungle.

Put simply, we will give you the tools and the advice that should revolutionise your punting, taking the guesswork and bias out of your selections.

JULY
29 Start of French Le Championnat

AUGUST
2 UEFA Champions League Second Qualifying Round, second-legs
3 UEFA Intertoto Cup Semi Final, second-legs
5 Start of the German Bundesliga
6 Start of the Coca-Cola Football League
  Start of the Bell's Scottish Football League
7 English FA Community Shield
  Arsenal v Chelsea
9 UEFA Champions League Third Qualifying Round, first-legs
  UEFA Intertoto Cup Finals, first-legs
  CIS Insurance Cup First Round
11 UEFA Cup Second Qualifying Round, first-legs
13 Start of the FA Barclaycard Premier League
23 UEFA Champions League Third Qualifying Round, second-legs
  UEFA Intertoto Cup Finals, second-legs
  CIS Insurance Cup Second Round
24 Carling Cup First Round
25 UEFA Cup Second Qualifying Round, second-legs
26 UEFA Super Cup
  CSKA Moscow v Liverpool
27 FA Cup Preliminary Round
28 Start of Spanish La Liga
30 Bell's Challenge Cup Second round

SEPTEMBER
3 World Cup Qualifiers
  Northern Ireland v Azerbaijan
  Scotland v Italy
  Wales v England
7 World Cup Qualifiers
  Northern Ireland v England
  Norway v Scotland
  Republic of Ireland v France
  Poland v Wales
10 FA Cup First Qualifying Round
13 UEFA Champions League Group stage, match day one
  Bell's Challenge Cup Third Round
14 UEFA Champions League Group stage, match day one
15 UEFA Cup First round, first-legs
20 CIS Insurance cup Third Round
21 Carling Cup Second Round
24 FA Cup Second Qualifying Round
27 UEFA Champions League Group stage, match day two
  Bell's Challenge Cup Semi-Finals
28 UEFA Champions League Group stage, match day two
29 UEFA Cup First Round, second-legs

OCTOBER

8 FA Cup Third Qualifying Round
World Cup Qualifiers
   Cyprus v Republic of Ireland
   England v Austria
   Northern Ireland v Wales
   Scotland v Belarus
12 World Cup Qualifiers
   Austria v Northern Ireland
   England v Poland
   Republic of Ireland v Switzerland
   Slovenia v Scotland
   Wales v Azerbaijan
17 LDV Vans Trophy First Round
18 UEFA Champions League Group stage, match day three
19 UEFA Champions League Group stage, match day three
20 UEFA Cup Group stage, match day one
22 FA Cup Fourth Qualifying Round
26 Carling Cup Third Round

NOVEMBER

1 UEFA Champions League Group stage, match day four
2 UEFA Champions League Group stage, match day four
3 UEFA Cup Group stage, match day two
5 FA Cup First Round
6 Bell's Challenge Cup Final
8 CIS Insurance Cup Fourth Round
19 Tennent's Scottish Cup First Round
21 LDV Vans Trophy Second Round
22 UEFA Champions League Group stage, match day five
23 UEFA Champions League Group stage, match day five
24 UEFA Cup Group stage, match day three
30 Carling Cup Fourth Round
   UEFA Cup Group stage, match day four

DECEMBER

1 UEFA Cup Group stage, match day four
3 FA Cup Second Round
6 UEFA Champions League Group stage, match day six
7 UEFA Champions League Group stage, match day six
10 Tennent's Scottish Cup Second Round
14 UEFA Cup Group stage, match day five
15 UEFA Cup Group stage, match day five
19 LDV Vans Trophy Area Quarter-Finals
21 Carling Cup Fifth Round

JANUARY

7 FA Cup Third Round
   Tennent's Scottish Cup Third Round
11 Carling Cup Semi-Finals, first-legs

23 LDV Vans Trophy Area Semi-Finals
25 Carling Cup Semi-Finals, second-legs
28 FA Cup Fourth Round

FEBRUARY

1 CIS Insurance Cup Semi-Finals
4 Tennent's Scottish Cup Fourth Round
15 UEFA Cup First knockout round, first-legs
16 UEFA Cup First knockout round, first-legs
18 FA Cup Fifth Round
20 LDV Vans Trophy Area Finals, first-legs
21 UEFA Champions League First knockout round, first-legs
22 UEFA Champions League First knockout round, first-legs
23 UEFA Cup First knockout round, second-legs
25 Tennent's Scottish Cup Quarter-Finals
26 Carling Cup Final

MARCH

6 LDV Vans Trophy Area Finals, second-legs
7 UEFA Champions League First knockout round, second-legs
8 UEFA Champions League First knockout round, second-legs
9 UEFA Cup Second knockout round, first-legs
15 UEFA Cup Second knockout round, second-legs
16 UEFA Cup Second knockout round, second-legs
19 CIS Insurance Cup Final
22 FA Cup Sixth Round
28 UEFA Champions League Quarter-Finals, first-legs
29 UEFA Champions League Quarter-Finals, first-legs
30 UEFA Cup Quarter-Finals, first-legs

APRIL

1 Tennent's Scottish Cup Semi-Finals
2 LDV Vans Trophy Final
  Tennent's Scottish Cup Semi-Finals
4 UEFA Champions League Quarter-Finals, second-legs
5 UEFA Champions League Quarter-Finals, second-legs
6 UEFA Cup Quarter-Finals, second-legs
18 UEFA Champions League Semi-Finals, first-legs
19 UEFA Champions League Semi-Finals, first-legs
20 UEFA Cup Semi Finals, first-legs
22 FA Cup Semi-Finals
25 UEFA Champions League Semi-Finals, second-legs
26 UEFA Champions League Semi-Finals, second-legs
27 UEFA Cup Semi-Finals, second-legs

MAY

10 UEFA Cup Final
13 FA Cup Final
17 UEFA Champions League Final
27 Tennent's Scottish Cup Final

JUNE

9 World Cup Finals until 9 July

SCHEDULED LIVE MATCHES

LIVE ON SKY SPORTS

August

Sat 6	Sheffield Utd v Leicester City	ko 12.45 pm	Championship
	Southampton v Wolves	ko 5.15 pm	Championship
Sun 7	Leeds Utd v Millwall	ko 12.15 pm	Championship
	Arsenal v Chelsea	ko 3.00 pm	Community Shield
Mon 8			
	Preston North End v Derby County	ko 7.45 pm	Championship
Fri 12			
	Cardiff City v Watford	ko 7.45 pm	Championship
Sat 13	Everton v Manchester Utd	ko 12.45 pm*	Premiership
	Middlesbrough v Liverpool	ko 5.15 pm*	Premiership
Sun 14	Arsenal v Newcastle Utd	ko 1.30 pm	Premiership
	Wigan Athletic v Chelsea	ko 4.00pm	Premiership
Mon 15	Port Vale v Brentford		ko 7.45 pm
League 1			
Wed 17	Republic of Ireland v Italy	ko 7.30 pm	Int Friendly
	Denmark v England	ko 7.00pm	Int Friendly
	Wales v Slovenia	ko 7.45 pm	Int Friendly
Sat 20	Manchester Utd v Aston Villa	ko 12.45 pm*	Premiership
	Birmingham city v Manchester City	ko 5.15 pm*	Premiership
Sun 21	Bolton Wanderers v Everton	ko 1.30 pm	Premiership
	Chelsea v Arsenal	ko 4.00 pm	Premiership
Mon 22	Southend Utd v Southampton	ko 8.00 pm	Carling Cup
Fri 26	QPR v Sheffield Wednesday	ko 7.45 pm	Championship
Sat 27	WBA v Birmingham City	ko 12.15 pm*	Premiership
	Watford v Reading	ko 5.15 pm	Championship
Sun 28	Middlesbrough v Charlton Athletic	ko 1.30 pm	Premiership
	Newcastle Utd v Manchester Utd	ko 4.00 pm	Premiership
Mon 29	Ipswich Town v Preston North End	ko TBC	Championship
	Coventry City v Southampton	ko TBC	Championship
Tues 30	Leeds Utd v Crystal Palace	ko 7.45 pm	Championship

September

Sat 3	Bristol City v Colchester Utd	ko 12.05 pm	League 1
	Wales v England	ko 3.00pm	World Cup Qualifier
	Scotland v Italy	ko 5.30 pm	World Cup Qualifier
Wed 7	Republic of Ireland v France	ko 7.45 pm	World Cup Qualifier
	Poland v Wales	ko 7.30 pm	World Cup Qualifier
Sat 10	Norwich City v Plymouth Argyle	ko 12.45 pm	Premiership
	Middlesbrough v Arsenal	ko 5.15 pm*	Premiership
Sun 11	Crewe Alexandra v Derby County	ko 1.30 pm	Championship
	Bolton W v Blackburn Rovers	ko 4.00 pm	Premiership
Mon 12	West Ham Utd v Aston Villa	ko 8.00 pm	Premiership
Fri 16	Preston North End v Stoke City	ko 7.45 pm	Championship
Sat 17	Hull v Luton Town	ko 12.45 pm	Championship
	Aston Villa v Tottenham Hotspur	ko 5.15 pm*	Premiership
Sun 18	Liverpool v Manchester Utd	ko 12.00 noon	Premiership
	Blackburn Rovers v Newcastle Utd	ko 2.00 pm*	Premiership
	Derby County v Southampton	ko 4.00 pm	Championship
Mon 19	Arsenal v Everton	ko 8.00 pm	Premiership
Fri 23	Luton Town v Sheffield Wednesday	ko 7.45 pm	Championship
Sat 24	Birmingham City v Liverpool	ko 12.45 pm*	Premiership
	Bolton W v Portsmouth	ko 5.15 pm*	Premiership
Sun 25	Middlesbrough v Sunderland	ko 4.00 pm	Premiership
Mon 26	Tottenham Hotspur v Fulham	ko 8.00 pm	Premiership

Fri 30	Wolves v Burnley	ko 7.45 pm	Championship

October

Sat 1	Manchester City v Everton	ko 12.45 pm*	Premiership
	Sunderland v West Ham Utd	ko 5.15 pm*	Premiership
Sun 2	Arsenal v Birmingham City	ko 1.30 pm	Premiership
	Liverpool v Chelsea ko 4.00 pm	Premiership	
Mon 3	QPR v Crystal Palace	ko 7.45 pm	Championship
Sat 8	Scotland v Belarus	TBC	World Cup Qualifier
	England v Austria (BBC)	TBC	World Cup Qualifier
Sun 9	Southend Utd v Nottingham Forest	ko 4.00 pm	League 1
Mon 10	Bradford City v Huddersfield Town	ko 7.45 pm	League 1
Wed 12	Republic of Ireland v Switzerland	TBC	World Cup Qualifier
	Wales v Azerbaijan	TBC	World Cup Qualifier
	Austria v Northern Ireland	TBC	World Cup Qualifier
	England v Poland (BBC)	TBC	World Cup Qualifier
Sat 15	Wigan Athletic v Newcastle Utd	ko 12.45 pm*	Premiership
	Middlesbrough v Portsmouth	ko 5.15 pm	Premiership
Sun 16	Reading v Ipswich Town	ko 1.30 pm	Championship
	Manchester City v West Ham Utd	ko 4.00 pm	Premiership
Mon 17	Charlton Athletic v Fulham	ko 8.00 pm	Premiership
Fri 21	Leeds Utd v Sheffield Utd	ko 7.45 pm	Championship
Sat 22	Blackburn R v Birmingham City	ko 12.45 pm	Premiership
	Portsmouth v Charlton Athletic	ko 5.15 pm*	Premiership
Sun 23	Newcastle Utd v Sunderland	ko 1.30 pm*	Premiership
	Everton v Chelsea	ko 4.00 pm	Premiership
Fri 28	Burnley v Hull City	ko 7.45 pm	Championship
Sat 29	Wigan Athletic v Fulham	ko 12.45 pm*	Premiership
	Middlesbrough v Manchester Utd	ko 5.15 pm*	Premiership
Sun 30	Plymouth Argyle v Millwall	ko 1.30 pm	Championship
	WBA v Newcastle Utd	ko 4.00 pm	Premiership
Mon 31	Manchester City v Aston Villa	ko 8.00 pm	Premiership

November

Sat 5	Aston Villa v Liverpool	ko 12.45 pm*	Premiership
	Portsmouth v Wigan Athletic	ko 5.15 pm	Premiership
Sun 6	Manchester Utd v Chelsea	ko 4.00 pm	Premiership
Mon 7	Bolton W v Tottenham Hotspur	ko 8.00 pm	Premiership
Fri 11	Swindon Town v Bristol City	ko 7.45 pm	League 1
Sun 13	Stockport County v Barnet	ko 1.30 pm	League 2
	Blackpool v Scunthorpe	ko 4.00 pm	League 1
Fri 18	Derby County v Wolvers	ko 7.45 pm	Championship
Sat 19	Wigan Athletic v Arsenal	ko 12.45 pm	Premiership
	WBA v Everton	ko 5.15 pm*	Premiership
Sun 20	Brighton v Crystal Palace	ko 1.30 pm	Championship
	Middlesbrough v Fulham	ko 4.00 pm	Premiership
Mon 21	Birmingham City v Bolton W	ko 8.00 pm	Premiership
Sat 26	Portsmouth v Chelsea	ko 5.15 pm*	Premiership
Sun 27	Everton v Newcastle Utd	ko 1.30 pm	Premiership
	West Ham Utd v Manchester Utd	ko 4.00 pm	Premiership

December

Sat 3	Manchester Utd v Portsmouth	ko 5.15 pm*	Premiership
Sun 4	Charlton Athletic v Manchester City	ko 4.00 pm	Premiership
Mon 5	Birmingham city v West Ham Utd	ko 8.00pm	Premiership
Sat 10	Liverpool v Middlesbrough	ko 12.45 pm	Premiership
	Newcastle Utd v Arsenal	ko 5.15 pm*	Premiership
Sun 11	Manchester Utd v Everton	ko 4.00 pm	Premiership

Sponsored by Stan James

Mon 12	Tottenham Hotspur v Portsmouth	ko 8.00 pm	Premiership
Sat 17	Aston Villa v Manchester Utd	ko 12.45 pm*	Premiership
	Sunderland v Liverpool	ko 5.15 pm*	Premiership
Sun 18	Middlesbrough v Tottenham H	ko 1.30 pm	Premiership
	Arsenal v Chelsea	ko 4 pm	Premiership
Mon 26	Charlton Athletic v Arsenal	ko 12.45 pm	Premiership
	Liverpool v Newcastle Utd	ko 3.00 pm*	Premiership
	Aston Villa v Everton	ko 5.15 pm	Premiership
Wed 28	Everton v Liverpool	ko 8.00 pm	Premiership
Sat 31	Aston Villa v Arsenal	ko 12.45 pm	Premiership
January 2006			
Mon 2	West Ham Utd v Chelsea	ko 12.45 pm	Premiership
Tue 3	Arsenal v Manchester Utd	ko 8.00 pm	Premiership
Sat 14	Manchester City v Manchester Utd	ko 12.45 pm	Premiership
	Blackburn Rovers v Bolton W	ko 5.15 pm*	Premiership
Sun 15	Wigan Athletic v WBA	ko 1.30 pm	Premiership
	Sunderland v Chelsea	ko 4.00 pm	Premiership

SHARP: Neil Warnock's Blades kick off this season's live coverage

FIGARO'S ANALYSIS

It's a game of two halves

THE bookies' quotes against HT/FT double results are often a rip off, but their weakness is that they apply a blanket set of odds for all nine possible double results that rests on just the two prices for the straight home win or away win. This means that they don't treat each match or team on their individual merits.

In the spring, we started putting half-time and second-half tables in the Outlook on an occasional basis, and a comparison of both 'Half' tables with the standard ones reveals many ways of exploiting this weakness: there is far less correspondence between the two halves than you might expect.

Comparing the half performances of teams can pinpoint strengths and weaknesses, and of course, you would have to question the fitness of those teams who repeatedly fall away after the break.

Punters should also be encouraged by the way trends are more solid and more likely to continue when you take a team's first-half and second-half records separately. All this is vital if you enjoy a bet in-running, too.

There is no space here to print the 'Half' tables in full, but a set of 2004/05 English Divisions is free if you send a s.a.e. to: Outlook Half Tables, PO Box 352, Oxford, OX2 0AF.

The point about the holes in the bookies' blanket cover policy is easy to prove. Look no further than the home records of Chelsea and Arsenal. The pricing of this pair at home would have been similar all year, from heavy odds-on against duffers coming up towards 5-4 when they were visited by others in the top six.

However, the first-half performance of the pair at home could hardly be more different. Arsenal always set off all guns blazing. At half time, their home record reads 14-4-1-24-6, so they went in ahead 74% of the time.

By contrast, Chelsea were far more patient. In nearly half their games, home and away, they were only drawing at the break and their home record at that points reads 9-10-0. Thus the WIN-WIN double home result was more viable for the runners-up than it was for the Champions, where the DRAW-WIN option (often paying 7-2) was better.

Another leading Premiership side where the DRAW-WIN home option paid off handsomely was Everton. The Toffees scored fewer first-half goals home and away than anyone else - a paltry 14. That's one goal every 122 minutes. The half-time home record was 2-14-3-7-9. But their second-half performances were second only to those of Chelsea, whose second-half away record, incidentally, was an amazing 13-6-0-24-4. That's where they won the title. Everton secured their Champions League spot on the strength of their second-half performances at Goodison, where the stats read 13-2-4-17-6.

Like Everton, Spurs were drawing at half-time in 24 of their 38 league games and in aways their interval stats read a remarkable 0-15-4-2-6. So double results using the half-time draw cover when Spurs were away would have been winning at the break 79% of the time.

That sort of stat can only occur when an away team goes out to stifle the game in the first instance. Even when visiting the likes of Norwich and Palace, it seems Tottenham cannot have set out to take charge early on.

How different Liverpool's away half-time record reads: 3-6-10-6-17. Arguably, their efforts to overhaul Everton got lost early in their away games where they left themselves a mountain to climb more than half the time - just as they did in the Champions League Final.

Here are some other surprising half result stats. The worst second-half performers in the Premiership were not the relegated sides but Charlton and Newcastle. The latter conceded 40 second half goals, more than any other team and their second-half record was 7-13-18. Again, one remembers how their final second-half performance in Europe repeated this story.

In the Championship, Millwall were second in the first-half table, but down at 18th in the second-half list. New boss Steve Claridge is famous for his stamina as a player, but clearly needs to pack more into his new charges.

Luton turned it on at home in the second-half to win League 1. Their record there was 16-7-0-24-4. By contrast, Huddersfield kept falling away badly. They had the best home and away first-half record, but were 21st in the second-half.

Oxford's game could hardly have been of two more different halves. Second at half-time with a 13-6-4 home record, they were bottom of the second half list. Eleven teams scored more in the second-half at the Kassam Stadium than Oxford - which is where you should send for the full tables!

FA BARCLAYCARD PREMIERSHIP FIRST-HALF TABLE

Pos		Home P	W	D	L	F	A	Away W	D	L	F	A	Pts	Goal Diff
1	Arsenal	38	14	4	1	24	6	7	10	2	13	4	77	+27
2	Chelsea	38	9	10	0	18	3	9	8	2	13	5	72	+23
3	Man Utd	38	9	8	2	11	4	7	9	3	10	5	65	+12
4	Man City	38	10	5	4	15	5	5	12	2	13	9	62	+14
5	Bolton	38	8	7	4	11	5	6	8	5	12	10	57	+8
6	Newcastle	38	5	10	4	11	8	8	7	4	13	9	56	+7
7	Charlton	38	9	5	5	15	10	4	10	5	7	9	54	+3
8	Middlesbro	38	6	8	5	11	8	5	11	3	9	9	52	+3
9	Birmingham	38	6	10	3	12	4	4	8	7	10	12	48	+6
10	Liverpool	38	8	8	3	16	7	3	6	10	6	17	47	-2
11	Blackburn	38	6	8	5	12	11	3	9	7	3	9	44	-5
12	WBA	38	2	14	3	5	6	5	6	8	10	19	41	-10
13	Fulham	38	6	6	7	11	9	2	10	7	9	15	40	-4
14	Portsmouth	38	2	13	4	17	17	4	9	6	8	15	40	-7
15	Tottenham	38	5	9	5	14	12	0	15	4	2	6	39	-2
16	Everton	38	2	14	3	7	9	3	10	6	7	13	39	-8
17	Crystal Pal	38	4	12	3	8	6	1	9	9	8	18	36	-8
18	Aston Villa	38	6	7	6	13	12	1	8	10	8	22	36	-13
19	Southampton	38	4	10	5	15	16	0	8	11	6	24	30	-19
20	Norwich	38	2	11	6	8	15	1	6	12	6	24	26	-25

FA BARCLAYCARD PREMIERSHIP SECOND-HALF TABLE

Pos		Home P	W	D	L	F	A	Away W	D	L	F	A	Pts	Goal Diff
1	Chelsea	38	8	10	1	17	3	13	6	0	24	4	79	+34
2	Everton	38	13	2	4	17	6	8	4	7	14	18	69	+7
3	Arsenal	38	11	5	3	30	13	7	9	3	20	13	68	+24
4	Man Utd	38	9	8	2	20	8	8	7	4	17	9	66	+20
5	Tottenham	38	10	6	3	22	10	5	7	7	9	13	58	+8
6	Liverpool	38	8	7	4	15	8	5	8	6	15	9	54	+13
7	Aston Villa	38	8	8	3	13	5	5	7	7	11	13	54	+6
8	Middlesbro	38	10	5	4	18	11	4	7	8	15	18	54	+4
9	Southampton	38	6	10	3	15	14	4	10	5	9	12	50	-2
10	Fulham	38	8	5	6	18	17	4	8	7	14	19	49	-4
11	Blackburn	38	6	7	6	9	11	5	9	5	8	12	49	-6
12	Bolton	38	5	9	5	14	13	6	4	9	12	16	46	-3
13	Norwich	38	8	6	5	21	17	3	5	11	7	21	44	-10
14	Portsmouth	38	8	5	6	13	9	1	9	9	5	18	41	-9
15	Man City	38	6	6	8	9	9	4	5	10	10	16	40	-6
16	Crystal Pal	38	5	8	6	13	13	2	9	8	12	25	38	-13
17	Birmingham	38	4	10	5	12	11	3	6	10	6	19	37	-12
18	WBA	38	5	8	6	12	18	4	2	13	9	18	37	-15
19	Charlton	38	7	5	7	14	19	1	8	10	6	20	37	-19
20	Newcastle	38	5	7	7	14	17	2	6	11	9	23	34	-17

ARSENAL

Nickname: The Gunners
Colours: Red and white
Ground: Highbury
Capacity: 38,500
Tel: 020 7704 4000
www.arsenal.com

FOR a man who has achieved as much as Arsene Wenger on a budget that makes renowned scrooge Doug Ellis look like Santa Claus, the Frenchman is deserving of far more credit than he gets.

Unfortunately for Arsenal, having all but seen off the Mancunian challenge, the Russian-fuelled Blue tidal wave may be a force of nature too powerful even for a man of Wenger's capabilities to overcome.

Despite noises to the contrary, I suspect the Gunners supremo will be forced to shop at bargain prices again this summer.

The Ashley Cole saga has not been an encouraging start to the close season, but expect the England full-back to play out at least one more year at Highbury.

Dennis Bergkamp has extended his contract for another year, but his playing days are numbered and his presence will be more vital in the development of Robin van Persie than anything he is likely to accomplish on the pitch.

Of course, the big story of the summer is the sale of Patrick Vieira to Juventus.

The Frenchman is always the subject of summer rumours, and this year they came true as Wenger opted to take what would probably have been the last chance to cash in on a player who has not performed at his peak over the past two seasons.

Alexander Hleb has joined from Stuttgart, but with Edu gone too, Cesc Fabregas and Mathieu Flamini are likely to be called upon to an even greater extent than they were last term. They have bags of potential but will have to settle for second best this time.

Longest run without loss: 16
Longest run without win: 3
High - low league position: 1-3
High - low Outlook form figure: 70-48
Final Outlook Index figure: 956

Key Stat: *The Gunners took just two points off Chelsea and Man Utd.*

2004/05 Premiership Stats

	Apps	Gls	YC	RC
J Aliadiere	0 (4)	0	0	0
M Almunia	10	0		0
D Bergkamp	20 (9)	8	1	0
S Campbell	16	1	1	0
G Clichy	7 (8)	0	2	0
A Cole	35	2	7	0
P Cygan	15	0	2	0
E Eboue	0 (1)	0	0	0
Edu	6 (6)	2	1	0
F Fabregas	24 (9)	2	4	0
M Flamini	9 (12)	1	0	0
T Henry	31 (1)	25	2	0
J Hoyte	4 (1)	0	0	0
Lauren	32 (1)	1	4	0
J Lehmann	28	0	0	0
F Ljungberg	24 (2)	10	2	0
Q Owusu-Abeyie	1	0	0	0
J Pennant	1 (6)	0	0	0
R Pires	26 (7)	14	2	0
J Reyes	25 (5)	9	3	0
P Senderos	12 (1)	0	1	0
G Silva	13	0	0	0
K Toure	35	0	1	0
R Van Persie	12 (14)	5	2	1
P Vieira	32	6	9	0

League and Cup Stats
Clean sheets 20
Yellow cards 49 Red cards 1
Players used 25
Leading scorer:
Thierry Henry 30 (25 league)

Outlook forecast: 2nd

Your forecast:

Sponsored by Stan James

ASTON VILLA

Nickname: The Villans
Colours: Claret and blue
Ground: Villa Park
Capacity: 42,584
Tel: 0121 327 2299
www.avfc.co.uk

AS long as Deadly Doug continues to body-swerve the grim reaper with more ease than any of his players do opposition full-backs, Aston Villa will remain an enigma of a football club.

Far be it from me to wish ill health on the old boy, but it seems that the longer Doug Ellis remains at the head of affairs, the longer the trophy cabinet will remain bare.

It's nearly five years since he shelled out any significant cash, when he gave John Gregory £7.5 million to spend securing the services of Juan Pablo Angel.

Whilst in that time the likes of Leeds have spent their way into oblivion, David O'Leary is left to wonder how the two time European Cup winners can even compete with the clubs pushing for a Uefa Cup spot on his limited budget. It's a quandary that O'Leary - the man who, lest we forget, was allowed to spend so irresponsibly at Elland Road - is unlikely to find the answer to.

The signings of Kevin Phillips and Patrik Berger for instance, are hardly likely to have the Villa faithful queuing three times around the block to get their season tickets renewed and Ellis must either move with the times or fall on his sword. He might face a challenge to his position this season as former Man City star turned entrepreneur Ray Ranson is considering a bid for the club.

O'Leary is an able manager and given the right tools would be capable of reviving this grand old club. Under the present regime, those tools are not in evidence, and should Villa start slowly, the 16-1 about the Irishman in the sack race looks tempting.

Longest run without loss: 6
Longest run without win: 6
High - low league position: 5-13
High - low Outlook form figure: 60-38
Final Outlook Index figure: 868
Key Stat: *Villa took four points from aways against other sides in the top twelve.*

2004/05 Premiership Stats

	Apps	Gls	YC	RC
J-P Angel	30 (5)	7	1	0
G Barry	33 (1)	7	2	0
M Berson	7 (4)	0	2	0
C Cole	18 (9)	3	1	0
S Davis	19 (9)	1	2	0
U De La Cruz	30 (4)	0	2	0
M Delaney	30	0	3	0
E Djemba-Djemba	4 (2)	0	2	0
L Hendrie	25 (4)	5	9	1
T Hitzlsperger	17 (11)	2	1	0
M Laursen	12	1	3	0
G McCann	20	1	3	0
O Mellberg	30	3	6	0
L Moore	5 (20)	1	1	0
S Moore	0 (1)	0	0	0
S Postma	2 (1)	0	1	0
L Ridgewell	12 (3)	1	3	1
J Samuel	34 (1)	0	6	0
N Solano	32 (4)	8	6	0
T Sorensen	36	0	1	0
D Vassell	17 (4)	2	0	0
P Whittingham	5 (8)	1	1	0

League and Cup Stats
Clean sheets 11
Yellow cards 55 Red cards 2
Players used 22
Leading scorer:
Nolberto Solano 9 (8 league)

Outlook forecast: 12th

Your forecast:

BIRMINGHAM CITY

Nickname: The Blues
Colours: Blue
Ground: St Andrews
Capacity: 30,016
Tel: 0121 772 0101
www.bcfc.com

IF you were to try and put together the perfect board to run a football club, then perhaps the last thing you would want to do would be to unite a single-minded, hard-nosed businesswoman like Karen Brady and put her to work alongside porn baron David Sullivan.

But as fate would have it, this odd couple have formed a successful enough partnership at Birmingham, a side that still has very obvious limitations but which, under the watchful eye of Steve Bruce, is making a decent fist at becoming an established Premiership club.

The disruptive figure of Robbie Savage is no longer about and although he did his bit for the Blues, they have now progressed to a level where they are no longer in need of his in-your-face style. There are better players out there then Sav to perform that task in a less obnoxious manner.

The spine of the side is solid - Maik Taylor remains one of the Premiership's best kept secrets, Matthew Upson and Kenny Cunningham are as honest as the day is long and in Mikael Forssell and Emile Heskey, they possess a pair of strikers who the word handful was made for.

If David Dunn can go five minutes without pinging a hamstring and spend more time out on the pitch than he does chatting to Tim Lovejoy and Helen Chamberlain on Soccer AM, then a push for Europe is a possibility.

However, the chances of the latter happening are limited at best, and Bruce's boys will have to settle for mid-table.

Longest run without loss: 6
Longest run without win: 6
High - low league position: 9-16
High - low Outlook form figure: 63-40
Final Outlook Index figure: 868

Key Stat: *More bullying please: they won just once against the bottom five sides.*

2004/05 Premiership Stats

	Apps	Gls	YC	RC
D Anderton	9 (11)	3	1	0
R Blake	2 (9)	2	0	0
D Carter	12 (3)	2	1	0
J Clapham	18 (9)	0	0	0
S Clemence	13 (9)	0	2	0
K Cunningham	36	0	3	0
S Diao	2	0	1	0
D Dunn	9 (2)	2	4	0
M Forssell	4	0	0	0
J Gray	18 (14)	2	0	0
J Gronkjaer	13 (3)	0	1	0
E Heskey	34	10	6	0
M Izzet	10	1	3	1
S John	0 (3)	0	0	0
D Johnson	36	0	7	2
S Lazaridis	15 (5)	0	1	0
M Melchiot	33	1	3	0
C Morrison	13 (13)	4	4	0
M Nafti	7 (3)	0	4	0
W Pandiani	13 (1)	4	2	0
J Pennant	12	0	3	0
R Savage	18	4	5	0
Maik Taylor	38	0	0	0
Martin Tayor	4 (3)	0	1	0
O Tebily	9 (6)	0	2	0
M Upson	36	2	5	0
D Yorke	4 (9)	2	1	0

League and Cup Stats
Clean sheets 10
Yellow cards 57   Red cards 3
Players used 27
Leading scorer:
Emile Heskey 11 (10 league)

Outlook forecast: 11th

Your forecast:

BLACKBURN ROVERS

Nickname: Rovers
Colours: Blue and white
Ground: Ewood Park
Capacity: 31,367
Tel: 08701 113 232
www.rovers.co.uk

THERE'S no point in beating around the bush. Last season Blackburn made watching a Grand Prix in slow motion seem like riding a roller coaster on ecstasy.

However, Mark Hughes would be the first to point out that when he filled the vacancy at Ewood Park, survival was the name of the game and by fair means or (as often as not) foul, the former Wales boss got the job done with room to spare.

At least Rovers could count themselves among the few sides with the stomach to stand up against Chelsea last term, and one particularly bruising encounter saw Arjen Robben's ankle shattered and Jose Mourinho accusing Hughes's men of employing bully boy tactics.

It is true that Blackburn are a little rough around the edges and any side that contains Robbie Savage is never going to endear themselves to the neutral audience, but in Morten Gamst Pedersen and Brett Emerton, Rovers are capable of being more than kick and rush merchants.

If Hughes can use his knowledge of the world transfer market as he did bringing in combative central defender Ryan Nelson and tough tackling midfielder Aaron Mokoena to embellish the side with players of a more aesthetic nature, Rovers are capable of making a significant move up the table.

Scoring goals was the major problem last season, but Hughes has recruited 20-goal Shefki Kuqi from Ipswich and Craig Bellamy will provide much needed flair if Hughes can rein in the former Newcastle man's worst excesses.

Longest run without loss: 6
Longest run without win: 9
High - low league position: 12-19
High - low Outlook form figure: 62-34
Final Outlook Index figure: 870

Key Stat: *No-one committed more fouls in the Premiership last season (595).*

2004/05 Premiership Stats

	Apps	Gls	YC	RC
L Amoruso	5 (1)	0	0	1
J Bothroyd	6 (5)	1	0	1
J De Pedro	1 (1)	0	0	0
M Derbyshire	0 (1)	0	0	0
P Dickov	27 (2)	9	7	0
Y Djorkaeff	3	0	0	0
J Douglas	0 (1)	0	0	0
B Emerton	33 (4)	4	4	0
B Ferguson	21	2	4	0
G Flitcroft	17 (2)	0	4	0
B Friedel	38	0	0	0
P Gallagher	5 (11)	2	0	0
M Gray	9	0	0	0
V Gresko	2 (1)	0	0	0
M Jansen	3 (4)	2	0	0
N Johansson	18 (4)	0	2	0
J Johnson	0 (3)	0	0	0
D Matteo	25 (3)	0	6	0
J McEveley	5	0	1	0
A Mokoena	16	0	5	0
L Neill	34 (2)	1	8	0
R Nelsen	15	0	2	0
M Pedersen	19	4	1	0
S Reid	23 (5)	2	3	0
R Savage	9	0	3	0
C Short	13 (1)	1	1	1
J Stead	19 (10)	2	6	0
D Thompson	11 (13)	0	2	1
A Todd	26	1	4	0
Tugay	13 (8)	0	6	1
D Yorke	2 (2)	0	0	0

League and Cup Stats

Clean sheets 18
Yellow cards 74 Red cards 5
Players used 31
Leading scorer:
Paul Dickov 10 (9 league)

Outlook forecast: 13th

Your forecast:

BOLTON WANDERERS

Nickname: The Trotters
Colours: Blue and white
Ground: Reebok Stadium
Capacity: 28,723
Tel: 01204 673673
www.bwfc.co.uk

NEVER judge a book by its cover is a proverb that fits Sam Allardyce like one of his snugly tailored suits.

On the face of it, Big Sam looks like one of those frustrated Alex Ferguson wannabes you see patrolling the touchlines at Hackney Marshes on a Sunday morning, but that rugged northern exterior does not even begin to do justice to one of the most forward thinking coaches in Europe, let alone the Premiership.

A strict fitness and dietary programme, the use of Prozone and an advanced scouting network are all overseen by the former Blackpool manager who is currently tied in to a ten-year contract.

In getting the best out of Liverpool flop (or should that be flob) El-Hadji Diouf, Allardyce has turned water into wine. The Senegalese striker lends genuine pace to an otherwise agricultural attack and along with underrated Greek schemer Stylianos Giannakopoulos, helps make Bolton a far more aesthetically pleasing unit than most give them credit for.

Bolton's recent record against the top sides is evidence enough to show they are more than just a side who rely on set pieces and centre forwards who would look more at home on a basketball court.

Their first European campaign provides a new challenge. Balancing the rigours of the Premiership against progress in the Uefa Cup has caused the likes of Middlesbrough and Ipswich problems in the recent past, but in Allardyce, Bolton have the man to ensure their rapid progress is maintained.

Longest run without loss: 10
Longest run without win: 10
High - low league position: 3-14
High - low Outlook form figure: 68-37
Final Outlook Index figure: 895
Key Stat: *Bolton shared a 2-2 draw with each of the top three.*

2004/05 Premiership Stats

	Apps	Gls	YC	RC
A Barness	5 (3)	0	0	0
Ben Haim	19 (2)	1	5	0
I Campo	20 (7)	0	4	0
V Candela	9 (1)	0	3	0
J Cesar	4 (1)	0	0	0
K Davies	33 (2)	8	5	0
E-H Diouf	23 (4)	9	7	0
K Fadiga	0 (5)	0	0	0
L Ferdinand	1 (11)	1	1	0
R Gardner	30 (3)	0	3	0
S Giannakopoulos	28 (6)	7	5	0
F Hierro	15 (14)	1	3	0
N Hunt	29	0	5	0
J Jaaskelainen	36	0	1	1
R Jaidi	20 (7)	5	2	0
B Kaku	0 (1)	0	0	0
B N'Gotty	37	0	4	1
K Nolan	27 (9)	4	5	0
J O'Brien	0 (1)	0	0	0
A Oakes	1	0	0	0
J Okocha	29 (2)	6	2	0
H Pedersen	13 (14)	6	0	0
K Poole	1 (1)	0	0	0
G Speed	37 (1)	1	1	0
R Vaz Te	1 (6)	0	1	0

League and Cup Stats
Clean sheets 11
Yellow cards 56 Red cards 2
Players used 25
Leading scorers: Davies, Pedersen & Diouf all 9, with Diouf's all league.

Outlook forecast: 5th

Your forecast:

CHARLTON ATHLETIC

Nickname: Addicks
Colours: Red and white
Ground: The Valley
Capacity: 26,875
Tel: 020 8333 4000
www.cafc.co.uk

OF all the clubs in the Premiership that would want fewer teams competing, Charlton would surely be the one most likely to cast their vote with the 'Ayes'.

Reducing the number of sides by say, four, would mean the Addicks could finish their season in early March, negating the chances of going to pieces in the Spring.

In all seriousness, the fact that in each of the last three seasons Charlton have been in a position to qualify for Europe before displaying a Paula Radcliffe-esque 'I've run 20 miles but cant be bothered to run the last six' attitude, is becoming a major source of annoyance to their supporters.

The ground and infrastructure are now firmly in place, and although expectations have risen, they are not at a level that could be deemed unreasonable. Nobody expects Charlton to win the Premiership, but a decent Cup run and a top eight finish is hardly the stuff of wild fantasy.

Some believe Alan Curbishley has taken the club as far as he can, and his record over the past few years would suggest that to be the case. However, you get the feeling that unless he does something unforgivable, like re-signing Francis Jeffers, he is forever going to be part of the furniture.

The manager has scoured the bargain bin and made full use of the loan system to bring in a host of defenders and midfielders, but a new striker is a must.

20 goals a season from a single player would make a huge difference, but do the Charlton board have the determination to bring an Andy Johnson type to the Valley?

Longest run without loss: 5
Longest run without win: 9
High - low league position: 4-13
High - low Outlook form figure: 62-37
Final Outlook Index figure: 860

Key Stat: *The Addicks registered just one league win after January.*

2004/05 Premiership Stats

	Apps	Gls	YC	RC
S Andersen	2	0	0	0
S Bartlett	25	6	0	1
T El Karkouri	28 (4)	5	5	1
J Euell	7 (19)	2	1	0
M Fish	6 (1)	0	0	0
J Fortune	28 (3)	2	1	0
M Holland	31 (1)	3	0	0
H Hreidarsson	33 (1)	1	4	0
B Hughes	10 (7)	1	1	0
F Jeffers	9 (11)	3	2	0
J Johansson	15 (11)	4	0	0
D Kiely	36	0	0	0
R Kishishev	27 (4)	0	4	0
P Konchesky	15 (13)	1	3	0
K Lisbie	12 (5)	1	0	0
D Murphy	37 (1)	3	3	0
C Perry	17 (2)	1	3	1
D Rommedahl	19 (7)	2	0	0
L Sam	0 (1)	0	0	0
G Stuart	4	0	3	0
J Thomas	21 (3)	3	2	0
L Young	36	2	4	0

League and Cup Stats
Clean sheets 13
Yellow cards 34 Red cards 3
Players used 22
Leading scorer:
Shaun Bartlett 8 (6 league)

Outlook forecast: 14th
Your forecast:

CHELSEA

Nickname: The Blues
Colours: Blue and white
Ground: Stamford Bridge
Capacity: 42,449
Tel: 0870 300 1212
www.chelseafc.co.uk

EVEN for a man who gives the impression he could go flower picking in a minefield and come up with something worthy of a gold medal at the Chelsea Flower Show, it will take something out of the ordinary for Jose Mourinho to surpass last season's achievements, and there is nothing in his track record to suggest that the self-styled 'special one' isn't capable of sweeping the board this time around.

A top-class striker aside, it's impossible to find a flaw in the squad assembled by the Portuguese master.

Much of the criticism hurled at Didier Drogba towards the tail end of last season was harsh in the extreme, and Mourinho is likely to maintain the selfless Ivorian as a key member of his attacking unit.

He has little choice since Samuel Eto'o and Andriy Shevchenko have resisted his attempts to lure them to the Bridge to supplement Damien Duff and Arjen Robben, but that has paved the way for Hernan Crespo to return after a season in Milan and Shaun Wright-Phillips is a solid signing.

Both his wing wizards have shown a propensity to pick up niggling injuries in the past, and Chelsea have proved easier to nullify when that explosive duo are absent.

If they stay fit and Lampard, Terry and Cole continue to blossom, it's hard to envisage either Arsenal or United - who have enough problems between them to fill a double bill of Trisha - making any significant inroads into the Blues' superiority.

Chelsea look more than deserving favourites to retain the trophy.

Longest run without loss: 25
Longest run without win: 2
High - low league position: 1-2
High - low Outlook form figure: 68-54
Final Outlook Index figure: 978
Key Stat: *The Blues dropped just four points against bottom-half sides.*

2004/05 Premiership Stats

	Apps	Gls	YC	RC
C Babayaro	3 (1)	0	2	0
W Bridge	12 (3)	0	0	0
P Cech	35	0	0	0
J Cole	19 (9)	8	5	0
C Cudicini	3	0	0	0
D Drogba	18 (8)	10	2	0
D Duff	28 (2)	6	1	0
M Forssell	0 (1)	0	0	0
W Gallas	28	2	1	0
Geremi	6 (7)	0	1	0
A Grant	0 (1)	0	0	0
E Gudjohnsen	30 (7)	12	1	0
R Huth	6 (4)	0	0	0
J Jarosik	3 (11)	0	1	0
G Johnson	13 (3)	0	2	0
M Kezman	6 (18)	4	2	0
F Lampard	38	13	6	0
C Makelele	36	1	6	0
A Mutu	0 (2)	0	0	0
Nuno Morais	0 (2)	0	0	0
F Oliveira	0 (1)	0	0	0
S Parker	1 (3)	0	1	0
Paulo Ferreira	29	0	2	0
L Pidgeley	0 (1)	0	0	0
Ricrado Carvalho	22 (3)	1	2	0
A Robben	14 (4)	7	5	0
A Smertin	11 (5)	0	2	0
J Terry	36	3	7	0
Tiago	21 (13)	4	4	0
S Watt	0 (1)	0	0	0

League and Cup Stats
Clean sheets 29
Yellow cards 52 Red cards 0
Players used 30
Leading scorer:
Frank Lampard 18 (12 league)

Outlook forecast: 1st

Your forecast:

EVERTON

Nickname: The Toffees
Colours: Blue and white
Ground: Goodison Park
Capacity: 40,260
Tel: 0151 330 2200
www.evertonfc.com

LAST season, Everton and David Moyes put a completely different spin on the words over achievement.

European football will be back at Goodison Park for the first time in ten years, and although that is very definitely cause for some celebration, the fact that up to twenty extra games could be added to an already hectic schedule will certainly be a double edged sword.

It would be unfair to suggest that the Toffees qualified for the Champions League beacuse Liverpool and the rest under performed to a degree that made it impossible for the Blues not to finish fourth. However, what is undeniable is the fact that towards the back end of last season, Everton were quite simply knackered.

Moyes' dealings in the summer transfer market will determine whether the Toffees can reproduce last term's efforts.

The early signs are not encouraging for the flame-haired Scot. Already the carrot of Champions League football has not been tasty enough to lure the likes of Mikael Forssell and Scott Parker and whilst he might have several Tim Cahill style bargains up his sleeve, those two rejections are a clear indication that Everton still lack the financial muscle even to compete with those sides languishing in mid-table mediocrity.

Simon Davies may turn out to be a useful addition, and the purchase of Danish international defender Per Kroldrup is a very shrewd investment, but much more is needed if Everton are to hold onto local bragging rights.

Longest run without loss: 7
Longest run without win: 3
High - low league position: 2-7
High - low Outlook form figure: 65-41
Final Outlook Index figure: 875

Key Stat: *The Toffees' second half of the season record? 6-3-10.*

2004/05 Premiership Stats

	Apps	Gls	YC	RC
M Arteta	10 (2)	1	5	0
J Beattie	7 (4)	1	1	1
M Bent	31 (6)	6	2	0
T Cahill	33	11	9	1
K Campbell	4 (2)	0	0	0
L Carsley	35 (1)	4	7	0
N Chadwick	0 (1)	0	0	0
D Ferguson	6 (29)	6	2	1
T Gravesen	20 (1)	4	3	0
T Hibbert	35 (1)	0	9	0
K Kilbane	37 (1)	1	3	0
N Martyn	32	0	0	0
J McFadden	7 (16)	1	1	0
G Naysmith	5 (6)	0	0	1
L Osman	24 (5)	6	3	0
A Pistone	32 (1)	0	2	0
A Stubbs	29 (2)	1	1	0
J Vaughan	0 (2)	1	0	0
S Watson	12 (13)	0	1	0
D Weir	34	1	3	0
R Wright	6 (1)	0	0	0
J Yobo	19 (8)	0	1	0

League and Cup Stats
Clean sheets 15
Yellow cards 49   Red cards 4
Players used 22
Leading scorer:
Tim Cahill 12 (11 league)

Outlook forecast: 8th
Your forecast:

FULHAM

Nickname: The Cottagers
Colours: Black and white
Ground: Craven Cottage
Capacity: 22,000
Tel: 020 7893 8383
www.fulhamfc.com

DOES anything stay the same at Fulham for more than five minutes these days?

It doesn't seem too long ago that crowds of 3,000 or so at Craven Cottage were being treated to the delights of Jim Stannard's comedy goalkeeping.

Back then, Fulham were a quiet, sleepy club, content with their place in the English footballing hierarchy. That was before the man who owns Britain's biggest corner shop got his hands on this traditional old club. Nowadays Fulham seem to change their kit, their sponsors, their players and even their ground at least twice a season.

But during the Al Fayed era, one man has remained a constant figure, whether it be as player, coach or manager. Chris Coleman has exerted a massive influence during his time at Craven Cottage.

After a successful first season in charge, last year's return to SW6 was something of an anti-climax and Coleman's main task this time around is to re-motivate players such as Steed Malbranque, Claus Jensen and Tomasz Radzinski, none of whom showed much relish for the job last season.

Edwin van der Sar, by any measure Fulham's most consistent performer last term, has left for one last shot at the big time with Manchester United and the untried, untested and barely pronounceable Jaroslav Drobny will have big gloves to fill.

With the arrival of Watford's 20-goal striker Heidar Helguson and with Pape Bouba Diop and Luis Boa Morte still among their ranks, the Fulham faithful can at least count on continued Premiership football.

Longest run without loss: 8
Longest run without win: 4
High - low league position: 10-17
High - low Outlook form figure: 64-37
Final Outlook Index figure: 871

Key Stat: *The Cottagers beat all the bottom five at home.*

2004/05 Premiership Stats

	Apps	Gls	YC	RC
L Boa Morte	29 (2)	8	7	0
C Bocanegra	26 (2)	1	4	0
L Clark	15 (2)	1	2	0
A Cole	29 (2)	12	4	1
M Crossley	5	0	0	0
P Diop	29	6	7	2
L Fontaine	0 (1)	0	0	0
A Goma	15 (1)	0	2	0
A Green	4	0	2	0
E Hammond	0 (1)	0	0	0
C Jensen	10 (2)	0	0	1
C John	13 (14)	4	2	0
Z Knight	35	1	3	1
S Legwinski	13 (2)	1	3	0
S Malbranque	22 (4)	6	0	0
B McBride	15 (16)	6	0	0
B McKinlay	1 (1)	0	0	0
I Pearce	11	0	0	1
M Pembridge	26 (2)	0	2	0
T Radzinski	25 (10)	6	1	0
Z Rehmen	15 (2)	0	4	0
L Rosenior	16 (1)	0	3	1
E Van der Sar	33 (1)	0	4	0
M Volz	31	0	5	0

League and Cup Stats
Clean sheets 10
Yellow cards 54   Red cards 7
Players used 25
Leading scorer:
Andrew Cole 13 (12 league)

Outlook forecast: 15th
Your forecast:

LIVERPOOL

Nickname: The Reds
Colours: Red
Ground: Anfield
Capacity: 45,362
Tel: 0151 263 2361
www.liverpoolfc.tv

HOW to soar like an eagle when you are surrounded by turkeys was a conundrum that Steven Gerrard somehow answered during Liverpool's improbable run to Champions League glory.

Whether he is the king of brinkmanship or the most indecisive natural leader in history is open to question, but he will be playing at Anfield after some tortuous and sometimes farcical negotiations. That's a major boost, but the fact that many of those who starred on the run to European glory are to be discarded gives an indication of the job that Rafa Benitez has on his hands.

They start their 2005/06 campaign in July, a consequence of their unconventional qualification for Europe's premier competition, and the chances of Benitez hauling the Reds closer to the Premiership top three will hardly be enhanced by a summer tour of unpronounceable eastern European outposts.

To redress the gap, the former Valencia boss has raided La Liga for Villarreal's Jose Reina, who will strengthen a competitive goalkeeping department, Mark Gonzalez (Albacete), Antonio Barragan (Seville) and Valencia's midfield prospect Mohamed Sissoko. Luis Figo and Peter Crouch are also on the wanted list.

Up front, Milan Baros may be on his way out, but Fernando Morientes will benefit from a more settled pre-season than he is used to, while, if Djibril Cisse can score half as many goals as he has tattoos, Liverpool will be in business. Anticipate further progress, but not nearly enough to satisfy Gerrard's ultimate ambitions.

Longest run without loss: 4
Longest run without win: 4
High - low league position: 5-12
High - low Outlook form figure: 65-43
Final Outlook Index figure: 891
Key Stat: *They lost away to all the other top-eight sides, scoring only twice.*

2004/05 Premiership Stats

	Apps	Gls	YC	RC
X Alonso	20 (4)	2	1	0
M Baros	22 (4)	9	2	1
I Biscan	8 (11)	2	0	0
J Carragher	38	0	4	0
S Carson	4	0	0	0
D Cisse	10 (6)	4	0	0
S Diao	4 (4)	0	1	0
J Dudek	24	0	0	0
S Finnan	29 (4)	1	3	0
S Gerrard	28 (2)	7	3	0
D Hamann	23 (7)	0	6	0
S Hyypia	32	2	2	0
Josemi	13 (2)	0	5	1
H Kewell	15 (3)	1	0	0
C Kirkland	10	0	0	0
A Le Tallec	2 (2)	0	0	0
Luis Garcia	26 (3)	8	6	0
N Mellor	6 (3)	2	0	0
F Morientes	12 (1)	3	1	0
A Nunez	8 (10)	0	2	0
M Pellegrino	11 (1)	0	1	0
D Potter	0 (2)	0	0	0
D Raven	0 (1)	0	0	0
J Riise	34 (3)	6	1	0
S-Pongolle	6 (10)	2	1	0
V Smicer	2 (8)	0	1	0
D Traore	18 (8)	0	1	0
S Warnock	11 (8)	0	1	0
J Welsh	2 (1)	0	0	0

League and Cup Stats
Clean sheets 11
Yellow cards 39 Red cards 2
Players used 29
Leading scorers: Baros, Gerrard & Garcia all 13, with Baros 9 in the league.

Outlook forecast: 4th
Your forecast:

MANCHESTER CITY

Nickname: The Citizens
Colours: Blue and white
Ground: City of Manchester Stadium
Capacity: 48,000
Tel: 0161 231 3200
www.mcfc.co.uk

JUST what is it about Man City that makes them so loveable?

Had Ricky Hatton pledged his allegiance to the red half of Manchester, he would be nowhere near as popular as he is. Most people despised Peter Schmeichel when he was at United, but once he switched to City, we forgot about his tantrums at Old Trafford to the extent that we now look forward to his 'echsperrrt' analysis on Match Of The Day.

Now with Stuart Pearce rightly installed as manager, the allure for the neutral is even greater. The quirkiest club of them all appear to have hired a quirky manager and I for one believe this could be a marriage made in heaven.

The thing that has always struck me about City has been their tolerance of defeat.

Players, managers and even the fans seem to take defeat in remarkably good spirit. Things are about to change though, because as his nickname suggests, Psycho is a man who eradicated the word 'lose' from his vocabulary the moment he first stepped onto a football pitch.

The loss of Shaun Wright-Phillips to Chelsea is a blow. He was City's best player by a country mile but the extra cash will come in handy. Pearce did nothing in the transfer market before the Wright-Phillips issue was resolved and at the time of writing, had only been able to extend Kiki Musampa's loan from Atletico Madrid.

Even so, a solid season is in prospect, as long as Pearce can resist the temptation to stick David James up front again.

Longest run without loss: 8
Longest run without win: 5
High - low league position: 8-18
High - low Outlook form figure: 62-42
Final Outlook Index figure: 884
Key Stat: *They had just two defeats against the bottom eight.*

2004/05 Premiership Stats

	Apps	Gls	YC	RC
N Anelka	18 (1)	7	0	0
J Barton	28 (3)	1	9	0
P Bosvelt	28	2	6	0
L Croft	0 (7)	0	0	0
S Distin	38	1	3	0
R Dunne	35	1	5	1
W Flood	4 (5)	1	1	0
R Fowler	28 (4)	10	3	0
D James	38	0	0	0
S Jordan	19	0	5	0
J Macken	16 (7)	1	0	0
S McManaman	5 (8)	0	1	0
D Mills	29 (3)	0	5	1
K Musampa	14	3	0	0
C Negouai	0 (1)	0	0	1
N Onuoha	11 (6)	0	0	0
C Reyna	16 (1)	2	0	0
A Sibierski	34 (1)	4	3	0
T Sinclair	2 (2)	1	0	0
D Sommeil	1	0	0	0
Sun Jihai	4 (2)	0	0	0
B Thatcher	17 (1)	0	2	0
N Weaver	0 (1)	0	0	0
B Wright-Phillips	0 (14)	1	0	0
S Wright-Phillips	33 (1)	10	0	0

League and Cup Stats
Clean sheets 11
Yellow cards 43 Red cards 2
Players used 25
Leading scorers: Fowler & Wright-Phillips, both 11 with 10 in the league.

Outlook forecast: 9th
Your forecast:

MANCHESTER UNITED

Nickname: The Red Devils
Colours: Red and white
Ground: Old Trafford
Capacity: 68,174
Tel: 0161 868 8000
www.manutd.com

FROM the outside looking in, this Malcolm Glazer business doesn't look anywhere near as desperate as the doom-mongers make out.

OK, so the fans might have to pay more to see their team in the flesh, but I don't recall any mutterings of discontent when their PLC status helped fund the transfers of Ruud van Nistelrooy, Rio Ferdinand, Wayne Rooney and the rest of their expensively assembled squad.

At the end of the day, if you swim with sharks, don't come crying to me if you get one of your legs bitten off. The fact that an American now runs the world's most famous club is far from United's biggest problem.

No Sir, the reason the Reds have won the Premiership only once in the past four seasons is this. In Roy Keane, David Beckham, Paul Scholes, Gary Neville and Ryan Giggs, United had an outstanding group of players who all peaked in 1999 and who have been steadily declining ever since.

And although Fergie may have found replacements of similar playing ability, he will never again be so lucky as to stumble upon such a talented group of men who are United to the core.

Wayne Rooney may be the one glittering exception, but Cristiano Ronaldo is bound to be attracted by the bright lights of Madrid one day, whilst Rio Ferdinand's grubby haggling over an extra 20 grand a week doesn't suggest he'd die for the club.

With that sort of attitude, Sir Alex will be forced to stand back and watch a young buck called Jose lap up the plaudits.

Longest run without loss: 18
Longest run without win: 3
High - low league position: 2-13
High - low Outlook form figure: 67-47
Final Outlook Index figure: 942
Key Stat: *United won 60 more corners than any other Premiership side.*

2004/05 Premiership Stats

	Apps	Gls	YC	RC
D Bellion	1 (9)	2	0	0
W Brown	18 (3)	1	1	1
R Carroll	26	0	0	0
E Djemba-Djemba	3 (2)	0	0	0
R Ferdinand	31	0	3	0
D Fletcher	18	3	0	0
D Forlan	0 (1)	0	0	0
Q Fortune	12 (5)	0	1	0
R Giggs	26 (6)	6	3	0
G Heinze	26	1	4	0
T Howard	12	0	0	0
R Keane	28 (3)	1	9	0
Kleberson	6 (2)	0	1	0
L Miller	3 (5)	0	0	0
G Neville	22	0	2	1
P Neville	12 (7)	0	3	0
J O'Shea	16 (7)	2	1	0
K Richardson	0 (2)	0	2	0
C Ronaldo	25 (8)	5	3	0
W Rooney	24 (5)	11	6	0
L Saha	7 (7)	1	0	0
P Scholes	29 (4)	9	3	1
M Silvestre	33 (2)	2	2	1
A Smith	22 (9)	6	2	1
J Spector	2 (1)	0	0	0
R van Nistelrooy	16 (1)	6	1	0

League and Cup Stats
Clean sheets 29
Yellow cards 44 Red cards 5
Players used 26
Leading scorer:
Wayne Rooney 17 (11 league)

Outlook forecast: 3rd
Your forecast:

MIDDLESBROUGH

Nickname: Boro
Colours: Red
Ground: The Riverside Stadium
Capacity: 35,100
Tel: 01642 877700
www.mfc.co.uk

HAS anyone ever earned so inflated a reputation on the back of so little achievement as Steve McClaren?

A season and a half as Fergie's yes-man and suggesting that it might be a good idea to chuck on Sheringham and Solksjaer with ten minutes of the Champions League final to go hardly make him the next Sir Alex.

Apparently, Steve has an excellent taste in red wine. Perhaps that's why the FA allow him to sit next to Sven during England games, for there's nothing else in his track record to suggest he's qualified for the job.

True, Boro are on the up having qualified for Europe two years on the trot, but the backing of a mini-Abramovic in the shape of Steve Gibson has undoubtedly aided the Smoggies' rise to the upper echelons of the Premiership. McClaren in particular has benefited from the chairman's goal of turning Boro into a consistent force at the top level, and if the early signs of the summer period are any indication, that desire burns as strongly as ever.

With Mark Viduka keeping fit the Darren Anderton way and Jimmy-Floyd Hasselbaink becoming moodier every year, new signing Aiyegbeni Yakubu will become the focal point of Boro's attack.

At £7.5 million, the capture of the Nigerian forward represents a massive gamble for McClaren. Should the muscular ex-Pompey man continue his progression, Boro will undoubtedly enjoy another successful season. Should he fail to settle in the north, McClaren's reputation may take an overdue buffeting.

Longest run without loss: 6
Longest run without win: 4
High - low league position: 4-10
High - low Outlook form figure: 63-42
Final Outlook Index figure: 882

Key Stat: *Boro scored a dozen in the final five minutes of games last season.*

2004/05 Premiership Stats

	Apps	Gls	YC	RC
M Bates	0 (2)	0	0	0
G Boateng	25	3	8	0
M Christie	2	1	0	0
C Cooper	11 (4)	0	0	0
A Davies	2 (1)	0	0	0
Doriva	15 (11)	0	4	0
S Downing	28 (7)	5	1	0
U Ehiogu	9 (1)	0	1	0
D Graham	0 (11)	1	0	0
J-F Hasselbaink	36	13	2	0
J-D Job	10 (13)	4	0	0
B Jones	5	0	0	0
J Kennedy	0 (1)	0	0	0
A McMahon	12 (1)	0	2	0
G Mendieta	7	0	1	0
J Morrison	4 (9)	0	1	0
C Nash	2	0	0	0
S Nemeth	18 (13)	4	1	0
R Parlour	32 (1)	0	10	1
S Parnaby	16 (3)	0	0	0
F Queudrue	31	5	6	1
M Reiziger	15 (3)	1	0	0
C Riggott	20 (1)	2	3	0
M Schwarzer	31	0	0	0
G Southgate	36	0	4	0
M Viduka	15 (1)	5	0	0
B Zenden	36	5	8	0

League and Cup Stats
Clean sheets 12
Yellow cards 52 Red cards 2
Players used 27
Leading scorer:
Jimmy-Floyd Hasselbaink 16 (13 league)

Outlook forecast: 6th
Your forecast:

NEWCASTLE

Nickname: The Magpies
Colours: Black and white
Ground: St James' Park
Capacity: 52,218
Tel: 0191 201 8425
www.nufc.co.uk

SOME people never learn their lesson. Throughout his eventful managerial career, one fact has become crystal clear about Graeme Souness - he just doesn't get on with flair players.

It should hardly come as a surprise when you consider that during his playing days he spent most of his time hacking lumps out of players of that ilk.

However, in ousting the likes of Craig Bellamy, Patrick Kluivert and Laurent Robert from St James' Park, Souness has left himself with a big problem - what he is left with isn't much cop.

If he is bidding to rid the club of big time Charlies and replace them with honest pros then fair enough, but by entering into negotiations with Luis Figo, king of the hissy fit, it looked for a while as though he was intent on replacing like for like.

However, the captures of Inter's highly-rated midfielder Emre and Scott Parker from Chelsea are definite signs of ambition, and an indication that Newcastle still have the necessary pulling power.

Parker's lack of football in the last 18 months is a concern, but with the World Cup looming, the 2004 PFA Young Player of the Year will do his best to ensure both he and his new club enjoy a successful season.

It is men with this workmanlike and ambitious attitude that the fiery Scot should be after, rather than the likes of Figo. Unfortunately, practicality and sense make uneasy bedfellows at St James' Park, and another season of false dawns and mediocrity is anticipated.

Longest run without loss: 8
Longest run without win: 8
High - low league position: 7-17
High - low Outlook form figure: 62-33
Final Outlook Index figure: 867

Key Stat: *They culled just four points from aways at the top twelve.*

2004/05 Premiership Stats

	Apps	Gls	YC	RC
D Ambrose	8 (4)	3	1	0
S Ameobi	17 (14)	2	3	1
C Babayaro	7	0	2	0
C Bellamy	21	7	2	0
O Bernard	19 (2)	0	4	0
J-A Boumsong	14	0	0	0
L Bowyer	26 (1)	3	5	2
T Bramble	18 (1)	1	2	0
N Butt	16 (2)	1	3	0
S Carr	26	1	5	0
M Chopra	0 (1)	0	0	0
K Dyer	20 (3)	4	0	1
R Elliott	15 (2)	1	5	0
A Faye	8 (1)	0	7	1
S Given	36	0	1	0
S Harper	2	0	0	0
A Hughes	18 (4)	1	0	0
J Jenas	28 (3)	1	4	0
R Johnsen	3	0	2	0
P Kluivert	15 (10)	6	3	0
J Milner	13 (12)	1	0	0
C N'Zogbia	8 (6)	0	2	0
A O'Brien	21 (2)	2	3	0
P Ramage	2 (2)	0	0	0
L Robert	20 (11)	3	4	0
A Shearer	26 (2)	7	0	0
S Taylor	11 (2)	0	5	1

League and Cup Stats
Clean sheets 9
Yellow cards 55 Red cards 6
Players used 27
Leading scorer:
Alan Shearer 19 (7 league)

Outlook forecast: 10th

Your forecast:

PORTSMOUTH

Nickname: Pompey
Colours: Blue
Ground: Fratton Park
Capacity: 20,101
Tel: 023 9273 1204
www.pompeyfc.co.uk

THE fixture list has been relatively kind to Portsmouth in that they will not have to face any of the big boys until late November.

However, if Pompey reach that stage of the campaign with a number of points that wouldn't prevent you from driving, a return to the Championship is inevitable.

The decision to shove Harry Redknapp to one side looks barmier and barmier with every passing month. Milan Mandaric is left with a manager in Alain Perrin who I'm not sure even he knows much about, while honest 'Arry is left in a job he never really wanted in the first place.

The whole Redknapp affair has thrown the club completely off course and heading for the sign marked Premiership trapdoor not long after they had finally found some semblance of stability and direction.

The loss of Yakubu is another sign that Fratton Park isn't a happy camp at present and quite what Laurent Robert is going to bring to the party is anyone's guess. Safe to say though, his work ethic doesn't exactly lend itself to a relegation dog fight.

Andy O'Brien, a man who could not oust Titus Bramble from Newcastle's defence, is hardly likely to shore things up at the back, and the jury is out on Collins Mbesuma, prolific up front for Kaizer Chiefs but rejected after a trial at Bolton.

Perrin did halt the Pompey slide to some extent when he arrived at the back-end of last term, but if his troops aren't ready from the off, it could be some time before we hear the Pompey chimes in the Premiership again.

Longest run without loss: 5
Longest run without win: 6
High - low league position: 9-16
High - low Outlook form figure: 59-39
Final Outlook Index figure: 854
Key Stat: *Pompey managed just 18 second-half goals last season.*

2004/05 Premiership Stats

	Apps	Gls	YC	RC
J Ashdown	16	0	0	0
P Berger	30 (2)	3	0	0
E Berkovic	6 (5)	1	0	0
K Chalkias	5	0	0	0
A Cisse	12 (8)	0	1	0
J Curtis	0 (1)	0	0	0
A De Zeeuw	32	3	3	0
A Faye	17 (3)	0	4	1
R Fuller	13 (18)	1	4	0
A Griffin	18 (4)	0	7	0
S Hislop	17	0	0	0
R Hughes	13 (3)	0	4	0
D Kamara	15 (10)	4	3	0
J Keene	1 (1)	0	0	0
L LuaLua	20 (5)	6	2	1
V Mezague	3 (8)	0	0	0
G O'Neil	21 (3)	2	3	0
L Primus	31 (4)	1	2	0
N Quashie	19	0	2	0
A Rodic	1 (3)	0	0	0
G Skopelitis	9 (4)	0	2	0
D Stefanovic	32	0	4	0
S Stone	22 (1)	3	1	0
M Taylor	21 (10)	1	4	0
D Unsworth	15	2	4	0
Yakubu	29 (1)	13	2	0

League and Cup Stats
Clean sheets 8
Yellow cards 43 Red cards 1
Players used 26
Leading scorer:
Aiyegbeni Yakubu 17 (13 league)

Outlook forecast: 18th

Your forecast:

Sponsored by Stan James

SUNDERLAND

Nickname: Mackems / Black Cats
Colours: Red and white
Ground: Stadium Of Light
Capacity: 48,300
Tel: 0191 551 5000
www.safc.com

SUNDERLAND could probably play with ten men in each of their Premiership games in the coming season and still find it hard to perform as badly as they did last time they dined at the top table of English football.

With 19 points from 38 games in 2003, the Wearsiders comfortably achieved the lowest points tally in Premiership history and that stat does not even begin to do justice to how awful that team really was.

The Black Cats open with a home game against Charlton and, in the corresponding fixture two years ago, three own goals in the space of eight first-half minutes gifted the Londoners victory.

Mick McCarthy has taken time to re-establish his reputation and restore some pride to a proud club, and in spite of their limitations you can be assured there will be no freebies this time around.

This is a side that has prevailed through hard work rather than fantasy football.

Big Mick has been busy in the transfer market already this summer. Jon Stead has much to prove after fading badly at Blackburn, both Nyron Nosworthy and Daryl Murphy will relish the challenge of a step up in class and Kelvin Davis was the best keeper in the Championship with Ipswich last term. He has the ability to make the impossible look routine but has serious problems in the kicking department.

The layers have not been too impressed with McCarthy's early signings and you can see why they have been installed as 3-1 favourites to finish bottom.

Longest run without loss: 8
Longest run without win: 2
High - low league position: 1-17
High - low Outlook form figure: 67-46
Final Outlook Index figure: 864
Key Stat: *The Black Cats won 11 of their last 13 league games.*

2004/05 Championship Stats

	Apps	Gls	YC	RC
B Alnwick	3	0	1	0
J Arca	39 (1)	9	8	0
G Breen	40	2	5	1
M Bridges	5 (14)	1	0	0
C Brown	13 (24)	5	3	0
S Caldwell	41	4	4	1
D Carter	8 (2)	1	1	0
B Clark	1 (1)	0	0	0
D Collins	6 (8)	0	0	0
N Collins	8 (3)	0	0	0
B Deane	0 (4)	0	0	0
S Elliott	29 (13)	15	1	0
M Ingham	1 (1)	0	0	0
S Johnson	1 (4)	0	0	0
K Kyle	5 (1)	0	2	0
L Lawrence	20 (12)	7	3	0
M Lynch	5 (6)	0	0	0
G McCartney	35 (1)	0	4	0
T Myhre	31	0	0	0
J Oster	6 (3)	0	0	0
M Piper	1 (1)	0	0	0
M Poom	11	0	0	0
C Robinson	40	4	9	0
M Stewart	40 (3)	16	2	0
S Thornton	3 (13)	4	5	0
A Welsh	3 (4)	1	0	0
D Whitehead	39 (3)	5	5	0
J Whitley	32 (3)	0	9	0
D Williams	1	0	1	0
S Wright	39	1	10	0

League and Cup Stats
Clean sheets 19
Yellow cards 73   Red cards 2
Players used 30
Leading scorer:
Marcus Stewart 17 (16 league)

Outlook forecast: 20th

Your forecast:

TOTTENHAM HOTSPUR

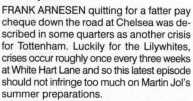

Nickname: Spurs
Colours: White and navy blue
Ground: White Hart Lane
Capacity: 36,236
Tel: 020 8365 5000
www.spurs.co.uk

FRANK ARNESEN quitting for a fatter pay cheque down the road at Chelsea was described in some quarters as another crisis for Tottenham. Luckily for the Lilywhites, crises occur roughly once every three weeks at White Hart Lane and so this latest episode should not infringe too much on Martin Jol's summer preparations.

Quite what Arnesen did to earn such kudos in the first place is beyond me. True, the likes of Tom Huddlestone, Wayne Routledge, Andy Reid and Michael Dawson all look like good signings, but the average student layabout with a serious Championship Manager addiction could have told Daniel Levy all of that for free.

The long-term loss to Spurs is difficult to ascertain but even if Arnesen was to unearth the next Ronaldo, it is unlikely he would be tempted by the outside possibility of Uefa Cup football with Tottenham, and in Jol, they have a decent enough head chef to cook the perfect broth.

Sorting out his strike partnership must be priority number one. It's strange since Jol hails from the land of total football that he seems to have it stuck in his mind that little man must play alongside big man.

In Jermain Defoe and Robbie Keane, Spurs have two international class strikers, but in Freddie Kanoute and Mido they possess two lazy sulkers.

Given the chance to shine together, I'm convinced Defoe and Keane can combine as a successful double act. It may not be Gilzean and Greaves, but let's walk before we can run Spurs fans.

Longest run without loss: 10
Longest run without win: 4
High - low league position: 5-15
High - low Outlook form figure: 65-40
Final Outlook Index figure: 876

Key Stat: *They won only once after falling behind last season.*

2004/05 Premiership Stats

	Apps	Gls	YC	RC
T Atouba	15	3	1	0
M Brown	20 (4)	1	8	0
G Bunjevcevic	2 (1)	0	1	0
M Carrick	26 (3)	0	1	0
R Cerny	2 (1)	0	0	0
C Davenport	0 (1)	0	0	0
S Davies	17 (4)	0	0	0
S Davis	11 (4)	0	4	0
M Dawson	5	0	2	0
J Defoe	28 (7)	13	5	0
G Doherty	0 (1)	0	0	0
E Edman	28	1	3	0
A Gardner	8 (9)	0	0	0
P Ifil	2	0	0	0
J Jackson	3 (5)	0	1	0
F Kanoute	22 (10)	7	2	1
R Keane	23 (12)	11	0	0
S Kelly	13 (4)	2	1	0
L King	38	2	2	0
M Mabizela	1	0	0	0
D Marney	3 (2)	2	3	0
Mido	4 (5)	2	1	0
N Naybet	27	1	4	0
N Pamarot	23	1	4	0
Pedro Mendes	22 (2)	1	3	0
J Redknapp	9 (5)	0	5	0
A Reid	13	1	2	0
R Ricketts	5 (1)	0	0	0
P Robinson	36	0	0	0
M Yeates	0 (2)	0	1	0
R Ziegler	12 (11)	1	1	0

League and Cup Stats

Clean sheets 16
Yellow cards 44 Red cards 1
Players used 31
Leading scorer:
Jermain Defoe 22 (13 league)

Outlook forecast: 7th

Your forecast:

WEST BROM

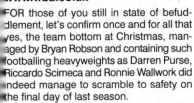

Nickname: The Baggies
Colours: Navy blue and white
Ground: The Hawthorns
Capacity: 27,877
Tel: 0121 525 8888
www.wba.co.uk

FOR those of you still in state of befuddlement, let's confirm once and for all that yes, the team bottom at Christmas, managed by Bryan Robson and containing such footballing heavyweights as Darren Purse, Riccardo Scimeca and Ronnie Wallwork did indeed manage to scramble to safety on the final day of last season.

One couldn't help feel more than a tad pleased for Robson after he helped to mastermind the Baggies' great escape, especially after he was all but written off in a managerial capacity from the moment Steve Gibson drafted in Terry Venables to hold his hand during the end of his tenure at Middlesbrough.

Refreshed and revitalised after a short spell at Bradford, Robson appears to have learnt from his mistakes while maintaining the same drive and enthusiasm that made him one of his country's greatest players.

His standing in the game is still such that players will always be attracted by the idea of playing for him. Kevin Campbell and Kieran Richardson were snapped up back in January and Robson has brought in more men with something to prove in Darren Carter, Steve Watson and Chris Kirkland.

However, Robson will be all too aware that one swallow does not a summer make. Much is required if they are to avoid the strain and heartache that made watching any game involving the bottom four last term border on the unhealthy.

However, with the experience of last season behind them, bank on the Baggies to still be boing-boinging come May 2006.

Longest run without loss: 4
Longest run without win: 14
High - low league position: 11-20
High - low Outlook form figure: 60-28
Final Outlook Index figure: 855

Key Stat: *Eight away score-draws last term, including at Arsenal and Man United.*

2004/05 Premiership Stats

	Apps	Gls	YC	RC
M Albrechtsen	20 (4)	0	1	0
K Campbell	16	3	0	0
R Chaplow	3 (1)	0	0	0
N Clement	35	3	1	1
C Contra	5	0	0	1
S Dobie	1 (4)	1	0	0
L Dyer	0 (4)	0	0	0
R Earnshaw	18 (13)	11	0	0
T Gaardsoe	25 (4)	0	2	1
Z Gera	31 (7)	6	4	0
J Greening	32 (2)	0	4	1
B Haas	9 (1)	0	1	0
G Horsfield	18 (11)	3	2	0
R Hoult	36	0	1	0
R Hulse	0 (5)	0	0	0
J Inamoto	0 (3)	0	0	0
A Johnson	22	0	3	0
N Kanu	21 (7)	2	2	0
J Koumas	5 (5)	0	1	0
T Kuszczak	2 (1)	0	0	0
D Moore	10 (6)	0	3	0
D Purse	22	0	2	1
K Richardson	11 (1)	3	2	0
P Robinson	28 (2)	1	6	0
A Sakiri	2 (1)	0	0	0
R Scimeca	27 (6)	0	3	0
R Wallwork	19 (1)	1	1	0

League and Cup Stats
Clean sheets 8
Yellow cards 40 Red cards 4
Players used 27
Leading scorer:
Robert Earnshaw 14 (11 league)

Outlook forecast: 16th
Your forecast:

WEST HAM

Nickname: Hammers / Irons
Colours: Claret and blue
Ground: Boleyn Ground
Capacity: 35,500
Tel: 020 8548 2748
www.whufc.co.uk

WITH zero games played in the 2005/06 season, West Ham sit second bottom by virtue of alphabetical order. The Iron's points tally will have improved by mid May, but it is unlikely that their final position will prevent them from making an immediate return to the Championship.

The coming season is likely to be a case of what might have been for the West Ham faithful as they visit the top Premiership grounds to catch up with old friends Frank, Joe, Rio and Jermain.

Had the Hammers kept those individuals together, they might be playing in the Champions League. However, thanks to chronic mismanagement, those England regulars found new homes and bigger wage packets and Upton Park regulars must content themselves with the limited skills of Bobby Zamora and Tomas Repka.

Alan Pardew is a likeable boss, but one who suffers from a chronic case of 'Henmanitis' - the ability to appear a winner who says the right things, that only serves to make him look an even bigger plonker when he is fated to end up a loser.

Promising youngsters are starting to roll off the production line again. Elliot Ward, Mark Noble and Rio Ferdinand's younger brother Anton all showed promise during West Ham's successful play-off campaign.

But, despite adding a smattering of Premiership know-how in Paul Konchesky and Roy Carroll, a lack of experience both on the pitch and in the dugout is sure to mean West Ham will be blowing bubbles in the Championship come 2006/07.

Longest run without loss: 8
Longest run without win: 5
High - low league position: 4-16
High - low Outlook form figure: 65-42
Final Outlook Index figure: 821

Key Stat: *They lost more than they won against other top-half sides last term.*

2004/05 Championship Stats

	Apps	Gls	YC	RC
R Brevett	10	1	2	1
S Bywater	36	0	1	0
L Chadwick	22 (10)	1	2	0
C Cohen	1 (10)	0	0	1
C Dailly	2 (1)	0	1	0
C Davenport	10	0	2	0
M Etherington	37 (2)	4	0	0
A Ferdinand	24 (5)	1	1	0
C Fletcher	26 (6)	2	6	0
R Garcia	0 (1)	0	0	0
M Harewood	45	17	7	1
D Hutchison	2 (3)	0	2	0
S Lomas	18 (5)	1	2	1
M Mackay	17 (1)	2	1	0
J McAnuff	0 (1)	0	0	0
T McClenahan	0 (2)	0	0	0
A Melville	3	0	0	0
H Mullins	32 (5)	1	4	1
S Newton	11	0	0	0
M Noble	10 (3)	0	2	0
A Nowland	3 (1)	1	0	0
C Powell	35 (1)	0	1	0
D Powell	5	1	1	0
S Rebrov	12 (14)	1	3	0
N Reo-Coker	34 (5)	3	10	0
T Repka	42	0	6	1
T Sheringham	26 (7)	20	1	0
M Taricco	1	0	0	0
J Walker	10	0	1	0

League and Cup Stats
Clean sheets 18
Yellow cards 65 Red cards 6
Players used 32
Leading scorer:
Marlon Harewood 22 (17 league)

Outlook forecast: 19th

Your forecast:

WIGAN

Nickname: The Latics
Colours: Blue
Ground: JJB Stadium
Capacity: 25,000
Tel: 01942 774000
www.wiganlatics.co.uk

"HOSTING Chelsea on the first day of the season, it's like all our Christmases have come at once", said a club spokeswoman on hearing the news that newly promoted Wigan will play Chelsea on the opening day of the season.

Now, I have never been anywhere near Wigan during the festive period, but I imagine it can't be a particularly happy location if December 25th on Wigan Pier bears any similarity to taking a beating from the champions in near 100 degree heat.

Luckily, the Latics' fate will not be determined by the margin of defeat they suffer on August 13th but what they accomplish in the remaining 37 fixtures.

In Paul Jewell, Wigan can count on a manager who somehow kept Bradford in the division, whilst chairman Dave Whelan has the ambition to ensure his club are here to stay in the manner that clubs like Barnsley and Swindon plainly weren't.

Despite Whelan's millions and promotion to the Premiership, Europe's finest have not exactly been quick to volunteer their services to the Wigan cause. Playing in front of a half empty stadium in a town more concerned with oval balls than round ones is hardly likely to entice the Carlos Kickaballs of this world.

Fancy-sounding foreign additions are not what Wigan require. Their young and inexperienced squad could do with a smattering of wise old men to help the likes of Bullard, Ellington and McCulloch develop. Should they find those men, Wigan may be more than just one-season wonders.

Longest run without loss: 13
Longest run without win: 4
High - low league position: 1-3
High - low Outlook form figure: 67-44
Final Outlook Index figure: 837

Key Stat: *They won just the one against others in the top four.*

2004/05 Championship Stats

	Apps	Gls	YC	RC
L Baines	41	1	3	0
I Breckin	42	0	4	0
J Bullard	46	3	5	0
N Eaden	33 (6)	0	3	0
N Ellington	43 (2)	24	0	0
J Filan	46	0	4	0
M Flynn	1 (12)	1	1	0
P Frandsen	9	1	0	0
D Graham	13 (17)	1	0	0
M Jackson	35 (1)	1	2	0
J Jarrett	4 (10)	0	1	0
A Johansson	0 (1)	0	0	0
G Kavanagh	11	0	3	0
A Mahon	21 (6)	7	2	0
L McCulloch	42	14	5	1
S McMillan	5 (3)	0	0	0
P Mitchell	0 (1)	0	0	0
B Ormerod	3 (3)	2	0	0
J Roberts	45	21	9	0
G Teale	29 (8)	3	1	0
E Thome	11 (4)	0	1	0
G Whalley	7 (1)	0	0	0
D Wright	19 (12)	0	1	0

League and Cup Stats
Clean sheets 20
Yellow cards 47 Red cards 1
Players used 23
Leading scorer:
Nathan Ellington 24 (all league)

Outlook forecast: 17th
Your forecast:

BRIGHTON & HOVE ALBION

Nickname: The Seagulls
Colours: Blue and white

Ground: Withdean Stadium
Capacity: 7,053

Tel: 01273 778 855

www.seagulls.co.uk

ONCE again, the Seagulls' pre-season is dominated by the question of whether John Prescott will allow Brighton to move to a purpose-built 23,000-capacity stadium in Falmer.

And once again there is prevarication with the original June deadline pushed back because of conflicting planning reports.

However, Mark McGhee did receive one piece of close-season good news when the club was the winner of Coca-Cola's 'Win A Player' promotion. Part of the £250,000 prize has been spent on Bury striker Colin Kazim-Richards, who will augment a toothless attack. Veteran defender Jason Dodd has also arrived after being released by Southampton.

They can stay up but their survival might depend on producing spirited displays like the ones that saw Brighton get results at West Ham, Leeds and Sheffield United last term.

Longest run without loss: 5
Longest run without win: 9
High - low league position: 13-22
High - low Outlook form figure: 56-34
Key Stat: *Albion managed wins against half the top ten. God knows how!*

Outlook forecast: 20th

Final Outlook Index figure: 780
Clean sheets 11
Yellow cards 62 Red cards 6
Players used 30

Leading scorer:
Adam Virgo 8 (all league)

Your forecast:

BURNLEY

Nickname: The Clarets
Colours: Claret and blue

Ground: Turf Moor
Capacity: 22,546

Tel: 0870 443 1882

www.burnleyfootballclub.com

AVOIDING the drop was Steve Cotterill's remit when taking charge of the Turf Moor reins last summer.

And that he did, taking the Clarets to the dizzy heights of 13th on the back of a miserly defence, as well as orchestrating the embarrassment of Aston Villa and Liverpool in the Carling Cup and FA Cup respectively.

What is the reward for the ex-Cheltenham and Stoke boss? A post-season spent rebuilding his squad, which has shrunk to less than a matchday XI.

To the Potteries he has returned to purchase Wayne Thomas and Gifton Noel-Williams, whilst raiding Bournemouth for attacking midfield pair Garreth O'Connor and Wade Elliott.

Full-back Danny Karbassiyoon has also signed after being released by Arsenal and more low-budget captures are expected to follow.

Longest run without loss: 8
Longest run without win: 6
High - low league position: 5-14
High - low Outlook form figure: 57-42
Key Stat: *They did not concede more than three in any league or Cup match.*

Outlook forecast: 11th

Final Outlook Index figure: 795
Clean sheets 22
Yellow cards 71 Red cards 5
Players used 24

Leading scorer:
Nathan Blake 13 (10 league)

Your forecast:

CARDIFF CITY

Nickname: The Bluebirds
Colours: Blue

Ground: Ninian Park
Capacity: 20,000

Tel: 02920 221001

www.cardiffcityfc.co.uk

BALANCING the books, not promotion pushes, is now the priority of colourful chairman Sam Hammam, vilified vice-chairman Peter Ridsdale and new boss Dave Jones this season.

14-goal striker Peter Thorne and midfielder Jobi McAnuff have already departed for title contenders Norwich and Crystal Palace, while defenders Danny Gabbidon and James Collins have been hawked to West Ham. More are likely to follow them out.

However, Willie Boland and Neal Ardley have been joined in the engine room by experienced Sunderland midfielder Jeff Whitley.

Cardiff survived the trapdoor last term only by virtue of their ten home wins.

Although Ninian Park is sure to remain a difficult venue to get a result, the proposed new 30,000-capacity stadium could well be hosting League 1 football next campaign.

Longest run without loss: 8
Longest run without win: 8
High - low league position: 3-23
High - low Outlook form figure: 60-37
Key Stat: *They drew 10 of their aways against others in the bottom half.*

Outlook forecast: 23rd

Final Outlook Index figure: 794
Clean sheets 12
Yellow cards 50 Red cards 4
Players used 32
Leading scorer:
Peter Thorne 14 (12 league)

Your forecast:

COVENTRY CITY

Nickname: The Sky Blues
Colours: Sky blue

Ground: Ricoh Arena
Capacity: 32,000

Tel: 024 76234000

www.ccfc.co.uk

NEW stadiums might tick all the right boxes with city money-men but football fans and punters are definitely wary.

In recent years, Leicester were relegated the season before their move to the Walkers, while both Southampton and West Ham took months to register home wins after leaving their spiritual home and redeveloping respectively.

However, the Sky Blues signed-off from Highfield Road in style, thumping Play-Off placed Derby in the penultimate game of the season to stave off relegation fears.

Micky Adams knows it will be improved away-form - only five wins last term compared with eight in 2003/04 - which will determine a return to the safety of mid-table.

Debts incurred by the move to the Ricoh Arena mean Jamie Scowcroft and Clayton Ince are the only new faces so far but key players have signed on for another campaign, which bodes well.

Longest run without loss: 4
Longest run without win: 7
High - low league position: 5-22
High - low Outlook form figure: 58-35
Key Stat: *They lost five and drew eight of the 22 games where they took the lead.*

Outlook forecast: 15th

Final Outlook Index figure: 789
Clean sheets 9
Yellow cards 58 Red cards 3
Players used 36
Leading scorer:
Gary McSheffrey 14 (12 league)

Your forecast:

CREWE ALEXANDRA

Nickname: The Railwaymen
Colours: Red and white

Ground: Gresty Road
Capacity: 10,066

Tel: 01270 213014

www.crewealex.net

EVERY year Crewe are condemned by the pundits and told to sacrifice their crisp, pass-and-move football to survive the rigours of a relegation battle.

Andy every year manager emeritus Dario Gradi, now 22 seasons at Gresty Road, resists the pundits, finds new gems and relies on miracle reverses of fortune.

Last season was no different. The Railwaymen lost David Wright and club captain Dave Brammer in the summer and ace striker Dean Ashton in the January transfer window before a remarkable final day saw them come from behind to beat Coventry and Gillingham pegged back by already relegated Forest.

Cat Clayton Ince and Colin Murdock have moved on and youngsters Gary Roberts and Chris McCready will play prominent roles.

There is, for once, some cash to spend but Juan Ugarte (free) and Eddie Johnson (loan) are the only early arrivals.

Longest run without loss: 8
Longest run without win: 20
High - low league position: 8-23
High - low Outlook form figure: 63-32
Key Stat: *Against the top 16 they won just once at home.*

Outlook forecast: 21st

Final Outlook Index figure: 777
Clean sheets 4
Yellow cards 25 Red cards 1
Players used 27
Leading scorer:
Dean Ashton 19 (17 league)

Your forecast:

CRYSTAL PALACE

Nickname: The Eagles
Colours: Claret and blue

Ground: Selhurst Park
Capacity: 26,309

Telephone: 0208 768 6000

www.cpfc.co.uk

DON'T expect the Eagles to be too bruised by relegation to push for immediate promotion back to the promised land of the Premiership, whether or not inspirational manager Iain Dowie remains at the helm.

The current most sought-after gaffer in the game has, with the definite and probable exceptions of Wayne Routledge and Andy Johnson respectively, largely kept hold of his squad from the top flight and, by the end of June, already made three decent captures.

There are two to perform on the pitch in the shape of proven striker Jon Macken and combative ex-Millwall stopper Darren Ward, and one, in Neil McDonald, to act as his number two.

The ex-Bolton coach is another devotee of innovative training methods so his arrival could be an effort at pre-empting any mid-season disruption of the Selhurst Park status quo.

Longest run without loss: 4
Longest run without win: 11
High - low league position: 14-19
High - low Outlook form figure: 61-35
Key Stat: *Apart from Andrew Johnson, no Palace player scored more than three!*

Outlook forecast: 1st

Final Outlook Index figure: 838
Clean sheets 10
Yellow cards 57 Red cards 3
Players used 27
Leading scorer:
Andrew Johnson 22 (21 league)

Your forecast:

DERBY COUNTY

Nickname: The Rams
Colours: White and black

Ground: Pride Park
Capacity: 33,597

Tel: 0870 444 1884

www.dcfc.co.uk

THE Rams are once again a club in turmoil after George Burley walked out weeks after taking them to a Play-Off semi-final and it's hard to see new man at the tiller Phil Brown achieving much more than mid-table respectability.

The exact reason for Burley's departure is still not known but what is certain is that there is much rebuilding work to be done.

Mainstays Ian Taylor, Marco Reich and Junior have all been released as the east Midlands club still has huge debts.

And last season's star men, midfielder Inigo Idiakez and 16-goal Grzegorz Raziak, are both likely to arouse interest.

Derby's fourth-place finish last term was won on the back of 12 away victories - including at rivals West Ham, Reading and Sheff United - but this campaign's travels start at post-season nemesis Preston.

Longest run without loss: 6
Longest run without win: 6
High - low league position: 4-19
High - low Outlook form figure: 66-41
Key Stat: *County won all 13 games that they led at half-time.*

Outlook forecast: 13th

Final Outlook Index figure: 826
Clean sheets 15
Yellow cards 55 Red cards 3
Players used 24
Leading scorer:
Grzegorz Rasiak 17 (16 league)

Your forecast:

HULL CITY

Nickname: The Tigers
Colours: Amber and black

Ground: Kingston Communications Stadium
Capacity: 25,404

Tel: 0870 8370003

www.hullcityafc.net

PETER TAYLOR'S stock never quite reached rock bottom but the former Leicester, England U-21 and England (1 game) boss has excelled himself in leading the Tigers back into the second tier of English football for the first time since 1991.

Plymouth survived fairly comfortably after back-to-back promotions and Hull should manage to do so as well if last term's meagre two home defeats is anything to go by.

However, 10 losses on the road suggest there is much for Taylor to work on pre-season and to that end he has made the capture of a new centre-half his prime transfer objective.

Former Sunderland full-back Mark Lynch and highly-rated Portuguese keeper Sergio Leite have already been snared.

So far, 27-goal Stuart Elliot has not been lured away and consolidation in the Championship is a realistic aim.

Longest run without loss: 9
Longest run without win: 6
High - low league position: 1-16
High - low Outlook form figure: 73-41
Key Stat: *They conceded three or more in six away games.*

Outlook forecast: 17th

Final Outlook Index figure: 759
Clean sheets 14
Yellow cards 45 Red cards 4
Players used 29
Leading scorer:
Stuart Elliott 29 (27 league)

Your forecast:

IPSWICH TOWN

Nickname: Town or Tractor Boys
Colours: Blue and white

Ground: Portman Road
Capacity: 30,300

Tel: 01473 400500

www.itfc.co.uk

JOE ROYLE has had a torrid time preparing the Tractor Boys for a fourth season in the Championship as the heartbreak of missing out on automatic promotion on the final day and a second successive Play-Off exit has meant another dismantling of his squad.

Consistent cat Kelvin Davis and Darren Bent at least brought in fees for seeking pastures new but Shefki Kuqi, Tommy Miller, Jim Magilton, Drissa Diallo and Pablo Counago have either exercised their right to walk or have been released.

Goals were Ipswich's most profitable currency last term - Championship top-notchers with 83 - and they appear well set again in attack with Nicky Forster and Sam Parkin in from Reading and Swindon alongside Dean Bowditch.

However, no significant steps to plug holes in defence could mean a campaign treading water.

Longest run without loss: 10
Longest run without win: 4
High - low league position: 1-9
High - low Outlook form figure: 66-41
Key Stat: *Just the one clean sheet against a top-ten side since last October.*
Outlook forecast: 8th

Final Outlook Index figure: 832
Clean sheets 12
Yellow cards 55 Red cards 1
Players used 21
Leading scorer:
Darren Bent 23 (19 league)
Your forecast:

LEEDS UNITED

Nickname: United
Colours: White

Ground: Elland Road
Capacity: 40,204

Tel: 0113 367 6000

www.leedsunited.com

KEITH BLACKWELL will argue that however good a coach he is, any promotion push was doomed to failure last term such was the mess the club was in after relegation and virtual administration.

However, there will be no excuses this time around even if Aaron Lennon is the latest talented youngster to leave Elland Road.

Goalkeeper Ian Bennett and wide midfielders Steve Stone and Eddie Lewis are solid if not spectacular summer additions - more are promised - to a squad that already contains the likes of Clarke Carlisle, David Healy, Rob Hulse and Jermaine Wright.

Indeed, it was not the better teams that Leeds had trouble dispatching last season but the small fry. They beat most of the top dogs but there were reverses at Gillingham, Rotherham and Brighton, and a home defeat by Crewe.

Longest run without loss: 5
Longest run without win: 5
High - low league position: 9-19
High - low Outlook form figure: 57-42
Key Stat: *They had four wins against the top five but none against the final five.*
Outlook forecast: 5th

Final Outlook Index figure: 809
Clean sheets 13
Yellow cards 82 Red cards 7
Players used 35
Leading scorer:
Brian Deane 7 (6 league)
Your forecast:

LEICESTER CITY

Nickname: The Foxes
Colours: Blue and white

Ground: The Walkers Stadium
Capacity: 32,500

Tel: 0870 0406000

www.lcfc.co.uk

LAST year's title tip were flattered in finishing 15th and on the face of it there is no reason why the Foxes should rise from mid-table mediocrity to promotion possibles on the strength of a recuperative off-season.

However, the problems on and off the pitch were underestimated by all - including Craig Levein on taking over from caretaker-manager Dave Bassett in November - and Leicester lost only two of 11 games after going down 1-0 to Blackburn in the FA Cup quarter-finals. Those were to Sunderland and Wigan, while West Ham and Wolves were held and Derby beaten.

The new boss has not been slow in re-shaping the squad.

Mark de Vries was nabbed in the January transfer window and Patrick Kisnorbo, Mo Sylla, Rab Douglas and Paul Henderson signed in the summer to offset the release of a number of last season's first-team regulars.

Longest run without loss: 7
Longest run without win: 7
High - low league position: 8-19
High - low Outlook form figure: 60-41
Key Stat: *The Foxes never won more than two in a row.*

Outlook forecast: 4th

Final Outlook Index figure: 803
Clean sheets 16
Yellow cards 78 Red cards 8
Players used 34
Leading scorer:
David Connolly 13 (all league)

Your forecast:

LUTON TOWN

Nickname: The Hatters
Colours: White and black

Ground: Kenilworth Road
Capacity: 9,975

Tel: 01582 411622

www.lutontown.co.uk

THERE was only one signature Hatters supporters really wanted this summer, that of Portsmouth loanee Rowan Vine, who netted nine times in 45 league games last term.

Mike Newell got his man and he will be joined at Kenilworth Road by Wrexham centre-half Carlos Edwards.

There is genuine optimism that the Bedfordshire boys can avoid an immediate return back down to League 1.

With just six defeats all last season - a better return than either Plymouth or QPR managed during their 2003/04 promotion campaigns - that optimism does not look misplaced.

Indeed, the only reason they are not taken to finish higher than fellow new boys Hull and Sheffield Wednesday is that they are bigger clubs and may be better placed to deal with any injuries or poor form once the enthusiasm of August has died down.

Longest run without loss: 8
Longest run without win: 4
High - low league position: 1-2
High - low Outlook form figure: 70-44
Key Stat: *Does crime pay? The champs committed the most fouls in League 1.*

Outlook forecast: 19th

Final Outlook Index figure: 792
Clean sheets 19
Yellow cards 65 Red cards 4
Players used 25
Leading scorer:
Steve Howard 22 (18 league)

Your forecast:

MILLWALL

Nickname: The Lions
Colours: Blue and white

Ground: The New Den
Capacity: 20,146

Tel: 020 7232 1222

www.millwallfc.co.uk

DENNIS WISE clearly thought he was going to get no financial support from Jeff Burnige - Theo Paphitis' short-lived successor as Lions chairman - and had no hesitation in walking minutes after the end of the last game of the season.

Former RFO columnist Steve Claridge has stepped up to the plate and after short spells in charge at Portsmouth and Weymouth, is out to prove he does more than just talk a good game these days. However, he'll have to make do without the services of Wise, Jody Morris, Kevin Muscat, Darren Ward, Peter Sweeney and Paul Ifill.

That's quite an exit list but last term's dozen home wins was better than any of the teams who finished out of the top-ten and it is a lack of away goals that needs the manager's attention first.

Only Stoke, Burnley and Forest scored fewer away than the Lions 18 last term.

Longest run without loss: 5
Longest run without win: 4
High - low league position: 5-18
High - low Outlook form figure: 68-38
Key Stat: *They conceded nine in the first-half but a whopping 39 in the second-half!*

Outlook forecast: 14th

Final Outlook Index figure: 804
Clean sheets 15
Yellow cards 81 Red cards 8
Players used 33
Leading scorer:
Barry Hayles 12 (all league)

Your forecast:

NORWICH CITY

Nickname: The Canaries
Colours: Yellow and green

Ground: Carrow Road
Capacity: 24,349

Tel: 01603 760 760

www.canaries.co.uk

DELIA SMITH might have shed her homely image with her inebriated "let's be having you", but don't expect Norwich boss Nigel Worthington to be given the boot if the Canaries suffer a slight relegation hangover.

Or for his team to swap their traditional pass-and-move football for kick-and-rush tactics to bounce straight back into the Premiership.

Worthington knows a passing game works at this level - they won the 2003/04 pennant with 94 points - and is bound to have the calibre of players to carry it off.

Dean Ashton is going nowhere and Jason Jarrett and Peter Thorne have already arrived from Wigan and Cardiff.

David Bentley may not return for another East Anglian tour of duty but even so, Robert Green, Thomas Helveg and anyone unsatisfied at Carrow Road can go elsewhere when the price, sure to be re-invested, is right.

Longest run without loss: 4
Longest run without win: 9
High - low league position: 16-20
High - low Outlook form figure: 55-34
Key Stat: *Slow starters? They scored once every 114 minutes in the first-half.*

Outlook forecast: 3rd

Final Outlook Index figure: 846
Clean sheets 7
Yellow cards 35 Red cards 2
Players used 25
Leading scorers: Huckerby, Ashton, Francis & Mckenzie all 7, last three all league.

Your forecast:

PLYMOUTH ARGYLE

Nickname: The Pilgrims
Colours: Green

Ground: Home Park
Capacity: 20,134

Tel: 01752 562561

www.pafc.co.uk

SURVIVAL was all that was required down at Home Park in their first season in the Championship following back-to-back promotions.

Now that has been achieved - by four places, but only three points - there is no doubting what Pilgrims boss Bobby Williamson sees as the key to pushing up the table or who the example to follow is.

It is a strong defence and the precedent set (by Stoke) is of signing veterans.

Anthony Barness and Rufus Brevett are the first two to arrive, from Bolton and West Ham respectively, while Taribo West - spells at Derby as well as Auxerre, Inter and Milan - has signed for a year.

The attack has not been neglected either, with Hungarian midfielder Akos Buzsaky signing a permanent deal and winger Bojan Djordjic also joining on a free from Rangers.

Longest run without loss: 9
Longest run without win: 4
High - low league position: 2-21
High - low Outlook form figure: 62-37
Key Stat: *Since Christmas, they've only beaten one side that finished above them.*

Outlook forecast: 12th

Final Outlook Index figure: 780
Clean sheets 15
Yellow cards 66 Red cards 4
Players used 37
Leading scorer:
Richard Cresswell 21 (16 league)

Your forecast:

PRESTON NORTH END

Nickname: Lillywhites
Colours: White and navy

Ground: Deepdale
Capacity: 22,225

Tel: 0870 442 1964

www.pnefc.net

THE Lilywhites - a few well-worked set-plays apart - froze on their big day out in the Play-Off final and it could well take the Lancashire outfit the best part of the new campaign to rediscover their best form.

Indeed, getting highly-touted manager Billy Davies to sign a new contract will be considered the biggest coup of the summer by the Deepdale board who, entering July, have resisted the temptation to make wholesale changes to their squad in anticipation of bids for impressive striker Dave Nugent and midfielder Chris Sedgwick.

Port Vale forward Dave Hibbert and Bristol City winger Joe Anyinsah have both signed but US international Eddie Lewis did not take up the offer of a new deal.

However, that loss probably will not affect the immediate stability of a team whose promotion push was built around a solid defence.

Longest run without loss: 9
Longest run without win: 5
High - low league position: 4-20
High - low Outlook form figure: 63-38
Key Stat: *They have failed to score in only one league game since Boxing Day.*

Outlook forecast: 7th

Final Outlook Index figure: 829
Clean sheets 15
Yellow cards 66 Red cards 4
Players used 37
Leading scorer:
Richard Cresswell 21 (16 league)

Your forecast:

QUEENS PARK RANGERS

Nickname: The R's
Colours: Blue and white hoops

Ground: Loftus Road
Capacity: 19,148

Tel: 020 8743 0262

www.qpr.co.uk

WHEN the R's won all five league games in September and the first two of October (including home victories over West Ham and Leicester), wide-eyed gaffer Ian Holloway said he'd had enough excitement and just wanted to go to sleep and wake up in May safe.

Despite a final position of 11th, that is pretty much the extent of the Super Hoops' achievements, except for occasional exceptional displays such as the November scalping of Wigan and a February success away at Ipswich.

Signings have been thin on the ground but Aston Villa striker Stefan Moore could be a hit despite failing to notch last season when on loan at Leicester and Millwall.

Tommy Doherty will strengthen the midfield and centre-back Dan Shittu has penned an extension despite speculation about a move to the top flight. He's joined at the back by Ian Evatt.

Longest run without loss: 6
Longest run without win: 8
High - low league position: 3-23
High - low Outlook form figure: 60-36
Key Stat: *They beat only relegated sides in their last 10 matches.*

Outlook forecast: 18th

Final Outlook Index figure: 795
Clean sheets 16
Yellow cards 69 Red cards 5
Players used 36
Leading scorer:
Paul Furlong 19 (all league)

Your forecast:

READING

Nickname: The Royals
Colours: Blue and white

Ground: Madejski Stadium
Capacity: 24,200

Tel: 01189 681100

www.readingfc.co.uk

THE Royals have done magnificently to rack up a hat-trick of top-ten Championship finishes since winning automatic promotion in 2002.

That trend should continue with Steve Coppell being allowed to set the dead wood adrift and promised funds by Reading chairman John Madejski.

However, entering July, Leroy Lita is the only major signing and the tag of 'nearly men' could be hard to shift.

There was defeat by Wolves in the 2003 Play-Off semis, the long-term disruption caused by Alan Pardew's defection to West Ham that meant missing out on the Play-Offs in 2004, and last term, a final-month collapse of three defeats in a row.

19-goal Dave Kitson is a contender for section top-scorer and Lita, who couldn't stop scoring for Bristol City last term, could make an excellent strike partner for him.

Longest run without loss: 5
Longest run without win: 8
High - low league position: 1-8
High - low Outlook form figure: 60-36
Key Stat: *Unpredictable or what? They lost at Rotherham but won at Sunderland.*

Outlook forecast: 9th

Final Outlook Index figure: 806
Clean sheets 21
Yellow cards 41 Red cards 0
Players used 20
Leading scorer:
Dave Kitson 19 (all league)

Your forecast:

SHEFFIELD UNITED

Nickname: The Blades
Colours: Red and white

Ground: Bramall Lane
Capacity: 30,936

Tel: 0114 2215757

www.sufc.co.uk

SEASON 2005/06 surely represents Neil Warnock's last chance to sup at the saloon that is Bramall Lane.

The game's most in-your-face manager is looking long on bluster but extremely short of delivery, as each summer he re-shapes his Blades for a promotion push only to see them fall short.

This campaign is no different. Sprightly forwards Danny Webber, a loanee last term, and Paul Ifill have already been snapped up for fees while veteran centre-half Craig Short signed up on a free with more captures imminent.

Premiership enquiries about the availability of tough-tackling Phil Jagielka have been rejected.

It is the Blades' home form that needs improving - only nine wins and just the one, over Sunderland, against major promotion rivals.

The fixture list has been quite kind. None of the relegated clubs visit pre-Christmas.

Longest run without loss: 9
Longest run without win: 7
High - low league position: 5-21
High - low Outlook form figure: 62-41
Key Stat: *The Blades were awarded just one penalty last season.*

Outlook forecast: 10th

Final Outlook Index figure: 798
Clean sheets 16
Yellow cards 51 Red cards 5
Players used 33
Leading scorer:
Andy Gray 18 (15 league)

Your forecast:

SHEFFIELD WEDNESDAY

Nickname: The Owls
Colours: Blue and white

Ground: Hillsborough
Capacity: 39,814

Tel: 0114 221 2121

www.swfc.co.uk

PAUL STURROCK has twice shown the managerial nous to take clubs into the Championship and it is highly likely he has the skills not only to keep the Owls up but to win them a berth in mid-table.

There was a marked failure to win at home against any of the four teams that finished above them in the main season but the squad upped their game in the Play-Offs, even if their roller-coaster victory over Hartlepool in the final was a little fortunate.

In the recess, Sturrock has concentrated on defensive acquisitions - Drissa Diallo from Ipswich, Jon Hills from Gillingham and Graham Coughlan from Plymouth - safe in the knowledge that Wednesday notched 43 away goals last term, the most in League 1 and more than promoted Hull got at home.

However, Northern Ireland international striker James Quinn has been released.

Longest run without loss: 10
Longest run without win: 7
High - low league position: 3-15
High - low Outlook form figure: 69-39
Key Stat: *Before the Play-Offs they won one in eight against the teams above them.*

Outlook forecast: 16th

Final Outlook Index figure: 742
Clean sheets 16
Yellow cards 48 Red cards 5
Players used 34
Leading scorer:
Steve MacLean 19 (18 league)

Your forecast:

SOUTHAMPTON

Nickname: The Saints
Colours: Red and white

Ground: St Mary's Stadium
Capacity: 32,800

Tel: 0870 2200 000

www.saintsfc.co.uk

HOW much has the drop taken out of the Saints and how much worse, with Sir Clive Woodward stirring things up behind the scenes, will morale get before it gets better?

It's hardly a case of rats leaving the sinking ship but Kevin Phillips was delighted at being snapped up by Villa, Peter Crouch effectively handed in a transfer request after the England tour of the USA and ace keeper Antti Niemi is sure to be poached by a Premiership club once the money offered is acceptable.

Short term measures have been taken in that the ever-enthusiastic Dave Bassett will coach the defence while the forever-fiesty Dennis Wise is on the payroll, although as a player and not as a prospective boss.

Regular victories at St Mary's are a given but decent away form - never Harry's forte - is a must from the off.

Longest run without loss: 6	*Final Outlook Index figure: 842*
Longest run without win: 9	*Clean sheets 8*
High - low league position: 14-20	*Yellow cards 49 Red cards 2*
High - low Outlook form figure: 55-35	*Players used 35*
Key Stat: *Saints came from behind to win or draw seven times last season.*	*Leading scorer:* *Peter Crouch 16 (12 league)*
Outlook forecast: 6th	**Your forecast:**

STOKE CITY

Nickname: The Potters
Colours: Red and white

Ground: Britannia Stadium
Capacity: 28,384

Tel: 01782 592222

www.stokecityfc.com

SACKING Tony Pulis just before pre-season, for allegedly refusing to sign foreign players, shows the mess Stoke have got themselves into.

Although new Britannia Stadium boss Johan Boskamp has managed to retain some key players like cat Ed de Goey and defender Gerry Taggart, as well as signing Peter Sweeney and Mamady Sidibe, they look like strugglers.

So far, he has turned down offers for club captain Clive Clarke, but Burnley have nabbed Wayne Thomas and Gifton Noel-Williams, and the likes of John Halls and Clint Hill could be ripe for poaching. Foreign targets such as Walter Baseggio are now swift to decline approaches.

Back-to-back mid-table finishes have been founded on a solid defence. This is unlikely to continue in the current climate and there is no obvious solution to just 36 goals scored.

Longest run without loss: 6	*Final Outlook Index figure: 788*
Longest run without win: 7	*Clean sheets 20*
High - low league position: 1-16	*Yellow cards 79 Red cards 6*
High - low Outlook form figure: 64-36	*Players used 32*
Key Stat: *Shut-out experts: Stoke won 15 of the 17 games where they took the lead.*	*Leading scorer:* *Gifton Noel-Williams 12 (all league)*
Outlook forecast: 22nd	**Your forecast:**

Sponsored by Stan James

WATFORD

Nickname: The Hornets
Colours: Yellow and black

Ground: Vicarage Road
Capacity: 22,000

Tel: 01923 496000

www.watfordfc.com

LAST July was a month of anticipation at Vicarage Road as Ray Lewington managed to drag the Hornets out of the depths of despair following the death of Jimmy Davis into a respectable mid-table position by virtue of some flowing football.

This pre-season, the atmosphere will be much more fraught following a mass exodus.

Name the player and he has gone - Heidar Helguson, Danny Webber, Jack Smith, Sean Dyche - although Marlon King is a loan signing.

Adrian Boothroyd was given the hotseat following Lewington's March sacking, and anticipating such a scenario pressed unproven youngsters into service.

They played pretty football and, with wins at Rotherham and Stoke, got the necessary results. However, eight defeats in the last 15 matches is a pretty plausible case for terminal decline.

Longest run without loss: 11
Longest run without win: 8
High - low league position: 6-21
High - low Outlook form figure: 67-33
Key Stat: *They managed a 1-6-1 record in games against the top four.*

Outlook forecast: 24th

Final Outlook Index figure: 783
Clean sheets 18
Yellow cards 59 Red cards 2
Players used 29
Leading scorer:
Heidar Helguson 20 (16 league)

Your forecast:

WOLVERHAMPTON W

Nickname: Wolves
Colours: Gold and black

Ground: Molineux
Capacity: 28,525

Tel: 0870 442 0123

www.wolves.co.uk

IF teams take on the manner of their managers, then no doubt Glenn Hoddle's Wolves will have been the Championship club most satisfied with itself after ending last term on an unbeaten league run of 18.

Punters have not been slow to back the men from Molineux - only £8 was traded at 11.00 on Betfair and VC Bet's 9-1 is long gone.

However, any preening will have to be left on the beach with newly-relegated Southampton and Crystal Palace two tough opening fixtures.

And the majority of the nine draws in this sequence must be converted into wins if a title challenge is to go full term.

Parkhead terrace hero Jackie McNamara is a solid early signing, and more are slated to arrive, but keeping the likes of Paul Ince and Mark Kennedy happy could be just as important to the Gold and Blacks' prospects.

Longest run without loss: 16
Longest run without win: 7
High - low league position: 9-21
High - low Outlook form figure: 62-45
Key Stat: *Godliness or Hodliness? Only Crewe committed fewer fouls.*

Outlook forecast: 2nd

Final Outlook Index figure: 831
Clean sheets 8
Yellow cards 54 Red cards 2
Players used 25
Leading scorer:
Kenny Miller 20 (19 league)

Your forecast:

AFC BOURNEMOUTH

Nickname: The Cherries
Colours: Red and black

Ground: Dean Court
Capacity: 10,770

Tel: 01202 726300

www.afcb.co.uk

THE Cherries were superb on the road last season and with 36 points only promoted Luton and Sheffield Wednesday did better. Their away form kept Sean O'Driscoll's side in Play-Off contention until the final day and only a late Hartlepool equaliser thwarted their ambitions.

Injuries proved as costly as some indifferent home form, with most of the defence visiting the treatment tables in the spring and star left-back Warren Cummings is set to miss the start of the new season thanks to a double leg fracture sustained against Swindon. James Hayter also suffered, missing two months of the season but again finished top scorer with 19 league goals.

Midfielders Wade Elliott and 13-goal Garreth O'Connor have both gone to Burnley, but O'Driscoll is looking to strengthen and made Stephen Cooke the first summer arrival after two successful loan spells from Villa.

Longest run without loss: 6
Longest run without win: 5
High - low league position: 4-20
High - low Outlook form figure: 63-42
Key Stat: *They won three of 14 games against the seven sides above them.*

Outlook forecast: 7th

Final Outlook Index figure: 742
Clean sheets 12
Yellow cards 35 Red cards 4
Players used 26
Leading scorer:
James Hayter 22 (19 league)

Your forecast:

BARNSLEY

Nickname: Tykes
Colours: Red and white

Ground: Oakwell
Capacity: 23,186

Tel: 01226 211211

www.barnsleyfc.co.uk

THANKS to the efforts of new boss Andy Ritchie, who replaced Paul Hart in March, the Tykes finished in mid-table, 10 points from the Play-Offs and 10 from the relegation zone.

Ritchie got the job after Hart endured a barren run of two wins in 13 games and promptly won Manager of the Month, taking 18 points from the final eight matches. Under Ritchie, Barnsley earned almost half a point per game more than under Hart.

Home form was a problem. The Tykes managed seven wins at Oakwell, as many as they won away from home and less than any other team that beat the drop.

They'll miss 17-goal Michael Chopra, whose loan spell from Newcastle is over, but Paul Hayes has joined after finding the net 19 times for Scunthorpe last term, and Daniel Nardiello has turned his loan from Man United into a permanent move.

Longest run without loss: 13
Longest run without win: 7
High - low league position: 12-20
High - low Outlook form figure: 67-37
Key Stat: *Pure mid-table mediocrity. Only most League 1 draws (19) stands out.*

Outlook forecast: 8th

Final Outlook Index figure: 743
Clean sheets 13
Yellow cards 74 Red cards 6
Players used 27
Leading scorer:
Michael Chopra 17 (all league)

Your forecast:

BLACKPOOL

Nickname: The Seasiders
Colours: Tangerine and white

Ground: Bloomfield Road
Capacity: 11,295

Tel: 0870 443 1953

www.blackpoolfc.co.uk

COLIN HENDRY made an inauspicious start to his first job in management as nine games passed without victory for the Seasiders, but a 3-0 win away at Port Vale broke Blackpool's duck and they finished out of trouble.

Hendry's side got better as the season went on and although the Seasiders seemed to run out of steam at the death and lost their final two games, they consistently produced results after Christmas.

Home form was again a problem and they lost as many as they won at Bloomfield Road, but away from Blackpool they performed respectably, earning more points on the road than Play-Off finalists Hartlepool.

Top scorer Scott Taylor went to Plymouth in the winter transfer window, but Keigan Parker adapted well to his first season south of the border and John Murphy also made a valuable contribution to the Blackpool goal tally.

Longest run without loss: 6
Longest run without win: 9
High - low league position: 14-24
High - low Outlook form figure: 61-27
Key Stat: *The Seasiders won only four against top-half teams.*

Outlook forecast: 20th

Final Outlook Index figure: 731
Clean sheets 14
Yellow cards 65 Red cards 3
Players used 36
Leading scorer:
Scott Taylor 14 (12 league)

Your forecast:

BRADFORD CITY

Nickname: The Bantams
Colours: Claret and amber

Ground: Valley Parade
Capacity: 25,000

Tel: 01274 773355

www.bradfordcityfc.co.uk

CONSIDERING the Bantams were reeling from relegation, parting with most of their senior players and in administration before the start of last season, narrowly missing out on a top-ten finish was quite an achievement.

City never let their problems off the pitch affect performances on it, winning five in a row in October.

They were only allowed to start the season after former chief executive Julian Rhodes stepped in with the money they

needed to pay the staff over the summer, and it was Rhodes who took over the club in December.

Now with a little cash for Colin Todd to spend, things are looking up at last. England U-19 defender Andrew Taylor is a loanee, Danny Cadamarteri has returned and Russell Howarth will challenge Donovan Ricketts between the sticks who, in turn, is joined at the back by Jamaican international colleague Damion Stewart.

Longest run without loss: 5
Longest run without win: 6
High - low league position: 2-17
High - low Outlook form figure: 65-37
Key Stat: *The Bantams won away at four of the top five.*

Outlook forecast: 14th

Final Outlook Index figure: 736
Clean sheets 11
Yellow cards 88 Red cards 4
Players used 30
Leading scorer:
Dean Windass 28 (27 league)

Your forecast:

BRENTFORD

Nickname: The Bees
Colours: Red, white and black

Ground: Griffin Park
Capacity: 12,763

Tel: 0208 847 2511

www.brentfordfc.co.uk

MARTIN ALLEN has worked miracles since arriving at Brentford. He arrived in March 2004 with the Bees deep in the mire and they made sure of their survival with just seven minutes of the season left. Last term, he transformed the survivors into contenders.

The Bees finished fourth, going out of the Play-Offs to promoted Sheffield Wednesday while a decent Cup run saw them take Southampton to a fifth-round replay. Brentford's away form undermined their ambitions, with just Milton Keynes and relegated Peterborough scoring fewer away. Unsatisfied, Allen had a summer clearout, with John Salako and Deon Burton notable casualties.

Popular striker Lloyd Owusu has returned to Griffin Park after a spell at Reading and perhaps the most interesting of a number of new faces is DJ Campbell, prolific in the Yeading attack.

Longest run without loss: 9
Longest run without win: 8
High - low league position: 2-13
High - low Outlook form figure: 63-40
Key Stat: *The Bees won just once away against at others in the top half.*
Outlook forecast: 4th

Final Outlook Index figure: 752
Clean sheets 22
Yellow cards 76 Red cards 5
Players used 35
Leading scorer:
Isaiah Rankin 10 (8 league)
Your forecast:

BRISTOL CITY

Nickname: The Robins
Colours: Red

Ground: Ashton Gate
Capacity: 21,479

Tel: 0117 9630630

www.bcfc.co.uk

DISAPPOINTING favourites after narrowly missing out on automatic promotion in 2004, City didn't even make the Play-Offs last season.

The problem was at Ashton Gate, where they won nine times as opposed to 15 in 2003/04.

It was a breakthrough season for striker Leroy Lita who formed a useful partnership with Steve Brooker and netted 29 times. Lita will be playing in the Championship with Reading this term, but with Marcus Stewart in from Sunderland after 17 goals in the Black Cats' title-winning season, Brian Tinnion looks to have an adequate replacement.

Tinnion's side are among the League 1 favourites again but will only justify their status with more consistency.

The Robins managed a maximum of three wins in a row, half as many as champions Luton and a poor total compared to Hull's eight.

Longest run without loss: 14
Longest run without win: 5
High - low league position: 5-21
High - low Outlook form figure: 63-39
Key Stat: *Bully boys - their record against the bottom six read 10-2-0.*
Outlook forecast: 1st

Final Outlook Index figure: 758
Clean sheets 17
Yellow cards 83 Red cards 2
Players used 32
Leading scorer:
Leroy Lita 29 (24 league)
Your forecast:

CHESTERFIELD

Nickname: Spireites
Colours: Blue and white

Ground: Recreation Ground
Capacity: 8,960

Tel: 01246 209765

www.chesterfield-fc.co.uk

AFTER avoiding the drop by the skin of their teeth in each of the previous two seasons, last term's 17th place was a welcome change for the Spireites and their highest league finish in six years.

They started fast but faded after Christmas, winning five of their last 24 matches and perhaps paying the price for having a small squad.

Chesterfield's away record was better than the previous year but goals were still hard to come by. Their total of 55 equalled that of relegated Torquay. Few clubs did worse, although it was better than 2003/04's woeful tally of 49.

Tcham N'Toya was top scorer with eight goals and manager Roy McFarland has responded by recruiting Paul Hall and Colin Larkin, who scored 11 each for Tranmere and Mansfield respectively last season. They'll need to do the same again to keep Chesterfield out of trouble.

Longest run without loss: 4
Longest run without win: 7
High - low league position: 2-17
High - low Outlook form figure: 56-38
Key Stat: *Ran out of steam. The Spireites won only two of their last 12.*

Outlook forecast: 23rd

Final Outlook Index figure: 719
Clean sheets 11
Yellow cards 69 Red cards 6
Players used 28
Leading scorer:
Tcham N'Toya 8 (all league)

Your forecast:

COLCHESTER UNITED

Nickname: The U's
Colours: Blue and white

Ground: Layer Road
Capacity: 7,556

Tel: 0845 330 2975

www.cu-fc.com

THE U's dropped back last season to finish 15th, but good Cup runs compensated for inconsistent league form. They were beaten by Blackburn in the FA Cup and pushed Southampton hard in the League Cup, losing 3-2 at St Mary's.

They were the only sides to score three times against the Essex club last term, and with an average of 1.08 goals conceded per league game, they could boast the best defensive record in the section after champions Luton.

At the other end however, only 12-goal Neil Danns broached double figures. The well-travelled Scot Chris Iwelumo will join him up front after a move from Alemannia Aachen.

The move to a new stadium in time for the 2007/08 season can't come soon enough. Colchester were terrible at Layer Road and their total of 30 points at home was the worst of all the clubs that beat the drop.

Longest run without loss: 11
Longest run without win: 9
High - low league position: 1-18
High - low Outlook form figure: 63-39
Key Stat: *Their average crowd was less than a sixth of Sheffield Wednesday's.*

Outlook forecast: 10th

Final Outlook Index figure: 745
Clean sheets 12
Yellow cards 56 Red cards 3
Players used 27
Leading scorer:
Neil Danns 12 (11 league)

Your forecast:

DONCASTER ROVERS

Nickname: Rovers
Colours: Red and white

Ground: Belle Vue
Capacity: 9,706

Tel: 01302 539441

www.doncasterroversfc.co.uk

IT was another good season for Doncaster who finished five points off the Play-Off zone after two successive promotions.

They adapted well to life in League 1 especially Michael McIndoe. The League 2 Player of the Season in Rovers' 2003/04 championship campaign enjoyed another good year, weighing in with 10 goals.

Rovers were particularly strong at Belle Vue, where only Sheffield Wednesday and Chesterfield left with three points.

Donny boss Dave Penney wants to build on this success and has been busy in the transfer market.

Penney broke the club transfer record twice over the summer, first landing striker Paul Heffernan from Bristol City for £125,000 in June and topping that in July, when he paid Sunderland £175,000 for gritty midfielder Sean Thornton.

Longest run without loss: 6
Longest run without win: 5
High - low league position: 8-19
High - low Outlook form figure: 62-42
Key Stat: *Donny scored nearly a quarter of their goals in the last ten minutes.*

Outlook forecast: 3rd

Final Outlook Index figure: 748
Clean sheets 15
Yellow cards 68 Red cards 5
Players used 35
Leading scorer:
Michael McIndoe 12 (10 league)

Your forecast:

GILLINGHAM

Nickname: The Gills
Colours: Blue and black

Ground: Priestfield Stadium
Capacity: 11,582

Tel: 01634 851854/300000

www.gillinghamfootballclub.com

IT'S no surprise to see the Gills back in League 1 after two cliffhanger campaigns even though they were a Championship side until Eugen Bopp's 85th minute heartbreaker for Forest on the final day.

In the end, it was only goal difference that ended four seasons in the Championship.

Neale Cooper, who took Hartlepool to the Play-Offs last term, has taken over from outgoing manager Stan Ternent.

His first task is to rebuild the team. With a dozen players out of contract and chairman Paul Scally out to balance the books, this season's side will bear little resemblance to last season's, and the likes of Mamady Sidibe and Nyron Nosworthy have already left Priestfield.

Cooper must get his new side performing on the road. Away form was not Hartlepool's strongest suit last term but the Gills were awful away, winning just twice.

Longest run without loss: 9
Longest run without win: 9
High - low league position: 2-23
High - low Outlook form figure: 60-33
Key Stat: *They lost only one of their last twelve in the league.*

Outlook forecast: 18th

Final Outlook Index figure: 784
Clean sheets 8
Yellow cards 68 Red cards 3
Players used 34
Leading scorer:
Darius Henderson 9 (all league)

Your forecast:

HARTLEPOOL UNITED

Nickname: Pools
Colours: White and blue

Ground: Victoria Park
Capacity: 7,629

Tel: 01429 272584

www.hartlepoolunited.co.uk

HARTLEPOOL reached the Play-Offs for the fifth time in six seasons but the campaign finished in disappointment after a bright start.

Pools were especially strong at home, winning 2.7 points per game in their first 14 outings at Victoria Park.

However, after Luton ended a 10-match winning streak at home in the middle of February, this dropped to 1.25 points per game in the Monkey Hangers'

last eight matches on their own turf.

The shock departure of manager Neale Cooper in the build-up to the Play-Offs didn't help much but reserve team boss Martin Scott stepped in to provide continuity and has taken the job on a permananent basis.

Hartlepool-born striker Adam Boyd scored almost a third of Pools' league goals last season and is joined up front by Martin Scott from Rotherham.

Longest run without loss: 12
Longest run without win: 9
High - low league position: 4-15
High - low Outlook form figure: 65-40

Key Stat: *Pools lost away at all the teams above them, goal tally 2-10.*

Outlook forecast: 11th

Final Outlook Index figure: 740
Clean sheets 16
Yellow cards 49 Red cards 1
Players used 30

Leading scorer:
Adam Boyd 27 (20 league)

Your forecast:

HUDDERSFIELD TOWN

Nickname: The Terriers
Colours: Blue and white

Ground: Galpharm Stadium
Capacity: 24,500

Tel: 01484 484100

www. htafc.com.

THE Terriers were back in League 1 last season thanks to a Play-Off final penalty shootout but never looked like a side that had scraped in by such a narrow margin.

They started with a win and were the division's strongest finishers, winning eight of their last nine games.

That run came too late though and they finished ninth as one of three teams just a point away from the Play-Offs.

Peter Jackson has a young side and it was Pawel Abbott who stole the limelight with 26 league goals. Andy Booth contributed a useful 10.

Jackson has persuaded some of his youngsters to stay at the renamed Galpharm Stadium including 22-year-old captain Jon Worthington who has signed a new contract. Gary Taylor-Fletcher arrives from Lincoln, where he netted 10 times in League 2 last season.

Longest run without loss: 9
Longest run without win: 6
High - low league position: 5-18
High - low Outlook form figure: 65-38

Key Stat: *Strong finishers. The Terriers won eight of their last nine.*

Outlook forecast: 2nd

Final Outlook Index figure: 759
Clean sheets 11
Yellow cards 70 Red cards 6
Players used 28

Leading scorer:
Pawel Abbot 27 (26 league)

Your forecast:

MILTON KEYNES DONS

Nickname: The Dons
Colours: White and gold

Ground: National Hockey Stadium
Capacity: 8,900

Tel: 01908 607090

www.mkdons.com

THE Dons beat the drop by the skin of their teeth, preserving their League 1 status on goal difference.

Danny Wilson's side won home and away in their last two games, beating first Peterborough and then Tranmere on the final day but they still needed Torquay to lose at Layer Road to stave off a second successive relegation.

They started badly and by the time Wilson took over in December, the Dons looked certainties for the drop. By February however, the Buckinghamshire outfit were embarking on an 11-match unbeaten run.

They saved their best for the National Hockey Stadium, where the average attendance nudged the 5,000 mark, not far below the average for the division, but were dreadful away with a meagre haul of just 17 points on the road. Significantly, 12 of those points were won under Wilson.

Longest run without loss: 11
Longest run without win: 8
High - low league position: 19-23
High - low Outlook form figure: 58-38
Key Stat: *They did not lose at home to any bottom-half side.*

Outlook forecast: 17th

Final Outlook Index figure: 730
Clean sheets 13
Yellow cards 71 Red cards 1
Players used 34
Leading scorer:
Izale McLeod 17 (15 league)

Your forecast:

NOTTINGHAM FOREST

Nickname: Forest
Colours: Red and white

Ground: City Ground
Capacity: 30,602

Tel: 0115 9824444

www.nottinghamforest.co.uk

IN the third tier for the first time in more than 50 years, Forest are as short as 7-2 with some of the layers to bounce straight back as champions.

They got off to a dreadful start, waiting 10 games for their first win and were already in deep trouble by the time Gary Megson replaced Joe Kinnear in January.

Forest were soon on a six-match unbeaten run and although they were a quarter point per game better in the 18 matches under Megson, it was too little too late.

Whilst the Reds undoubtedly improved in the run-in, they have a lot to find before they start looking like Championship material.

Megson is staying at the City Ground, but the inevitable fire sale means he is effectively starting from scratch. Chris Doig, David Johnson, Eoin Jess, Marlon King and Alan Rogers, all regulars last season, are on the way out along with a host of others.

Longest run without loss: 5
Longest run without win: 8
High - low league position: 17-23
High - low Outlook form figure: 57-36
Key Stat: *They culled just three points from aways at top-half teams.*

Outlook forecast: 13th

Final Outlook Index figure: 780
Clean sheets 16
Yellow cards 85 Red cards 8
Players used 35
Leading scorer:
Gareth Taylor 11 (7 league)

Your forecast:

OLDHAM ATHLETIC

Nickname: The Latics
Colours: Blue

Ground: Boundary Park
Capacity: 13,659

Tel: 0870 753 2000

www.oldhamathletic.co.uk

IT was another trying season for Oldham. They were haunted by the spectre of relegation until beating Bradford on the final day and finished 19th, a point off the drop zone.

Manager Brian Talbot didn't make it that far. He was shown the door after a run of seven consecutive defeats and replaced by former Rotherham boss Ronnie Moore. With Moore in charge, they lost just four of the remaining 12 league matches.

The Latics have lost midfielder Kevin Betsy and 21-year-old striker Scott Vernon, who scored an FA Cup winner against Man City, a rare highlight.

Loanee Luke Beckett takes his place after scoring six in nine towards the end of last season whilst on loan from Sheffield United.

Other new faces include Grimsby stopper Terrell Forbes, and midfielders Richard Butcher from Lincoln and Richie Wellens from Blackpool.

Longest run without loss: 7
Longest run without win: 9
High - low league position: 14-21
High - low Outlook form figure: 66-31
Key Stat: They won just two penalties last season.

Outlook forecast: 5th

Final Outlook Index figure: 719
Clean sheets 9
Yellow cards 76 Red cards 1
Players used 40
Leading scorer:
Chris Killen 15 (10 league)

Your forecast:

PORT VALE

Nickname: The Valiants
Colours: White and black

Ground: Vale Park
Capacity: 23,.000

Tel: 01782 655800

www.port-vale.co.uk

LAST season will not be remembered as a classic by the Vale Park faithful, as the Valiants stuttered on the road and in front of goal to finish 18th.

Only bottom club Stockport were worse away from home, and only Stockport and Peterborough (second from bottom) equalled Vale's dismal tally of 49 goals.

Vale's season compared poorly to their 2003/04 campaign when they finished seventh with 73 goals, a total that would have put them third in the 2004/05 divisional scorer's list.

Stephen McPhee's 25 league goals were sorely missed after he swapped League 1 for the Portugese Superliga last summer. Billy Paynter and Bristol City signing Lee Matthews both scored 10, but elsewhere goals were hard to come by. Martin Foyle has drafted in Hector Sam from Wrexham in the hope that his goals can keep Vale out of trouble.

Longest run without loss: 4
Longest run without win: 3
High - low league position: 3-19
High - low Outlook form figure: 57-37
Key Stat: They had the worsts goals to shots ratio in League 1 - 10.6%.

Outlook forecast: 22nd

Final Outlook Index figure: 724
Clean sheets 12
Yellow cards 67 Red cards 6
Players used 33
Leading scorer:
Billy Paynter 13 (10 league)

Your forecast:

ROTHERHAM UNITED

Nickname: The Millers
Colours: Red and white

Ground: Millmoor
Capacity: 11,514

Tel: 01709 512434

www.themillers.co.uk

IT was the end of November and the season was already 21 games old before Rotherham got their first win last term and that's why they find themselves back in League 1 after four years in the Championship.

They managed just five wins all season and only two were at Millmoor. Averaging a little over half a point per game at their own ground, they were the worst home team in the Championship by some distance.

Manager Ronnie Moore finished his eight-year tenure at the club in January with the Millers 12 points adrift at the bottom of the table.

By the time Mick Harford took over in April, it was far too late to salvage the situation and he plans to rebuild.

A number of players have already gone, with defenders Colin Murdock (Crewe), David Worrell (Plymouth) and Jon Otsemobor (Liverpool) coming in.

Longest run without loss: 3
Longest run without win: 17
High - low league position: 18-24
High - low Outlook form figure: 52-33

Key Stat: *The Millers never beat any of the eight teams just above them.*

Outlook forecast: 19th

Final Outlook Index figure: 743
Clean sheets 8
Yellow cards 69 Red cards 1
Players used 30

Leading scorer:
Martin Butler 6 (all league)

Your forecast:

SCUNTHORPE UNITED

Nickname: The Iron
Colours: Claret and white

Ground: Glanford Park
Capacity: 9,183

Tel: 01724 848077

www.scunthorpe-united.co.uk

AFTER fighting relegation for much of the 2003/04 season, Brian Laws' side came from out of the blue to finish second and win automatic promotion last term.

16 wins at Glanford Park were the foundation upon which their successful campaign was built but the Iron also proved difficult to beat away from home.

With just 10 defeats all season they lost fewer games than any team in the section.

It looked like Laws was putting together a Masters team when Paul Musselwhite, Ian Baraclough and Andy Crosby joined with a combined age of 102, but between them they started 134 league games.

Paul Hayes will be missed next season after his 19 goals last term but another veteran in the well-travelled Tommy Johnson is in after playing for Gillingham and Sheffield United in the Championship last term.

Longest run without loss: 13
Longest run without win: 4
High - low league position: 1-4
High - low Outlook form figure: 67-40

Key Stat: *They won more points per game against top-half teams than bottom-half.*

Outlook forecast: 24th

Final Outlook Index figure: 692
Clean sheets 21
Yellow cards 58 Red cards 4
Players used 27

Leading scorer:
Paul Hayes 19 (17 league)

Your forecast:

SOUTHEND UNITED

Nickname: The Shrimpers
Colours: Blue

Ground: Roots Hall
Capacity: 12,392

Tel: 01702 304050

www.southendunited.co.uk

SOUTHEND won promotion from League 2 through the Play-Offs, but their season looked like it might end badly when they lost the LDV Vans Trophy final and their league form dropped away at a crucial time.

Just one win in their final five games left the Shrimpers in fourth place, an agonising two points away from automatic promotion.

They also started badly, going six games before recording their first win, but fortu-nately for Steve Tilson's side, the bits in the middle weren't bad at all.

Player of the Season Adam Barrett wants to stay after an excellent first season at his hometown club when he scored 11 goals from the heart of the Blues defence.

Che Wilson has also inked a new deal and they are desperate to hang on to 21-year-old striker Freddy Eastwood (19 league goals) having already turned down some sizeable offers.

Longest run without loss: 17
Longest run without win: 6
High - low league position: 1-24
High - low Outlook form figure: 66-38
Key Stat: *They won 20 of the 22 games in which they scored first.*

Outlook forecast: 21st

Final Outlook Index figure: 701
Clean sheets 21
Yellow cards 58 Red cards 2
Players used 26
Leading scorer:
Freddy Eastwood 24 (19 league)

Your forecast:

SWANSEA CITY

Nickname: The Swans
Colours: White

Ground: TBC pending sponsors
Capacity: 20,000

Tel: 01792 633 400

www.swanseacity.net

THE Swans ended 103 years at Vetch Field in style, beating Wrexham in the final of the FAW Premier Cup and adding a handy £100,000 to the coffers for next season.

More importantly, a run of four home wins in their league run-in helped earn a third-place finish and promotion.

Boss Kenny Jackett, who along with his assistant Kevin Nugent has extended his contract, doesn't have a great deal of money to strengthen the squad but the addition of 16-goal Adebayo Akinfenwa from Torquay in the face of stiff competition is something of a coup.

Nevertheless, Jackett has some quality players in his side, notably defender Sam Ricketts, who has flourished in his first season of league football, and League 2 Player of the Season Lee Trundle, whose 22 strikes last term showed how he combines trickery with an eye for goal.

Longest run without loss: 6
Longest run without win: 5
High - low league position: 1-19
High - low Outlook form figure: 66-40
Key Stat: *They collected just one point from aways against other top-eight sides.*

Outlook forecast: 16th

Final Outlook Index figure: 704
Clean sheets 21
Yellow cards 81 Red cards 7
Players used 27
Leading scorer:
Lee Trundle 22 (21 league)

Your forecast:

SWINDON TOWN

Nickname: The Robins
Colours: Red and white

Ground: County Ground
Capacity: 15,728

Tel: 0870 443 1969

www.swindontownfc.co.uk

THE Robins couldn't emulate their 2003/04 Play-Off appearance last term and, sabotaged by travel sickness, finished comfortably in mid-table.

That might be the extent of their ambitions this season as financial difficulties mean Andy King is having as much trouble keeping his existing players as he is attracting new ones.

A number of first-teamers have turned their backs on the County Ground this summer and none will be missed more than Sam Parkin, whose 24 goals last term earned him a move to Ipswich.

Grant Smith got 10 from midfield but he is now at Bristol City and there were few goals elsewhere.

QPR duo Jamie Cureton and Tony Thorpe are now Robins, but will need to do better than four goals between them in the Championship last term, whilst Kyle Lapham and Michael Pook are recent youth team graduates.

Longest run without loss: 6
Longest run without win: 5
High - low league position: 6-19
High - low Outlook form figure: 63-37
Key Stat: *They beat five of the top six at home and lost to five of the top six away.*

Outlook forecast: 15th

Final Outlook Index figure: 733
Clean sheets 12
Yellow cards 59 Red cards 6
Players used 32

Leading scorer:
Sam Parkin 24 (23 league)

Your forecast:

TRANMERE ROVERS

Nickname: Rovers
Colours: White

Ground: Prenton Park
Capacity: 16,789

Tel: 0151 609 3333

www.tranmererovers.co.uk

ROVERS managed to keep up the momentum that saw them surge towards the Play-Offs in 2003/04 for much of last season, but their promotion push ended in the worst possible way, finishing third before going out of the Play-Offs on penalties.

They stuttered at the final stages - one win from their last five matches in the run-in - and finished a distant third, 19 points behind Luton and seven points from automatic promotion. There was disappointment in the FA Cup too, the customary Cup run ending at Peterborough in the first round.

Winger Paul Hall has gone to Chesterfield and promising defender Ryan Taylor has left to play in the Premiership with Wigan, but on a positive note, young Congolese striker Calvin Zola, who played just 15 times for the club before running into visa problems, has been given the all-clear to play in England.

Longest run without loss: 9
Longest run without win: 4
High - low league position: 2-11
High - low Outlook form figure: 66-44
Key Stat: *Nine started 39+ league games where they never lost successive matches.*

Outlook forecast: 6th

Final Outlook Index figure: 756
Clean sheets 17
Yellow cards 69 Red cards 4
Players used 24

Leading scorer:
Iain Hume 15 (14 league)

Your forecast:

WALSALL

Nickname: The Saddlers
Colours: Red, white and black

Ground: Bescot Stadium
Capacity: 9,000

Tel: 01922 622791

www.saddlers.co.uk

IT took a while for Paul Merson's side to get going following their relegation from the Championship.

The Saddlers beat Port Vale on the opening day but won just one of their next 11. However, they did improve, even beating eventual champions Luton in October.

They might even have been in the hunt for the Play-Offs if not for a run of five defeats in a row in March that threatened to get them involved at the wrong end of the table. The arrival of Julian Joachim on deadline day turned things around - he scored six times in Walsall's last eight games but has moved on to play in League 2 with Boston.

Coventry defender Craig Pead was another who arrived on loan in March and he has made the switch to the Saddlers permanent. If Merson can build on his side's five wins from five in the run-in, a top-half finish will be a reasonable target.

Longest run without loss: 6
Longest run without win: 9
High - low league position: 10-21
High - low Outlook form figure: 67-36
Key Stat: *Player-manager Paul Merson managed most League 1 assists (18).*

Final Outlook Index figure: 737
Clean sheets 10
Yellow cards 56 Red cards 3
Players used 37
Leading scorer:
Matt Fryatt 14 (all league)

Outlook forecast: 12th

Your forecast:

YEOVIL TOWN

Nickname: The Glovers
Colours: Green and white

Ground: Huish Park
Capacity: 9,107

Tel: 01935 423662

www.ytfc.net

YEOVIL were as short as 7-1 to win League 2 last summer and duly obliged on the final day of the season.

It was their second title in three seasons after winning the Conference in 2003, but they are a much bigger price to follow up in League 1.

Gary Johnson's decision to stay with the Glovers after talking to Derby about their managerial vacancy is a major fillip for the Somerset club and assistant boss Steve Thompson has also signed a new deal, making for consistency in the dugout.

Yeovil already have some decent players - Phil Jevons was League 2's top scorer last season and Darren Way was excellent with 45 appearances and seven goals from midfield - but expect some new faces before the season kicks off.

Johnson has already signed David Poole, Matt Harrold and Luke Oliver.

Longest run without loss: 9
Longest run without win: 6
High - low league position: 1-9
High - low Outlook form figure: 71-39
Key Stat: *They scored nearly a third of their goals in the last ten minutes.*

Final Outlook Index figure: 707
Clean sheets 10
Yellow cards 47 Red cards 2
Players used 32
Leading scorer:
Phil Jevons 29 (27 league)

Outlook forecast: 9th

Your forecast:

BARNET

Nickname: The Bees
Colours: Amber and black

Ground: Underhill Stadium
Capacity: 4,057

Tel: 020 8441 6932

www.barnetfc.com

HAVING won the Conference by a commanding 12 points, the Bees have high hopes of success in League 2.

Chairman Tony Kleanthous believes the Bees should be pushing for a Play-Off spot following the example of Yeovil, but the Conference graduates that followed the West Country side fared less well.

Both Shrewsbury and Chester struggled last season, casting doubt over the ease of transition between the two tables.

Their promotion marks a return after four seasons in the Conference during which the London club made steady progress. However, Paul Fairclough has never managed above Conference level and last season was his first coaching players full-time.

Famous for its sloping pitch, Underhill is a tricky venue and the Bees will have to use that to their advantage, but it looks like an uphill struggle.

Longest run without loss: 8
Longest run without win: 3
High - low league position: 1-3
High - low Outlook form figure: 71-42
Key Stat: *Bees won seven games coming from behind last season.*

Final Outlook Index figure: 672
Clean sheets 14
Yellow cards 52 Red cards 4
Players used 24
Leading scorer:
Guliano Grazioli 29 (all league)

Outlook forecast: 20th

Your forecast:

BOSTON UNITED

Nickname: The Pilgrims
Colours: Amber and black

Ground: York Street
Capacity: 6,643

Tel: 01205 364406

www.bufc.co.uk

IN the three seasons since promotion in 2002, the Pilgrims have finished 15th, 11th and 16th, comfortably ensuring their league status without troubling either end of the table.

Poor away form has sabotaged the lofty aspirations their York Street form might hint at.

They earned the same home points tally last season as Play-Off contenders Lincoln and Steve Evans has poached the towering Ben Futcher from these local rivals. The former Imps captain brings experience and leadership as well as a threat from set-pieces.

The loss of top-scorer Andy Kirk to league rivals Northampton last March was a blow but Evans has bought well over the summer.

Not far into his second stint at the club, the manager guided them to a Conference title and there is a real feeling that he can lead them to further progress this season.

Longest run without loss:
Longest run without win:
High - low league position: 7-19
High - low Outlook form figure: 57-40
Key Stat: *They failed to win after taking the lead 12 times.*

Final Outlook Index figure: 663
Clean sheets 12
Yellow cards 98 Red cards 3
Players used 38
Leading scorer:
Andy Kirk 20 (18 league)

Outlook forecast: 7th

Your forecast:

BRISTOL ROVERS

Nickname: The Pirates
Colours: Blue and white

Ground: The Memorial Stadium
Capacity: 11,916

Tel: 0117 909 6648

www.bristolrovers.co.uk

IF a team loses just once at home all season success should follow, but Rovers managed to draw 12 times at the Memorial Stadium and finished slap-bang in mid-table - 12/24.

Given the investment in players and facilities (1200 extra seats are planned), improvement will be expected this term, particularly away, where Rovers won just three.

Ian Atkins is close to completing his Uefa Pro Licence course and must impart this knowledge to his under-achieving side.

The future of top-scorer Junior Agogo is uncertain. The striker has only a year on his contract and his further commitment to the club will be significant for their prospects of improvement.

Though the bookies have gone cold on the Pirates' chances this term, they have the potential to make an impact if they can turn draws into wins. However, they are a team to be wary of.

Longest run without loss: 8
Longest run without win: 9
High - low league position: 1-17
High - low Outlook form figure: 63-37
Key Stat: *They did not manage to win two in a row after August.*

Outlook forecast: 9th

Final Outlook Index figure: 680
Clean sheets 18
Yellow cards 48 Red cards 8
Players used 30
Leading scorer:
Junior Agogo 21 (19 league)

Your forecast:

BURY

Nickname: The Shakers
Colours: White and blue

Ground: Gigg Lane
Capacity: 11,841

Tel: 0161 764 4881

www.buryfc.co.uk

THOUGH the Shakers finished a few places further down the League than in 2003/04, they upped their points tally and showed marked improvement defensively at Gigg Lane which remained a hard ground to get a result.

Graham Barrow's team shipped fewer goals at home than any team bar those that gained promotion.

It's not long since Bury were in administration and a whisker from folding completely and that experience has forced the club to live within their means. They are boosted by a deal to regain ownership of Gigg Lane, completing the turn-around from those dark days.

The loss of David Nugent and Danny Swailes mid-season came with a dip in form and the Shakers have also lost young prospect Colin Kazim-Richards to Brighton but there are some new faces at the club. Another mid-table finish is likely.

Longest run without loss: 6
Longest run without win: 9
High - low league position: 4-20
High - low Outlook form figure: 61-37
Key Stat: *Unusually, most of Bury's goals, for and against, came in the first-half.*

Outlook forecast: 16th

Final Outlook Index figure: 674
Clean sheets 11
Yellow cards 53 Red cards 6
Players used 28
Leading scorer:
Dave Nugent 12 (11 league)

Your forecast:

CARLISLE UNITED

Nickname: Cumbrians / Blues
Colours: Blue and white

Ground: Brunton Park
Capacity: 16,651

Tel: 01228 526237

www.carlisleunited.co.uk

AFTER a season in the Conference, the Blues bounced back via the Play-Offs.

However, in six seasons before relegation, their average League 2 finish was 22nd and they face another relegation battle.

It's no surprise that those years coincided with dire financial problems which took the club into administration. The formation of a supporters trust was a step in the right direction but they are currently fighting a cost-

ly legal battle with a local property developer who bought the club.

Five key players have so far failed to sign one-year contract extensions on reduced terms, the same number have gone, and no new signings are planned.

Manager Paul Simpson has a very difficult task ahead of him and last term's Conference graduates will need every ounce of their resilience to avoid dropping straight back down.

Longest run without loss: 14
Longest run without win: 9
High - low league position: 2-10
High - low Outlook form figure: 70-43
Key Stat: *The Cumbrians scored 13 in the last five minutes of games.*

Outlook forecast: 22nd

Final Outlook Index figure: 669
Clean sheets 18
Yellow cards 28 Red cards 1
Players used 27
Leading scorer:
Karl Hawley 13 (all league)

Your forecast:

CHELTENHAM TOWN

Nickname: The Robins
Colours: Red and white

Ground: Whaddon Road
Capacity: 7,407

Tel: 01242 573558

www.ctfc.com

THE launch of the Robins Supporters Trust in pre-season is an encouraging step forward for a club that, like so many, has struggled financially.

However, the implication of its financial position is that manager John Ward is unlikely to sign more than two new players, with more going out than coming in.

Cheltenham must therefore look to existing resources to improve on their goal-scoring problem (they finished in mid-table

respectability but with a negative goal-difference), and have renewed the contracts of strikers Damien Spencer and Kayode Odejayi who managed just 11 goals between them.

The Robins' position in League 2 has been consistent since relegation in 2002/03 but, given the lack of funds, progress toward a Play-Off challenge is unlikely unless they can somehow improve on their meek offensive play.

Longest run without loss: 7
Longest run without win: 5
High - low league position: 6-20
High - low Outlook form figure: 61-37
Key Stat: *They won only once away at the 10 sides who finished below them.*

Outlook forecast: 15th

Final Outlook Index figure: 666
Clean sheets 14
Yellow cards 46 Red cards 2
Players used 23
Leading scorer:
Martin Devaney 11 (10 league)

Your forecast:

CHESTER CITY

Nickname: City
Colours: Blue and white

Ground: Deva Stadium
Capacity: 6,012

Tel: 01244 371376

www.chestercityfc.net

HOPEFULLY for the Blues, this season will be more about what happens on the pitch than off.

The departure of manager Mark Wright before a ball was kicked was the worst possible start for their first season back in the Football League.

Two gaffers have been and gone since and now Keith Curle, who left Mansfield under a cloud, is in the hot seat.

Curle is an unabashed disciplinarian,

whose first task is to shore up his defence. City's defensive record was the division's worst bar Kidderminster, who now play in the Conference. If Curle can't improve the back line, Chester will soon be joining them.

The sales of Kevin Ellison and Danny Collins were disappointing but generated much needed cash.

Curle has lured talented midfielder Craig Dove from Rushden but his other signings are unlikely to set the section alight.

Longest run without loss: 10
Longest run without win: 6
High - low league position: 14-24
High - low Outlook form figure: 60-32
Key Stat: *Only Kidderminster had fewer shots on target than Chester's 198.*

Outlook forecast: 18th

Final Outlook Index figure: 660
Clean sheets 12
Yellow cards 103 Red cards 11
Players used 35
Leading scorer:
Michael Branch 13 (11 league)

Your forecast:

DARLINGTON

Nickname: The Quakers
Colours: Black and white

Ground: Feethams
Capacity: 8,500

Tel: 01325 240240

www.darlington-fc.net

DARLO finished the season with a flourish, losing just three of their last 13 games only to miss out on the Play-Offs on goal-difference, their best finish in five seasons.

It's hard to judge whether that performance was a one-off or a springboard to better things.

They achieved despite manager Dave Hodgson's frustration over inconsistent line-ups and he wants to add another four players, particularly a forward.

If Hodgson can find the right faces, he will be confident of building on last season's near miss and 22-year-old striker Simon Johnson, who failed to make an impact at Leeds, has been brought in with that in mind.

Having kept the nucleus of the squad that took them so close to the Play-Offs intact and provided they continue this season as they finished the last, the Quakers could go one better in a division that lacks depth.

Longest run without loss: 5
Longest run without win: 6
High - low league position: 5-19
High - low Outlook form figure: 62-42
Key Stat: *Their last eight matches were all level at half-time.*

Outlook forecast: 4th

Final Outlook Index figure: 699
Clean sheets 16
Yellow cards 61 Red cards 2
Players used 30
Leading scorer:
Clyde Wijnhard 14 (all league)

Your forecast:

GRIMSBY TOWN

Nickname: The Mariners
Colours: Black and white

Ground: Blundell Park
Capacity: 10,003

Tel: 01472 605050

www.gtfc.co.uk

MARINERS' fans are fearful they have too many inexperienced hands on deck. So far Russell Slade has been knocked back by all his close season targets, and most of those coming in are untested in League 2.

The supporters expect more than survival but in present circumstances Grimsby could be heading for choppy waters.

In front of their own fans, they are a difficult side to take on - just five defeats at Blundell Park last term - but woeful away form was the major factor in consecutive relegations and their slump to 18th in League 2.

Close season transactions offer little cause for optimism of any change in this proud club's trajectory.

Exciting midfielder Jason Crowe has rejected a new contract in favour of title favourites Northampton and a mid-table finish would be considered a success.

Longest run without loss: 4
Longest run without win: 7
High - low league position: 7-21
High - low Outlook form figure: 61-39
Key Stat: *The Mariners missed six penalties last season.*

Outlook forecast: 19th

Final Outlook Index figure: 679
Clean sheets 14
Yellow cards 54 Red cards 4
Players used 31
Leading scorers: Parkinson and Reddy both 9, the former all league.

Your forecast:

LEYTON ORIENT

Nickname: The O's
Colours: Red and black

Ground: Brisbane Road
Capacity: 13,842

Tel: 020 8926 1111

www.leytonorient.com

O'S fans must have thought their team might finally fulfil its potential, as by mid-October they were top of the table.

They stayed there for just a week and held a Play-Off position until the wheels fell off in late November and they won just once in the next ten league games.

Martin Ling prepares for a new campaign seeking the four or five players he feels will strengthen his squad enough to allow a more sustained assault on the top of the division, and lose the one-week-wonder tag.

A few more in the mould of Gary Alexander or 16-goal forward Lee Steele would certainly help.

Their injuries were blamed for their slump in form along with the inexperience of a youthful side.

With 200 games under his belt for Colchester, Joe Keith is a useful addition and Orient seem to be building rather than battling. Play-Off material.

Longest run without loss: 5
Longest run without win: 6
High - low league position: 1-16
High - low Outlook form figure: 61-38
Key Stat: *They failed to hang on to a lead eleven times.*

Outlook forecast: 6th

Final Outlook Index figure: 677
Clean sheets 11
Yellow cards 69 Red cards 5
Players used 29
Leading scorer:
Lee Steele 17 (16 league)

Your forecast:

LINCOLN CITY

Nickname: The Red Imps
Colours: Red, white and black

Ground: Sincil Bank
Capacity: 10,918

Tel: 01522 880011

www.redimps.com

THE signs are that the Imps side Keith Alexander guided to three unsuccessful Play-Off campaigns is dismantling.

The experienced quartet of Simon Yeo, Gary Taylor-Fletcher, Ben Futcher and Peter Gain are all quiting the club and Yeo, top scorer last season with 21 goals, will be tough to replace.

On his way out of the door, Yeo accused the board of not rewarding their players properly. Lincoln earned a big pay day by reaching Cardiff, but their Community Supporters Trust was not prepared to gamble with the club's future in the way that others in a similar position have lived to regret.

The club's bigger names may be disgruntled but the Imps have moved out of administration and into the black.

Nevertheless, Lincoln look a weaker side this time around, and a fourth straight Play-Off looks a tall order.

Longest run without loss: 4
Longest run without win: 6
High - low league position: 5-22
High - low Outlook form figure: 63-42
Key Stat: *The Imps lost 10 of the 12 games in which they fell behind.*

Outlook forecast: 13th

Final Outlook Index figure: 701
Clean sheets 20
Yellow cards 59 Red cards 2
Players used 33
Leading scorer:
Simon Yeo 23 (21 league)

Your forecast:

MACCLESFIELD TOWN

Nickname: The Silkmen
Colours: Blue

Ground: Moss Rose
Capacity: 6,335

Tel: 01625 264686

www.mtfc.co.uk

ONE of the surprise packages of last season, the Silkmen were fancied to struggle but instead made the Play-Offs.

It remains to be seen whether that was a one-off or an indication of a progressive side, but with skipper Matthew Tipton and keeper Steve Wilson - who between them have made over 300 league appearances - leading a minor exodus (nine players have been released) caution is advised.

Brian Horton will have a smaller squad, albeit one with a great deal of collective experience.

They retain lanky striker Jon Parkin who along with those remaining squad members should take a great deal from last season's experience of the Play-Offs.

However, they may struggle to emulate last term's success which came after five consecutive seasons finishing in the bottom half of the table.

Longest run without loss: 8
Longest run without win: 5
High - low league position: 1-10
High - low Outlook form figure: 69-42
Key Stat: *Macc have scored only three in their last nine aways.*

Outlook forecast: 14th

Final Outlook Index figure: 691
Clean sheets 16
Yellow cards 49 Red cards 2
Players used 28
Leading scorer:
Jon Parkin 26 (22 league)

Your forecast:

MANSFIELD TOWN

Nickname: The Stags
Colours: Amber and blue

Ground: Field Mill
Capacity: 10,000

Tel: 0870 7563160

www.mansfieldtown.net

THE Stags were thrown into turmoil early last season when manager Keith Curle was suspended and eventually dismissed. Carlton Palmer has the difficult task of steadying the ship.

He couldn't save Stockport from Championship relegation in 2002 in his only previous appointment, and didn't last long the following season.

The former England player may have been handed a poisoned chalice as Stockport were relegated again last season.

Palmer has made some useful signings, none more so than Matthew Tipton who scored bags of goals for Macclesfield last season, and with Welsh U-21 striker Adam Birchall joining from Arsenal the Stags' front line looks promising.

Whilst Palmer must replace experienced keeper Kevin Pilkington, his useful signings could help put the Stags back on an upward curve.

Longest run without loss: 4
Longest run without win: 11
High - low league position: 4-17
High - low Outlook form figure: 63-38
Key Stat: *Conceded more than 25% of goals against in the first or last five minutes.*

Outlook forecast: 10th

Final Outlook Index figure: 670
Clean sheets 16
Yellow cards 49 Red cards 4
Players used 38
Leading scorer:
Colin Larkin 11 (all league)

Your forecast:

NORTHAMPTON TOWN

Nickname: The Cobblers
Colours: Claret and white

Ground: Sixfields Stadium
Capacity: 7,653

Tel: 01604 757773

www.ntfc.co.uk

THE Cobblers were many pundits' fancies for this division last season, having made the Play-Offs the year before.

The team had bags of experience and the right man in charge in the well-regarded Scot Colin Calderwood.

Northampton never looked genuine title contenders, drawing more games at home than any side in the top ten, but made the Play-Offs for the second consecutive season. They only missed out on the final thanks to a dubious penalty against eventual winners Southend.

The loss of Chris Willmott is a blow, but the new additions to the squad far outweigh any defections.

Northampton are one of the section's few progressive clubs, and the bookies rate them favourites with good reason.

With the high calibre of new signings and their Play-Off pedigree, the Cobblers look good to deliver on their potential.

Longest run without loss: 6
Longest run without win: 6
High - low league position: 5-17
High - low Outlook form figure: 64-40
Key Stat: *Including Play-Offs, they won one in 10 games against the top four.*

Outlook forecast: 1st

Final Outlook Index figure: 700
Clean sheets 18
Yellow cards 70 Red cards 4
Players used 36
Leading scorer:
Scott McGleish 15 (11 league)

Your forecast:

NOTTS COUNTY

Nickname: The Magpies
Colours: Black and white

Ground: Meadow Lane
Capacity: 20,300

Tel: 0115 9529000

www.nottscountyfc.co.uk

SEASONED manager Gudjon Thordarson is the Magpies' new boss, filling the vacancy left by former player-boss Ian Richardson.

But he won't be bringing any big names to Meadow Lane.

The Notts County Supporters Trust stepped in with a £50,000 loan in June to keep the club going during the off-season, a measure of the problems the club faces and, sadly, the situation in the boardroom is reflected on the pitch. The Black and Whites finished 19th last season and were relegated the season before.

Midfielder Paul Bolland has moved to Grimsby and the moves in the other direction are hardly inspiring. So far, Thordarson has moved for Mansfield cat Kevin Pilkington, Lewis McMahon, released by Sheffield Wednesday and Brian O'Callaghan from Icelandic outfit Kevlavik. This season will be about survival.

Longest run without loss: 5
Longest run without win: 5
High - low league position: 17-24
High - low Outlook form figure: 60-35
Key Stat: *They won more points on the road than at home.*

Outlook forecast: 21st

Final Outlook Index figure: 663
Clean sheets 16
Yellow cards 64 Red cards 4
Players used 30
Leading scorer:
Glynn Hurst 15 (14 league)

Your forecast:

OXFORD UNITED

Nickname: The U's
Colours: Yellow and navy blue

Ground: The Kassam Stadium
Capacity: 12,573

Tel: 01865 337 533

www.oufc.co.uk

INSTALLED for one game at the end of last season (which they lost), Brian Talbot became Oxford's fifth manager in just over a year, which even in an era of brief stewardships is an appalling statistic.

The rot started when Ian Atkins was poached in March 2004 and hasn't stopped. South American coach Ramon Diaz brought flair, bewilderment (having coached River Plate and Monaco) and an immediate impact with February's Manager of the Month award. However, success was short-lived as the U's slipped out of Play-Off contention and he quickly left through the revolving door.

Talbot clearly wants to start afresh and has made a positive signing in Northampton skipper Chris Willmott, but the loss of Tommy Mooney is a negative.

Stability is what Oxford need but the pressure is on Talbot to turn things around.

Longest run without loss: 6
Longest run without win: 6
High - low league position: 4-21
High - low Outlook form figure: 62-37
Key Stat: *They won just four of 18 games against the top nine.*

Outlook forecast: 11th

Final Outlook Index figure: 672
Clean sheets 9
Yellow cards 83 Red cards 6
Players used 37
Leading scorer:
Tommy Mooney 14 (all league)

Your forecast:

PETERBOROUGH UNITED

Nickname: Posh
Colours: Blue

Ground: London Road
Capacity: 15,314

Tel: 08700 550 442

www.theposh.com

IT'S sad that Barry Fry's nine-year stint as Peterborough manager ended in relegation.

He has moved into a director of football role, handing over the reins to Mark Wright.

Wright did a fantastic job taking Southport to fourth place in the Conference at a time when Yeovil and Rushden had full-time squads, and then took Chester into the league, leaving abruptly before the adventure started.

He has raided his former club for Paul Carden, Chester's Player of the Season last term, and signed Oldham stopper Dean Holden, but he has a real task on his hands.

Posh won just nine games last season and finished behind Wrexham who had a 10-point handicap.

Although they undoubtedly have a good man at the helm, Posh may suffer under the burden of expectation. Midtable looks realistic.

Longest run without loss: 4
Longest run without win: 6
High - low league position: 5-23
High - low Outlook form figure: 55-32
Key Stat: *Posh managed just one goal per game aginst other bottom-half outfits.*

Outlook forecast: 12th

Final Outlook Index figure: 690
Clean sheets 11
Yellow cards 58 Red cards 2
Players used 34

Leading scorer:
Callum Willock 13 (11 league)

Your forecast:

ROCHDALE

Nickname: The Dale
Colours: Blue

Ground: Spotland Stadium
Capacity: 10,249

Tel: 01706 644648

www.rochdaleafc.co.uk

THE Dale's league history stretches back almost half a century, the last thirty years of which have been spent campaining at this level, but only once have they finished in the Play-Off positions.

In that context, last season's top-ten finish was a good showing, particularly as they lost fewer games than Champions Yeovil and all bar Scunthorpe.

One of the reasons Rochdale are so hard

to beat is Steve Parkin's skill as a defensive coach and issues are in order at the other end of the field too, Dale having held on to prolific striker Grant Holt, as well as the core of the rest of last season's squad.

Rochdale are financially sound and have been for some time.

In a section that won't take much winning, they are a good bet to improve upon last season's placing and worth considering in the handicap markets.

Longest run without loss: 6
Longest run without win: 6
High - low league position: 7-21
High - low Outlook form figure: 68-41
Key Stat: *Just one home defeat and one away win against the eight above them.*

Outlook forecast: 5th

Final Outlook Index figure: 687
Clean sheets 21
Yellow cards 80 Red cards 9
Players used 29

Leading scorer:
Grant Holt 24 (17 league)

Your forecast:

RUSHDEN & DIAMONDS

Nickname: Diamonds
Colours: White and blue

Ground: Nene Park
Capacity: 6,553

Tel: 01933 652000

www.thediamondsfc.com

DIAMONDS' recent league history is looking increasingly boomerang-shaped.

They won the Conference and League 2 titles in three seasons before dropping straight back down two years ago, and have since been fighting for survival.

It's no secret that the club have struggled financially, and the imminent sale of star turn Andy Burgess is symptomatic of this, as is the type of player coming in - cast-offs and journeymen.

If Rushden are to stop the rot, they must start winning away - they won just twice away from Nene Park last season.

The club's historic debt-free transfer to a supporters' trust is positive, as is the £750,000 fund the former owners have pledged over the next two seasons.

Those funds have not been spent on better players and are therefore unlikely to have an immediate impact on the pitch. Relegation is looming large.

Longest run without loss: 3
Longest run without win: 12
High - low league position: 4-22
High - low Outlook form figure: 58-37

Key Stat: *Only Cambridge had a lower goals to shots ratio of 1/12.1.*

Outlook forecast: 23rd

Final Outlook Index figure: 644
Clean sheets 16
Yellow cards 54 Red cards 5
Players used 32

Leading scorer:
Billy Sharp 9 (all league)

Your forecast:

SHREWSBURY TOWN

Nickname: The Shrews
Colours: Blue and amber

Ground: Gay Meadow
Capacity: 8,700

Tel: 01743 360111

www.shrewsburytown.co.uk

THE Shrews narrowly avoided an immediate return to the Conference, ending last term with just one win from their last eleven games.

Their Gay Meadow form was crucial to their survival, where they conceded 10 fewer goals than the champions did at home.

Gary Peters has acknowledged the need for root and branch change, offering new contracts to just two of his first team. Top-scorer Luke Rodgers had already

signalled his intention to leave, though his tally of six was miserable.

New boy Colin McMenamin was hardly more prolific in Scotland, but getting so many new players to gel will be the gaffer's biggest job.

Peters has signed two experienced professionals in Barnsley striker Mark Stallard and Crewe midfielder Neil Sorvel. Neither are long term prospects but will carry the fight in what looks sure to be a tough season.

Longest run without loss: 4
Longest run without win: 5
High - low league position: 17-24
High - low Outlook form figure: 61-38

Key Stat: *Too bright or too slow? Shrews were offside less than any English team.*

Outlook forecast: 24th

Final Outlook Index figure: 662
Clean sheets 15
Yellow cards 63 Red cards 8
Players used 32

Leading scorer:
Luke Rodgers 8 (6 league)

Your forecast:

STOCKPORT COUNTY

Nickname: County
Colours: Blue

Ground: Edgeley Park
Capacity: 11,540

Tel: 0161 286 8888

www.stockportcounty.com

CHRIS TURNER has an unenviable task as County are a club in serious decline.

As recently as the 2001/02 season they were playing in the Championship and last term were relegated after finishing rock bottom in League 1, with fewer points than any club in the four professional divisions and the worst defensive record.

Turner must find a way to succeed where others have failed, while dealing with the financial consequences of such a rapid fall from grace.

With several out of contract players released, Turner's squad will inevitably be smaller, and he is looking to bring in versatile players to compensate.

Turner says promotion is "possible but not probable" but, with the players and resources available to him, he'll do well to avoid the nether regions of this division.

Longest run without loss: 3
Longest run without win: 11
High - low league position: 15-24
High - low Outlook form figure: 55-32
Key Stat: *They conceded in the first five minutes seven times.*

Outlook forecast: 17th

Final Outlook Index figure: 665
Clean sheets 7
Yellow cards 68 Red cards 2
Players used 38

Leading scorer:
Warren Feeney 16 (14 league)

Your forecast:

TORQUAY UNITED

Nickname: The Gulls
Colours: Yellow and blue

Ground: Plainmoor
Capacity: 6,003

Tel: 01803 328666

www.torquayunited.com

THE Gulls have had plenty of time to reflect on how close they were to remaining in League 1.

Gareth Edds' late goal kept Milton Keynes up in their place, as they lost to Colchester on the back of a four-game winning run.

Now Leroy Rosenior must wipe that disappointment from the collective memory.

Plainmoor will be one of the tougher venues in the section as its location often deters significant away support and if the Gulls can retain the resilience that enabled them to lose fewer away than Hull (now a Championship side), then a swift return is possible.

16-goal striker Adebayo Akinfenwa will be missed, but while there are stronger candidates for promotion, the Gulls should be capable of something better than midtable, especially since they were so close to surviving in League 1 last season.

Longest run without loss: 5
Longest run without win: 9
High - low league position: 17-23
High - low Outlook form figure: 63-32
Key Stat: *They won just once against sides in the top eight.*

Outlook forecast: 8th

Final Outlook Index figure: 728
Clean sheets 8
Yellow cards 70 Red cards 2
Players used 37

Leading scorer:
Adebayo Akinfenwa 16 (14 league)

Your forecast:

Sponsored by Stan James

WREXHAM

Nickname: Dragons
Colours: Red and white

Ground: Racecourse Ground
Capacity: 15,500

Tel: 01978 262129/290793

www.wrexhamafc.co.uk

THE Dragons' drop into League 2 was the result of problems off the field.

But for a10-point penalty after going into administration, the Welsh club would still be one rung further up the ladder.

The administrators, who are still running the club, took the current owners to court in June over ownership of the Racecourse Ground.

Against that backdrop Denis Smith must use all his experience to start the new campaign without the team carrying a chip on its shoulder over the points deduction.

Demotion has brought its consequences. Top scorer Juan Ugarte is now in the Championship with Crewe and Welsh U-21 Craig Morgan rejected a new deal in favour of a move to Milton Keynes. Wrexham have lost some influential players but aren't in this division on merit. Relative heavyweights, they should be Play-Off material at least.

Longest run without loss: 7
Longest run without win: 4
High - low league position: 5-22
High - low Outlook form figure: 60-39

Key Stat: *The LDV winners' away games generated on average 3.43 goals.*

Outlook forecast: 3rd

Final Outlook Index figure: 715
Clean sheets 11
Yellow cards 64 Red cards 3
Players used 27

Leading scorer:
Juan Ugarte 19 (14 league)

Your forecast:

WYCOMBE WANDERERS

Nickname: The Chairboys
Colours: Sky and navy blue

Ground: Causeway Stadium
Capacity: 10,000

Tel: 01494 472100

www.wycombewanderers.co.uk

AFTER Tony Adams's short-lived management career, John Gorman resumed the hot-seat last November, steering the Chairboys to within touching distance of the Play-Offs.

Gorman will wonder why Wycombe took more points and scored more goals on the road than at the Causeway Stadium.

Nathan Tyson's 22 goals were significant and his likely departure will leave the Scotsman with a problem up front, but

Wanderers' five new signings include Tommy Mooney who scored 15 times for Oxford last season.

Wycombe have renewed their ground-share with rugby league outfit Wasps which should help financially and, with an experienced man in charge, some useful new players, and having had a season to adjust to the rigours of League 2 football, they are likely to make a bigger impact this time around.

Longest run without loss: 4
Longest run without win: 6
High - low league position:
High - low Outlook form figure:

Key Stat: *Despite finishing 10th, they had the division's best away record.*

Outlook forecast: 2nd

Final Outlook Index figure: 682
Clean sheets
Yellow cards 50 Red cards 2
Players used 33

Leading scorer:
Nathan Tyson 22 (all league)

Your forecast:

CELTIC

Nickname: The Bhoys
Colours: Green and white
Ground: Celtic Park
Capacity: 60,506
Tel: 0141 556 2611
www.celticfc.co.uk

LAST season Celtic failed to cope with life without Henrik Larsson and this year they may struggle to deal with life after Martin O'Neill.

The Bhoys' spectacular collapse against injury-hit Motherwell in the final two minutes of last term gifted Rangers the title and although they won the Scottish Cup the following weekend there are some serious questions to answer at Parkhead.

It had long been suggested that O'Neill was sticking with a side that were past their peak and in the end the doubters were proved correct.

Never under O'Neill had Celtic folded so easily and they looked a bundle of nerves during the closing weeks of the campaign, losing three of their last eight matches.

Gordon Strachan is the new boss and his first job will be to rejuvenate the ageing team.

Strachan has already lost Craig Bellamy and club captain Jackie McNamara. The latter will be a concern due to a lack of fullbacks at Parkhead, although Mo Camara has arrived from Burnley.

O'Neill was often guilty of choosing players over formation last term, with the likes of Stilian Petrov and Chris Sutton playing away from their preferred positions, and it will be interesting to see what Strachan does with the side this season.

For the first time this decade Celtic's midfield was outplayed by Rangers last season and the Bhoys can no longer out-muscle sides as they used to do two seasons ago.

Longest run without loss: 11
Longest run without win: 2
High - low league position: 1-2
High - low Outlook form figure: 75-50
Final Outlook Index figure: 904
Key Stat: *Like Rangers, they won all games where they led at half-time (23).*

2004/05 SPL Stats

	Apps	Gls	YC	RC
D Agathe	14 (2)	0	1	0
B Balde	34	2	5	0
C Beattie	0 (11)	4	0	0
C Bellamy	12	7	3	0
H Camara	12 (6)	8	2	0
R Douglas	14	0	1	0
D Fernandez	0 (1)	0	0	0
J Hartson	38	25	5	0
M Hedman	6	0	0	0
S Henchoz	2 (4)	0	0	0
Juninho	9 (5)	1	0	0
P Lambert	0 (4)	0	0	0
U Laursen	12 (6)	0	0	0
N Lennon	38	0	6	0
S Maloney	1 (1)	0	0	0
D Marshall	18	0	0	0
A McGeady	20 (7)	4	0	0
S McManus	2	0	0	0
J McNamara	34	1	0	0
S Pearson	1 (7)	0	1	0
S Petrov	37	11	2	0
C Sutton	25 (2)	12	2	1
M Sylla	1 (5)	0	0	0
A Thompson	32	7	5	1
J Valgaeren	18 (1)	0	1	0
S Varga	34	3	2	0
R Wallace	4 (12)	0	0	0

League Stats
Clean sheets 21
Yellow cards 41 Red cards 2
Players used 27
Leading scorer:
John Hartson 30 (25 league)

Outlook forecast: 2nd
Your forecast:

RANGERS

Nickname: The Gers
Colours: Blue, white and black
Ground: Ibrox Stadium
Capacity: 50,403
Tel: 0870 600 1972
www.rangers.co.uk

AFTER their dramatic final day title win, the Gers will be aiming to do far better in their title defence then they did two seasons ago. Then, after also having won the championship on the last day, they trailed home 17 points behind Celtic.

This term looks set to be a different story for the Light Blues as for the first time in five years, Rangers have a better and more settled side than Celtic.

It was said, probably rightly, that Alex McLeish was within one defeat of getting the sack towards the start of last season but that would have been harsh on Big Eck, as he was in the process of building a strong side. That potential is now on the way towards being fulfilled, and with Celtic currently the team having to do the rebuilding, Rangers can hold onto the SPL flag.

Although Greek international defender Sotirios Kyrgiakos might be on the way out, with most of the important members of the squad staying together, Gers can only improve.

McLeish has added to the squad well during the summer, bringing Ian Murray from Hibs and former Marseille captain Brahim Hemdani, who is expected to become the lynchpin of this season's team.

The return of Barry Ferguson was a big boost and he helped the Gers get the monkey off their back by winning 2-0 at Parkhead in February - their first victory at Celtic Park in five years.

They are rightful favourites and a second consecutive title awaits Big Eck and his Rangers team.

Longest run without loss: 19
Longest run without win: 2
High - low league position: 1-5
High - low Outlook form figure: 74-50
Final Outlook Index figure: 906
Key Stat: *The champions have won their last ten aways.*

2004/05 SPL Stats

	Apps	Gls	YC	RC
C Adam	0 (1)	0	0	0
M Andrews	30	4	1	0
S Arveladze	11 (13)	6	0	0
M Ball	12 (2)	0	0	0
J-A Boumsong	18	2	1	0
T Buffel	13 (2)	4	1	0
C Burke	7 (5)	0	1	0
R Davidson	0 (1)	0	0	0
B Djordjic	4	0	1	0
B Ferguson	13	2	0	1
S Hughes	6 (5)	2	0	0
A Hutton	8 (2)	0	2	0
Z Khizanishvili	14 (2)	0	4	0
S Klos	23	0	0	0
S Kyrgiakos	15	0	5	0
P Lovenkrands	12 (5)	3	1	0
R Malcolm	18 (3)	1	3	0
R McCormack	0 (1)	0	0	0
A McGregor	2	0	0	0
D Mladenovic	6 (1)	0	0	0
C Moore	3	0	2	0
H Namouchi	13 (7)	2	2	0
N Novo	34 (1)	19	4	1
D Prso	33 (1)	18	3	1
A Rae	17 (8)	1	4	0
F Ricksen	38	4	3	0
M Ross	14	0	1	0
S Smith	2 (2)	0	0	0
S Thompson	7 (17)	5	3	0
P Vanoli	3 (2)	0	1	0
G Vignal	29 (1)	3	6	0
R Waterreus	13	0	0	0

League Stats
Clean sheets 20
Yellow cards 52   Red cards 3
Players used 32
Leading scorer:
Nacho Novo 25 (19 league)

Outlook forecast: 1st

Your forecast:

ABERDEEN

Nickname: The Dons
Colours: Red

Ground: Pittodrie
Capacity: 22,199

Tel: 01224 650400

www.afc.co.uk

IMPROVING from 11th to fourth, the Dons took dramatic steps forward last season and look set to continue their progress this term.

Much of this success can be put down to the organisation that manger Jimmy Calderwood has instilled in the side and having plugged a leaky defence, they kept 15 clean sheets last term.

They have a very solid central defensive pairing in Russell Anderson and Zander Di-amond, while Scott Severin does a great job as the holding midfielder.

It was when going forward that Aberdeen struggled last term. They found the net just 44 times in the league and only Darren Mackie got more than five goals.

Calderwood has already added attacking midfielder Barry Nicholson from Dunfermline, ex-Celtic winger Jamie Smith, and former Dundee striker Steve Lovell will lead the line next season.

Longest run without loss: 7
Longest run without win: 4
High - low league position: 2-5
High - low Outlook form figure: 63-39
Key Stat: *Dons conceded just the one in their first seven matches.*

Outlook forecast: 4th

Final Outlook Index figure: 827
Clean sheets 17
Yellow cards 60 Red cards 4
Players used 26
Leading scorer:
Darren Mackie 15 (12 league)

Your forecast:

DUNDEE UNITED

Nickname: The Terrors
Colours: Orange and black

Ground: Tannadice Park
Capacity: 14,209

Tel: 01382 833166

www.dundeeunitedfc.co.uk

DUNDEE UNITED were the biggest disappointments in the SPL last season. They should have been challenging for third place rather than dodging the drop on the final day.

The Arabs have one of the best all-round squads outside of the Old Firm and should prove it this season under Gordon Chisholm.

They showed the promise they have in the Cups last season, reaching the final of the Scottish Cup and semis of the League Cup, and it's hard to work out why that form deserted them in the league.

They've added Lee Miller to their attack, who impressed with Hearts in the second-half of last term, and he should form a useful partnership with Stevie Crawford.

Left-sided midfielder Barry Robson is one of the best deadball specialists in the SPL and, along with Mark Wilson on the right, will provide the ammunition for the front two.

Longest run without loss: 6
Longest run without win: 7
High - low league position: 7-12
High - low Outlook form figure: 63-41
Key Stat: *United had 7-0-2 record in Cup ties, losing only to the Old Firm.*

Outlook forecast: 3rd

Final Outlook Index figure: 791
Clean sheets 7
Yellow cards 52 Red cards 4
Players used 26
Leading scorer:
Jim McIntyre 15 (10 league)

Your forecast:

DUNFERMLINE

Nickname: The Pars
Colours: Black and white

Ground: East End Park
Capacity: 12,509

Tel: 01383 724295

www.dafc.co.uk

DUNFERMLINE will lose their biggest advantage this season when their plastic pitch is ripped up and replaced by grass.

The Pars lost only eight of the 37 matches they played at East End Park since the installation of the artificial surface in September 2003 and their fellow SPL clubs voted against the use of the XL Turf.

The Fifers will now have to improve their away form that saw them take full points only when travelling to the city of Dundee. They have lost first choice goalkeeper Derek Stillie who has quit to move south and so far the Pars have failed to attract any new players to the club.

Legendary manager Jim Leishman took over with two games remaining last season and kept the club in the SPL. Having been given the job on a permanent basis, he will require all his skills to repeat the trick.

Longest run without loss: 3
Longest run without win: 10
High - low league position: 3-11
High - low Outlook form figure: 62-35
Key Stat: *Pars were awarded just one penalty last season. They missed it.*

Outlook forecast: 11th

Final Outlook Index figure: 782
Clean sheets 12
Yellow cards 46   Red cards 1
Players used 28
Leading scorer:
Andy Tod 8 (7 league)

Your forecast:

FALKIRK

Nickname: The Bairns
Colours: Dark blue and white

Ground: Falkirk Stadium
Capacity: 6,500

Tel: 01324 624121

www.falkirkfc.co.uk

FALKIRK were denied entry to the top flight two years ago after old ground Brockville fell short of SPL regulations, but following the move to a new stadium at the beginning of last season, the Bairns wasted little time setting the record straight and ran away with the First Division.

They might have won it by a more than an impressive 15-point margin had they not eased off towards the end of the campaign and the Bairns can take heart from the fact that the last three sides promoted to the SPL have avoided relegation in their first season.

Darryl Duffy is a talented striker who scored 27 times last term, while Russell Latapy runs the show from midfield.

However, the Bairns have released their central defensive pairing and their chances could hinge on how new signings Craig Ireland, Kenny Milne and Tiago Rodrigues settle in.

Longest run without loss: 17
Longest run without win: 3
High - low league position: 1-6
High - low Outlook form figure: 76-48
Key Stat: *They were unbeaten in the league this year until they won promotion.*

Outlook forecast: 10th

Final Outlook Index figure: 770
Clean sheets 17
Yellow cards 45   Red cards 1
Players used 27
Leading scorer:
Darryl Duffy 27 (17 league)

Your forecast:

HEARTS

Nickname: Jam Tarts
Colours: Claret and white

Ground: Tynecastle
Capacity: 18,000

Tel: 0131 200 7200

www.heartsfc.co.uk

IT'S difficult to know what to make of Hearts at the moment as their Lithuanian owners have yet to fulfil their promise to turn the Jambos into realistic challengers to the Old Firm.

So far their major contribution has been to oust John Robertson from the manger's job, although they've also brought in three useful looking Lithuanian internationals.

And, for now at least, the Jam Tarts will continue to play their home matches at Tynecastle, the most intimate venue in Scotland and a ground which provides a big advantage for Hearts.

On the pitch, Hearts have the best defence outside the Old Firm, with Scottish internationals Craig Gordon, Steven Pressley and Andy Webster providing a strong backbone.

George Burley was appointed manager at the beginning of July and immediately set about trying to attract new talent.

Longest run without loss: 7
Longest run without win: 8
High - low league position: 3-7
High - low Outlook form figure: 67-41
Key Stat: *The Jambos conceded two in seven of their last eight games.*

Outlook forecast: 5th

Final Outlook Index figure: 823
Clean sheets 13
Yellow cards 78 Red cards 4
Players used 34

Leading scorer:
Paul Hartley 15 (11 league)

Your forecast:

HIBERNIAN

Nickname: Hibs
Colours: Green and white

Ground: Easter Road
Capacity: 17,500

Tel: 0131 661 2159

www.hibs.co.uk

HIBS proved style and success can go hand-in-hand as Tony Mowbray's side won plaudits for their football and finished best of the rest in the SPL.

When Mowbray took over last summer, it looked as though he would need at least a couple of years to blend the club's brilliant youngsters into a winning team.

The fact he did it in one season tells you all you need to know about the man and his players, but this season may prove more difficult since last season's success means that clubs are queuing up to take their best players.

Captain Ian Murray has already gone to Rangers, star striker Derek Riordan looks set to join Celtic and more may follow.

The sheer number of players Mowbray brought through last year should leave them with a healthy squad, but a defence that kept only three clean sheets will need to sharpen up.

Longest run without loss: 8
Longest run without win: 3
High - low league position: 3-9
High - low Outlook form figure: 64-44
Key Stat: *Their current run without a clean sheet is 13 matches.*

Outlook forecast: 6th

Final Outlook Index figure: 822
Clean sheets 10
Yellow cards 57 Red cards 4
Players used 29

Leading scorer:
Derek Riordan 23 (20 league)

Your forecast:

INVERNESS CT

Nickname: Caley
Colours: Blue

Ground: Caledonian Stadium
Capacity: 6,500

Tel: 01463 222880

www.caleythistleonline.com

INVERNESS were the success story of last season as they overcame every obstacle in front of them to comfortably avoid relegation, having started favourites to go straight back down to Division One.

Caley Thistle had to play their first 11 'home' games 100 miles away in Aberdeen as their own ground failed to meet SPL criteria, but made the best of a bad situation by winning three and drawing four of their 11 matches in the Granite City.

They showed their true form once they were back at the Caledonian Stadium where they have had an excellent record over the years.

Caley start the campaign there this season and should continue to improve.

Craig Brewster has fostered a strong team spirit with all the squad on equal pay and this should help them beat the drop for a second year.

Longest run without loss: 4
Longest run without win: 8
High - low league position: 7-12
High - low Outlook form figure: 62-32
Key Stat: *They won just two points from 15 against the dross after the league split.*

Outlook forecast: 8th

Final Outlook Index figure: 791
Clean sheets 11
Yellow cards 52 Red cards 4
Players used 24
Leading scorer:
Barry Wilson 10 (all league)

Your forecast:

KILMARNOCK

Nickname: Killie
Colours: Blue and white

Ground: Rugby Park
Capacity: 18,128

Tel: 01563 545 300

www.kilmarnockfc.co.uk

KILLIE ended last season with a bang to finish best of the bottom half but look a difficult team to place this season.

Leading goalscorer Kris Boyd, who netted 17 times in the league - the next highest was four - looks set to be on his way to England and, at the moment, Killie don't have the quality in their squad to cope without him.

Due to financial constraints it is unlikely that they will make any major signings

and it might only be the weakness of the teams around them that will save them.

They improved their defensive displays last term to keep ten clean sheets (compared with three the season before) but they are a side who lack fight and they collected one only point from the 16 games in which they conceded first.

If Boyd does leave, it's hard to see where the goals will come from and this looks like being a difficult campaign.

Longest run without loss: 6
Longest run without win: 7
High - low league position: 5-11
High - low Outlook form figure: 62-32
Key Stat: *Their longest unbeaten run was against other duffers after the league split.*

Outlook forecast: 9th

Final Outlook Index figure: 804
Clean sheets 12
Yellow cards 52 Red cards 2
Players used 24
Leading scorer:
Kris Boyd 19 (17 league)

Your forecast:

LIVINGSTON

Nickname: Livi Lions
Colours: White and orange

Ground: Almondvale
Capacity: 10,016

Tel: 01506 417000

www.livingstonfc.co.uk

LIVI are on their fourth manager in 12 months and the musical chairs hasn't made for consistency at the club.

They did remarkably well to avoid relegation last season after a run of seven defeats in January and February left them looking certainties for the drop. However, Richard Gough came in and with a couple of signings helped turn the fortunes of the side around.

It has been a difficult summer though.

Gough quit as soon the season ended and the club were found guilty of paying Hassan Kachloul despite the Moroccan signing as an amateur.

Paul Lambert has now taken over the reins and is currently working on rebuilding the squad for the new campaign.

So far his only signings have been keeper Ludovic Roy from Ayr and left-back Paul Tierney but, even if there's more to come, a relegation battle is in store.

Longest run without loss: 4
Longest run without win: 7
High - low league position: 5-12
High - low Outlook form figure: 63-28
Key Stat: *Tey gained 11 points from their last six to stay up.*

Outlook forecast: 12th

Final Outlook Index figure: 786
Clean sheets 12
Yellow cards 70 Red cards 1
Players used 34
Leading scorer:
Burton O'Brian 8 (all league)

Your forecast:

MOTHERWELL

Nickname: The Well
Colours: Amber and claret

Ground: Fir Park
Capacity: 13,742

Tel: 01698 333333

www.motherwellfc.co.uk

TERRY BUTCHER has performed miracles since taking over at Motherwell to lead them into the top six for the second successive season.

It is worth remembering that only two years ago the club were in administration and beat the drop only because Falkirk's ground did not meet SPL criteria.

Their last-minute win over Celtic must have given Butcher great satisfaction, as not only is he a Rangers legend but his

young side have truly arrived in the big time. The Steelmen have a good blend of youth and experience and it must have been pleasing for the Well faithful to see a side missing seven first-team regulars compete with a team gunning for the title.

Success this season will depend on how many of the youngsters they can hold onto but, even if they keep them all, with clubs improving around them they may just miss out on a top-six finish.

Longest run without loss: 8
Longest run without win: 6
High - low league position: 3-7
High - low Outlook form figure: 7-35
Key Stat: *Well were winless for six before beating Celtic to deny them the title.*

Outlook forecast: 7th

Final Outlook Index figure: 810
Clean sheets 12
Yellow cards 55 Red cards 2
Players used 24
Leading scorer:
Scott McDonald 13 (all league)

Your forecast:

Our ratings expose the media hype

THE Outlook Index is our exclusive ratings system and a regular feature in the Racing & Football Outlook.

It's a tool that offers punters the best way to take an objective look at the relative strength of teams in England and Scotland, all of the major European leagues and summer leagues as well as at international level.

This means we can accurately compare teams from different divisions and national leagues and across national borders and Fifa continental zones - vital in a World Cup year.

The Index is especially useful at the beginning of the season when we can use it to get a handle on how the newly promoted and recently relegated sides will fare in their new divisions as well as gaining an insight into the opening exchanges in European competition.

Domestically, Chelsea are head and shoulders above the rest and worryingly for the competition, their Index Trend value shows they were improving as the season went on.

What's more, with Jose Mourinho taking full advantage of the deepest pockets in Russia, they look set to go on improving in the coming season. It might not be the most left-field tip you'll read in the build up to next season, but to my mind they look unopposable in the Premiership at around even money.

For those who want to see the old order of Man United and Arsenal restored to the top of the tree, the signs are not

Alex Deacon

so positive. They've fallen a long way behind the Blues and both ended the season with their Trend values in decline.

It's easy to use the Index to see how teams have performed and where they have been going wrong, but it's also possible to use it to see at a glance where they might go right in the future.

Liverpool are one of the more interesting sides in the chasing pack in that they would seem to have the potential to step up a level and at least compete for third place again.

Rafa Benitez's side punched above their weight in Europe last season but let themselves down domestically. Their Home Index rating shows that, basically, they are not far off either United or Arsenal. Away from Anfield, however, we

BAYERN MUNICH: the Index suggests that the Germany champions are very underrated

see a different picture and the Reds performed at a similar level to teams like Charlton, Blackburn or even newly promoted Sunderland.

This is obviously an area where they can - and must - raise their game.

The fact that they managed to turn this form on its head in Europe with memorable results at the BayArena, Stadio Delle Alpi and Stamford Bridge on the way to their unforgettable victory in Istanbul meant that few sides were more frustrating than Liverpool from a betting point of view, but it does show that with a little more consistency in domestic football, the Reds could be crashing the party before too much longer.

Their European Cup win must have a positive effect, and Benitez has kept the talismanic Steven Gerrard on board, as well as completing a handful of decent-looking signings. For the most part, last term's new faces settled in well at Anfield and we can expect to see further progress this season.

Whether Chelsea are as deserving of their status as favourites in the Champions League is a more debatable question than their domestic supremacy.

The Premiership nurtures itself within a cocoon of hype and if one relies solely on the majority of media coverage - which has a vested interest in perpetuating that hype and the view that the Premiership is the best league in the world - it's impossible to look at the odds objectively.

This is where the Index comes into its own. Although the Premiership's fifth best team lifted the trophy last term, the Index suggests that Barcelona and Milan are marginally better equipped than the English champions.

Whether time proves that assertion right or not, there is now little to choose between the top clubs in the top leagues and either of the Spanish pair of Barca and Real Madrid offer decent alternatives whilst the improving Inter and Bayern Munich certainly should not be counted out.

Bayern rate firmly alongside Europe's best, including Chelsea, and yet some of the bookmakers rate them almost twice the price of Man United or Arsenal.

Clearly the bookies have overrated the Premiership as a league and the Index is the perfect tool to highlight the discrepancies between the odds and a team's true chances.

League tables are, quite simply, one of the mos deceptive tools a punter can employ in makin selections each week, showing as they do the state of a competi tion at any given point in time.

In their usual format they reveal nothing as to the quality of th opponents each side has met until then. That's where the Outloo Index comes in, showing as it does the relative strength of eac side determined by the results of over 38,000 matches an weighted by the strength of the opposition.

Detailed 60-match form is also given for each side so that an trends in a side's playing strength can be readily identified.

Each week of the football season, the Outlook will print update Index ratings, with the best analysis to help your football betting.

WORK TO DO? Charlton have the biggest negative trend figure in the Premiership

FA PREMIERSHIP 2004-05

Previous match form

	Curr	1-6	7-12	13-18	19-24	25-30	31-36	37-42	43-48	49-54	55-60	Home	Away	Trend
Chelsea	978	978	974	967	953	943	942	934	942	934	932	948	949	4
Arsenal	956	963	958	963	962	972	974	969	977	969	964	968	926	-3
Man Utd	942	944	959	949	937	932	930	936	946	957	967	948	924	-4
Bolton	895	895	892	878	886	902	900	893	878	889	883	892	877	4
Liverpool	891	892	897	903	902	904	905	905	900	904	911	919	859	-3
Man City	884	873	864	867	866	861	859	860	865	860	864	894	861	11
Middlesboro	882	878	882	889	894	885	879	876	882	879	877	904	850	0
Tottenham	876	878	875	880	867	866	874	861	866	870	858	900	841	0
Everton	875	880	882	891	896	883	869	864	876	870	876	911	832	-6
Fulham	871	862	858	859	860	864	874	877	874	879	886	901	837	8
Blackburn	870	877	872	869	864	863	870	878	870	874	881	877	871	-1
Birmingham	868	861	863	869	865	868	870	876	883	885	878	904	834	3
Aston Villa	868	879	876	880	894	892	893	897	886	884	876	900	840	-7
Newcastle U	867	866	879	876	882	891	892	902	904	910	908	938	814	-4
Charlton	860	866	881	884	878	874	877	875	883	887	885	860	853	-10
WBA	855	847	832	824	828	838	838	848	850	833	834	891	838	13
Portsmouth	854	860	859	871	875	870	870	870	848	840	844	892	817	-6
Norwich	846	844	835	843	852	849	853	854	842	840	835	890	796	3
Southampton	842	845	846	842	850	854	863	870	876	874	879	905	813	-2
C Palace	838	830	830	826	827	827	819	828	812	808	789	867	824	7

CHAMPIONSHIP 2004-2005

Previous match form

	Curr	1-6	7-12	13-18	19-24	25-30	31-36	37-42	43-48	49-54	55-60	Home	Away	Trend
Sunderland	864	859	849	841	841	837	828	819	822	826	818	878	848	9
Wigan	837	832	837	830	829	838	832	826	812	808	818	832	836	3
Ipswich	832	836	834	846	841	838	829	822	815	816	810	864	804	-3
Wolves	831	820	815	808	808	816	823	833	843	837	842	864	804	11
Preston	829	835	829	823	801	793	787	782	788	790	804	889	792	2
Derby	826	825	819	813	806	806	800	787	782	783	782	836	832	5
West Ham	821	819	810	818	826	825	833	839	835	829	838	849	818	3
Leeds	809	814	821	816	810	815	827	835	845	852	845	846	824	-4
Reading	806	814	804	816	830	830	832	820	817	813	814	856	797	-4
Millwall	804	794	794	803	809	803	802	810	808	828	832	838	800	5
Leicester	803	799	800	815	820	824	830	835	850	850	853	856	800	-1
Sheffield Utd	798	811	807	817	823	813	807	807	804	810	818	839	804	-9
QPR	795	798	801	786	790	805	804	779	777	780	786	853	787	0
Burnley	795	790	798	806	807	796	796	787	787	790	790	846	802	-1
Cardiff	794	787	789	793	778	784	781	783	797	799	788	823	790	5
Coventry	789	791	781	779	794	796	792	801	800	799	804	834	808	3
Stoke	788	794	806	796	810	806	812	818	810	803	813	828	790	-7
Gillingham	784	787	772	762	754	756	756	772	770	770	779	837	768	7
Watford	783	781	798	801	798	810	806	804	792	788	788	830	818	-5
Plymouth	780	782	780	776	787	790	787	797	786	781	785	855	762	0
Brighton	780	772	785	786	773	776	780	772	768	762	758	835	771	1
Nottingham F	780	781	791	777	782	786	798	802	807	790	784	862	776	-2
Crewe	777	778	785	798	802	780	776	772	777	778	782	814	817	-6
Rotherham	743	750	752	761	754	751	761	774	788	785	793	797	795	-6

LEAGUE 1 2004-2005

Previous match form

	Curr	1-6	7-12	13-18	19-24	25-30	31-36	37-42	43-48	49-54	55-60	Home	Away	Trend
Luton	792	787	782	774	774	767	770	766	746	749	758	828	774	7
Hull	759	773	772	760	766	742	731	727	715	708	704	812	746	-6
Huddersfield	759	746	725	724	727	730	725	718	722	724	723	813	753	18
Bristol City	758	750	754	756	759	768	759	760	770	771	790	794	772	4
Tranmere	756	765	770	774	774	778	770	765	760	745	738	817	746	-8
Brentford	752	749	746	745	735	734	746	733	729	719	708	810	750	5
Doncaster	748	742	739	740	730	727	716	712	706	702	698	803	738	6
Colchester	745	736	721	730	727	733	739	750	750	736	735	784	768	11
Barnsley	743	744	739	742	746	733	736	736	737	738	732	795	772	1
Sheffield W	742	747	760	757	751	737	734	730	724	742	755	771	772	-7
Bournemouth	742	749	751	744	755	752	747	740	740	744	746	794	766	-4
Hartlepool	740	749	748	770	762	750	749	753	756	751	748	790	745	-9
Walsall	737	721	728	737	744	742	746	762	770	777	775	804	745	6
Bradford	736	737	736	747	752	754	750	742	742	754	754	781	774	-2
Swindon	733	733	744	741	741	747	753	756	752	761	769	800	775	-3
Blackpool	731	737	741	726	715	723	722	712	725	735	730	779	775	-1
MK Dons	730	726	724	713	710	713	726	724	736	738	736	801	757	6
Torquay	728	719	714	717	713	715	702	699	707	698	706	782	743	8
Port Vale	724	725	723	718	727	734	738	754	750	742	738	803	723	1
Oldham	719	718	706	722	735	731	728	742	747	742	737	788	733	2
Chesterfield	719	718	725	724	730	735	732	736	723	715	723	792	727	-2
Wrexham	715	719	721	715	718	723	733	732	728	729	737	753	764	-2
Peterborough	690	692	694	698	703	720	727	736	740	736	722	738	758	-3
Stockport	665	672	688	692	696	700	716	723	741	741	720	719	763	-12

LEAGUE 2 2004-2005

Previous match form

	Curr	1-6	7-12	13-18	19-24	25-30	31-36	37-42	43-48	49-54	55-60	Home	Away	Trend
Yeovil	707	699	714	719	718	701	702	708	700	696	704	768	726	-1
Swansea	704	699	688	698	694	689	682	666	656	668	677	768	716	6
Southend	701	712	706	693	691	680	676	663	666	674	660	753	727	-2
Lincoln	701	708	701	705	696	700	690	686	704	710	706	733	731	-2
Northampton	700	696	704	706	712	699	702	703	714	703	690	758	733	-1
Darlington	699	693	696	689	684	686	677	675	676	670	664	763	724	5
Scunthorpe	692	689	687	691	702	696	675	672	656	659	678	783	686	2
Macclesfield	691	693	706	692	678	677	673	678	676	658	650	763	712	-2
Rochdale	687	687	688	682	678	669	657	659	660	658	656	771	704	2
Wycombe	682	685	694	689	692	692	703	717	711	707	698	727	746	-4
Bristol Rvrs	680	675	670	677	674	677	684	688	674	658	654	792	688	5
Grimsby	679	675	689	687	690	691	702	703	714	718	724	775	719	-2
Leyton Orient	677	670	668	668	674	678	679	668	655	666	682	764	704	6
Bury	674	668	658	665	672	683	673	675	670	672	670	756	712	7
Oxford U	672	678	676	678	663	662	673	680	674	688	703	747	697	-2
Mansfield	670	674	675	682	680	679	689	690	686	698	696	742	703	-4
Cheltenham	666	667	676	686	685	684	673	669	677	679	694	741	715	-6
Boston	663	667	671	681	682	680	683	684	688	682	668	771	676	-6
Notts County	663	672	677	677	678	682	686	690	703	714	718	746	722	-8
Shrewsbury	662	660	660	651	645	640	636	635	632	655	675	743	704	4
Chester	660	659	651	658	660	666	661	643	648	640	630	742	712	3
Cambridge U	653	646	640	631	636	648	658	660	664	653	652	734	707	9
Rushden	644	653	649	648	659	669	683	689	694	709	727	737	684	-4
Kidderminster	634	643	639	633	637	640	659	671	678	675	670	725	695	-3

CONFERENCE 2004-2005

Previous match form

	Curr	1-6	7-12	13-18	19-24	25-30	31-36	37-42	43-48	49-54	55-60	Home	Away	Trend
Hereford	678	674	662	665	668	668	667	664	666	667	660	724	680	7
Morecambe	677	674	660	652	640	645	636	638	640	634	634	675	655	10
Exeter	675	665	664	670	659	663	665	664	657	648	654	730	692	7
Barnet	672	677	669	680	684	668	660	640	641	652	669	736	672	-2
Carlisle	669	670	661	668	680	679	668	666	663	656	641	721	676	1
Stevenage	667	661	658	656	652	638	638	636	630	640	638	664	659	6
Woking	658	656	666	655	654	648	640	638	640	642	638	679	649	0
Aldershot	657	644	632	625	631	628	619	604	615	623	622	710	641	15
Accrington	654	655	658	641	641	643	656	650	658	652	651	664	639	2
Dag and Red	651	640	631	636	629	632	639	643	640	637	632	658	632	11
Halifax	645	652	664	652	651	644	643	633	631	634	646	716	658	-7
Tamworth	644	643	628	636	640	626	630	630	632	635	627	666	654	5
Burton	635	631	640	631	628	637	628	626	628	632	634	636	653	2
Scarborough	634	644	643	655	658	659	660	659	653	657	642	714	654	-8
Northwich	631	628	623	625	626	622	622	630	634	640	643	669	630	4
Gravesend	626	640	646	631	636	656	655	658	663	662	661	656	640	-9
Crawley	622	634	642	640	646	642	646	652	648	652	642	671	602	-11
Forest Green	618	622	621	621	609	600	612	610	620	618	612	635	658	-1
Canvey Island	613	606	617	625	632	644	643	648	642	637	632	666	622	-1
York	613	614	620	618	622	628	620	629	645	663	685	709	658	-2
Farnborough	588	588	603	622	630	628	628	633	628	631	635	638	626	-10
Leigh RMI	567	572	578	574	585	602	620	622	612	618	623	598	613	-5

BANK OF SCOTLAND SPL 2004-2005

Previous match form

	Curr	1-6	7-12	13-18	19-24	25-30	31-36	37-42	43-48	49-54	55-60	Home	Away	Trend
Rangers	906	905	911	900	898	886	881	889	897	910	913	917	884	1
Celtic	904	914	917	918	915	924	928	938	959	956	949	912	909	-7
Aberdeen	827	818	813	808	819	806	790	786	797	802	803	808	830	9
Hearts	823	824	835	843	843	854	856	856	844	849	846	849	788	-6
Hibernian	822	832	829	834	818	809	800	798	802	803	802	820	817	-5
Motherwell	810	801	805	802	805	797	799	796	797	790	780	845	775	5
Kilmarnock	804	791	794	798	797	804	803	797	794	798	807	833	772	7
Inverness CT	791	806	802	788	784	777	778	765	754	762	760	808	762	-5
Dundee Utd	791	788	784	788	792	803	817	818	813	803	800	798	792	3
Livingston	786	782	769	772	778	786	792	795	792	797	800	806	786	7
Dundee	784	780	787	786	785	790	802	808	796	796	800	822	784	1
Dunfermline	782	781	790	795	802	806	804	820	818	821	827	851	750	-4

BELL'S SCOTTISH DIVISION ONE 2004-2005

Previous match form

	Curr	1-6	7-12	13-18	19-24	25-30	31-36	37-42	43-48	49-54	55-60	Home	Away	Trend
Falkirk	770	784	790	788	775	762	744	746	749	756	770	774	772	-10
St Mirren	748	737	727	722	737	733	716	694	694	704	704	814	705	12
Clyde	746	756	769	768	774	782	784	786	789	790	776	789	742	-12
Queen OTS	741	733	730	735	738	744	740	736	736	745	744	775	743	6
Ross County	725	724	714	712	714	717	718	728	726	724	719	750	747	5
Hamilton	722	717	706	702	688	690	694	680	669	672	664	728	749	10
Airdrie Utd	721	724	732	734	719	712	715	708	693	680	678	736	718	-4
Partick	718	713	725	720	734	747	764	753	743	746	745	790	709	-1
St Johnstone	716	720	727	738	728	729	730	756	760	752	760	721	749	-7
Raith	648	651	651	654	663	658	670	681	677	673	677	726	656	-3

BELL'S SCOTTISH DIVISION TWO 2004-2005

Previous match form

	Curr	1-6	7-12	13-18	19-24	25-30	31-36	37-42	43-48	49-54	55-60	Home	Away	Trend
Brechin	702	707	706	713	699	677	671	670	670	657	652	728	700	-3
Morton	688	684	676	672	673	669	664	683	686	686	692	740	661	7
Stranraer	675	681	684	694	695	686	667	656	652	650	649	712	687	-7
Alloa	668	660	671	674	650	652	656	678	681	678	667	705	695	2
Forfar	668	658	650	646	654	672	669	675	673	669	674	685	708	11
Dumbarton	658	656	658	658	671	674	691	677	671	668	659	723	670	0
Stirling	656	664	665	660	666	672	650	634	638	637	638	714	681	-5
Arbroath	651	650	645	633	636	636	645	650	645	651	648	688	694	5
Ayr	646	652	663	678	692	686	694	691	690	694	700	739	671	-12
Berwick	645	649	640	637	625	632	650	656	659	666	668	681	712	3

BELL'S SCOTTISH DIVISION THREE 2004-2005

Previous match form

	Curr	1-6	7-12	13-18	19-24	25-30	31-36	37-42	43-48	49-54	55-60	Home	Away	Trend
Gretna	688	684	671	666	659	643	631	628	620	620	615	712	702	10
Peterhead	640	639	656	660	655	644	628	630	626	629	627	697	663	-6
C'denbeath	597	585	593	608	603	602	608	622	622	626	626	655	656	3
Queen's Park	585	580	582	579	580	582	580	574	574	568	565	665	656	4
Montrose	581	582	568	576	592	586	584	582	585	581	571	626	642	3
St'housemuir	577	583	586	591	595	596	602	603	615	624	634	659	639	-6
East Fife	574	580	589	602	594	613	632	628	634	638	648	652	635	-9
Elgin	563	562	560	551	554	552	545	548	536	540	547	671	598	4
Albion	562	563	560	550	557	575	579	583	598	594	607	610	656	3
East Stirling	503	509	495	494	489	481	486	484	491	499	508	605	554	3

BUNDESLIGA 2004-2005

Previous match form

	Curr	1-6	7-12	13-18	19-24	25-30	31-36	37-42	43-48	49-54	55-60	Home	Away	Trend
B Munich	974	966	957	956	954	953	956	964	962	962	959	991	935	10
W Bremen	933	933	941	934	936	939	953	956	954	942	931	925	931	-1
Dortmund	932	922	907	901	909	915	917	919	914	916	931	946	888	14
Leverkusen	928	922	927	927	922	927	930	913	900	920	926	936	884	3
H Berlin	928	930	924	919	902	899	900	888	889	886	898	953	889	4
Stuttgart	926	940	937	932	932	945	939	939	931	945	950	945	899	-7
Schalke	924	927	939	931	922	900	903	917	916	903	900	935	911	-4
Hamburg	904	918	925	913	905	898	910	908	910	909	900	931	870	-9
Mainz	889	877	876	883	904	905	595	0	0	0	0	906	877	6
Wolfsburg	887	880	882	888	903	902	882	878	888	894	902	923	864	2
Bochum	885	878	871	877	888	904	914	910	915	900	901	922	862	6
Hannover	882	876	881	898	898	880	877	879	880	891	893	899	889	-1
K'slautern	880	889	898	893	871	871	875	882	884	881	893	914	862	-7
B M'gladbach	874	872	875	878	877	876	878	874	872	875	866	946	823	0
H Rostock	869	870	858	857	861	876	885	886	887	880	861	906	852	5
A Bielefeld	866	876	879	878	881	870	864	882	879	877	876	902	854	-7
Nuremburg	863	866	856	861	856	852	850	863	862	868	865	888	885	2
Freiburg	826	831	840	849	856	870	871	874	876	878	876	896	822	-9

LE CHAMPIONNAT 2004-2005

Previous match form

	Curr	1-6	7-12	13-18	19-24	25-30	31-36	37-42	43-48	49-54	55-60	Home	Away	Trend
Lyon	947	941	944	948	951	950	946	944	943	936	936	952	908	2
Monaco	912	913	915	924	914	917	919	924	928	935	942	932	863	-2
Lille	906	902	898	910	910	908	892	888	893	879	874	911	876	2
Paris St-G	899	900	896	910	915	916	921	936	931	922	910	940	858	-2
Rennes	888	891	884	876	874	880	886	877	870	876	871	944	833	3
Strasbourg	884	879	865	858	860	849	853	863	854	864	872	912	842	11
Lens	881	878	880	871	879	872	882	885	892	891	901	940	841	3
St Etienne	880	877	873	864	852	831	822	820	818	823	825	926	812	7
Ajaccio	876	869	854	852	853	848	849	858	854	857	856	913	829	11
Marseille	875	884	902	896	882	883	884	882	893	900	904	903	862	-11
Sochaux	875	878	882	881	890	896	901	910	920	918	920	905	838	-4
Nice	874	867	868	872	876	882	868	871	888	893	894	918	821	4
Auxerre	874	884	893	911	910	914	914	910	912	926	915	926	854	-13
Bordeaux	874	872	878	886	892	888	893	897	900	906	903	913	850	-3
Nantes	870	872	872	872	880	898	897	910	902	900	888	923	848	-1
Metz	864	865	864	863	864	876	880	866	851	846	848	904	850	0
Bastia	852	848	840	840	850	864	868	861	868	861	869	912	808	6
Toulouse	852	871	892	889	880	880	885	870	865	852	846	898	846	-19
Caen	851	846	844	839	848	847	837	832	839	835	806	873	834	5
Istres	823	818	817	808	804	800	803	804	806	804	811	847	823	6

SERIE A 2004-2005

Previous match form

	Curr	1-6	7-12	13-18	19-24	25-30	31-36	37-42	43-48	49-54	55-60	Home	Away	Trend
Juventus	975	970	966	966	974	974	967	957	972	976	976	991	947	5
AC Milan	971	979	984	974	984	981	978	981	984	971	960	978	952	-6
Inter Milan	963	956	946	945	938	935	939	937	926	936	956	950	931	10
Udinese	928	926	922	926	936	922	913	922	923	925	923	935	923	2
Sampdoria	922	925	926	922	910	900	896	905	913	913	911	936	889	0
Parma	904	906	904	908	904	916	924	934	928	933	937	968	873	-1
Siena	902	898	888	882	875	877	876	882	887	888	897	926	899	9
Palermo	902	905	918	914	915	908	911	453	0	0	0	917	889	-6
Lazio	900	905	914	910	920	926	933	935	934	940	945	937	907	-6
Livorno	900	902	900	898	894	901	891	451	0	0	0	932	884	1
Messina	899	903	896	897	900	911	918	301	0	0	0	937	872	0
Roma	895	894	912	927	932	932	938	954	961	960	961	944	888	-9
Chievo	894	886	884	898	902	917	924	906	903	908	910	930	894	4
Lecce	891	887	892	895	893	905	909	894	872	869	850	948	872	1
Reggina	888	886	891	902	892	886	892	887	881	887	892	930	869	-2
Fiorentina	885	874	870	866	872	862	846	847	861	866	872	952	871	10
Brescia	884	880	868	873	884	890	890	893	895	897	892	902	894	6
Atalanta	883	892	882	867	876	886	892	893	891	893	876	940	861	1
Bologna	882	890	908	909	886	886	893	897	905	905	894	926	856	-11
Cagliari	880	883	879	881	882	872	861	858	870	874	871	974	836	0

PRIMERA LIGA 2004-2005

Previous match form

	Curr	1-6	7-12	13-18	19-24	25-30	31-36	37-42	43-48	49-54	55-60	Home	Away	Trend
Barcelona	983	988	985	985	986	982	974	972	968	950	933	978	954	-2
Real Madrid	979	976	962	967	956	952	948	961	986	994	986	990	948	8
Villarreal	950	941	943	940	920	916	912	914	900	906	917	994	890	8
Real Betis	946	941	938	938	934	930	920	923	922	928	914	966	908	5
Valencia	938	942	952	957	964	952	966	968	968	960	961	975	898	-8
Seville	935	942	940	947	945	940	940	931	926	919	923	950	916	-5
Espanyol	929	925	929	926	934	924	919	908	894	883	874	974	881	2
Malaga	926	913	909	900	893	906	911	912	914	898	904	946	918	13
Deportivo	920	931	942	940	947	955	954	957	955	966	964	966	900	-11
Ath Bilbao	917	932	935	936	922	917	922	931	930	936	923	962	889	-10
Getafe	916	920	920	913	909	905	908	305	0	0	0	952	895	-1
R Zaragoza	911	918	911	900	903	918	920	906	904	892	892	966	880	1
Mallorca	910	895	889	898	903	906	920	920	904	908	923	935	916	11
Atl Madrid	910	913	921	914	918	919	921	911	917	918	922	979	868	-4
R Sociedad	908	915	910	902	912	906	904	910	914	918	922	956	891	-1
R Santander	903	898	900	892	894	901	891	896	904	905	906	939	902	4
Osasuna	898	905	893	905	910	906	910	906	925	920	924	937	890	-2
Levante	881	886	899	900	907	923	921	306	0	0	0	906	896	-9
Numancia	877	870	876	875	882	885	899	897	892	896	896	949	876	2
Albacete	872	875	888	906	913	911	906	914	910	901	899	925	884	-11

Real value is to be found in lower leagues

SO, hands up anyone who backed Chelsea, Sunderland, Luton, Yeovil, Rangers, Falkirk, Brechin and Gretna in handy little accas last season?

Of that set, Chelsea and Rangers improved by just the one place to land their titles and both Sunderland and Gretna (a gimme) by just the two.

Falkirk finished one further back in fourth in 2003/04 and Brechin were a bounce-back after relegation.

Luton and Yeovil were back in tenth and eighth at the end of that year though with 23 away defeats between them. And between them, they killed off tens of thousands of accas.

The final pair of English Divisions are traditionally the most volatile. No fewer than seven different teams including the eventual winners topped League Two after the first three games last season, only four of the 24 sides were never in the Play-Off zone, and champions Yeovil were not even in there at the end of October.

So while you might gain more kudos amongst your pals by picking the winners of the Premiership and the SPL back in August, you're more likely to get value looking for possibilities in the lower divisions.

You'll find the fullest treatment of the ante-post markets - taking all the summer transfers into account - in the Outlook supplements in August, but one thing that won't change between now and then is the certainty that one of the Big Three will win the Premiership.

Chelsea deserve to be favourites and if you can get odds-against for them anywhere, you've got yourself a deal. A bigger price about them retaining the Carling Cup could be an even better piece of business. They have filled a possible hole at left back, strengthening a squad that was already the best, and if they can keep Arjen Robben and Damien Duff fit throughout the season, it will hardly matter whether Didier Drogba proves himself worth £24 million or not.

Man United are more likely than Arsenal to wrest the title from them in my view. The takeover won't affect the team in the short term. A good businessman has bought a good business - 'nuff said.

Chelsea are privately owned and it hasn't done them any harm and once you cease to be a PLC, it can be easier to raise funds quickly to buy players. One that they have bought early in the summer could make a key difference, too.

Edwin van der Sar may not be much of a showman, but he's generally a safer pair of hands than any of the nine others used since Peter Schmeichel and as I write, the Gunners have stuck with the pair of dodgy cats that cost them goals last season. Man United outplayed them in the Cup Final and United at 10-3 each-way with Skybet (one third the odds a place 1,2) seems a fair way to cover your stake on them to regain the title at a decent price.

A more interesting market is teams to finish in the top six. Hills opened in June and others have followed suit.

LEEDS! LEEDS! LEEDS! Figaro believes the Yorkshire outfit represent the each-way value

There are two sides that stand out: Middlesbrough (11-4) and the perennially underestimated Bolton (7-2).

New boy Aiyegbeni Yakubu gives Steve McLaren a handy 'any two or three from EIGHT' striking options and it's hard to believe Boro will be hit by such awful injury problems two years running. Having Ugo Ehiogu, Gaizka Mendieta, George Boateng and Malcolm Christie back should be one hell of a boost.

I see no reason to expect Newcastle to break into the top six and there's a slight chance that Liverpool might drop out, especially given their fixture pile up.

Meanwhile, Everton's signings should help them improve on their late season league

form, but that will make them only a mid-table team.

For Premiership relegation, the three promoted sides all rightly start well odds-on in most places, so with all the stars choosing not to flock to Wigan, Totesport's evens against them going back looks a steal to me when Ladbrokes go 4-6. The other big differences of opinion involve Charlton (4-1 up to 8-1 with Skybet) and Blackburn (6-1 up to 10-1 with VC or Blue Square). With Darren Bent unlikely to make that much difference, the Addicks are tempting at 8-1.

The Coca-Cola markets are swarming with false favourites for both promotion and relegation. By early July, Saints boss Harry Redknapp was saying "I have lost six of my best

16 players and could lose more", while even if Palace have clung on to Andrew Johnson, they'll have a similar squad to the one that finished seventh at this level two years ago. Norwich have a great pair of strikers, but they also have a defence that shipped six in their last must-win game at Fulham. Last season, none of the relegated Premiership trio even reached the Play-Offs.

Let's go instead with two sleeping giants responding to a wake-up call. In Jackie Mc-Namara (free from Celtic), Glenn Hoddle looks to have found just the kind of player that could turn all those draws within Wolves' long unbeaten run into wins. They are the pick of those in the 13-2 bracket.

At a bigger price you have to like Leeds, where Rob Hulse and David Healey will now be drawing on supplies from Steve Stone and Eddie Lewis down the flanks.

With Ken Bates holding the purse strings, guaranteed massive support and other new boys like promising England U-21 international Danny Harding on board, United are each-way value at around 18-1.

Ipswich have shed their best players and Derby their whole management team while Reading will have a very different squad too, so pass on those. Hull have the set-up, manager and top scorer to press that trio, plus Sheffield United and Preston for a Play-Off place. Look out for Burnley as well.

Relegation? Brighton's fate could be determined by whether '4-4-2 Jags' Prescott decides to play for them and agrees to their Falmer Stadium project. If it is agreed in time, they might attract new players in the January window. If it's thrown out, the club could be knocked back down two or three Divisions, let alone one.

Crewe, with £3 million from the sale of Dean Ashton to invest, are more likely to survive. Wrexham's top scorer Juan Ugarte could flourish with Dario Gradi's coaching. By contrast, Cardiff and Watford have been shedding players and look sure to struggle.

In League One, it's all change at favourites Forest, as well as leading contenders Bournemouth, Brentford and Gillingham so swerve them, but Marcus Stewart looks an adequate replacement for Reading-bound striker Leroy Lita at well-supported Bristol City, widely available at 7s.

The most interesting activity has been at Oldham where Ronnie Moore, who took Rotherham up from this Division, has made some shrewd signings. For once, the teams coming up from League Two look less threatening here, but expect improvement from both Walsall and progressive Colchester who should not be amongst the favourites for relegation.

MK Dons under Danny Wilson are unlikely to drop either, while Oldham and Bradford may not be out at 28-1 or 25-1 for the title when you read this. Bradford's signing of Danny Cadamarteri and Russell Howarth will help push them up and the new faces Moore has recruited to the Oldham cause have got that town buzzing with confidence.

In League Two, Northampton (now with Eion Jess) just about deserve to be general favourites, but there are huge disagreements about nearly every other side.

Tommy Mooney is the pick of a great set of new boys at John Gorman's Wycombe (12-1 SportingBet) while Torquay (16-1 with Skybet, but 8-1 elsewhere) have the best chance amongst the relegated teams.

Darlington and Rochdale have kept their best players from last season while this year's Lincoln will be largely unrecognisable from last year's with five new signings after a clearout. Boston have acquired experience in the form of Brentford captain Stewart Talbot, Noel Whelan and Ben Futcher and are the best handicap bet of the year.

Debt-free Rushden are now run by a Supporters Trust who have been given 20 acres of land and promised £750,000 next season by departing Doc Martens supremo Max Griggs. They should not be favourites for the drop.

In Scotland, favourites more frequently oblige and we'll go with Rangers, Dundee and Gretna.

Recommended bets

20 points each on **Middlesbrough** and **Bolton** to be in the top six.
10 points on **Wolves**.
5 points e-w on **Leeds**.
10 points on **Bristol City**.
5 points e-w on **Oldham** and **Bradford**.
10 points on **Wycombe**.
5 points e-w on b.
HANDICAPS: **Middlesbrough**, **Leeds**, **Bradford** and **Boston**.
Scotland: **Rangers**, **Dundee**, **Gretna**.
Acca: Any 3 of **Chelsea**, **Wigan** (to be relegated) **Wolves**, **Bristol City**, **Wycombe**, **Rangers**, **Dundee** and **Gretna** = 70 bets at 0.5 points per bet.

FA Premier League 2005/06

	BET365	BLUE S	VC BET	CORAL	HILLS	LADS	SKYBET	S SOC	S JAMES	STANLEY	TOT
Chelsea	10-11	5-6	5-6	5-6	9-10	4-5	4-5	5-6	5-6	10-11	4-5
Arsenal	5-2	5-2	5-2	5-2	13-5	5-2	11-4	13-5	5-2	12-5	9-4
Man United	11-4	3	3	3	3	3	10-3	3	3	11-4	10-
Liverpool	20	16	20	16	16	14	14	25	20	20	16
Tottenham	150	150	150	125	100	125	200	150	100	125	150
Newcastle	100	150	150	125	100	100	200	150	200	125	250
Everton	250	100	150	150	150	100	150	200	150	150	250
Middlesbrough	200	300	250	300	200	200	300	200	250	300	300
Aston Villa	350	400	300	300	250	250	300	500	300	300	350
Bolton	350	300	300	400	200	350	300	500	350	300	350
Birmingham	500	500	300	400	250	500	300	500	500	500	500
Man City	350	300	500	500	200	350	500	500	300	400	500
Charlton	1000	750	500	750	750	750	750	1000	1000	750	100
Blackburn	1500	500	1000	750	500	750	750	750	500	750	1000
Fulham	1500	1500	1250	1000	750	1000	1000	1500	1000	1000	150
Portsmouth	2000	1500	1250	1250	750	1250	2000	2000	1500	1500	200
West Brom	2000	1500	2000	1500	1000	1500	3000	3000	2000	1500	350
Sunderland	2000	2000	1500	1500	1000	2000	5000	3000	1500	1500	500
West Ham	2500	2000	2500	1500	1000	5000	5000	3000	2000	2500	500
Wigan	2000	1500	3000	1500	750	3500	5000	3000	2000	2000	250

Win or each-way (*terms available from individual bookmakers*)

Coca-Cola Championship 2005/06

	BET365	BLUE S	VC BET	CORAL	HILLS	LADS	SKYBET	S SOC	S JAMES	STANLEY	TOTE
Southampton	5	11-2	11-2	5	9-2	5	11-2	5	11-2	5	9-2
Wolves	6	11-2	6	5	11-2	6	9-2	11-2	6	6	9-2
Crystal Palace	6	11-2	5	6	11-2	5	11-2	6	6	6	9-2
Norwich	6	13-2	11-2	6	13-2	6	11-2	11-2	11-2	6	11-2
Ipswich	11	14	10	12	10	12	14	10	12-1	10	14
Leeds	12	14	12	14	16	12	14	14	12	14	16
Sheffield Utd	16	14	16	16	14	16	14	16	14	16	18
Preston	18	16	14	14	16	14	16	18	18	16	16
Leicester	14	14	14	16	20	16	16	14	20	16	20
Derby	20	16	16	16	20	14	20	20	16	16	20
Reading	20	20	25	20	18	20	20	20	18	20	25
Hull	22	20	28	20	20	20	20	20	25	22	25
Coventry	33	33	28	40	33	25	40	33	25	33	33
Sheffield Wed	50	40	33	33	50	50	40	33	50	40	50
Luton	66	40	33	66	40	50	50	50	50	50	66
QPR	50	50	33	40	33	40	33	50	40	50	66
Millwall	50	40	33	66	50	66	66	40	66	40	66
Burnley	66	50	66	66	50	50	66	50	66	50	50
Stoke	40	40	40	33	33	50	100	50	50	40	100
Cardiff	100	50	50	80	50	50	100	50	66	50	100
Watford	80	66	50	80	66	66	50	66	66	66	100
Plymouth	100	80	100	80	50	50	100	66	80	80	150
Brighton	250	200	150	150	150	150	150	150	150	150	500
Crewe	250	200	200	150	150	250	150	150	150	200	500

Win or each-way (*terms available from individual bookmakers*)

ANTE-POST PRICES

Sponsored by Stan James

Coca-Cola League 1 2005/06

	BET365	BLUE S	VC BET	CORAL	HILLS	LADS	SKYBET	S SOC	S JAMES	STANLEY	TOTE
Nottm Forest	4	5	4	9-2	9-2	4	5	9-2	6	9-2	4
Bristol City	6	7	7	13-2	13-2	7	6	8	13-2	7	6
Tranmere	9	7	9	8	10	8	8	8	9	8	8
Huddersfield	12	12	11	12	10	8	12	12	10	12	9
Gillingham	12	10	14	11	12	11	12	10	10	11	9
Hartlepool	16	16	14	14	16	14	16	18	18	14	16
Brentford	20	14	14	16	16	14	16	16	20	16	20
Yeovil	20	18	16	20	16	20	20	18	18	18	20
Barnsley	14	14	20	16	16	14	12	14	20	16	20
Doncaster	16	16	18	20	20	20	16	22	20	20	22
Walsall	18	20	22	20	20	20	25	18	16	20	25
Rotherham	20	18	20	20	25	25	14	16	20	20	25
Oldham	16	25	20	25	20	28	25	28	16	28	20
Bournemouth	25	20	22	20	20	25	33	20	22	20	25
Swindon	25	28	25	20	20	25	25	28	33	25	33
Bradford	25	20	20	20	16	14	25	20	22	20	40
Swansea	33	33	20	20	20	18	40	25	25	25	33
Blackpool	40	33	33	33	28	25	50	33	40	33	40
MK Dons	40	40	40	40	50	50	40	40	20	40	40
Southend	50	50	33	33	25	33	40	40	33	33	40
Port Vale	50	33	50	40	40	50	50	40	50	40	50
Colchester	50	40	33	40	40	40	50	40	40	40	40
Scunthorpe	40	50	33	33	40	28	50	33	50	33	40
Chesterfield	80	66	40	50	80	50	50	50	66	50	80

Win or each-way (*terms available from individual bookmakers*)

Coca-Cola League 2 2005/06

	BET365	BLUE S	VC BET	CORAL	HILLS	LADS	SKYBET	S SOC	S JAMES	STANLEY	TOTE
Northampton	6	6	6	6	13-2	6	6	13-2	6	7	6
Wycombe	8	9	9	8	8	8	7	10	8	10	8
Wrexham	9	10	12	10	8	8	14	11	12	8	10
Darlington	9	14	12	10	14	12	11	10	12	10	11
Peterborough	12	12	10	12	12	12	12	12	14	14	10
Macclesfield	12	16	12	14	12	11	14	14	14	14	14
Lincoln	14	12	12	12	16	10	16	12	14	10	14
Torquay	12	12	12	12	11	12	16	12	12	11	14
Oxford Utd	14	12	14	14	18	16	16	16	14	16	14
Bristol Rovers	20	14	14	16	16	14	16	14	20	16	14
Carlisle	20	20	20	16	18	14	20	20	20	20	16
Leyton Orient	20	18	18	16	16	16	25	20	18	16	16
Barnet	25	20	18	20	16	14	16	20	20	20	18
Rochdale	25	25	20	25	22	25	25	25	22	25	25
Boston	20	16	25	25	18	18	16	28	25	25	20
Notts County	25	25	28	25	25	20	20	25	25	22	25
Stockport	25	20	20	20	18	20	14	16	20	16	28
Mansfield	25	28	25	25	33	20	33	25	28	25	33
Grimsby	25	28	28	25	28	25	20	25	25	28	33
Cheltenham	25	28	28	33	33	25	33	28	33	33	33
Chester	33	25	33	40	28	25	25	33	33	28	25
Bury	50	33	40	40	40	40	40	33	40	40	40
Shrewsbury	66	50	40	50	50	50	66	66	66	50	66
Rushden	80	50	40	66	66	50	50	50	66	50	100

Win or each-way (*terms available from individual bookmakers*)

Nationwide Conference 2005/06

	BET365	CHANDLR	CORAL	HILLS	LADS	PREMIER	SKYBET	S SOC	SJAMES	TOTE
Hereford	5	7-2	4	5	9-2	9-2	5	9-2	5	5
Aldershot	7	9	8	8	7	7	8	8	9	6
Stevenage	10	9	8	10	8	10	8	8	8	8
Exeter	12	6	10	12	10	10	12	9	12	7
Morecambe	10	10	10	15-2	12	12	10	11	12	10
Grays Athletic	10	9	10	9	8	12	10	10	10	10
Accrington Stan	16	14	14	10	14	10	10	12	14	14
Kidderminster	12	12	12	14	12	12	20	16	12	14
Halifax	20	20	14	16	16	16	14	12	18	20
Dagenham & R	20	16	16	16	20	20	16	16	20	16
Woking	25	16	16	16	16	25	16	16	16	20
Cambridge Utd	20	25	20	20	12	16	25	22	16	20
Scarborough	25	33	25	20	25	20	25	25	25	33
Crawley Town	20	25	25	25	25	33	16	25	25	25
Southport	20	25	25	25	28	33	33	28	28	25
York	20	25	25	28	33	33	25	33	28	40
Burton Albion	33	40	33	33	33	40	33	33	33	40
Gravesend	33	33	40	40	40	40	33	33	28	50
Tamworth	50	40	40	33	50	50	33	50	40	50
Canvey Island	33	33	40	33	40	50	40	40	33	66
Altrincham	33	33	50	50	40	66	50	50	33	50
Forest Green	33	66	66	50	66	66	50	66	33	80

Win or each-way (*terms available from individual bookmakers*)

STUART WATKISS: his Kidderminster side could find it tough going in the Conference

FA Cup 2005/06

	BET365	CHANDLER	VC BET	HILLS	LADS	P POWER	SKYBET	S SOCCER	S.JAMES	TOTE
Chelsea	4	7-2	4	7-2	4	7-2	7-2	4	4	7-2
Man Utd	6	4	4	5	6	5	9-2	9-2	9-2	9-2
Arsenal	9-2	4	5	5	15-2	9-2	4	9-2	8	5
Liverpool	8	8	7	9	9	8	8	9	11-2	9
Newcastle	12	14	12	16	14	14	16	14	16	20
Tottenham	14	16	12	16	14	18	20	14	12	16
Everton	14	25	20	18	16	22	20	14	25	20
Middlesbrough	25	25	25	22	20	22	25	22	25	28
Bolton	25	33	33	25	25	33	33	33	33	33
Aston Villa	25	33	33	28	25	28	33	33	33	33
Man City	25	33	33	22	20	28	33	33	33	40
Birmingham	50	33	50	28	25	33	25	33	40	40
Blackburn	50	40	50	33	28	40	33	40	40	66
Charlton	50	50	66	50	33	50	66	40	66	66
Fulham	50	50	50	50	33	50	50	66	50	66
Portsmouth	50	50	80	50	33	50	66	80	100	80
Sunderland	66	66	80	66	50	66	66	80	66	100
West Brom	80	66	80	66	50	66	66	80	100	100
West Ham	80	66	80	66	50	80	66	80	66	100
Wigan	80	66	80	66	-	80	100	80	66	100
Southampton	100	66	100	66	50	80	100	100	100	100
Crystal Palace	125	80	125	100	80	100	100	125	66	100
Norwich	80	80	100	100	80	100	100	125	66	100
Wolves	125	80	100	80	66	100	125	125	100	100
Ipswich	125	100	150	125	80	125	150	150	100	150
Derby	200	150	150	150	125	200	150	150	100	200
Leeds	150	125	150	100	80	150	200	150	100	200
Leicester	200	150	150	150	125	150	200	150	150	200
Preston	150	150	150	150	125	200	150	150	200	200
Sheffield Utd	50	150	150	125	100	150	150	150	150	200
Hull	250	-	200	150	125	200	-	200	200	250
Reading	225	-	150	125	100	200	200	150	150	250
Burnley	250	-	250	250	200	250	200	250	250	300
Cardiff	100	-	300	200	150	300	300	250	250	300
Coventry	200	200	200	250	150	250	250	200	200	300
Luton	400	-	250	200	150	250	-	200	300	300
QPR	100	-	200	200	150	250	200	250	300	300
Sheff Wed	200	-	200	200	200	200	-	200	250	300
Stoke	250	-	200	150	125	300	250	200	300	300
Millwall	250	-	150	200	150	200	200	200	300	300
Plymouth	250	-	-	250	200	300	250	250	300	400
Watford	250	-	250	250	200	300	250	250	300	400
Bristol City	-	-	-	250	200	-	-	-	400	400
Nottm Forest	-	-	-	250	200	250	250	-	300	400
Brighton	400	-	-	300	200	-	300	300	400	500
Crewe	500	-	300	300	200	-	300	300	350	500
Gillingham	-	-	-	-	-	-	300	-	300	500

Win or each-way (*terms available from individual bookmakers*)

Carling Cup 2005/06

	BET365	VC BET	HILLS	LADS	SKYBET	SP ODDS	S.JAMES	S SOCCER	TOTE
Chelsea	9-2	4	4	7-2	9-2	9-2	9-2	4	4
Man Utd	8	13-2	6	9	8	8	9	8	7
Liverpool	8	9	9	9	6	8	8	8	7
Arsenal	8	12	15-2	12	8	10	10	9	9
Newcastle	10	10	14	12	10	10	12	11	14
Tottenham	12	12	14	10	14	10	9	10	11
Middlesbrough	16	20	20	16	16	14	16	16	20
Everton	14	25	16	10	16	20	25	20	20
Bolton	20	18	25	16	20	25	25	22	25
Aston Villa	20	20	25	16	20	20	20	22	25
Man City	20	20	20	16	16	20	25	20	28
Birmingham	25	25	25	16	20	28	25	25	28
Blackburn	33	28	28	25	33	33	25	33	33
Charlton	33	33	33	25	33	40	50	40	40
Fulham	50	40	33	40	33	50	40	40	40
Portsmouth	50	28	33	50	40	50	50	50	50
Sunderland	40	40	50	50	50	66	50	50	80
West Brom	66	50	50	50	50	66	50	50	80
West Ham	50	40	50	50	50	66	66	66	80
Wigan	50	40	50	66	50	80	66	66	80
Southampton	66	50	50	80	66	80	100	66	80
Crystal Palace	80	50	80	80	66	100	80	80	80
Norwich	66	66	80	100	66	80	100	80	80
Wolves	66	66	66	66	66	80	100	80	80
Ipswich	100	66	80	100	100	125	125	100	100
Derby	150	80	125	-	-	150	150	125	150
Leeds	100	66	80	100	100	125	125	125	150
Leicester	125	80	125	125	-	150	150	125	150
Preston	100	66	125	125	-	150	150	150	150
Sheffield Utd	125	125	100	125	125	150	100	125	150
Hull	150	-	125	-	-	200	200	200	200
Reading	150	-	100	125	-	200	125	200	200
Burnley	200	-	200	-	-	250	250	200	250
Cardiff	200	-	150	-	-	250	250	200	250
Coventry	150	150	150	-	-	200	150	150	250
Luton	200	-	150	-	-	250	250	250	250
QPR	200	-	150	-	-	250	150	200	250
Sheffield Wed	150	125	200	150	-	200	150	200	250
Stoke	150	-	125	-	-	250	200	200	250
Plymouth	250	-	200	-	-	250	250	250	300
Watford	200	-	200	-	-	300	200	200	300
Millwall	150	-	150	-	-	300	350	200	300
Bristol City	-	-	200	-	-	300	400	-	300
Nottm Forest	-	-	200	-	-	-	400	-	300
Brighton	250	-	200	-	-	-	500	300	500
Crewe	250	-	200	-	-	350	500	350	500
Gillingham	-	-	-	-	-	-	500	-	500

Win or each-way (terms available from individual bookmakers)

Sponsored by Stan James

Scottish Premier League 2005/06

	BET365	CORAL	VC BET	HILLS	LADS	PREMIER	SKYBET	SP ODDS	S JAMES	STANLEY	TOTE
Rangers	5-6	5-6	5-6	4-6	5-6	8-11	4-6	8-11	4-6	5-6	8-11
Celtic	5-6	5-6	5-6	11-10	5-6	11-10	11-10	Evs	11-10	5-6	Evs
Hearts	400	250	300	250	250	250	250	400	400	400	300
Hibernian	250	250	200	250	200	300	150	250	400	250	250
Aberdeen	500	200	250	250	200	500	200	300	300	300	250
Dundee Utd	1000	1500	500	1000	1000	1000	1000	1500	800	1000	1000
Kilmarnock	1000	1000	1000	1000	1000	1500	1000	1500	500	1500	1500
Motherwell	500	500	1000	500	1000	1500	750	1500	500	1000	1500
Inverness	2000	2000	2000	1000	1000	2500	2000	2500	800	2000	2500
Dunfermline	2000	2500	2500	1000	2500	2500	2500	3000	1000	2500	3000
Livingston	2500	2500	2000	1500	2500	3000	3000	3000	1000	2000	3000
Falkirk	2500	2500	3000	1500	2500	3000	4000	4000	1000	2500	3500

Win only

Scottish Cup 2005/06

	CORAL	VC BET	HILLS	LADS	SKYBET	S JAMES	TOTE
Rangers	5-4	11-8	11-8	5-4	11-8	11-8	5-4
Celtic	5-4	11-8	11-8	5-4	6-4	6-4	11-8
Hearts	14	14	14	16	14	14	14
Hibernian	14	14	14	14	14	14	14
Aberdeen	14	14	12	14	12	12	12
Dundee Utd	33	25	40	33	25	33	33
Kilmarnock	33	33	33	33	25	25	33
Motherwell	-	33	25	25	20	25	33
Inverness	40	33	50	40	33	33	50
Dunfermline	50	40	50	66	40	40	50
Livingston	50	40	100	66	50	66	80
Falkirk	66	50	80	66	-	50	100

Win or each-way (*terms available from individual bookmakers*)

CIS Cup 2005/06

	CORAL	VC BET	LADS	SKYBET	TOTE
Rangers	11-8	6-4	11-8	13-8	6-4
Celtic	11-8	6-4	11-8	7-4	6-4
Aberdeen	12	12	12	10	11
Hibernian	12	12	12	12	12
Hearts	12	12	14	12	12
Dundee Utd	25	20	33	20	33
Kilmarnock	25	28	33	20	25
Motherwell	-	28	20	16	25
Inverness	33	28	33	25	33
Dunfermline	50	33	66	33	33
Livingston	50	33	66	40	50
Falkirk	66	40	66	-	66

Win or each-way (*individual bookmakers terms apply*)

RANGERS: *favourites for the lot*

Primera Liga

	BET365	SPORTING B	SKYBET	SSOC	S JAMES	TOTE
Barcelona	Evs	Evs	Evs	Evs	5-6	Evs
Real Madrid	11-8	7-5	11-10	5-4	6-4	13-8
Valencia	12	8	10	10	10	8
Real Betis	25	22	25	33	33	16
Deportivo	25	20	25	25	33	20
Seville	25	33	33	33	25	33
Villarreal	12	25	33	16	16	18
Atletico Madrid	66	50	33	40	33	80
Athletic Bilbao	100	80	100	100	150	80
Espanyol	100	66	100	125	150	80
Real Zaragoza	200	200	100	200	200	250
Real Sociedad	200	150	200	250	250	200
Celta Vigo	250	250	500	400	300	400
Malaga	150	150	500	300	250	200
Mallorca	300	300	500	400	400	400
Osasuna	500	300	500	500	300	500
Alaves	500	400	750	1000	1000	750
R Santander	500	750	1000	-	750	1000
Cadiz	1000	1500	2000	2000	1000	2000
Getafe	1000	1500	2000	2000	1000	2000

Win or each-way (*terms available from individual bookmakers*)

LYON: *going for a nap hand of titles*

Le Championnat

	BET365	SKYBET	S SOC	TOTE
Lyon	13-8	11-10	10-11	6-5
Monaco	4	7-2	9-2	4
Marseille	13-2	7	6	11-2
Paris St-G	7	7	7	9
Lille	7	10	9	8
Auxerre	14	14	12	16
Lens	33	33	33	40
Rennes	33	33	40	33
Nantes	40	40	50	40
St Etienne	50	66	66	80
Bordeaux	66	50	80	80
Sochaux	80	80	50	66
Strasbourg	100	150	150	150
Toulouse	100	150	150	150
Metz	200	200	200	300
Nice	200	200	150	250
Ajaccio	500	500	500	500
Le Mans	500	500	500	750
Nancy	500	500	500	750
Troyes	1000	1000	500	1000

Win or e-w (*individual bookmakers terms apply*)

Bundesliga

	BET365	SKYBET	S.SOC	TOTE
B Munich	5-6	1-2	8-13	8-13
Schalke	5	5	5	11-2
W Bremen	8	13-2	7	15-2
H Berlin	12	12	11	12
B Leverkusen	14	14	12	14
Hamburg	16	20	20	14
Stuttgart	20	12	18	14
B Dortmund	10	33	14	12
Wolfsburg	50	80	100	80
Hannover	200	200	250	250
K'slautern	500	500	500	500
Mainz	500	500	500	500
B M'gladbach	200	750	300	300
Cologne	250	750	-	400
A Bielefeld	500	750	750	750
Frankfurt	500	750	1000	1000
MSV Duisburg	500	750		1000
Nuremberg	500	750	-	500

Win or e-w (*individual bookmakers terms apply*)

SCHALKE: can they deny Bayern?

ADRIANO: can fire Inter to Serie A glory

Serie A

	BET365	SKYBET	S SOC	TOTE
AC Milan	5-4	10-11	6-5	Evs
Juventus	11-8	6-5	5-4	6-4
Inter Milan	3	4	3	11-4
Udinese	50	33	40	50
Roma	40	80	40	40
Sampdoria	66	40	50	80
Lazio	100	80	80	100
Fiorentina	125	150	150	300
Parma	125	200	150	200
Messina*	350	250	400	400
Genoa	500	500	500	500
Lecce	500	500	500	500
Palermo	125	750	500	500
Cagliari	500	750	600	600
Torino*	500	750	500	750
Chievo	350	150	300	1000
Siena	1000	750	1000	1000
Livorno	1000	1000	1000	1000
Reggina	1000	1500	1500	1500
Empoli	1500	2000	2000	1500

*Serie A status subject to appeal
Win or e-w (*individual bookmakers terms apply*)

Back status quo in Spain, but Inter look ready to rock

LIVERPOOL winning the Champions League last season has, to some extent, disguised the fact that the top flight of English football would make a fight between Mike Tyson and Jimmy Cranky look competitive.

Anyone with a decent satellite connection would confirm that where our Premiership is concerned, all that glitters is not always gold.

Eurosport's coverage of European football might have distinctly low budget production values, but that cannot hide the fact that our game is still somewhat primitive in comparison to the rest of Europe.

In an era dominated by player power and clever marketing, the role of the manager has been dumbed down to the extent that if his team wins, he is regarded as no more than a cog in the wheel, whilst in defeat, he may be subjected to anything just shy of public execution.

Season 2004/05 went some way to redressing that balance, and the upcoming campaign is sure to again underline the importance of men such as Frank Rijkaard, Fabio Capello and Felix Magath.

In Spain last year, only four coaches survived the entire season but of those that swerved the white handkerchief wavers, one lifted the title, two more delivered Champions League football and the last a Uefa cup position. Proof indeed that stability brings success.

Having secured their first title in six years, Barcelona will take some shifting from the La Liga summit.

Frank Rijkaard has spent a mountain of cash, but unlike his counterparts at Madrid, has spread it evenly throughout his team.

An injury to Samuel Eto'o may leave the Catalans slightly exposed in terms of strikers, but in captain Xavi, a fusion of the metronomic Pep Guardiola and the artistry of Hristo Stoichkov, they can boast Europe's most complete midfielder. Throw in World Player of the Year Ronaldinho, the rugged Carlos Puyol, the decadence of Deco and the guile of Giuly and you begin to realise the challenge facing the rest.

A new era of dominance may be about to start in Spain and in Italy the tide might also be about to turn.

Kaka aside, Milan are a team growing old together, Juve's success last year owed ten times as much to Capello's organisational skills as it did to the waning powers of Alessandro Del Piero and David Trezeguet, and the capital clubs Roma and Lazio are now little more than illustrious names.

With that in mind, back Inter to end what seems like a lifetime of underachievement and claim their first Scud-

INTER MILAN: Mancini's Nerazzuri can emerge from the wilderness to grab Serie A glory

etto since 1989. Sharing a bath with an electric toaster may have been a better idea than parting with your hard-earned in support of the Nerazzurri this time last year, and you would be more than entitled to ask what has changed, especially as Inter finished last term 14 points adrift of Juventus last season.

The key is the coach. Roberto Mancini's attacking philosophies have helped replace any feelings of inadequacy with a fresh impetus.

Inter may have drawn a staggering 18 times in Serie A last year, but many of those points were achieved via miraculous comebacks and stoppage time equalisers, which suggests that Mancini has control of the dressing room - unlike a long line of his predecessors.

A couple of defensive reinforcements will no doubt be made to give the men from the San Siro the necessary steel that championship winning sides need, but Mancini has proved a worthy judge of talent thus far, and 4-1 is too good to miss.

In France, the resignation of Paul Le Guen could signal the end of Lyon's four-year reign as French champions.

The appointment of Gerard Houllier as his replacement is a puzzling one. Lyon have been one of the continent's most vibrant attacking sides in recent years but Gerard, as we know, is hardly renowned for producing teams of an aesthetically pleasing nature.

Houllier's arrival will no doubt give encouragement to traditional heavyweights Marseille and Paris St-Germain who deserve to be supported.

At around 13-2 the pair they represent massive value as opposed to the 13-8 about the Lyonnais under new management.

Both these sides improved towards the back-end of last season and will be aided by a bumper new Premiership-style TV deal which will give French sides cash to burn.

Watch too for Marseille's teenage sensation Samir Nasri, whose breathtaking ability and Algerian roots have inevitably drawn comparisons with Zinedine Zidane.

Finally, in Germany, Bayern Munich are banker material once again. Magath, once thought of as little more than Germany's answer to Dave Bassett, is revelling in his new position of power.

Schalke threatened to run Kahn and co. close last time before running out of puff, whilst Stuttgart and Bremen have already been weakened this summer by the loss of key personnel.

The new Allianz Arena which Bayern now call home, is an all-singing, all-dancing modern stadium fit for champions and that's exactly what the Bavarians will be again come May.

FA Barclaycard Premiership

Champions:	Chelsea
Runners-up:	Arsenal
Relegated:	Crystal Palace
	Norwich
	Southampton

Coca-Cola Championship

Champions:	Sunderland
Runners-up:	Wigan
Play-off champions:	West Ham Utd
Relegated:	Gillingham
	Nottm Forest
	Rotherham

Coca-Cola League 1

Champions:	Luton
Runners-up:	Hull
Play-off champions:	Sheff Wed
Relegated:	Torquay
	Wrexham*
	Peterborough
	Stockport

Coca-Cola League 2

Champions:	Yeovil
Runners-up:	Scunthorpe
Third:	Swansea
Play-off champions:	Southend
Relegated:	Kidderminster
	Cambridge Utd*

Bank of Scotland Premier League

Champions:	Rangers
Runners-up:	Celtic
Relegated:	Dundee

Bell's Scottish Division One

Champions:	Falkirk
Runners-up:	St Mirren
Relegated:	Partick
	Raith Rovers

Bell's Scottish Division Two

Champions:	Brechin
Runners-up:	Stranraer
Relegated:	Arbroath
	Berwick

Bell's Scottish Third Division

Champions:	Gretna
Runners-up:	Peterhead
Bottom:	East Stirling

Nationwide Conference

Champions:	Barnet
Play-off champions:	Carlisle
Relegated:	Northwich*
	Farnborough
	Leigh RMI

Nationwide Conference North

Champions:	Southport
Runners-up:	Nuneaton
Relegated:	Runcorn
	Ashton Utd
	Bradford Pk

Nationwide Conference South

Champions:	Grays Athletic
Runners-up:	Cambridge City
Relegated:	Hornchurch*
	Margate*
	Redbridge+

FA Cup

Winners:	Arsenal
Runners-up:	Man United

Carling Cup

Winners:	Chelsea
Runners-up:	Liverpool

LDV Vans Trophy

Winners:	Wrexham
Runners-up:	Southend

FA Trophy

Winners:	Grays Athletic
Runners-up:	Hucknall

Tennent's Scotttish FA Cup

Winners:	Celtic
Runners-up:	Dundee Utd

CIS Insurance Cup

Winners:	Rangers
Runners-up:	Motherwell

Bell's Scottish Challenge Cup

Winners:	Falkirk
Runners-up:	Ross County

*10 points deducted +Three points deducted

Sponsored by Stan James

Referees can be the bane of players and managers alike but the bookings market is increasingly where spread betting and fixed odds punters look to make some profit.

Below are the stats for last sesaon's select group of referees. Their card counts are exclusive to the Premiership and that should be borne in mind when weighing up their final scores.

Name	Games	Yellow	Red	Pts	Ave
Bennett	26	98	5	1,155	**44.4**
Dowd	20	62	7	805	**40.3**
Messias	11	43	0	430	**39.1**
Styles	23	66	7	875	**38.0**
Poll	31	101	4	1,140	**36.8**
Dean	11	28	4	400	**36.4**
D'urso	12	35	3	435	**36.3**
Riley	27	77	7	975	**36.1**
Webb	23	72	2	770	**33.5**
Wiley	21	50	4	640	**30.5**
Walton	16	45	1	475	**29.7**
Gallagher	20	48	3	555	**27.8**
Knight	16	31	4	410	**25.6**
Halsey	22	50	1	525	**23.9**
Dunn	22	49	1	515	**23.4**
Barry	20	38	2	90	**22.5**
Rennie	15	27	1	305	**20.3**
Foy	16	31	0	310	**19.4**

Points are awarded on the basis of ten points for a yellow card and 25 for a red. In the case of a second yellow followed by red the number of points rises to 35, the usual practice in spread betting.

THE GOOD? Chris Foy *THE BAD? Andy D'urso* *THE UGLY? Steve Bennett*

FA BARCLAYCARD PREMIER LEAGUE

	Team	Pld	W	D	L	F	GFA	PGA	Pts
1	Arsenal (2)	38	25	8	5	87	**2.29**	2.2	83
2	Chelsea (1)	38	29	8	1	72	**1.89**	2.5	95
3	Man Utd (3)	38	22	11	5	58	**1.53**	2.0	77
4	Middlesbro (7)	38	14	13	11	53	**1.39**	1.4	55
5	Liverpool (5)	38	17	7	14	52	**1.37**	1.5	58
6	Fulham (13)	38	12	8	18	52	**1.37**	1.2	44
7	Bolton (6)	38	16	10	12	49	**1.29**	1.5	58
8	Man City (8)	38	13	13	12	47	**1.24**	1.4	52
9	Tottenham (9)	38	14	10	14	47	**1.24**	1.4	52
10	Newcastle (14)	38	10	14	14	47	**1.24**	1.2	44
11	Everton (4)	38	18	7	13	45	**1.18**	1.6	61
12	Aston Villa (10)	38	12	11	15	45	**1.18**	1.2	47
13	Southampton (20)	38	6	14	18	45	**1.18**	0.8	32
14	Portsmouth (16)	38	10	9	19	43	**1.13**	1.0	39
15	Charlton (11)	38	12	10	16	42	**1.11**	1.2	46
16	Norwich (19)	38	7	12	19	42	**1.11**	0.9	33
17	C Palace (18)	38	7	12	19	41	**1.08**	0.9	33
18	Birmingham (12)	38	11	12	15	40	**1.05**	1.2	45
19	West Brom (17)	38	6	16	16	36	**0.95**	0.9	34
20	Blackburn (15)	38	9	15	14	32	**0.84**	1.1	42

- Number in brackets refers to final league finishing position
- GFA: Goals for average per match
- PGA: Average points gained per match

COCA-COLA CHAMPIONSHIP

	Team	Pld	W	D	L	F	GFA	PGA	Pts
1	Ipswich (3)	46	24	13	9	85	**1.85**	1.8	85
2	Wigan (2)	46	25	12	9	79	**1.72**	1.9	87
3	Sunderland (1)	46	29	7	10	76	**1.65**	2.0	94
4	Wolves (9)	46	15	21	10	72	**1.57**	1.4	66
5	Derby (4)	46	22	10	14	71	**1.54**	1.7	76
6	Preston (5)	46	21	12	13	67	**1.46**	1.6	75
7	West Ham (6)	46	21	10	15	66	**1.43**	1.6	73
8	Crewe (21)	46	12	14	20	68	**1.40**	1.1	50
9	Coventry (19)	46	13	13	20	61	**1.33**	1.1	52
10	Sheff Utd (8)	46	18	13	15	57	**1.24**	1.5	67
11	QPR (11)	46	17	11	18	54	**1.17**	1.3	62
12	Plymouth (17)	46	14	11	21	52	**1.13**	1.2	53
13	Watford (18)	46	12	16	18	52	**1.13**	1.1	52
14	Reading (7)	46	19	13	14	51	**1.11**	1.5	70
15	Millwall (10)	46	18	12	16	51	**1.11**	1.4	66
16	Leeds (14)	46	14	18	14	49	**1.07**	1.3	60
17	Leicester (15)	46	12	21	13	49	**1.07**	1.2	57
18	Cardiff (16)	46	13	15	18	48	**1.04**	1.2	54
19	Gillingham (22)	46	12	14	20	45	**0.98**	1.1	50
20	Nottm Forest (23)	46	9	17	20	42	**0.91**	1.0	44
21	Brighton (20)	46	13	12	21	40	**0.87**	1.1	51
22	Burnley (13)	46	15	15	16	58	**0.83**	1.3	60
23	Stoke (12)	46	17	10	19	36	**0.78**	1.3	61
24	Rotherham (24)	46	5	14	27	35	**0.76**	0.6	29

Sponsored by Stan James

FA BARCLAYCARD PREMIER LEAGUE

	Team	Pld	W	D	L	A	GAA	PGA	Pts
1	Chelsea (1)	38	29	8	1	15	**0.39**	2.5	95
2	Arsenal (2)	38	25	8	5	26	**0.68**	2.2	83
3	Man Utd (3)	38	22	11	5	26	**0.68**	2.0	77
4	Man City (9)	38	13	13	12	39	**1.03**	1.4	52
5	Liverpool (6)	38	17	7	14	41	**1.08**	1.5	58
6	Tottenham (9)	38	14	10	14	41	**1.08**	1.4	52
7	Blackburn (15)	38	9	15	14	43	**1.13**	1.1	42
8	Bolton (6)	38	16	10	12	44	**1.16**	1.5	58
9	Everton (4)	38	18	7	13	46	**1.21**	1.6	61
10	Middlesbro (7)	38	14	13	11	46	**1.21**	1.4	55
11	Birmingham (12)	38	11	12	15	46	**1.21**	1.2	45
12	Aston Villa (10)	38	12	11	15	52	**1.37**	1.2	47
13	Newcastle (14)	38	10	14	14	57	**1.50**	1.2	44
14	Charlton (11)	38	12	10	16	58	**1.53**	1.2	46
15	Portsmouth (16)	38	10	9	19	59	**1.55**	1.0	39
16	Fulham (14)	38	12	8	18	60	**1.58**	1.2	44
17	West Brom (17)	38	6	16	16	61	**1.60**	0.9	34
18	C Palace (19)	38	7	12	19	62	**1.63**	0.9	33
19	Southampton (20)	38	6	14	18	66	**1.74**	0.8	32
20	Norwich (19)	38	7	12	19	77	**2.03**	0.9	33

- Number in brackets refers to final league finishing position
- GAA: Goals against average per match
- PGA: Average points gained per match

COCA-COLA CHAMPIONSHIP

	Team	Pld	W	D	L	A	GAA	PGA	Pts
1	Wigan (2)	46	25	12	9	35	**0.76**	1.9	87
2	Stoke (12)	46	17	10	19	38	**0.83**	1.3	61
3	Burnley (14)	46	15	15	16	39	**0.85**	1.3	60
4	Reading (7)	46	19	13	14	44	**0.96**	1.5	70
5	Millwall (10)	46	18	12	16	45	**0.98**	1.4	66
6	Leicester (15)	46	12	21	13	46	**1.00**	1.2	57
7	Cardiff (16)	46	13	15	18	51	**1.11**	1.2	54
8	Sunderland (1)	46	29	7	10	41	**1.12**	2.0	94
9	Ipswich (3)	46	24	13	9	56	**1.22**	1.8	85
10	West Ham (6)	46	21	10	15	56	**1.22**	1.6	73
11	Sheff Utd (8)	46	18	13	15	56	**1.22**	1.5	67
12	Preston (5)	46	21	12	13	58	**1.26**	1.6	75
13	QPR (11)	46	17	11	18	58	**1.26**	1.3	62
14	Wolves (10)	46	15	21	10	59	**1.28**	1.4	66
15	Watford (19)	46	12	16	18	59	**1.28**	1.1	52
16	Derby (4)	46	22	10	14	60	**1.30**	1.7	76
17	Plymouth (17)	46	14	11	21	64	**1.39**	1.2	53
18	Brighton (20)	46	13	12	21	65	**1.39**	1.1	51
19	Gillingham (22)	46	12	14	20	66	**1.43**	1.1	50
20	Nottm Forest (23)	46	9	17	20	66	**1.43**	1.0	44
21	Leeds (14)	46	14	18	14	52	**1.44**	1.3	60
22	Coventry (19)	46	13	13	20	73	**1.59**	1.1	52
23	Rotherham (24)	46	5	14	27	69	**1.50**	0.6	29
24	Crewe (22)	46	12	14	20	86	**1.87**	1.1	50

COCA-COLA LEAGUE 1

	Team	Pld	W	D	L	F	GFA	PGA	Pts
1	Luton (1)	46	29	11	6	87	**1.89**	2.1	98
2	Hull City (2)	46	26	8	12	80	**1.74**	1.9	86
3	Sheff Wed (5)	46	19	15	12	77	**1.67**	1.6	72
4	Bournemouth (8)	46	20	10	16	77	**1.67**	1.5	70
5	Hartlepool (6)	46	21	8	17	76	**1.65**	1.5	71
6	Bristol C (7)	46	18	16	12	74	**1.61**	1.5	70
7	Huddersfield (9)	46	20	10	16	74	**1.61**	1.5	70
8	Tranmere (3)	46	22	13	11	73	**1.59**	1.7	79
9	Barnsley (13)	46	14	19	13	69	**1.50**	1.3	61
10	Swindon (12)	46	17	12	17	66	**1.43**	1.4	63
11	Doncaster (10)	46	16	18	12	65	**1.41**	1.4	66
12	Walsall (14)	46	16	12	18	65	**1.41**	1.3	60
13	Bradford (11)	46	17	14	15	64	**1.39**	1.4	65
14	Wrexham (22)	46	13	14	19	62	**1.35**	1.2	43
15	Colchester (15)	46	14	17	15	60	**1.30**	1.3	59
16	Oldham (19)	46	14	10	22	60	**1.30**	1.1	52
17	Brentford (4)	46	22	9	15	57	**1.24**	1.6	75
18	Chesterfield (17)	46	14	15	17	55	**1.20**	1.2	57
19	Torquay (21)	46	12	15	19	55	**1.20**	1.1	51
20	Blackpool (16)	46	15	12	19	54	**1.17**	1.2	57
21	Milton Keynes (20)	46	12	15	19	54	**1.17**	1.1	51
22	Port Vale (18)	46	17	5	24	49	**1.07**	1.2	56
23	Peterborough (23)	46	9	12	25	49	**1.07**	0.8	39
24	Stockport (24)	46	6	8	32	49	**1.07**	0.6	26

COCA-COLA LEAGUE 2

	Team	Pld	W	D	L	F	GFA	PGA	Pts
1	Yeovil (1)	46	25	8	13	90	**1.96**	1.8	83
2	Scunthorpe (2)	46	22	14	10	69	**1.50**	1.7	80
3	Southend (4)	46	22	12	12	65	**1.41**	1.7	78
4	Leyton Orient (11)	46	16	15	15	65	**1.41**	1.4	63
5	Lincoln (6)	46	20	12	14	64	**1.39**	1.6	72
6	Swansea (3)	46	24	8	14	62	**1.35**	1.7	80
7	Northampton (7)	46	20	12	14	62	**1.35**	1.6	72
8	Boston Utd (16)	46	14	16	16	62	**1.35**	1.3	58
9	Macclesfield (5)	46	22	9	15	60	**1.30**	1.6	75
10	Bristol R (12)	46	13	21	12	60	**1.30**	1.3	60
11	Wycombe (10)	46	17	14	15	58	**1.26**	1.4	65
12	Darlington (8)	46	20	12	14	57	**1.24**	1.6	72
13	Mansfield (13)	46	15	15	16	56	**1.22**	1.3	60
14	Rochdale (9)	46	16	18	12	54	**1.17**	1.4	66
15	Bury (17)	46	14	16	16	54	**1.17**	1.3	58
16	Cheltenham (14)	46	16	12	18	51	**1.11**	1.3	60
17	Grimsby (18)	46	14	16	16	51	**1.11**	1.3	58
18	Oxford (15)	46	16	11	19	50	**1.09**	1.3	59
19	Shrewsbury (21)	46	11	16	19	48	**1.04**	1.1	49
20	Notts Co (19)	46	13	13	20	46	**1.00**	1.1	52
21	Chester (20)	46	12	16	18	43	**0.93**	1.1	52
22	Rushden (22)	46	10	14	22	42	**0.91**	1.0	44
23	Kidderminster (23)	46	10	8	28	39	**0.85**	0.8	38
24	Cambridge (24)	46	8	16	22	39	**0.85**	0.9	30

Sponsored by Stan James

COCA-COLA LEAGUE 1

	Team	Pld	W	D	L	A	GAA	PGA	Pts
1	Luton (1)	46	29	11	6	48	**1.04**	2.1	98
2	Colchester (15)	46	14	17	15	50	**1.09**	1.3	59
3	Hull City (2)	46	26	8	12	53	**1.15**	1.9	86
4	Tranmere (3)	46	22	13	11	55	**1.20**	1.7	79
5	Bristol C (7)	46	18	16	12	57	**1.24**	1.5	70
6	Sheff Wed (5)	46	19	15	12	59	**1.26**	1.6	72
7	Blackpool (16)	46	15	12	19	59	**1.26**	1.2	57
8	Port Vale (18)	46	17	5	24	59	**1.26**	1.2	56
9	Brentford (4)	46	22	9	15	60	**1.30**	1.6	75
10	Doncaster (10)	46	16	18	12	60	**1.30**	1.4	66
11	Bradford (11)	46	17	14	15	62	**1.35**	1.4	65
12	Chesterfield (17)	46	14	15	17	62	**1.35**	1.2	57
13	Bournemouth (8)	46	20	10	16	64	**1.39**	1.5	70
14	Huddersfield (9)	46	20	10	16	65	**1.41**	1.5	70
15	Hartlepool (6)	46	21	8	17	66	**1.43**	1.5	71
16	Swindon (12)	46	17	12	17	68	**1.48**	1.4	63
17	Milton Keynes (20)	46	12	15	19	68	**1.48**	1.1	51
18	Barnsley (13)	46	14	19	13	64	**1.39**	1.3	61
19	Walsall (14)	46	16	12	18	69	**1.50**	1.3	60
20	Oldham (19)	46	14	10	22	73	**1.59**	1.1	52
21	Peterborough (23)	46	9	12	25	73	**1.59**	0.8	39
22	Torquay (21)	46	12	15	19	79	**1.72**	1.1	51
23	Wrexham (22)	46	13	14	19	80	**1.74**	1.2	43
24	Stockport (24)	46	6	8	32	98	**2.13**	0.6	26

COCA-COLA LEAGUE 2

	Team	Pld	W	D	L	A	GAA	PGA	Pts
1	Scunthorpe (3)	46	22	14	10	42	**0.91**	1.7	80
2	Southend (4)	46	22	12	12	46	**1.00**	1.7	78
3	Lincoln (6)	46	20	12	14	47	**1.02**	1.6	72
4	Rochdale (9)	46	16	18	12	48	**1.04**	1.4	66
5	Macclesfield (5)	46	22	9	15	49	**1.07**	1.6	75
6	Darlington (8)	46	20	12	14	49	**1.07**	1.6	72
7	Northampton (7)	46	20	12	14	51	**1.11**	1.6	72
8	Wycombe (10)	46	17	14	15	52	**1.13**	1.4	65
9	Grimsby (18)	46	14	16	16	52	**1.13**	1.3	58
10	Shrewsbury (21)	46	11	16	19	53	**1.15**	1.1	49
11	Cheltenham (14)	46	16	12	18	54	**1.17**	1.3	60
12	Bury (17)	46	14	16	16	54	**1.17**	1.3	58
13	Swansea (3)	46	24	8	14	43	**1.19**	1.7	80
14	Mansfield (13)	46	15	15	16	56	**1.22**	1.3	60
15	Bristol R (12)	46	13	21	12	57	**1.24**	1.3	60
16	Boston Utd (16)	46	14	16	16	58	**1.26**	1.3	58
17	Notts Co (19)	46	13	13	20	62	**1.35**	1.1	52
18	Cambridge (24)	46	8	16	22	62	**1.35**	0.9	30
19	Oxford (15)	46	16	11	19	63	**1.37**	1.3	59
20	Rushden (22)	46	10	14	22	63	**1.37**	1.0	44
21	Yeovil (1)	46	25	8	13	65	**1.41**	1.8	83
22	Leyton Orient (11)	46	16	15	15	67	**1.46**	1.4	63
23	Chester (20)	46	12	16	18	69	**1.50**	1.1	52
24	Kidderminster (23)	46	10	8	28	85	**1.85**	0.8	38

NATIONWIDE CONFERENCE

	Team	Pld	W	D	L	F	GFA	PGA	Pts
1	Barnet (1)	42	26	8	8	90	**2.14**	2.0	86
2	Carlisle (3)	42	20	13	9	74	**1.76**	1.7	73
3	Halifax (9)	42	19	9	14	74	**1.76**	1.6	66
4	Accrington (10)	42	18	11	13	72	**1.71**	1.5	65
5	Exeter (6)	42	20	11	11	71	**1.69**	1.7	71
6	Morecambe (7)	42	19	14	9	69	**1.64**	1.7	71
7	Hereford (2)	42	21	11	10	68	**1.62**	1.8	74
8	Aldershot (4)	42	21	10	11	68	**1.62**	1.7	73
9	Dag & Red (11)	42	19	8	15	68	**1.62**	1.5	65
10	Stevenage (5)	42	22	6	14	65	**1.55**	1.7	72
11	Scarborough (13)	42	14	14	14	60	**1.43**	1.3	56
12	Woking (8)	42	18	14	10	58	**1.38**	1.6	68
13	Gravesend (14)	42	13	11	18	58	**1.38**	1.2	50
14	Northwich (19)	42	14	10	18	58	**1.38**	1.2	42
15	Tamworth (15)	42	14	11	17	53	**1.26**	1.3	50
16	Canvey Isl (18)	42	9	15	18	53	**1.26**	1.0	42
17	Crawley (12)	42	16	9	17	50	**1.19**	1.4	57
18	Burton (16)	42	13	11	18	50	**1.19**	1.2	50
19	Forest Green (20)	42	6	15	21	41	**0.98**	0.8	33
20	York (17)	42	11	10	21	39	**0.93**	1.0	43
21	Farnborough (21)	42	6	11	25	35	**0.83**	0.7	29
22	Leigh RMI (22)	42	4	6	32	31	**0.74**	0.4	18

BANK OF SCOTLAND SCOTTISH PREMIER LEAGUE

	Team	Pld	W	D	L	F	GFA	PGA	Pts
1	Celtic (2)	38	30	2	6	85	**2.24**	2.4	92
2	Rangers (1)	38	29	6	3	78	**2.05**	2.4	93
3	Hibernian (3)	38	18	7	13	64	**1.68**	1.6	61
4	Kilmarnock (6)	38	15	4	19	49	**1.29**	1.3	49
5	Motherwell (7)	38	13	9	16	46	**1.21**	1.3	48
6	Aberdeen (4)	38	18	7	13	44	**1.16**	1.6	61
7	Hearts (5)	38	13	11	14	43	**1.13**	1.3	50
8	Inverness CT (8)	38	11	11	16	41	**1.08**	1.2	44
9	Dundee Utd (9)	38	8	12	18	41	**1.08**	0.9	36
10	Dundee (12)	38	8	9	21	37	**0.97**	0.9	33
11	Livingston (10)	38	9	8	21	34	**0.89**	0.9	35
12	Dunfermline (11)	38	8	10	20	34	**0.89**	0.9	34

CLOSE BUT NO CIGAR: John Hartson top-scored but Celtic still finished second

NATIONWIDE CONFERENCE

	Team	Pld	W	D	L	A	GAA	PGA	Pts
1	Carlisle (3)	42	20	13	9	37	**0.88**	1.7	73
2	Hereford (2)	42	21	11	10	41	**0.98**	1.8	74
3	Barnet (1)	42	26	8	8	44	**1.05**	2.0	86
4	Woking (8)	42	18	14	10	45	**1.07**	1.6	68
5	Scarborough (13)	42	14	14	14	46	**1.10**	1.3	56
6	Exeter (6)	42	20	11	11	50	**1.19**	1.7	71
7	Morecambe (7)	42	19	14	9	50	**1.19**	1.7	71
8	Crawley (12)	42	16	9	17	50	**1.19**	1.4	57
9	Aldershot (4)	42	21	10	11	52	**1.24**	1.7	73
10	Stevenage (5)	42	22	6	14	52	**1.24**	1.7	72
11	Halifax (9)	42	19	9	14	56	**1.33**	1.6	66
12	Accrington (10)	42	18	11	13	58	**1.38**	1.5	65
13	Dag & Red (11)	42	19	8	15	60	**1.43**	1.5	65
14	Tamworth (15)	42	14	11	17	63	**1.50**	1.3	50
15	Gravesend (14)	42	13	11	18	64	**1.52**	1.2	50
16	Canvey Isl (18)	42	9	15	18	65	**1.55**	1.0	42
17	Burton (16)	42	13	11	18	66	**1.57**	1.2	50
18	York (17)	42	11	10	21	66	**1.57**	1.0	43
19	Northwich (19)	42	14	10	18	72	**1.71**	1.2	42
20	Forest Green (20)	42	6	15	21	81	**1.93**	0.8	33
21	Farnborough (21)	42	6	11	25	89	**2.12**	0.7	29
22	Leigh RMI (22)	42	4	6	32	98	**2.33**	0.4	18

BANK OF SCOTLAND SCOTTISH PREMIER LEAGUE

	Team	Pld	W	D	L	A	GAA	PpG	Pts
1	Rangers (1)	38	29	6	3	17	**0.45**	2.4	93
2	Celtic (2)	38	30	2	6	28	**0.74**	2.4	92
3	Aberdeen (4)	38	18	7	13	33	**0.87**	1.6	61
4	Hearts (5)	38	13	11	14	33	**0.87**	1.3	50
5	Motherwell (7)	38	13	9	16	41	**1.08**	1.3	48
6	Inverness CT (8)	38	11	11	16	42	**1.11**	1.2	44
7	Hibernian (3)	38	18	7	13	49	**1.29**	1.6	61
8	Kilmarnock (6)	38	15	4	19	53	**1.40**	1.3	49
9	Dunfermline (11)	38	8	10	20	54	**1.41**	0.9	34
10	Dundee Utd (9)	38	8	12	18	55	**1.45**	0.9	36
11	Livingston (10)	38	9	8	21	57	**1.50**	0.9	35
12	Dundee (12)	38	8	9	21	61	**1.61**	0.9	33

DOWN AND OUT: Dundee's porous defence cost them their place in the SPL

FA BARCLAYCARD PREMIER LEAGUE

	Team	Pld	CS	CS%
1	Chelsea (1)	38	25	**65.8**
2	Man Utd (3)	38	19	**50.0**
3	Arsenal (2)	38	16	**42.1**
4	Blackburn (15)	38	15	**39.5**
5	Everton (4)	38	13	**34.2**
6	Tottenham (9)	38	13	**34.2**
7	Charlton (11)	38	12	**31.6**
8	Man City (9)	38	11	**28.9**
9	Middlesbro (7)	38	11	**28.9**
10	Aston Villa (10)	38	11	**28.9**
11	C Palace (19)	38	10	**26.3**
12	Birmingham (12)	38	9	**23.7**
13	Bolton (6)	38	8	**21.1**
14	Fulham (14)	38	8	**21.1**
15	Liverpool (6)	38	7	**18.4**
16	West Brom (17)	38	7	**18.4**
17	Southampton (20)	38	7	**18.4**
18	Norwich (19)	38	6	**15.8**
19	Newcastle (14)	38	6	**15.8**
20	Portsmouth (16)	38	5	**13.2**

PETR CECH: clean sheet king

RECORD WHEN KEEPING A CLEAN SHEET

	Team	Pld	W	D	L	F	GFA	PGA	Pts
1	Arsenal (2)	16	15	1	0	34	2.13	**2.9**	46
2	Bolton (6)	8	7	1	0	7	0.88	**2.8**	22
3	Fulham (14)	8	7	1	0	15	1.88	**2.8**	22
4	Chelsea (1)	25	21	4	0	40	1.60	**2.7**	67
5	Everton (4)	13	11	2	0	15	1.15	**2.7**	35
6	Liverpool (6)	7	6	1	0	15	2.14	**2.7**	19
7	Middlesbro (7)	11	9	2	0	20	1.82	**2.6**	29
8	Portsmouth (16)	5	4	1	0	5	1.00	**2.6**	13
9	Aston Villa (10)	11	8	3	0	17	1.55	2.5	27
10	Man Utd (3)	19	13	6	0	26	1.37	**2.4**	45
11	Tottenham (9)	13	9	4	0	12	0.92	**2.4**	31
12	C Palace (19)	10	7	3	0	14	1.40	**2.4**	24
13	Charlton (11)	12	8	4	0	15	1.25	**2.3**	28
14	Man City (9)	11	7	4	0	14	1.27	**2.3**	25
15	Birmingham (12)	9	6	3	0	12	1.33	**2.3**	21
16	Blackburn (15)	15	9	6	0	14	0.93	**2.2**	33
17	West Brom (17)	7	4	3	0	7	1.00	**2.1**	15
18	Norwich (19)	6	3	3	0	4	0.67	**2.0**	12
19	Newcastle (14)	6	3	3	0	6	1.00	**2.0**	12
20	Southampton (20)	7	2	5	0	3	0.43	**1.6**	11

- Number in brackets refers to final league finishing position
- GFA: Goals against average per match
- PGA: Average points gained per match

COCA-COLA LEAGUE CHAMPIONSHIP

	Team	Pld	CS	CS%
1	Wigan (2)	46	20	**43.5**
2	Stoke (12)	46	20	**43.5**
3	Reading (7)	46	19	**41.3**
4	Burnley (14)	46	19	**41.3**
5	Sunderland (1)	46	18	**39.1**
6	QPR (11)	46	15	**32.6**
7	Millwall (10)	46	15	**32.6**
8	Leicester (15)	46	15	**32.6**
9	Derby (4)	46	14	**30.4**
10	Watford (19)	46	14	**30.4**
11	West Ham (6)	46	14	**30.4**
12	Sheff Utd (8)	46	14	**30.4**
13	Plymouth (17)	46	13	**28.3**
14	Preston (5)	46	12	**26.1**
15	Cardiff (16)	46	12	**26.1**
16	Nottm Forest (23)	46	12	**26.1**
17	Leeds (14)	46	11	**23.9**
18	Ipswich (3)	46	11	**23.9**
19	Brighton (20)	46	11	**23.9**
20	Rotherham (24)	46	8	**17.4**
21	Gillingham (22)	46	8	**17.4**
22	Wolves (10)	46	7	**15.2**
23	Coventry (19)	46	6	**13.0**
24	Crewe (22)	46	4	**8.7**

PAUL JEWELL: his Wigan side kept it tight at the back

RECORD WHEN KEEPING A CLEAN SHEET

	Team	Pld	W	D	L	F	GFA	PGA	Pts
1	Crewe (22)	4	4	0	0	9	2.25	**3.0**	12
2	Sunderland (1)	18	17	1	0	26	1.44	**2.9**	52
3	West Ham (6)	14	13	1	0	22	1.57	**2.9**	40
4	Preston (5)	12	11	1	0	24	2.00	**2.8**	34
5	Ipswich (3)	11	10	1	0	21	1.91	**2.8**	31
6	Derby (4)	14	12	2	0	23	1.64	**2.7**	38
7	Wigan (2)	20	16	4	0	37	1.85	**2.6**	52
8	Brighton (20)	11	9	2	0	9	0.82	**2.6**	29
9	Millwall (10)	15	11	4	0	18	1.20	**2.5**	37
10	Stoke (12)	20	14	6	0	19	0.95	**2.4**	48
11	Sheff Utd (8)	14	10	4	0	19	1.36	**2.4**	34
12	Plymouth (17)	13	9	4	0	17	1.31	**2.4**	31
13	Wolves (10)	7	5	2	0	9	1.29	**2.4**	17
14	Reading (7)	19	12	7	0	18	0.95	**2.3**	43
15	Burnley (14)	19	12	7	0	18	0.95	**2.3**	43
16	QPR (11)	15	10	5	0	14	0.93	**2.3**	35
17	Cardiff (16)	12	8	4	0	14	1.17	**2.3**	28
18	Coventry (19)	6	4	2	0	6	1.00	**2.3**	14
19	Nottm Forest (23)	12	7	5	0	9	0.75	**2.2**	26
20	Leicester (15)	15	8	7	0	15	1.00	**2.1**	31
21	Watford (19)	14	8	6	0	14	1.00	**2.1**	30
22	Leeds (14)	11	6	5	0	8	0.73	**2.1**	23
23	Rotherham (24)	8	3	5	0	3	0.38	**1.8**	14
24	Gillingham (22)	8	3	5	0	3	0.38	**1.8**	14

COCA-COLA LEAGUE 1

	Team	Pld	CS	CS%
1	Brentford (4)	46	18	**39.1**
2	Luton (1)	46	17	**37.0**
3	Tranmere (3)	46	15	**32.6**
4	Bristol C (9)	46	15	**32.6**
5	Hull City (2)	46	14	**30.4**
6	Sheff Wed (5)	46	14	**30.4**
7	Doncaster (10)	46	13	**28.3**
8	Barnsley (13)	46	12	**26.1**
9	Bournemouth (9)	46	12	**26.1**
10	Bradford (11)	46	11	**23.9**
11	Blackpool (17)	46	11	**23.9**
12	Port Vale (18)	46	11	**23.9**
13	Colchester (15)	46	11	**23.9**
14	Chesterfield (17)	46	11	**23.9**
15	Swindon (12)	46	10	**21.7**
16	Hartlepool (6)	46	10	**21.7**
17	Huddersfield (9)	46	10	**21.7**
18	Walsall (14)	46	9	**19.6**
19	Peterborough (23)	46	9	**19.6**
20	Milton Keynes (22)	46	9	**19.6**
21	Torquay (22)	46	8	**17.4**
22	Oldham (20)	46	6	**13.0**
23	Wrexham (19)	46	6	**13.0**
24	Stockport (24)	46	6	**13.0**

BRENTFORD: still managed to miss out on promotion

RECORD WHEN KEEPING A CLEAN SHEET

	Team	Pld	W	D	L	F	GFA	PGA	Pts
1	Luton (1)	17	15	2	0	26	1.53	**2.8**	47
2	Bournemouth (9)	12	11	1	0	27	2.25	**2.8**	34
3	Hull City (2)	14	12	2	0	25	1.79	**2.7**	38
4	Brentford (4)	18	14	4	0	19	1.06	**2.6**	46
5	Tranmere (3)	15	12	3	0	22	1.47	**2.6**	39
6	Sheff Wed (5)	14	11	3	0	25	1.79	**2.6**	36
7	Blackpool (17)	11	9	2	0	18	1.64	**2.6**	29
8	Port Vale (18)	11	9	2	0	19	1.73	**2.6**	29
9	Swindon (12)	10	8	2	0	15	1.50	**2.6**	26
10	Hartlepool (6)	10	8	2	0	18	1.80	**2.6**	26
11	Huddersfield (9)	10	8	2	0	16	1.60	**2.6**	26
12	Walsall (14)	9	7	2	0	15	1.67	**2.6**	23
13	Peterborough (23)	9	7	2	0	14	1.56	**2.6**	23
14	Torquay (22)	8	6	2	0	9	1.13	**2.5**	20
15	Bradford (11)	11	7	4	0	9	0.82	**2.3**	25
16	Chesterfield (17)	11	7	4	0	10	0.91	**2.3**	25
17	Milton Keynes (22)	9	6	3	0	11	1.22	**2.3**	21
18	Oldham (20)	6	4	2	0	8	1.33	**2.3**	14
19	Bristol C (9)	15	9	6	0	22	1.47	**2.2**	33
20	Doncaster (10)	13	8	5	0	17	1.31	**2.2**	29
21	Barnsley (13)	12	7	5	0	13	1.08	**2.2**	26
22	Wrexham (19)	6	3	3	0	4	0.67	**2.0**	12
23	Stockport (24)	6	3	3	0	6	1.00	**2.0**	12
24	Colchester (15)	11	5	6	0	15	1.36	**1.9**	21

COCA-COLA LEAGUE 2

	Team	Pld	CS	CS%
1	Rochdale (9)	46	20	**43.5**
2	Lincoln (8)	46	19	**41.3**
3	Swansea (3)	46	19	**41.3**
4	Scunthorpe (3)	46	19	**41.3**
5	Southend (4)	46	16	**34.8**
6	Rushden (22)	46	15	**32.6**
7	Bristol R (14)	46	15	**32.6**
8	Darlington (8)	46	15	**32.6**
9	Mansfield (14)	46	15	**32.6**
10	Northampton (8)	46	15	**32.6**
11	Shrewsbury (21)	46	15	**32.6**
12	Notts Co (20)	46	14	**30.4**
13	Cheltenham (14)	46	14	**30.4**
14	Macclesfield (5)	46	14	**30.4**
15	Grimsby (18)	46	13	**28.3**
16	Bury (18)	46	11	**23.9**
17	Cambridge (23)	46	11	**23.9**
18	Boston Utd (18)	46	11	**23.9**
19	Chester (20)	46	10	**21.7**
20	Oxford (15)	46	9	**19.6**
21	Wycombe (10)	46	9	**19.6**
22	Yeovil (1)	46	8	**17.4**
23	Kidderminster (24)	46	8	**17.4**
24	Leyton Orient (11)	46	8	**17.4**

YEOVIL: won the section but couldn't defend for toffee!

RECORD WHEN KEEPING A CLEAN SHEET

	Team	Pld	W	D	L	F	GFA	PGA	Pts
1	Yeovil (1)	8	8	0	0	13	1.63	**3.0**	24
2	Swansea (3)	19	18	1	0	30	1.58	**2.9**	55
3	Wycombe (10)	9	8	1	0	13	1.44	**2.8**	25
4	Darlington (8)	15	13	2	0	24	1.60	**2.7**	41
5	Northampton (8)	15	13	2	0	20	1.33	**2.7**	41
6	Lincoln (8)	19	15	4	0	26	1.37	**2.6**	49
7	Southend (4)	16	13	3	0	25	1.56	**2.6**	42
8	Cheltenham (14)	14	11	3	0	20	1.43	**2.6**	36
9	Macclesfield (5)	14	11	3	0	19	1.36	**2.6**	36
10	Boston Utd (18)	11	8	3	0	18	1.64	**2.5**	27
11	Scunthorpe (3)	19	12	7	0	24	1.26	**2.3**	43
12	Oxford (15)	9	6	3	0	8	0.89	**2.3**	21
13	Kidderminster (24)	8	5	3	0	7	0.88	**2.3**	18
14	Leyton Orient (11)	8	5	3	0	7	0.88	**2.3**	18
15	Rochdale (9)	20	12	8	0	24	1.20	**2.2**	44
16	Mansfield (14)	15	9	6	0	14	0.93	**2.2**	33
17	Shrewsbury (21)	15	9	6	0	22	1.47	**2.2**	33
18	Bristol R (14)	15	8	7	0	16	1.07	**2.1**	31
19	Bury (18)	11	6	5	0	12	1.09	**2.1**	23
20	Chester (20)	10	5	5	0	7	0.70	**2.0**	20
21	Notts Co (20)	14	6	8	0	12	0.86	**1.9**	26
22	Grimsby (18)	13	6	7	0	11	0.85	**1.9**	25
23	Rushden (22)	15	6	9	0	10	0.67	**1.8**	27
24	Cambridge (23)	11	4	7	0	4	0.36	**1.7**	19

NATIONWIDE CONFERENCE

	Team	Pld	CS	CS%
1	Hereford (2)	42	19	**45.2**
2	Woking (8)	42	16	**38.1**
3	Carlisle (4)	42	16	**38.1**
4	Aldershot (4)	42	15	**35.7**
5	Barnet (1)	42	14	**33.3**
6	Dag & Red (11)	42	13	**31.0**
7	Scarborough (13)	42	13	**31.0**
8	Halifax (9)	42	12	**28.6**
9	Stevenage (5)	42	12	**28.6**
10	Tamworth (14)	42	12	**28.6**
11	York (18)	42	11	**26.2**
12	Burton (17)	42	11	**26.2**
13	Crawley (12)	42	11	**26.2**
14	Morecambe (7)	42	11	**26.2**
15	Northwich (15)	42	11	**26.2**
16	Accrington (11)	42	11	**26.2**
17	Exeter (7)	42	10	**23.8**
18	Gravesend (17)	42	8	**19.0**
19	Canvey Isl. (19)	42	8	**19.0**
20	Forest Green (20)	42	7	**16.7**
21	Farnborough (21)	42	5	**11.9**
22	Leigh RMI (22)	42	4	**9.5**

EXETER: a leaking defence cost Alex Inglethorpe dearly

RECORD WHEN KEEPING A CLEAN SHEET

	Team	Pld	W	D	L	F	GFA	PGA	Pts
1	Barnet (1)	14	13	1	0	33	2.36	**2.9**	40
2	Stevenage (5)	12	11	1	0	22	1.83	**2.8**	34
3	Scarborough (13)	13	11	2	0	26	2.00	**2.7**	35
4	Halifax (9)	12	10	2	0	21	1.75	**2.7**	32
5	Northwich (15)	11	9	2	0	18	1.64	**2.6**	29
6	Hereford (2)	19	14	5	0	33	1.74	**2.5**	47
7	Woking (8)	16	12	4	0	20	1.25	**2.5**	40
8	Carlisle (4)	16	12	4	0	34	2.13	**2.5**	40
9	Aldershot (4)	15	11	4	0	24	1.60	**2.5**	37
10	Dag & Red (11)	13	10	3	0	23	1.77	**2.5**	33
11	Tamworth (14)	12	9	3	0	16	1.33	**2.5**	30
12	Crawley (12)	11	8	3	0	16	1.45	**2.5**	27
13	Leigh RMI (22)	4	3	1	0	4	1.00	**2.5**	10
14	Exeter (7)	10	7	3	0	15	1.50	**2.4**	24
15	York (18)	11	7	4	0	16	1.45	**2.3**	25
16	Burton (17)	11	7	4	0	11	1.00	**2.3**	25
17	Morecambe (7)	11	7	4	0	17	1.55	**2.3**	25
18	Accrington (11)	11	7	4	0	24	2.18	**2.3**	25
19	Gravesend (17)	8	5	3	0	14	1.75	**2.3**	18
20	Canvey Isl. (19)	8	5	3	0	12	1.50	**2.3**	18
21	Forest Green (20)	7	3	4	0	3	0.43	**1.9**	13
22	Farnborough (21)	5	1	4	0	2	0.40	**1.4**	7

BANK OF SCOTLAND SCOTTISH PREMIER LEAGUE

Team	Pld	CS	CS%
1. Rangers (1)	38	19	**50.0**
2. Celtic (2)	38	18	**47.4**
3. Aberdeen (4)	38	15	**39.5**
4. Hearts (5)	38	13	**34.2**
5. Kilmarnock (6)	38	10	**26.3**
6. Motherwell (7)	38	10	**26.3**
7. Livingston (10)	38	10	**26.3**
8. Inverness CT (8)	38	9	**23.7**
9. Hibernian (4)	38	6	**15.8**
10.Dunfermline (11)	38	6	**15.8**
11.Dundee Utd (9)	38	5	**13.2**
12.Dundee (12)	38	4	**10.5**

SAFE: Rangers' Stefan Klos

RECORD WHEN KEEPING A CLEAN SHEET

Team	Pld	W	D	L	F	GFA	PGA	Pts
1 Celtic (2)	18	18	0	0	44	2.44	3.0	54
2 Kilmarnock (6)	10	10	0	0	19	1.90	3.0	30
3 Hibernian (4)	6	6	0	0	13	2.17	3.0	18
4 Dundee Utd (9)	5	5	0	0	8	1.60	3.0	15
5 Rangers (1)	19	17	2	0	38	2.00	2.8	53
6 Inverness CT (8)	9	7	2	0	13	1.44	2.6	23
7 Aberdeen (4)	15	11	4	0	17	1.13	2.5	37
8 Dundee (12)	4	3	1	0	3	0.75	2.5	10
9 Hearts (5)	13	9	4	0	18	1.38	2.4	31
10 Motherwell (7)	10	7	3	0	13	1.30	2.4	24
11 Livingston (10)	10	7	3	0	13	1.30	2.4	24
12 Dunfermline (11)	6	3	3	0	7	1.17	2.0	12

DAVID MARSHALL: when Celtic kept a clean sheet they collected three points. Fact!

FA BARCLAYCARD PREMIER LEAGUE

	Team	Pld	FS	FS%
1	Arsenal (2)	38	**30**	78.9
2	Chelsea (1)	38	**29**	76.3
3	Man Utd (3)	38	**24**	63.2
4	Bolton (6)	38	**23**	60.5
5	Newcastle (14)	38	**20**	52.6
6	Everton (4)	38	**18**	47.4
7	Man City (9)	38	**18**	47.4
8	Charlton (11)	38	**18**	47.4
9	Liverpool (6)	38	**17**	44.7
10	Tottenham (9)	38	**17**	44.7
11	Middlesbro (7)	38	**16**	42.1
12	Birmingham (12)	38	**15**	39.5
13	Portsmouth (16)	38	**15**	39.5
14	Aston Villa (10)	38	**15**	39.5
15	Fulham (14)	38	**14**	36.8
16	C Palace (19)	38	**14**	36.8
17	Blackburn (15)	38	**14**	36.8
18	West Brom (17)	38	**13**	34.2
19	Southampton (20)	38	**11**	28.9
20	Norwich (19)	38	**10**	26.3

PROLIFIC: the Gunners

RECORD WHEN FIRST TO SCORE

	Team	Pld	W	D	L	F	A	PGA	Pts
1	Chelsea (1)	29	27	2	0	64	9	**2.9**	83
2	Everton (4)	18	16	1	1	31	11	**2.7**	49
3	Man Utd (3)	24	20	3	1	50	15	**2.6**	63
4	Arsenal (2)	30	23	6	1	76	23	**2.5**	75
5	Liverpool (6)	17	13	4	0	36	13	**2.5**	43
6	Tottenham (9)	17	13	3	1	37	14	**2.5**	42
7	Fulham (14)	14	10	3	1	31	12	**2.4**	33
8	Middlesbro (7)	16	11	4	1	30	9	**2.3**	37
9	Birmingham (12)	15	10	4	1	25	12	**2.3**	34
10	Bolton (6)	23	15	5	3	37	21	**2.2**	50
11	Charlton (11)	18	12	4	2	34	16	**2.2**	40
12	Man City (9)	18	11	6	1	30	13	**2.2**	39
13	Aston Villa (10)	15	9	5	1	28	11	**2.1**	32
14	Blackburn (15)	14	9	2	3	20	12	**2.1**	29
15	Portsmouth (16)	15	9	2	4	30	23	**1.9**	29
16	C Palace (19)	14	7	5	2	26	15	**1.9**	26
17	West Brom (17)	13	6	5	2	21	12	**1.8**	23
18	Newcastle (14)	20	8	10	2	35	27	**1.7**	34
19	Norwich (19)	10	4	4	2	18	15	**1.6**	16
20	Southampton (20)	11	5	2	4	20	17	**1.5**	17

- Number in brackets refers to final league finishing position
- PGA: Average points gained per match

Sponsored by Stan James

COCA-COLA LEAGUE CHAMPIONSHIP

Team	Pld	FS	FS%
1. Wigan (2)	46	33	71.7
2. West Ham (6)	46	27	58.7
3. Millwall (10)	46	27	58.7
4. Ipswich (3)	46	26	56.5
5. Sunderland (1)	46	26	56.5
6. Coventry (19)	46	23	50.0
7. Leicester (15)	46	23	50.0
8. QPR (11)	46	22	47.8
9. Derby (4)	46	22	47.8
10. Preston (5)	46	22	47.8
11. Reading (7)	46	21	45.7
12. Gillingham (22)	46	21	45.7
13. Crewe (22)	46	20	43.5
14. Watford (19)	46	20	43.5
15. Plymouth (17)	46	20	43.5
16. Stoke (12)	46	19	41.3
17. Wolves (10)	46	19	41.3
18. Cardiff (16)	46	19	41.3
19. Leeds (14)	46	18	39.1
20. Burnley (14)	46	18	39.1
21. Sheff Utd (8)	46	17	37.0
22. Rotherham (24)	46	17	37.0
23. Nottm Forest (23)	46	15	32.6
24. Brighton (20)	46	13	28.3

RARITY: Mark McGhee's Brighton scoring the first goal

RECORD WHEN FIRST TO SCORE

	Team	Pld	W	D	L	F	A	PGA	Pts
1	Sunderland (1)	26	24	1	1	52	12	2.8	73
2	Derby (4)	22	17	4	1	45	18	2.5	55
3	Preston (5)	22	17	4	1	44	15	2.5	55
4	Stoke (12)	19	15	2	2	24	7	2.5	47
5	Sheff Utd (8)	17	13	4	0	32	10	2.5	43
6	Wigan (2)	33	25	5	3	72	21	2.4	80
7	Reading (7)	21	16	2	3	36	14	2.4	50
8	Burnley (14)	18	13	5	0	27	7	2.4	44
9	Ipswich (3)	26	18	7	1	60	24	2.3	61
10	West Ham (6)	27	18	5	4	43	22	2.2	59
11	Millwall (10)	27	18	5	4	44	21	2.2	59
12	Cardiff (16)	19	12	5	2	35	15	2.2	41
13	Wolves (10)	19	11	6	2	40	24	2.1	39
14	Brighton (20)	13	8	3	2	15	10	2.1	27
15	QPR (11)	22	14	3	5	36	25	2.0	45
16	Crewe (22)	20	10	9	1	41	24	2.0	39
17	Leeds (14)	18	10	6	2	29	17	2.0	36
18	Gillingham (22)	21	11	6	4	32	23	1.9	39
19	Watford (19)	20	10	8	2	35	21	1.9	38
20	Nottm Forest (23)	15	8	5	2	19	11	1.9	29
21	Leicester (15)	23	11	9	3	39	23	1.8	42
22	Plymouth (17)	20	11	1	8	35	24	1.7	34
23	Coventry (19)	23	9	8	6	41	33	1.5	35
24	Rotherham (24)	17	4	5	8	21	26	1.0	17

COCA-COLA LEAGUE 1

	Team	Pld	FS	FS%
1	Tranmere (3)	46	**30**	65.2
2	Sheff Wed (5)	46	**30**	65.2
3	Barnsley (13)	46	**29**	63.0
4	Luton (1)	46	**28**	60.9
5	Hull City (2)	46	**25**	54.3
6	Huddersfield (9)	46	**25**	54.3
7	Bradford (11)	46	**24**	52.2
8	Hartlepool (6)	46	**24**	52.2
9	Bournemouth (9)	46	**24**	52.2
10	Torquay (22)	46	**23**	50.0
11	Oldham (20)	46	**22**	47.8
12	Bristol C (9)	46	**21**	45.7
13	Doncaster (10)	46	**21**	45.7
14	Swindon (12)	46	**19**	41.3
15	Brentford (4)	46	**19**	41.3
16	Blackpool (17)	46	**19**	41.3
17	Peterborough (23)	46	**19**	41.3
18	Wrexham (19)	46	**18**	39.1
19	Colchester (15)	46	**18**	39.1
20	Chesterfield (17)	46	**18**	39.1
21	Milton Keynes (22)	46	**18**	39.1
22	Walsall (14)	46	**17**	37.0
23	Port Vale (18)	46	**14**	30.4
24	Stockport (24)	46	**11**	23.9

CHRIS TURNER: hoping to turn it around at Stockport

RECORD WHEN FIRST TO SCORE

	Team	Pld	W	D	L	F	A	PGA	Pts
1	Luton (1)	28	23	4	1	61	21	**2.6**	73
2	Hull City (2)	25	21	2	2	55	17	**2.6**	65
3	Brentford (4)	19	16	1	2	27	10	**2.6**	49
4	Port Vale (18)	14	11	3	0	28	6	**2.6**	36
5	Bristol C (9)	21	16	5	0	54	16	**2.5**	53
6	Huddersfield (9)	25	19	2	4	51	25	**2.4**	59
7	Tranmere (3)	30	20	8	2	57	23	**2.3**	68
8	Bradford (11)	24	16	6	2	50	27	**2.3**	54
9	Bournemouth (9)	24	16	6	2	51	21	**2.3**	54
10	Swindon (12)	19	13	4	2	37	18	**2.3**	43
11	Doncaster (10)	21	14	5	2	46	23	**2.2**	47
12	Blackpool (17)	19	12	5	2	37	19	**2.2**	41
13	Chesterfield (17)	18	12	4	2	34	21	**2.2**	40
14	Sheff Wed (5)	30	18	8	4	64	33	**2.1**	62
15	Hartlepool (6)	24	16	2	6	54	32	**2.1**	50
16	Colchester (15)	18	11	5	2	42	19	**2.1**	38
17	Barnsley (13)	29	14	10	5	59	39	**1.8**	52
18	Oldham (20)	22	12	4	6	38	26	**1.8**	40
19	Milton Keynes (22)	18	10	3	5	29	18	**1.8**	33
20	Wrexham (19)	18	9	5	4	33	25	**1.8**	32
21	Walsall (14)	17	9	4	4	30	18	**1.8**	31
22	Peterborough (23)	19	9	6	4	33	20	**1.7**	33
23	Torquay (22)	23	9	10	4	36	30	**1.6**	37
24	Stockport (24)	11	5	1	5	20	18	**1.5**	16

COCA-COLA LEAGUE 2

	Team	Pld	FS	FS%
1	Yeovil (1)	46	**28**	60.9
2	Lincoln (8)	46	**27**	58.7
3	Swansea (3)	46	**27**	58.7
4	Macclesfield (5)	46	**26**	56.5
5	Oxford (15)	46	**24**	52.2
6	Darlington (8)	46	**24**	52.2
7	Boston Utd (18)	46	**24**	52.2
8	Leyton Orient (11)	46	**24**	52.2
9	Scunthorpe (3)	46	**23**	50.0
10	Cheltenham (14)	46	**23**	50.0
11	Northampton (8)	46	**23**	50.0
12	Rochdale (9)	46	**22**	47.8
13	Southend (4)	46	**22**	47.8
14	Grimsby (18)	46	**20**	43.5
15	Notts Co (20)	46	**19**	41.3
16	Bury (18)	46	**18**	39.1
17	Bristol R (14)	46	**18**	39.1
18	Mansfield (14)	46	**18**	39.1
19	Wycombe (10)	46	**16**	34.8
20	Shrewsbury (21)	46	**16**	34.8
21	Rushden (22)	46	**15**	32.6
22	Kidderminster (24)	46	**15**	32.6
23	Cambridge (23)	46	**14**	30.4
24	Chester (20)	46	**13**	28.3

YEOVIL: conceded plenty but were also quick off the mark

RECORD WHEN FIRST TO SCORE

	Team	Pld	W	D	L	F	A	PGA	Pts
1	Southend (4)	22	20	0	2	47	13	**2.7**	60
2	Swansea (3)	27	22	3	2	48	13	**2.6**	69
3	Scunthorpe (3)	23	17	4	2	47	17	**2.4**	55
4	Wycombe (10)	16	12	3	1	27	11	**2.4**	39
5	Macclesfield (5)	26	19	2	5	45	21	**2.3**	59
6	Northampton (8)	23	17	3	3	37	15	**2.3**	54
7	Yeovil (1)	28	19	5	4	61	31	**2.2**	62
8	Lincoln (8)	27	17	8	2	48	20	**2.2**	59
9	Rochdale (9)	22	14	6	2	43	19	**2.2**	48
10	Bristol R (14)	18	12	4	2	36	17	**2.2**	40
11	Mansfield (14)	18	12	4	2	34	16	**2.2**	40
12	Shrewsbury (21)	16	10	5	1	33	9	**2.2**	35
13	Chester (20)	13	8	4	1	22	13	**2.2**	28
14	Darlington (8)	24	15	6	3	39	19	**2.1**	51
15	Cheltenham (14)	23	14	6	3	36	20	**2.1**	48
16	Oxford (15)	24	15	4	5	41	25	**2.0**	49
17	Grimsby (18)	20	11	7	2	35	20	**2.0**	40
18	Rushden (22)	15	9	3	3	28	17	**2.0**	30
19	Boston Utd (18)	24	13	7	4	46	26	**1.9**	46
20	Leyton Orient (11)	24	12	10	2	40	27	**1.9**	46
21	Notts Co (20)	19	11	3	5	32	19	**1.9**	36
22	Bury (18)	18	9	6	3	33	22	**1.8**	33
23	Kidderminster (24)	15	7	3	5	21	18	**1.6**	24
24	Cambridge (23)	14	6	3	5	20	20	**1.5**	21

NATIONWIDE CONFERENCE

	Team	Pld	FS	FS%
1	Halifax (9)	42	**29**	69.0
2	Barnet (1)	42	**28**	66.7
3	Hereford (2)	42	**26**	61.9
4	Morecambe (7)	42	**25**	59.5
5	Carlisle (4)	42	**23**	54.8
6	Accrington (11)	42	**23**	54.8
7	Scarborough (13)	42	**23**	54.8
8	Stevenage (5)	42	**22**	52.4
9	Woking (8)	42	**21**	50.0
10	Aldershot (4)	42	**21**	50.0
11	Burton (17)	42	**20**	47.6
12	Tamworth (14)	42	**20**	47.6
13	Exeter (7)	42	**19**	45.2
14	Northwich (15)	42	**19**	45.2
15	York (18)	42	**17**	40.5
16	Dag & Red (11)	42	**17**	40.5
17	Crawley (12)	42	**16**	38.1
18	Gravesend (17)	42	**16**	38.1
19	Canvey Isl. (19)	42	**12**	28.6
20	Forest Green (20)	42	**12**	28.6
21	Farnborough (21)	42	**10**	23.8
22	Leigh RMI (22)	42	**9**	21.4

BARNET: were second best in this table but took the title

RECORD WHEN FIRST TO SCORE

	Team	Pld	W	D	L	F	A	PGA	Pts
1	Stevenage (5)	22	20	1	1	46	13	2.8	61
2	Dag & Red (11)	17	14	3	0	41	10	2.6	45
3	Barnet (1)	28	21	6	1	65	20	2.5	69
4	Crawley (12)	16	12	4	0	32	12	2.5	40
5	Carlisle (4)	23	17	5	1	60	16	2.4	56
6	Woking (8)	21	16	3	2	36	11	2.4	51
7	Gravesend (17)	16	12	3	1	40	14	2.4	39
8	Hereford (2)	26	19	3	4	56	23	2.3	60
9	Accrington (11)	23	16	5	2	61	25	2.3	53
10	Aldershot (4)	21	15	4	2	42	17	2.3	49
11	Northwich (15)	19	14	2	3	38	16	2.3	44
12	Canvey Isl. (19)	12	8	3	1	31	13	2.3	27
13	Morecambe (7)	25	17	4	4	50	27	2.2	55
14	Exeter (7)	19	12	5	2	38	19	2.2	41
15	York (18)	17	11	4	2	33	14	2.2	37
16	Scarborough (13)	23	14	5	4	48	20	2.0	47
17	Tamworth (14)	20	11	7	2	40	24	2.0	40
18	Halifax (9)	29	17	5	7	57	36	1.9	56
19	Burton (17)	20	11	4	5	33	25	1.9	37
20	Farnborough (21)	10	4	4	2	15	17	1.6	16
21	Leigh RMI (22)	9	4	1	4	14	18	1.4	13
22	Forest Green (20)	12	4	4	4	18	21	1.3	16

BANK OF SCOTLAND SCOTTISH PREMIER LEAGUE

	Team	Pld	FS	FS%
1	Celtic (2)	38	**30**	78.9
2	Rangers (1)	38	**29**	76.3
3	Kilmarnock (6)	38	**23**	60.5
4	Dunfermline (11)	38	**18**	47.4
5	Aberdeen (4)	38	**17**	44.7
6	Hibernian (4)	38	**17**	44.7
7	Dundee Utd (9)	38	**16**	42.1
8	Motherwell (7)	38	**16**	42.1
9	Inverness CT (8)	38	**16**	42.1
10	Hearts (5)	38	**15**	39.5
11	Dundee (12)	38	**11**	28.9
12	Livingston (10)	38	**9**	23.7

LIVI: were hardly ever ahead

RECORD WHEN FIRST TO SCORE

	Team	Pld	W	D	L	F	A	PGA	Pts
1	Rangers (1)	29	27	2	0	70	13	2.9	83
2	Celtic (2)	30	28	1	1	73	17	2.8	85
3	Hibernian (4)	17	14	3	0	37	13	2.6	45
4	Aberdeen (4)	17	14	2	1	30	10	2.6	44
5	Livingston (10)	9	7	1	1	16	4	2.4	22
6	Inverness CT (8)	16	11	3	2	29	12	2.3	36
7	Hearts (5)	15	11	2	2	28	9	2.3	35
8	Kilmarnock (6)	23	15	3	5	44	24	2.1	48
9	Motherwell (7)	16	10	4	2	28	13	2.1	34
10	Dundee (12)	11	5	6	0	18	12	1.9	21
11	Dundee Utd (9)	16	7	5	4	24	21	1.6	26
12	Dunfermline (11)	18	7	5	6	28	23	1.4	26

POOR EFFORT: going ahead was something of a poisoned chalice for Dunfermline

FINAL

ARSENAL	0-0	MAN UTD

(aet Arsenal won 5-4 on penalties)

SEMI-FINALS

NEWCASTLE	1-4	MAN UTD
ARSENAL	3-0	BLACKBURN

QUARTER-FINALS

BLACKBURN	1-0	LEICESTER
NEWCASTLE	1-0	TOTTENHAM
BOLTON	0-1	ARSENAL
SOUTHAMPTON	0-4	MAN UTD

FIFTH ROUND REPLAYS

NOTTM FOREST	0-3	TOTTENHAM
BLACKBURN	2-1	BURNLEY
BRENTFORD	1-3	SOUTHAMPTON
SHEFF UTD	0-0	ARSENAL

(aet Arsenal won 4-2 on penalties)

FIFTH ROUND

BURNLEY	0-0	BLACKBURN
NEWCASTLE	1-0	CHELSEA
TOTTENHAM	1-1	NOTTM FOREST
ARSENAL	1-1	SHEFF UTD
BOLTON	1-0	FULHAM
CHARLTON	1-2	LEICESTER
EVERTON	0-2	MAN UTD
SOUTHAMPTON	2-2	BRENTFORD

FOURTH ROUND REPLAYS

SHEFF UTD	1-1	WEST HAM

(aet Sheff Utd won 3-1 on penalties)

FULHAM	4-2	DERBY
HARTLEPOOL	0-1	BRENTFORD
TOTTENHAM	3-1	WEST BROM

FOURTH ROUND

CHELSEA	2-0	BIRMINGHAM
OLDHAM	0-1	BOLTON
ARSENAL	2-0	WOLVES
BLACKBURN	3-0	COLCHESTER
BRENTFORD	0-0	HARTLEPOOL
BURNLEY	2-0	BOURNEMOUTH
CHARLTON	3-2	YEOVIL
DERBY	1-1	FULHAM
EVERTON	3-0	SUNDERLAND
MAN UTD	3-0	MIDDLESBRO
NEWCASTLE	3-1	COVENTRY
NOTTM FOREST	1-0	PETERBOROUGH
READING	1-2	LEICESTER
SOUTHAMPTON	2-1	PORTSMOUTH
WEST BROM	1-1	TOTTENHAM
WEST HAM	1-1	SHEFF UTD

THIRD ROUND REPLAYS

BLACKBURN	3-2	CARDIFF
BOSTON UTD	0-1	HARTLEPOOL
EXETER	0-2	MAN UTD
FULHAM	2-0	WATFORD
BLACKPOOL	0-1	LEICESTER
SWANSEA	0-1	READING

THIRD ROUND

BURNLEY	1-0	LIVERPOOL
ARSENAL	2-1	STOKE
YEADING	0-2	NEWCASTLE
BIRMINGHAM	3-0	LEEDS

BOURNEMOUTH	2-1	CHESTER
CARDIFF	1-1	BLACKBURN
CHARLTON	4-1	ROCHDALE
CHELSEA	3-1	SCUNTHORPE
COVENTRY	3-0	CREWE
DERBY	2-1	WIGAN
HARTLEPOOL	0-0	BOSTON UTD
HULL CITY	0-2	COLCHESTER
IPSWICH	1-3	BOLTON
LEICESTER	2-2	BLACKPOOL
LUTON	0-2	BRENTFORD
MAN UTD	0-0	EXETER
MK DONS	0-2	PETERBOROUGH
NORTHAMPTON	1-3	SOUTHAMPTON
NOTTS CO	1-2	MIDDLESBRO
OLDHAM	1-0	MAN CITY
PLYMOUTH	1-3	EVERTON
PORTSMOUTH	1-0	GILLINGHAM
PRESTON	0-2	WEST BROM
QPR	0-3	NOTTM FOREST
READING	1-1	SWANSEA
ROTHERHAM	0-3	YEOVIL
SHEFF UTD	3-1	ASTON VILLA
SUNDERLAND	2-1	C PALACE
TOTTENHAM	2-1	BRIGHTON
WATFORD	1-1	FULHAM
WEST HAM	1-0	NORWICH
WOLVES	2-0	MILLWALL

SECOND ROUND REPLAYS

NOTTS CO	2-0	SWINDON
BRENTFORD	2-1	HINCKLEY UTD
SWANSEA	2-1	STOCKPORT

SECOND ROUND

HINCKLEY UTD	0-0	BRENTFORD
BLACKPOOL	1-0	PORT VALE
BOURNEMOUTH	2-1	CARLISLE
CAMBRIDGE C	0-1	MILTON KEYNES
EXETER	2-1	DONCASTER
HALIFAX	1-3	CHESTER
HARTLEPOOL	5-1	ALDERSHOT
HEREFORD	2-3	BOSTON UTD
HISTON	1-3	YEOVIL
HULL CITY	4-0	MACCLESFIELD
NORTHAMPTON	1-0	BURY
OLDHAM	4-0	LEYTON ORIENT
PETERBOROUGH	2-0	BATH CITY
RUSHDEN	2-5	COLCHESTER
SCUNTHORPE	2-0	WREXHAM
SLOUGH T	1-3	YEADING
STEVENAGE	0-2	ROCHDALE
STOCKPORT	0-0	SWANSEA
SWINDON	1-1	NOTTS CO
WYCOMBE	0-3	LUTON

FIRST ROUND REPLAYS

BRENTFORD	1-1	BRISTOL C

(aet Brentford won 4-3 on penalties)

BOURNEMOUTH	3-1	FOREST GREEN
CARLISLE	1-0	BRISTOL R
COLCHESTER	4-1	MANSFIELD
MACCLESFIELD	2-0	ALFRETON
YEOVIL	1-0	DARLINGTON

FIRST ROUND

ALDERSHOT	4-0	CANVEY ISL
ALFRETON	1-1	MACCLESFIELD
BARNET	1-2	BATH CITY
BILLERICAY	0-1	STEVENAGE
BLACKPOOL	3-0	TAMWORTH
BOSTON UTD	5-2	HORNCHURCH
BRADFORD	0-1	RUSHDEN
BRISTOL C	1-1	BRENTFORD
BRISTOL R	1-1	CARLISLE
BURY	5-2	VAUXHALL M
CAMBRIDGE C	2-1	LEIGH RMI
CHELTENHAM	1-3	SWANSEA
DARLINGTON	3-3	YEOVIL
EXETER	1-0	GRIMSBY
FOREST GREEN	1-1	BOURNEMOUTH
HALIFAX	3-1	CAMBRIDGE
HARTLEPOOL	3-0	LINCOLN
HAYES	0-4	WREXHAM
HINCKLEY UTD	2-0	TORQUAY
HISTON	2-0	SHREWSBURY
HULL CITY	3-2	MORECAMBE
LEYTON ORIENT	3-1	DAG & RED
MANSFIELD	1-1	COLCHESTER
MILTON KEYNES	1-0	LANCASTER
NORTHAMPTON	1-0	BARNSLEY
NOTTS CO	2-0	WOKING
PETERBOROUGH	2-1	TRANMERE
PORT VALE	3-1	KIDDERMINSTER
ROCHDALE	2-1	OXFORD
SCUNTHORPE	2-0	CHESTERFIELD
SLOUGH T	2-1	WALSALL
SOUTHEND	0-3	LUTON
SOUTHPORT	1-3	HEREFORD
STAFFORD RAN	0-2	CHESTER
STOCKPORT	3-1	HUDDERSFIELD
SWINDON	4-1	SHEFF WED
THURROCK	0-1	OLDHAM
TIVERTON	1-3	DONCASTER
WYCOMBE	1-0	COALVILLE
YEADING	2-1	HALESOWEN

CAPTAIN FANTASTIC: the ex-Arsenal skipper will ply his trade in Serie A

FOURTH QUALIFYING ROUND REPLAYS

ALFRETON	2-1	WORKSOP
BURTON	1-1	HINCKLEY UTD

(aet Hinckley Utd won 4-1 on penalties)

COALVILLE	2-0	LIVERSEDGE
SCARBOROUGH	0-1	LANCASTER
WOKING	4-2	LYMINGTON
LEEK TOWN	0-1	HALIFAX

FOURTH QUALIFYING ROUND

ACCRINGTON	0-2	LEIGH RMI
ALDERSHOT	2-1	MAIDENHEAD
BARNET	2-1	FARNBOROUGH
BATH CITY	1-0	LEATHERHEAD
BILLERICAY	3-0	FLACKWELL H
BOGNOR REGIS	0-2	YEADING
BRIGG TOWN	1-4	HALESOWEN
BROMLEY	0-3	CAMBRIDGE C
CANVEY ISL	4-1	HALLEN
CARLISLE	3-1	YORK
DAG & RED	2-1	CRAWLEY
EXETER	2-0	BRAINTREE
HALIFAX	2-2	LEEK TOWN
HAYES	4-0	ASHFORD TOWN
HEREFORD	2-1	RADCLIFFE BORO
HINCKLEY UTD	0-0	BURTON
HORNCHURCH	3-2	GRAVESEND
LANCASTER	1-1	SCARBOROUGH
LIVERSEDGE	0-0	COALVILLE
LYMINGTON	1-1	WOKING
MORECAMBE	5-1	HUCKNALL
NORTHWICH	1-2	VAUXHALL M
SLOUGH T	3-2	SALISBURY
SOUTHPORT	3-1	HYDE
STAFFORD RAN	2-0	GATESHEAD
STEVENAGE	5-0	HENDON
TAMWORTH	2-1	BURSCOUGH
THAME UTD	0-5	FOREST GREEN
THURROCK	6-0	SPALDING UTD
TIVERTON	4-1	NEWPORT CO
WEALDSTONE	0-2	HISTON
WORKSOP	1-1	ALFRETON

FINAL

LIVERPOOL	2-3	CHELSEA

(aet 1-1 after 90 minutes)

SEMI-FINAL SECOND-LEGS

MAN UTD	1-2	CHELSEA
WATFORD	0-1	LIVERPOOL

SEMI-FINAL FIRST-LEGS

CHELSEA	0-0	MAN UTD
LIVERPOOL	1-0	WATFORD

QUARTER-FINALS

FULHAM	1-2	CHELSEA
MAN UTD	1-0	ARSENAL
TOTTENHAM	1-1	LIVERPOOL

(aet Liverpool won 4-3 on penalties)

WATFORD	3-0	PORTSMOUTH

FOURTH ROUND

ARSENAL	3-1	EVERTON
BURNLEY	0-3	TOTTENHAM
CARDIFF	0-2	PORTSMOUTH
LIVERPOOL	2-0	MIDDLESBRO
MAN UTD	2-0	C PALACE
NEWCASTLE	0-2	CHELSEA
NOTTM FOREST	2-4	FULHAM
WATFORD	5-2	SOUTHAMPTON

THIRD ROUND

BIRMINGHAM	0-1	FULHAM
BOLTON	3-4	TOTTENHAM
BOURNEMOUTH	3-3	CARDIFF

(aet Cardiff won 5-4 on penalties)

BURNLEY	3-1	ASTON VILLA
CHARLTON	1-2	C PALACE
CHELSEA	1-0	WEST HAM
CREWE	0-3	MAN UTD
DONCASTER	0-2	NOTTM FOREST
EVERTON	2-0	PRESTON
MAN CITY	1-2	ARSENAL
MIDDLESBRO	3-0	COVENTRY
MILLWALL	0-3	LIVERPOOL
NEWCASTLE	2-1	NORWICH
PORTSMOUTH	2-1	LEEDS
SHEFF UTD	0-0	WATFORD

(aet Watford won 4-2 on penalties)

SOUTHAMPTON	3-2	COLCHESTER

SECOND ROUND

ASTON VILLA	3-1	QPR
BIRMINGHAM	3-1	LINCOLN
BLACKBURN	3-3	BOURNEMOUTH

(aet Bournemouth win 7-6 on penalties)

BOSTON UTD	1-4	FULHAM
BRISTOL C	2-2	EVERTON

(aet Everton won 4-3 on penalties)

BURNLEY	1-1	WOLVES

(aet Burnley won 4-2 on penalties)

COLCHESTER	2-1	WEST BROM
COVENTRY	1-0	SHEFF WED

CREWE	3-3	SUNDERLAN

(aet Crewe won 4-2 on penalties)

C PALACE	2-1	HARTLEPOO
DONCASTER	2-0	IPSWIC
GRIMSBY	0-2	CHARLTO
LEEDS	1-0	SWINDO
LEICESTER	2-3	PRESTO
MAN CITY	7-1	BARNSLE
MK DONS	1-4	CARDIF
NORWICH	1-0	BRISTOL
NORTHAMPTON	0-3	SOUTHAMPTO
NOTTM FOREST	2-1	ROTHERHA
OLDHAM	0-6	TOTTENHA
READING	0-3	WATFOR
TRANMERE	0-1	PORTSMOUTH
WEST HAM	3-2	NOTTS C
WREXHAM	2-3	SHEFF UT
YEOVIL	0-2	BOLTO

FIRST ROUND

MANSFIELD	0-4	PRESTO
BOSTON UTD	4-3	LUTO
BRADFORD	1-2	NOTTS C
COVENTRY	4-1	TORQUA
NOTTM FOREST	2-0	SCUNTHORPE
OXFORD	0-2	READING
SHEFF WED	1-0	WALSALL
BRIGHTON	1-2	BRISTOL
BURY	2-3	BURNLEY
COLCHESTER	2-1	CHELTENHAM
CREWE	4-1	BLACKPOOL
DARLINGTON	0-2	BARNSLEY
DONCASTER	3-1	PORT VALE
GILLINGHAM	1-2	NORTHAMPTON
GRIMSBY	1-0	WIGAN
HARTLEPOOL	2-1	MACCLESFIELD
HULL CITY	2-2	WREXHAM

(aet Wrexham win 3-1 on penalties)

IPSWICH	2-0	BRENTFORD
KIDDERMINSTER	1-1	CARDIFF
LEEDS	1-0	HUDDERSFIELD
LEYTON ORIENT	1-3	BOURNEMOUTH
LINCOLN	3-1	DERBY
OLDHAM	2-1	STOKE
PETERBOROUGH	0-3	MK DONS
QPR	3-0	SWANSEA
ROCHDALE	2-4	WOLVES
ROTHERHAM	2-1	CHESTERFIELD
RUSHDEN	0-1	SWINDON
SHEFF UTD	4-1	STOCKPORT
SUNDERLAND	3-0	CHESTER
TRANMERE	2-1	SHREWSBURY
WATFORD	1-0	CAMBRIDGE
WEST HAM	2-0	SOUTHEND
WYCOMBE	0-1	BRISTOL C
YEOVIL	3-2	PLYMOUTH

FINAL
SOUTHEND	0-2	WREXHAM

NORTHERN FINAL
WREXHAM	1-0	OLDHAM
OLDHAM	3-5	WREXHAM

SOUTHERN FINAL
SOUTHEND	2-2	BRISTOL R
BRISTOL R	1-2	SOUTHEND

NORTHERN SEMI-FINALS
HEREFORD	1-2	WREXHAM
OLDHAM	1-1	TRANMERE

(aet Oldham won 5-4 on penalties)

SOUTHERN SEMI-FINALS
LEYTON ORIENT	1-2	BRISTOL R
SOUTHEND	2-0	SWINDON

NORTHERN QUARTER-FINALS
CHESTER	0-1	WREXHAM
HEREFORD	2-1	BLACKPOOL
MACCLESFIELD	0-1	TRANMERE
OLDHAM	3-1	HARTLEPOOL

SOUTHERN QUARTER-FINALS
BRISTOL R	1-0	WYCOMBE
LEYTON ORIENT	1-0	WALSALL
NORTHAMPTON	0-2	SOUTHEND
SWINDON	1-0	BRISTOL C

NORTHERN SECOND ROUND
BLACKPOOL	6-3	HUDDERSFIELD
CARLISLE	0-1	HARTLEPOOL
CHESTER	1-0	ROCHDALE
HEREFORD	1-1	DONCASTER

(aet Hereford won 3-1 on penalties)

MACCLESFIELD	4-0	MANSFIELD
OLDHAM	3-2	ACCRINGTON
TRANMERE	2-1	PORT VALE
WREXHAM	2-0	STOCKPORT

SOUTHERN SECOND ROUND
BRISTOL R	2-0	BARNET
BRISTOL C	2-1	MK DONS
CAMBRIDGE	0-2	LEYTON ORIENT
CHELTENHAM	2-2	WALSALL

(aet Cheltenham won 4-3 on penalties)

EXETER	1-2	SWINDON
SOUTHEND	4-1	SHREWSBURY
TORQUAY	1-3	NORTHAMPTON
WYCOMBE	1-0	SWANSEA

NORTHERN FIRST ROUND
BRADFORD	1-2	ACCRINGTON
SHEFF WED	1-2	CHESTER
YORK	0-2	BLACKPOOL
CARLISLE	2-1	GRIMSBY
HARTLEPOOL	3-3	HULL CITY

(aet Hartlepool won 4-1 on penalties)

HEREFORD	1-1	SCUNTHORPE

(aet Hereford win 4-3 on penalties)

HUDDERSFIELD	3-0	MORECAMBE
LINCOLN	0-1	DONCASTER
MACCLESFIELD	2-1	CHESTERFIELD
MANSFIELD	0-0	DARLINGTON

(aet Mansfield won 4-3 on penalties)

NOTTS CO	2-3	WREXHAM
PORT VALE	1-0	BARNSLEY
ROCHDALE	4-1	SCARBOROUGH
STOCKPORT	3-1	BURY

SOUTHERN FIRST ROUND
ALDERSHOT	0-1	WYCOMBE
BARNET	3-1	STEVENAGE
BRENTFORD	0-3	MILTON KEYNES
BOSTON UTD	0-1	CAMBRIDGE
BRISTOL C	1-0	PETERBOROUGH
BRISTOL R	1-0	KIDDERMINSTER
CHELTENHAM	5-1	DAG & RED
COLCHESTER	1-1	SOUTHEND

(aet Southend won 5-3 on penalties)

OXFORD	2-2	EXETER

(aet Exeter win 3-1 on penalties)

SHREWSBURY	3-2	BOURNEMOUTH
SWANSEA	2-0	LUTON
TORQUAY	4-3	YEOVIL
WALSALL	1-0	RUSHDEN
WOKING	0-3	LEYTON ORIENT

WELSH WIZARDS: Wrexham were too good for Southend at the Millennium Stadium

FINAL

GRAYS	1-1	HUCKNALL

(aet Grays won 6-5 on penalties)

SEMI-FINAL SECOND-LEGS

BURTON	0-2	GRAYS
HUCKNALL	3-2	BISHOP'S ST

SEMI-FINAL FIRST-LEGS

BISHOP'S ST	1-2	HUCKNALL
GRAYS	5-0	BURTON

QUARTER-FINAL REPLAYS

GRAVESEND	2-3	BISHOP'S ST
HUCKNALL	1-0	HEREFORD

QUARTER-FINALS

BISHOP'S ST	1-1	GRAVESEND
BURTON	1-0	WOKING
GRAYS	4-1	EXETER
HEREFORD	2-2	HUCKNALL

FIFTH ROUND REPLAY

BISHOP'S ST	2-1	CANVEY ISL
HEREFORD	4-2	EASTWOOD T

FIFTH ROUND

ALTRINCHAM	2-4	GRAYS
BURTON	1-0	MORECAMBE
CAMBRIDGE C	0-1	HUCKNALL
CANVEY ISL	2-2	BISHOP'S ST
EASTWOOD T	1-1	HEREFORD
GRAVESEND	3-2	SLOUGH T
STAMFORD	0-1	EXETER
WOKING	1-0	CARLISLE

FOURTH ROUND REPLAYS

CRAWLEY	1-2	CAMBRIDGE C
WALTON & H	3-3	STAMFORD

(aet Stamford won 2-0 on penalties)

FOURTH ROUND

ALFRETON	0-3	WOKING
ALTRINCHAM	1-0	BARROW
AYLESBURY	0-1	CANVEY ISL
BISHOP'S ST	3-0	LEYTON
BURTON	2-0	HEDNESFORD
CAMBRIDGE C	3-3	CRAWLEY
CARLISLE	4-1	BARNET
EASTWOOD T	1-0	HAYES
GRAVESEND	2-1	HISTON
GRAYS	5-0	HAVANT & W
HEREFORD	3-0	HYDE
LANCASTER	1-2	MORECAMBE
NORTHWICH	0-2	HUCKNALL
SLOUGH T	1-0	THURROCK
STAMFORD	0-0	WALTON & H
TAMWORTH	0-3	EXETER

THIRD ROUND REPLAYS

ALFRETON	2-1	KETTERING
CHESHUNT	0-3	LEYTON
EASTBOURNE	0-1	GRAVESEND
EXETER	2-0	BILLERICAY
HAYES	7-2	YATE TOWN
HEREFORD	4-0	ACCRINGTON
HUCKNALL	1-0	SOUTHPORT

INVOLVED: action from the Trophy Final

LANCASTER	3-0	VAUXHALL M
WHITBY	0-1	HYDE
WALTON & H	1-1	TONBRIDGE

(aet Walton & H won 3-2 on penalties)

THIRD ROUND

ACCRINGTON	0-0	HEREFORD
BARNET	1-0	FARNBOROUGH
BARROW	2-1	SCARBOROUGH
BATH CITY	0-3	CANVEY ISL
BILLERICAY	2-2	EXETER
BURTON	3-0	YORK
CARLISLE	3-1	REDDITCH
CRAWLEY	3-2	WORTHING
DAG & RED	1-2	BISHOP'S ST
FOREST GREEN	1-2	AYLESBURY
GRAVESEND	0-0	EASTBOURNE
HALIFAX	0-1	NORTHWICH
HEDNESFORD	1-0	WORCESTER
HYDE	3-3	WHITBY
KETTERING	0-0	ALFRETON
LEIGH RMI	1-2	ALTRINCHAM
LEYTON	0-0	CHESHUNT
MORECAMBE	2-1	SUTTON C
REDBRIDGE	1-5	CAMBRIDGE C
SLOUGH T	4-3	HENDON
SOUTHPORT	1-2	HUCKNALL
ST ALBANS	0-1	HAVANT & W
STAMFORD	2-0	WILLENHALL
SUTTON UTD	0-2	GRAYS
TAMWORTH	5-0	GRESLEY R
TEAM BATH	1-2	HISTON
THURROCK	1-0	ALDERSHOT
TONBRIDGE	1-1	WALTON & H
VAUXHALL M	1-1	LANCASTER
WOKING	1-0	STEVENAGE
YATE TOWN	1-1	HAYES

MICK CHANNON
THE AUTHORISED BIOGRAPHY

BY PETER BATT

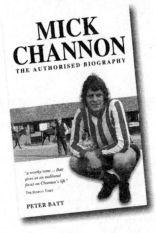

SPECIAL OFFER
£6.99
Save £1 off RRP of £7.99
plus free p&p

Fully authorised biography of a truly unique sporting talent, and one of the most popular people in sport.
Now in paperback.

"a worthy tome ... Batt gives us an undiluted focus on Channon's life" The Sunday Times

"the subject is fascinating and this is a book worth reading" Racing Post

ORDER A COPY TODAY

call Highdown's credit/debit card orderline on
01635 578080
and quote ref MSFG05
or order online at www.highdownbooks.co.uk

HIGHDOWN, RFM HOUSE, COMPTON, NEWBURY RG20 6NL

SCOTTISH CUP 2004-2005

FINAL

CELTIC	1-0	DUNDEE UTD

SEMI-FINALS

HEARTS	1-2	CELTIC
DUNDEE UTD	2-1	HIBERNIAN

QUARTER-FINALS

CLYDE	0-5	CELTIC
DUNDEE UTD	4-1	ABERDEEN
HEARTS	2-1	LIVINGSTON
HIBERNIAN	2-0	ST MIRREN

FOURTH ROUND REPLAYS

KILMARNOCK	1-3	HEARTS
CLYDE	2-1	ROSS COUNTY

FOURTH ROUND

ABERDEEN	2-1	INVERNESS CT
ALLOA	0-1	LIVINGSTON
AYR	0-2	ST MIRREN
DUNFERMLINE	0-3	CELTIC
HEARTS	2-2	KILMARNOCK
HIBERNIAN	4-0	BRECHIN
QUEEN OF STH	0-3	DUNDEE UTD
ROSS COUNTY	0-0	CLYDE

THIRD ROUND REPLAYS

STRANRAER	0-2	AYR
HEARTS	2-1	PARTICK
DUNFERMLINE	3-1	EAST FIFE

THIRD ROUND

ARBROATH	0-2	ABERDEEN
AYR	3-3	STRANRAER
BERWICK	0-3	BRECHIN
CELTIC	2-1	RANGERS
CLYDE	3-0	FALKIRK
EAST FIFE	0-0	DUNFERMLINE

GRETNA	3-4	DUNDEE UTD
INVERNESS CT	1-0	ST JOHNSTONE
HIBERNIAN	2-0	DUNDEE
KILMARNOCK	2-0	MOTHERWELL
LIVINGSTON	2-1	MORTON
MONTROSE	1-2	QUEEN OF STH
PARTICK	0-0	HEARTS
RAITH	0-2	ALLOA
ROSS COUNTY	4-1	AIRDRIE UTD
ST MIRREN	3-0	HAMILTON

SECOND ROUND REPLAYS

BERWICK	3-1	DUMBARTON
EAST FIFE	3-3	HUNTLY
(aet East Fife won 4-3 on penalties)		

SECOND ROUND

ALBION	0-1	ARBROATH
ALLOA	2-1	STENH'SEMUIR
AYR	3-0	EDINBURGH C
BRECHIN	1-0	STIRLING
COVE RANGERS	1-7	MORTON
DUMBARTON	1-1	BERWICK
GRETNA	3-0	ELGIN CITY
HUNTLY	0-0	EAST FIFE
KEITH	0-1	MONTROSE
STRANRAER	1-0	QUEEN'S PARK

FIRST ROUND

COVE RANGERS	4-1	DALBEATTIE S
COWDENBEATH	2-3	DUMBARTON
FORFAR	1-5	MONTROSE
HUNTLY	3-1	PETERHEAD
GLASGOW UNIV	0-3	BRECHIN
MORTON	3-1	EAST STIRLING
EAST FIFE	3-0	WHITEHILL W
INVERURIE L	1-2	KEITH

END OF AN ERA: ex-Celtic boss Martin O'Neill with his final piece of silverware

Sponsored by Stan James

CIS CUP FINAL

RANGERS	5-1	MOTHERWELL

SEMI-FINALS

RANGERS	7-1	DUNDEE UTD
MOTHERWELL	3-2	HEARTS

QUARTER-FINALS

DUNFERMLINE	1-3	HEARTS
RANGERS	2-1	CELTIC
DUNDEE UTD	2-1	HIBERNIAN
LIVINGSTON	0-5	MOTHERWELL

THIRD ROUND

ABERDEEN	0-2	RANGERS
ALBION	1-3	HIBERNIAN
CELTIC	8-1	FALKIRK
DUNDEE UTD	4-0	CLYDE
DUNFERMLINE	3-1	PARTICK
HEARTS	2-1	KILMARNOCK
INVERNESS CT	1-3	MOTHERWELL
LIVINGSTON	2-1	DUNDEE

SECOND ROUND

ABERDEEN	3-0	BERWICK
AIRDRIE UTD	0-1	CLYDE
ALBION	1-1	BRECHIN

(aet Albion won 4-3 on penalties)

DUNDEE	4-0	FORFAR
DUNDEE UTD	3-1	STRANRAER
HIBERNIAN	4-0	ALLOA
KILMARNOCK	3-0	HAMILTON
MORTON	0-3	MOTHERWELL
PETERHEAD	1-6	FALKIRK
ROSS COUNTY	0-1	INVERNESS CT
STENH'SEMUIR	2-5	PARTICK
STIRLING	0-2	LIVINGSTON

FIRST ROUND

HAMILTON	4-1	AYR
MORTON	1-0	GRETNA
QUEEN OF STH	1-2	ALBION
STIRLING	3-2	QUEEN'S PARK
AIRDRIE UTD	3-0	EAST FIFE
BERWICK	3-2	ELGIN CITY
BRECHIN	5-2	COWDENBEATH
DUMBARTON	1-3	ROSS COUNTY
FALKIRK	4-1	MONTROSE
PETERHEAD	3-2	EAST STIRLING
ST JOHNSTONE	2-3	ALLOA
ST MIRREN	2-5	FORFAR
STENH'SEMUIR	2-1	ARBROATH
STRANRAER	2-1	RAITH

BELL'S CHALLENGE CUP FINAL

FALKIRK	2-1	ROSS COUNTY

SEMI-FINALS

ROSS COUNTY	5-2	FORFAR
ST JOHNSTONE	1-2	FALKIRK

QUARTER-FINALS

CLYDE	1-2	FORFAR
ROSS COUNTY	1-1	PARTICK
BERWICK	0-1	ST JOHNSTONE
FALKIRK	3-0	GRETNA

SECOND ROUND

ALBION	1-2	PARTICK
ALLOA	1-2	BERWICK
CLYDE	1-0	STRANRAER
FALKIRK	5-3	STIRLING
FORFAR	2-2	QUEEN'S PARK
GRETNA	1-0	COWDENBEATH
PETERHEAD	1-2	ROSS COUNTY
ST JOHNSTONE	3-0	QUEEN OF STH

FIRST ROUND

AIRDRIE UTD	0-2	QUEEN OF STH
ALLOA	2-0	ELGIN CITY
ARBROATH	2-4	PETERHEAD
AYR	0-3	FALKIRK
DUMBARTON	1-2	STIRLING
EAST FIFE	0-0	COWDENBEATH
EAST STIRLING	1-2	BERWICK
FORFAR	3-1	MORTON
GRETNA	3-0	MONTROSE
PARTICK	3-0	BRECHIN
QUEEN'S PARK	1-1	STENH'SEMUIR
RAITH	0-2	ALBION
ROSS COUNTY	2-1	ST MIRREN
ST JOHNSTONE	2-0	HAMILTON

VICTORIOUS: Falkirk's John Hughes

FINAL

AC MILAN	3-3	LIVERPOOL

(aet Liverpool won 3-2 on penalties)

SEMI-FINAL SECOND-LEGS

PSV EINDHOVEN	3-1	AC MILAN
LIVERPOOL	1-0	CHELSEA

SEMI-FINAL FIRST-LEGS

CHELSEA	0-0	LIVERPOOL
AC MILAN	2-0	PSV EINDHOVEN

QUARTER-FINAL SECOND-LEGS

B MUNICH	3-2	CHELSEA
INTER MILAN	A-A	INTER MILAN

(AC Milan awarded a 3-0 win)

JUVENTUS	0-0	LIVERPOOL
PSV EINDHOVEN	1-1	LYON

(PSV Eindhoven won 4-2 on penalties)

QUARTER-FINAL FIRST-LEGS

AC MILAN	2-0	INTER MILAN
CHELSEA	4-2	B MUNICH
LIVERPOOL	2-1	JUVENTUS
LYON	1-1	PSV EINDHOVEN

LAST 16 SECOND-LEGS

AC MILAN	1-0	MAN UTD
ARSENAL	1-0	B MUNICH
B LEVERKUSEN	1-3	LIVERPOOL
CHELSEA	4-2	BARCELONA
INTER MILAN	3-1	PORTO
JUVENTUS	2-0	REAL MADRID
LYON	7-2	W BREMEN
MONACO	0-2	PSV EINDHOVEN

LAST 16 FIRST-LEGS

BARCELONA	2-1	CHELSEA
B MUNICH	3-1	ARSENAL
LIVERPOOL	3-1	B LEVERKUSEN
MAN UTD	0-1	AC MILAN
PORTO	1-1	INTER MILAN
PSV EINDHOVEN	1-0	MONACO
REAL MADRID	1-0	JUVENTUS
W BREMEN	0-3	LYON

GROUP A

DEPORTIVO	0-5	MONACO
LIVERPOOL	3-1	OLYMPIAKOS
MONACO	1-0	LIVERPOOL
OLYMPIAKOS	1-0	DEPORTIVO
DEPORTIVO	0-1	LIVERPOOL
OLYMPIAKOS	1-0	MONACO
LIVERPOOL	0-0	DEPORTIVO
MONACO	2-1	OLYMPIAKOS
MONACO	2-0	DEPORTIVO
OLYMPIAKOS	1-0	LIVERPOOL
DEPORTIVO	0-0	OLYMPIAKOS
LIVERPOOL	2-0	MONACO

GROUP B

B LEVERKUSEN	3-0	DYNAMO KIEV
ROMA	0-3	REAL MADRID
DYNAMO KIEV	2-0	ROMA
REAL MADRID	1-1	B LEVERKUSEN
DYNAMO KIEV	2-2	REAL MADRID
ROMA	1-1	B LEVERKUSEN
B LEVERKUSEN	3-1	ROMA
REAL MADRID	1-0	DYNAMO KIEV
DYNAMO KIEV	4-2	B LEVERKUSEN
REAL MADRID	4-2	ROMA
B LEVERKUSEN	3-0	REAL MADRID
ROMA	0-3	DYNAMO KIEV

GROUP C

AJAX	2-2	B MUNICH
M TEL AVIV	1-1	JUVENTUS
B MUNICH	5-1	M TEL AVIV
JUVENTUS	1-0	AJAX
B MUNICH	0-1	JUVENTUS
M TEL AVIV	2-1	AJAX
AJAX	3-0	M TEL AVIV
JUVENTUS	1-0	B MUNICH
B MUNICH	4-0	AJAX
JUVENTUS	1-0	M TEL AVIV
AJAX	0-1	JUVENTUS
M TEL AVIV	0-1	B MUNICH

GROUP D

FENERBAHCE	3-0	MAN UTD
LYON	5-0	SPARTA PRAGUE
MAN UTD	2-1	LYON
SPARTA PRAGUE	0-1	FENERBAHCE
LYON	4-2	FENERBAHCE
MAN UTD	4-1	SPARTA PRAGUE
FENERBAHCE	1-3	LYON
SPARTA PRAGUE	0-0	MAN UTD
MAN UTD	6-2	FENERBAHCE
SPARTA PRAGUE	1-2	LYON
FENERBAHCE	1-0	SPARTA PRAGUE
LYON	2-2	MAN UTD

GROUP E

ARSENAL	5-1	ROSENBORG
PANATHINAIKOS	4-1	PSV EINDHOVEN
PSV EINDHOVEN	1-1	ARSENAL
ROSENBORG	2-2	PANATHINAIKOS
ARSENAL	1-1	PANATHINAIKOS
PSV EINDHOVEN	1-0	ROSENBORG
PANATHINAIKOS	2-2	ARSENAL
ROSENBORG	1-2	PSV EINDHOVEN
PSV EINDHOVEN	1-0	PANATHINAIKOS
ROSENBORG	1-1	ARSENAL
ARSENAL	1-0	PSV EINDHOVEN
PANATHINAIKOS	2-1	ROSENBORG

GROUP F

CELTIC	0-0	AC MILAN
S DONETSK	2-0	BARCELONA
BARCELONA	1-1	CELTIC
AC MILAN	4-0	S DONETSK
BARCELONA	2-1	AC MILAN
CELTIC	1-0	S DONETSK
AC MILAN	1-0	BARCELONA
S DONETSK	3-0	CELTIC
BARCELONA	3-0	S DONETSK
AC MILAN	3-1	CELTIC
CELTIC	1-3	BARCELONA
S DONETSK	0-1	AC MILAN

GROUP G

INTER MILAN	3-0	ANDERLECHT
VALENCIA	0-2	W BREMEN
ANDERLECHT	1-2	VALENCIA
W BREMEN	1-1	INTER MILAN
INTER MILAN	0-0	VALENCIA
W BREMEN	5-1	ANDERLECHT
ANDERLECHT	1-2	W BREMEN
VALENCIA	1-5	INTER MILAN
ANDERLECHT	1-3	INTER MILAN
W BREMEN	2-1	VALENCIA
INTER MILAN	2-0	W BREMEN
VALENCIA	2-0	ANDERLECHT

GROUP H

PARIS ST-G	1-3	CSKA MOSCOW
PORTO	2-1	CHELSEA
CSKA MOSCOW	0-1	PORTO
CHELSEA	0-0	PARIS ST-G
CSKA MOSCOW	0-1	CHELSEA
PORTO	0-0	PARIS ST-G
CHELSEA	2-0	CSKA MOSCOW
PARIS ST-G	2-0	PORTO
CSKA MOSCOW	2-0	PARIS ST-G
CHELSEA	3-1	PORTO
PARIS ST-G	0-3	CHELSEA
PORTO	0-0	CSKA MOSCOW

THIRD QUALIFYING ROUND
SECOND-LEGS

BANIK OSTRAVA	2-1	B LEVERKUSEN
DJURGAARDENS	1-4	JUVENTUS
FC BRUGES	2-2	S DONETSK
M TEL AVIV	1-0	PAOK SALONIKA
MAN UTD	3-0	DIN BUCHAREST
PSV EINDHOVEN	5-0	RED STAR B
RANGERS	1-1	CSKA MOSCOW
REAL MADRID	3-1	WISLA KRAKOW
SPARTA PRAGUE	2-0	FERENCVAROS
TRABZONSPOR	0-2	DYNAMO KIEV
ANDERLECHT	3-0	BENFICA
DEPORTIVO	3-0	SHELBOURNE
INTER MILAN	4-1	FC BASLE
LIVERPOOL	0-1	GRAZ AK
MACCABI HAIFA	2-3	ROSENBORG
MONACO	6-0	NK HIT GORICA

THIRD QUALIFYING ROUND
FIRST-LEGS

B LEVERKUSEN	5-0	BANIK OSTRAVA
DIN BUCHAREST	1-2	MAN UTD
FC BASLE	1-1	INTER MILAN
FERENCVAROS	1-0	SPARTA PRAGUE
NK HIT GORICA	0-3	MONACO
RED STAR B	3-2	PSV EINDHOVEN
ROSENBORG	2-1	MACCABI HAIFA
S DONETSK	4-1	FC BRUGES
SHELBOURNE	0-0	DEPORTIVO
WISLA KRAKOW	0-2	REAL MADRID
BENFICA	1-0	ANDERLECHT
CSKA MOSCOW	2-1	RANGERS
DYNAMO KIEV	1-2	TRABZONSPOR

GRAZ AK	0-2	LIVERPOOL
JUVENTUS	2-2	DJURGAARDENS
PAOK SALONIKA	0-3	MACCABI TEL AVIV

SECOND QUALIFYING ROUND
SECOND-LEGS

CSKA MOSCOW	2-0	NEFTCHI BAKU
DIN BUCHAREST	1-0	ZILINA
FBK KAUNAS	0-2	DJURGAARDENS
FC COPENHAGEN	0-5	NK HIT GORICA
FERENCVAROS	0-1	SK TIRANA
L PLOVDIV	0-4	FC BRUGES
M TEL AVIV	1-0	HJK HELSINKI
RED STAR B	3-0	YOUNG BOYS
SERIF TIRASPOL	0-2	ROSENBORG
S DONETSK	1-0	PYUNIK YEREVAN
SHELBOURNE	2-0	HAJDUK SPLIT
SPARTA PRAGUE	2-1	APOEL NICOSIA
TRABZONSPOR	3-0	SKONTO RIGA
WISLA KRAKOW	3-0	WIT-GEO TBILISI

SECOND QUALIFYING ROUND
SECOND-LEGS

APOEL NICOSIA	2-2	SPARTA PRAGUE
DJURGAARDENS	0-0	FBK KAUNAS
FC BRUGES	2-0	L PLOVDIV
HAJDUK SPLIT	3-2	SHELBOURNE
ROSENBORG	2-1	SERIF TIRASPOL
SKONTO RIGA	1-1	TRABZONSPOR
YOUNG BOYS	2-2	RED STAR B
ZILINA	0-1	DIN BUCHAREST
HJK HELSINKI	0-0	MACCABI TEL AVIV
NK HIT GORICA	1-2	FC COPENHAGEN
NEFTCHI BAKU	0-0	CSKA MOSCOW
PYUNIK YEREVAN	1-3	S DONETSK
SK TIRANA	2-3	FERENCVAROS
WIT-GEO TBILISI	2-8	WISLA KRAKOW

FIRST QUALIFYING ROUND
SECOND-LEGS

FBK KAUNAS	4-1	SLIEMA W
HB TORSHAVN	3-0	WIT-GEO TBILISI
HJK HELSINKI	1-0	LINFIELD
JEUNESSE ESCH	1-0	SERIF TIRASPOL
NK HIT GORICA	3-1	FLORA TALLINN
NEFTCHI BAKU	1-0	NK SIROKI BRIJEG
PYUNIK YEREVAN	1-1	POBEDA PRILEP
RHYL	1-3	SKONTO RIGA
SK TIRANA	0-1	GOMEL
SHELBOURNE	0-0	KR REYKJAVIK

FIRST QUALIFYING ROUND
FIRST-LEGS

FLORA TALLINN	2-4	NK HIT GORICA
GOMEL	0-2	SK TIRANA
KR REYKJAVIK	2-2	SHELBOURNE
LINFIELD	0-1	HJK HELSINKI
SERIF TIRASPOL	2-0	JEUNESSE ESCH
SKONTO RIGA	4-0	RHYL
WIT-GEO TBILISI	5-0	HB TORSHAVN
NK SIROKI BRIJEG	2-1	NEFTCHI BAKU
POBEDA PRILEP	1-3	PYUNIK YEREVAN
SLIEMA W	0-2	FBK KAUNAS

FINAL

SP LISBON	1-3	CSKA MOSCOW

SEMI-FINAL SECOND-LEGS

AZ ALKMAAR	3-2	SP LISBON
CSKA MOSCOW	3-0	PARMA

SEMI-FINAL FIRST-LEGS

PARMA	0-0	CSKA MOSCOW
SP LISBON	2-1	AZ ALKMAAR

QUARTER-FINAL SECOND-LEGS

AZ ALKMAAR	1-1	VILLARREAL
AUXERRE	2-0	CSKA MOSCOW
PARMA	0-0	AUSTRIA VIENNA
SP LISBON	4-1	NEWCASTLE

QUARTER-FINAL FIRST-LEGS

AUSTRIA VIENNA	1-1	PARMA
CSKA MOSCOW	4-0	AUXERRE
NEWCASTLE	1-0	SP LISBON
VILLARREAL	1-2	AZ ALKMAAR

LAST 16 SECOND-LEGS

VILLARREAL	2-0	S BUCHAREST
AUXERRE	0-0	LILLE
CSKA MOSCOW	2-0	P BELGRADE
PARMA	1-0	SEVILLE
REAL ZARAGOZA	2-2	AUSTRIA VIENNA
SP LISBON	1-0	MIDDLESBRO
AZ ALKMAAR	2-1	S DONETSK
NEWCASTLE	4-0	OLYMPIAKOS

LAST 16 FIRST-LEGS

S BUCHAREST	0-0	VILLARREAL
AUSTRIA VIENNA	1-1	REAL ZARAGOZA
LILLE	0-1	AUXERRE
MIDDLESBRO	2-3	SP LISBON
OLYMPIAKOS	1-3	NEWCASTLE
P BELGRADE	1-1	CSKA MOSCOW
SEVILLE	0-0	PARMA
S DONETSK	1-3	AZ ALKMAAR

LAST 32 SECOND-LEGS

ATH BILBAO	1-2	AUSTRIA VIENNA
AZ ALKMAAR	2-1	A AACHEN
AUSTRIA VIENNA	0-0	ATH BILBAO
AUXERRE	3-1	AJAX
BENFICA	1-1	CSKA MOSCOW
DNIPRO	0-1	P BELGRADE
FEYENOORD	1-2	SP LISBON
LILLE	2-0	FC BASLE
MIDDLESBRO	2-1	GRAZ AK
NEWCASTLE	2-1	HEERENVEEN
REAL ZARAGOZA	2-1	FENERBAHCE
SCHALKE	0-1	S DONETSK
SEVILLE	2-0	PANATHINAIKOS
SOCHAUX	0-1	OLYMPIAKOS
S BUCHAREST	2-0	VALENCIA
STUTTGART	0-2	PARMA
VILLARREAL	2-0	DYNAMO KIEV

LAST 32 FIRST-LEGS

A AACHEN	0-0	AZ ALKMAAR
CSKA MOSCOW	2-0	BENFICA
DYNAMO KIEV	0-0	VILLARREAL
FC BASLE	0-0	LILLE
FENERBAHCE	0-1	REAL ZARAGOZA
GRAZ AK	2-2	MIDDLESBRO
HEERENVEEN	1-2	NEWCASTLE
OLYMPIAKOS	1-0	SOCHAUX
AJAX	1-0	AUXERRE
PANATHINAIKOS	1-0	SEVILLE
PARMA	0-0	STUTTGART
P BELGRADE	2-2	DNIPRO
S DONETSK	1-1	SCHALKE
SP LISBON	2-1	FEYENOORD
VALENCIA	2-0	S BUCHAREST

GROUP A

FC BASLE	1-0	FEYENOORD
HEARTS	0-1	FERENCVAROS
FERENCVAROS	1-2	FC BASLE
FEYENOORD	2-1	SCHALKE
FC BASLE	1-2	HEARTS
SCHALKE	2-0	FERENCVAROS
FERENCVAROS	1-1	FEYENOORD
HEARTS	0-1	SCHALKE
FEYENOORD	3-0	HEARTS
SCHALKE	1-1	FC BASLE

GROUP B

PARMA	3-2	BESIKTAS
STANDARD LIEGE	1-7	ATH BILBAO
ATH BILBAO	1-0	S BUCHAREST
BESIKTAS	1-1	STANDARD LIEGE
STANDARD LIEGE	2-1	PARMA
S BUCHAREST	2-1	BESIKTAS
BESIKTAS	3-1	ATH BILBAO
PARMA	1-0	S BUCHAREST
ATH BILBAO	2-0	PARMA
S BUCHAREST	2-0	STANDARD LIEGE

GROUP C

FC BRUGES	1-1	REAL ZARAGOZA
FC UTRECHT	1-2	AUSTRIA VIENNA
AUSTRIA VIENNA	1-1	FC BRUGES
REAL ZARAGOZA	2-1	DNIPRO
DNIPRO	1-0	AUSTRIA VIENNA
FC BRUGES	1-0	FC UTRECHT
AUSTRIA VIENNA	1-0	REAL ZARAGOZA
FC UTRECHT	1-2	DNIPRO
DNIPRO	3-2	FC BRUGES
REAL ZARAGOZA	2-0	FC UTRECHT

GROUP D

NEWCASTLE	1-1	SP LISBON
SOCHAUX	1-0	PANIONIOS
PANIONIOS	5-2	DYNAMO TBILISI
SP LISBON	0-1	SOCHAUX
DYNAMO TBILISI	0-4	SP LISBON
SOCHAUX	0-4	NEWCASTLE
NEWCASTLE	2-0	DYNAMO TBILISI
SP LISBON	4-1	PANIONIOS
DYNAMO TBILISI	0-2	SOCHAUX
PANIONIOS	0-1	NEWCASTLE

GROUP E

MIDDLESBRO	3-0	P BELGRADE
VILLARREAL	4-0	EGALEO
EGALEO	2-2	LAZIO
P BELGRADE	1-1	VILLARREAL
LAZIO	2-2	P BELGRADE
VILLARREAL	2-0	MIDDLESBRO
MIDDLESBRO	2-0	LAZIO
P BELGRADE	4-0	EGALEO

EGALEO	0-1	MIDDLESBRO
LAZIO	1-1	VILLARREAL

GROUP F

GRAZ AK	2-0	AZ ALKMAAR
RANGERS	0-2	AUXERRE
AZ ALKMAAR	1-0	RANGERS
AUXERRE	5-1	AMICA WRONKI
AMICA WRONKI	1-3	AZ ALKMAAR
RANGERS	3-0	GRAZ AK
AZ ALKMAAR	2-0	AUXERRE
GRAZ AK	3-1	AMICA WRONKI
AMICA WRONKI	0-5	RANGERS
AUXERRE	0-0	GRAZ AK

GROUP G

HEERENVEEN	1-0	BEVEREN
STUTTGART	2-1	D ZAGREB
BEVEREN	0-3	BENFICA
D ZAGREB	2-2	HEERENVEEN
BENFICA	2-0	D ZAGREB
HEERENVEEN	1-0	STUTTGART
D ZAGREB	6-1	BEVEREN
STUTTGART	3-0	BENFICA
BENFICA	4-2	HEERENVEEN
BEVEREN	1-5	STUTTGART

GROUP H

AEK ATHENS	0-2	A AACHEN
LILLE	1-0	SEVILLE
A AACHEN	2-2	ZENIT ST P'BURG
SEVILLE	3-2	AEK ATHENS
AEK ATHENS	1-2	LILLE
ZENIT ST P'BURG	1-1	SEVILLE
LILLE	2-1	ZENIT ST P'BURG
SEVILLE	2-0	A AACHEN
A AACHEN	1-0	LILLE
ZENIT ST P'BURG	5-1	AEK ATHENS

FIRST ROUND SECOND-LEGS

AEK ATHENS	1-0	NK HIT GORICA
AZ ALKMAAR	2-1	PAOK SALONIKA
A AACHEN	0-0	FH H'JORDUR
AMICA WRONKI	1-0	VENTSPILS
ATH BILBAO	2-0	TRABZONSPOR
AUXERRE	2-0	AALBORG
BANIK OSTRAVA	1-1	MIDDLESBRO
BENFICA	2-0	DUKLA BYSTRICA
BESIKTAS	1-0	BODO/GLIMT
BEVEREN	1-0	LEVSKI SOFIA
BNEI SACHNIN	1-5	NEWCASTLE
CSKA SOFIA	2-2	S BUCHAREST
CHATEAUROUX	1-2	FC BRUGES
DIN BUCHAREST	0-0	P BELGRADE
DJURGAARDENS	3-0	FC UTRECHT
DNIPRO	2-0	MACCABI HAIFA
DYNAMO TBILISI	2-1	WISLA KRAKOW
ELFSBORG	0-0	DYNAMO ZAGREB
FC BASLE	2-0	TEREK GROZNY
FC LOVECH	1-0	GRAZ AK
FERENCVAROS	3-1	MILLWALL
FEYENOORD	4-1	ODD GRENLAND
GENCLERBIRLIGI	1-1	EGALEO
HEERENVEEN	5-0	MACCABI PT
LAZIO	3-0	METALURG D
LEGIA WARSAW	1-3	AUSTRIA VIENNA

LILLE	2-0	SHELBOURNE
METALURGS L	0-4	SCHALKE
NK MARIBOR	0-0	PARMA
N MADEIRA	1-2	SEVILLE
RANGERS	1-0	MARITIMO
RAPID VIENNA	0-0	SP LISBON
RED STAR B	1-2	ZENIT ST P'BURG
SIGMA OLOMOUC	2-3	REAL ZARAGOZA
SP BRAGA	2-2	HEARTS
STABAEK	0-5	SOCHAUX
UDINESE	1-0	PANIONIOS
STUTTGART	4-0	UJPEST DOZSA
VFL BOCHUM	1-1	STANDARD LIEGE
VILLARREAL	3-0	HAMMARBY

FIRST ROUND FIRST-LEGS

AALBORG	1-1	AUXERRE
AUSTRIA VIENNA	1-0	LEGIA WARSAW
BODO/GLIMT	1-1	BESIKTAS
DUKLA BYSTRICA	0-3	BENFICA
DYNAMO ZAGREB	2-0	ELFSBORG
EGALEO	1-0	GENCLERBIRLIGI
FC BRUGES	4-0	CHATEAUROUX
FC UTRECHT	4-0	DJURGAARDENS
FH H'JORDUR	1-5	A AACHEN
GRAZ AK	5-0	FC LOVECH
HAMMARBY	1-2	VILLARREAL
HEARTS	3-1	SP BRAGA
LEVSKI SOFIA	1-1	BEVEREN
MACCABI HAIFA	1-0	DNIPRO
MARITIMO	1-0	RANGERS
METALURG D	0-3	LAZIO
MIDDLESBRO	3-0	BANIK OSTRAVA
MILLWALL	1-1	FERENCVAROS
NK HIT GORICA	1-1	AEK ATHENS
NEWCASTLE	2-0	BNEI SACHNIN
ODD GRENLAND	0-1	FEYENOORD
PAOK SALONIKA	2-3	AZ ALKMAAR
PANIONIOS	3-1	UDINESE
PARMA	3-2	NK MARIBOR
P BELGRADE	3-1	DIN BUCHAREST
REAL ZARAGOZA	1-0	SIGMA OLOMOUC
SCHALKE	5-1	METALURGS L
SEVILLE	2-0	N MADEIRA
SHELBOURNE	2-2	LILLE
SOCHAUX	4-0	STABAEK
SP LISBON	2-0	RAPID VIENNA
STANDARD LIEGE	0-0	VFL BOCHUM
S BUCHAREST	2-1	CSKA SOFIA
TEREK GROZNY	1-1	FC BASLE
TRABZONSPOR	3-2	ATH BILBAO
UJPEST DOZSA	1-3	STUTTGART
VENTSPILS	1-1	AMICA WRONKI
WISLA KRAKOW	4-3	DYNAMO TBILISI
ZENIT ST P'BURG	4-0	RED STAR B

SECOND QUALIFYING ROUND
SECOND-LEGS

AALBORG	0-0	ZALGIRIS VILNIUS
AUSTRIA VIENNA	3-0	ILLICHIVETS
BRONDBY	1-1	VENTSPILS
CSKA SOFIA	3-1	OMONIA NICOSIA
DNIPRO	1-1	PETRZALKA
DUNFERMLINE	1-2	FH H'JORDUR

DYNAMO TBILISI	2-0	SLAVIA PRAGUE
EKRANAS	2-1	ODD GRENLAND
ELFSBORG	2-1	GLENTORAN
FC HAKA	1-3	STABAEK
FC LOVECH	7-0	ZELJEZNICAR
FC TIRASPOL	1-2	METALURG D.
FC WIL	1-1	DUKLA BYSTRICA
HONVED	1-0	AMICA WRONKI
IA AKRANES	1-2	HAMMARBY
LECH POZNAN	0-1	TEREK GROZNY
LEGIA WARSAW	6-0	FC TBILISI
LEVADIA TALLINN	2-1	BODO/GLIMT
MACCABI PT	4-0	AEK LARNACA
METALURGS L	1-1	OSTERS
MODRICA	0-3	LEVSKI SOFIA
NK MARIBOR	0-1	BUDUCNOST
P BELGRADE	1-0	OTELUL GALATI
PARTIZAN TIRANA	1-3	BNEI SACHNIN
PRIMORJE	2-0	DYNAMO ZAGREB
RIJEKA	2-1	GENCLERBIRLIGI
RUBIN	0-3	RAPID VIENNA
SERVETTE	0-2	UJPEST DOZSA
SIGMA OLOMOUC	4-0	NISTRU OTACI
S BUCHAREST	1-2	ZELEZNIK
VADUZ	1-2	BEVEREN
ZENIT ST P'BURG	2-0	S PASCHING

SECOND QUALIFYING ROUND

FIRST-LEGS

| AEK LARNACA | 3-0 | MACCABI PT |
| AMICA WRONKI | 1-0 | HONVED |

BEVEREN	3-1	VADUZ
BNEI SACHNIN	3-0	PARTIZAN TIRANA
BODO/GLIMT	2-1	LEVADIA TALLINN
BUDUCNOST	1-2	NK MARIBOR
DUKLA BYSTRICA	3-1	FC WIL
DYNAMO ZAGREB	4-0	PRIMORJE
FC TBILISI	0-1	LEGIA WARSAW
FH H'JORDUR	2-2	DUNFERMLINE
GENCLERBIRLIGI	1-0	RIJEKA
GLENTORAN	0-1	ELFSBORG
HAMMARBY	2-0	IA AKRANES
ILLICHIVETS	0-0	AUSTRIA VIENNA
LEVSKI SOFIA	5-0	MODRICA
METALURG D.	3-0	FC TIRASPOL
NISTRU OTACI	1-2	SIGMA OLOMOUC
ODD GRENLAND	3-1	EKRANAS
OMONIA NICOSIA	1-1	CSKA SOFIA
OSTERS	2-2	METALURGS L
OTELUL GALATI	0-0	P BELGRADE
PETRZALKA	0-3	DNIPRO
RAPID VIENNA	0-2	RUBIN
S PASCHING	3-1	ZENIT ST P'BURG
SLAVIA PRAGUE	3-1	DYNAMO TBILISI
STABAEK	3-1	FC HAKA
TEREK GROZNY	1-0	LECH POZNAN
UJPEST DOZSA	3-1	SERVETTE
VENTSPILS	0-0	BRONDBY
ZALGIRIS VILNIUS	1-3	AALBORG
ZELEZNIK	2-4	S BUCHAREST
ZELJEZNICAR	1-2	FC LOVECH

CSKA MOSCOW: beat Sporting to become the first Russian side to lift the Uefa Cup

Sponsored by Stan James

Pos		P	Home W	D	L	F	A	Away W	D	L	F	A	Pts	Goal Diff
1	Chelsea	38	14	5	0	35	6	15	3	1	37	9	95	+57
2	Arsenal	38	13	5	1	54	19	12	3	4	33	17	83	+51
3	Man Utd	38	12	6	1	31	12	10	5	4	27	14	77	+32
4	Everton	38	12	2	5	24	15	6	5	8	21	31	61	-1
5	Liverpool	38	12	4	3	31	15	5	3	11	21	26	58	+11
6	Bolton	38	9	5	5	25	18	7	5	7	24	26	58	+5
7	Middlesbro	38	9	6	4	29	19	5	7	7	24	27	55	+7
8	Man City	38	8	6	5	24	14	5	7	7	23	25	52	+8
9	Tottenham	38	9	5	5	36	22	5	5	9	11	19	52	+6
10	Aston Villa	38	8	6	5	26	17	4	5	10	19	35	47	-7
11	Charlton	38	8	4	7	29	29	4	6	9	13	29	46	-16
12	Birmingham	38	8	6	5	24	15	3	6	10	16	31	45	-6
13	Fulham	38	8	4	7	29	26	4	4	11	23	34	44	-8
14	Newcastle	38	7	7	5	25	25	3	7	9	22	32	44	-10
15	Blackburn	38	5	8	6	21	22	4	7	8	11	21	42	-11
16	Portsmouth	38	8	4	7	30	26	2	5	12	13	33	39	-16
17	WBA	38	5	8	6	17	24	1	8	10	19	37	34	-25
18	Crystal Pal	38	6	5	8	21	19	1	7	11	20	43	33	-21
19	Norwich	38	7	5	7	29	32	0	7	12	13	45	33	-35
20	Southampton	38	5	9	5	30	30	1	5	13	15	36	32	-21

Pos		P	Home W	D	L	F	A	Away W	D	L	F	A	Pts	Goal Diff
1	Sunderland	46	16	4	3	45	21	13	3	7	31	20	94	+35
2	Wigan	46	13	5	5	42	15	12	7	4	37	20	87	+44
3	Ipswich	46	17	3	3	53	26	7	10	6	32	30	85	+29
4	Derby	46	10	7	6	38	30	12	3	8	33	30	76	+11
5	Preston	46	14	7	2	44	22	7	5	11	23	36	75	+9
6	West Ham	46	12	5	6	36	24	9	5	9	30	32	73	+10
7	Reading	46	13	7	3	33	15	6	6	11	18	29	70	+7
8	Sheff Utd	46	9	7	7	28	23	9	6	8	29	33	67	+1
9	Wolves	46	9	11	3	40	26	6	10	7	32	33	66	+13
10	Millwall	46	12	5	6	33	22	6	7	10	18	23	66	+6
11	QPR	46	10	7	6	32	26	7	4	12	22	32	62	-4
12	Stoke	46	11	2	10	22	18	6	8	9	14	20	61	-2
13	Burnley	46	10	7	6	26	19	5	8	10	12	20	60	-1
14	Leeds	46	7	10	6	28	26	7	8	8	21	26	60	-3
15	Leicester	46	8	8	7	24	20	4	13	6	25	26	57	+3
16	Cardiff	46	10	4	9	24	19	3	11	9	24	32	54	-3
17	Plymouth	46	9	8	6	31	23	5	3	15	21	41	53	-12
18	Watford	46	5	10	8	25	25	7	6	10	27	34	52	-7
19	Coventry	46	8	7	8	32	28	5	6	12	29	45	52	-12
20	Brighton	46	7	7	9	24	29	6	5	12	16	36	51	-25
21	Crewe	46	6	8	9	37	38	6	6	11	29	48	50	-20
22	Gillingham	46	10	6	7	22	23	2	8	13	23	43	50	-21
23	Nottm F	46	7	10	6	26	28	2	7	14	16	38	44	-24
24	Rotherham	46	2	7	14	17	34	3	7	13	18	35	29	-34

Sponsored by Stan James

COCA-COLA LEAGUE 1

Pos		P	Home W	D	L	F	A	Away W	D	L	F	A	Pts	Goal Diff
1	Luton	46	17	4	2	46	16	12	7	4	41	32	98	+39
2	Hull	46	16	5	2	42	17	10	3	10	38	36	86	+27
3	Tranmere	46	14	5	4	43	23	8	8	7	30	32	79	+18
4	Brentford	46	15	4	4	34	22	7	5	11	23	38	75	-32
5	Sheff Weds	46	10	6	7	34	28	9	9	5	43	31	72	+18
6	Hartlepool	46	15	3	5	51	30	6	5	12	25	36	71	+10
7	Bristol C	46	9	8	6	42	25	9	8	6	32	32	70	+17
8	Bournemouth	46	9	7	7	40	30	11	3	9	37	34	70	+13
9	Huddersfield	46	12	6	5	42	28	8	4	11	32	37	70	+9
10	Doncaster	46	10	11	2	35	20	6	7	10	30	40	66	+5
11	Bradford	46	9	6	8	40	35	8	8	7	24	27	65	+2
12	Swindon	46	12	5	6	40	30	5	7	11	26	38	63	-2
13	Barnsley	46	7	11	5	38	31	7	8	8	31	33	61	+5
14	Walsall	46	11	7	5	40	28	5	5	13	25	41	60	-4
15	Colchester	46	8	6	9	27	23	6	11	6	33	27	59	+10
16	Blackpool	46	8	7	8	28	30	7	5	11	26	29	57	-5
17	Chesterfield	46	9	9	6	32	28	5	7	11	23	34	57	-7
18	Port Vale	46	13	2	8	33	23	4	3	16	16	36	56	-10
19	Oldham	46	10	5	8	42	34	4	5	14	18	39	52	-13
20	Milton K	46	8	10	5	33	28	4	5	14	21	40	51	-14
21	Torquay	46	8	5	10	27	36	4	10	9	28	43	51	-24
22	Wrexham	46	6	8	9	26	37	7	6	10	36	43	43	-18
23	Peterboro	46	5	6	12	27	35	4	6	13	22	38	39	-24
24	Stockport	46	3	4	16	26	46	3	4	16	23	52	26	-49

Wrexham 10 points deducted

COCA-COLA LEAGUE 2

Pos		P	Home W	D	L	F	A	Away W	D	L	F	A	Pts	Goal Diff
1	Yeovil	46	16	4	3	57	28	9	4	10	33	37	83	+25
2	Scunthorpe	46	16	5	2	43	16	6	9	8	26	26	80	+27
3	Swansea	46	15	5	3	36	16	9	3	11	26	27	80	+19
4	Southend	46	13	5	5	31	14	9	7	7	34	32	78	+19
5	Macclesfield	46	15	3	5	39	24	7	6	10	21	25	75	+11
6	Lincoln	46	11	8	4	37	22	9	4	10	27	25	72	+17
7	Northampton	46	11	9	3	35	20	9	3	11	27	31	72	+11
8	Darlington	46	13	4	6	33	21	7	8	8	24	28	72	+8
9	Rochdale	46	11	8	4	34	21	5	10	8	20	27	66	+6
10	Wycombe	46	8	7	8	28	26	9	7	7	30	26	65	+6
11	Leyton O	46	10	8	5	40	30	6	7	10	25	37	63	-2
12	Bristol R	46	10	12	1	39	22	3	9	11	21	35	60	+3
13	Mansfield	46	9	8	6	29	24	6	7	10	27	32	60	0
14	Cheltenham	46	10	5	8	27	23	6	7	10	24	31	60	-3
15	Oxford Utd	46	11	4	8	29	24	5	7	11	21	39	59	-13
16	Boston	46	11	8	4	39	24	3	8	12	23	34	58	+4
17	Bury	46	8	9	6	26	18	6	7	10	28	36	58	0
18	Grimsby	46	8	10	5	28	19	6	6	11	23	33	58	-1
19	Notts Co	46	6	7	10	21	27	7	6	10	25	35	52	-16
20	Chester	46	7	8	8	25	33	5	8	10	18	36	52	-26
21	Shrewsbury	46	9	7	7	34	18	2	9	12	14	35	49	-5
22	Rushden & D	46	8	6	9	29	29	2	8	13	13	34	44	-21
23	Kidderminstr	46	6	6	11	21	39	4	2	17	18	46	38	-46
24	Cambridge U	46	7	6	10	22	27	1	10	12	17	35	30	-23

Cambridge U 10 points deducted

Sponsored by Stan James

Pos		P	Home W	D	L	F	A	Away W	D	L	F	A	Pts	Goal Diff
1	Barnet	42	16	2	3	56	20	10	6	5	34	24	86	+46
2	Hereford	42	10	7	4	28	14	11	4	6	40	27	74	+27
3	Carlisle	42	12	5	4	39	18	8	8	5	35	19	73	+37
4	Aldershot	42	13	3	5	38	22	8	7	6	30	30	73	+16
5	Stevenage	42	13	2	6	35	21	9	4	8	30	31	72	+13
6	Exeter	42	11	5	5	39	22	9	6	6	32	28	71	+21
7	Morecambe	42	12	5	4	38	23	7	9	5	31	27	71	+19
8	Woking	42	11	6	4	29	19	7	8	6	29	26	68	+13
9	Halifax	42	13	4	4	45	24	6	5	10	29	32	66	+18
10	Accrington	42	11	6	4	43	26	7	5	9	29	32	65	+14
11	Dagenham & R	42	12	4	5	39	27	7	4	10	29	33	65	+8
12	Crawley	42	13	4	4	35	18	3	5	13	15	32	57	0
13	Scarborough	42	9	12	0	42	17	5	2	14	18	29	56	+14
14	Gravesend	42	7	7	7	34	31	6	4	11	24	33	50	-6
15	Tamworth	42	10	3	8	22	22	4	8	9	31	41	50	-10
16	Burton	42	6	7	8	25	29	7	4	10	25	37	50	-16
17	York	42	7	6	8	22	23	4	4	13	17	43	43	-27
18	Canvey Islnd	42	6	10	5	34	31	3	5	13	19	34	42	-12
19	Northwich	42	9	5	7	37	29	5	5	11	21	43	42	-14
20	Forest G	42	2	9	10	19	40	4	6	11	22	41	33	-40
21	Farnborough	42	4	5	12	20	40	2	6	13	15	49	29	-54
22	Leigh RMI	42	2	2	17	18	52	2	4	15	13	46	18	-67

Tamworth three points deducted; Northwich 10 points deducted

SUPER BEES: Barnet will be plying their trade in the Football League after their title triumph

Sponsored by Stan James

CONFERENCE NORTH

Pos		Home P	W	D	L	F	A	Away W	D	L	F	A	Pts	Goal Diff
1	Southport	42	12	6	3	35	20	13	3	5	48	25	84	+38
2	Nuneaton	42	13	3	5	29	17	12	3	6	39	28	81	+23
3	Droylsden	42	13	3	5	46	26	11	4	6	36	26	79	+30
4	Kettering	42	10	4	7	22	21	11	3	7	34	29	70	+6
5	Altrincham	42	12	6	3	45	21	7	6	8	21	25	69	+20
6	Harrogate	42	13	5	3	40	22	6	6	9	22	27	68	+13
7	Worcester	42	10	5	6	32	25	6	7	8	27	28	60	+6
8	Stafford	42	8	10	3	33	20	6	7	8	19	24	59	+8
9	Redditch	42	11	3	7	36	32	7	5	9	29	27	59	+6
10	Hucknall T	42	7	8	6	31	32	8	6	7	28	25	59	+2
11	Gainsborough	42	7	8	6	27	22	9	1	11	28	33	57	0
12	Hinckley	42	8	5	8	29	31	7	6	8	26	31	56	-7
13	Lancaster	42	9	4	8	23	22	5	8	8	28	37	54	-8
14	Alfreton	42	7	5	9	24	23	8	3	10	29	32	53	-2
15	Vauxhall M	42	7	7	7	20	22	7	4	10	28	35	53	-9
16	Barrow	42	8	5	8	32	39	6	5	10	18	25	52	-14
17	Worksop	42	11	4	6	36	29	5	8	8	23	30	50	0
18	Moor Green	42	8	4	9	26	28	5	6	10	29	36	49	-9
19	Stalybridge	42	7	6	8	30	36	5	6	10	22	34	48	-18
20	Runcorn	42	7	6	8	24	26	3	6	12	20	37	42	-19
21	Ashton Utd	42	6	2	13	27	39	2	7	12	19	40	33	-33
22	Bradford Pk	42	3	5	13	20	37	2	4	15	17	33	24	-33

Redditch three points deducted; Worksop 10 points deducted

CONFERENCE SOUTH

Pos		Home P	W	D	L	F	A	W	D	L	F	A	Pts	Goal Diff
1	Grays	42	15	4	2	60	13	15	4	2	58	18	98	+87
2	Cambridge C	42	10	3	8	29	25	13	3	5	31	19	75	+16
3	Thurrock	42	9	3	9	29	32	12	3	6	32	24	69	+5
4	Lewes	42	11	6	4	42	29	7	5	9	31	35	65	+91
5	Eastbourne	42	10	5	6	38	26	8	5	8	27	21	64	+181
6	Basingstoke	42	12	3	6	37	20	7	3	11	20	32	63	+52
7	Weymouth	42	8	8	5	32	28	9	3	9	30	31	62	+35
8	Dorchester	42	11	5	5	40	33	6	6	9	37	48	62	-44
9	Bognor	42	11	4	6	46	31	6	5	10	24	34	60	+52
10	B Stortford	42	13	3	5	39	25	4	5	12	31	41	59	+4
11	Western SM	42	12	5	4	33	23	3	8	10	22	37	58	-52
12	Hayes	42	9	4	8	29	30	6	7	8	26	27	56	-2
13	Havant and W	42	12	3	6	38	26	4	4	13	26	43	55	-5
14	St Albans	42	8	3	10	34	37	8	3	10	30	39	54	-12
15	Sutton Utd	42	5	6	10	25	38	9	5	7	35	33	53	-11
16	Welling	42	5	5	11	23	30	10	2	9	41	38	52	-4
17	Hornchurch	42	11	5	5	44	24	6	5	10	27	39	51	+8
18	Newport AFC	42	8	5	8	36	34	5	6	10	20	27	50	-5
19	Carshalton	42	7	3	11	19	31	6	6	9	25	41	48	-28
20	Maidenhead	42	5	7	9	31	41	7	3	11	23	40	46	-27
21	Margate	42	9	3	9	30	29	3	5	13	24	46	34	-21
22	Redbridge	42	6	3	12	25	40	5	0	16	25	46	33	-36

Hornchurch 10 points deducted; Margate 10 points deducted; Redbridge three points deducted

BANK OF SCOTLAND SCOTTISH PREMIER LEAGUE

Pos		P	Home					Away					Pts	Goal
			W	D	L	F	A	W	D	L	F	A		Diff
1	Rangers	38	15	2	2	48	12	14	4	1	30	10	93	+56
2	Celtic	38	15	0	4	41	15	15	2	2	44	20	92	+50
3	Hibernian	38	9	4	6	32	26	9	3	7	32	31	61	+7
4	Aberdeen	38	8	4	7	22	17	10	3	6	22	22	61	+5
5	Hearts	38	9	4	6	25	15	4	7	8	18	26	50	+2
6	Motherwell	38	8	4	7	29	22	5	5	9	17	27	48	-3
7	Kilmarnock	38	10	2	7	32	20	5	2	12	17	35	49	-6
8	Inv CT	38	7	4	8	23	24	4	7	8	18	23	44	-6
9	Dundee Utd	38	4	7	8	22	28	4	5	10	19	31	36	-18
10	Livingston	38	5	4	10	22	34	4	4	11	12	27	35	-27
11	Dunfermline	38	5	9	5	23	19	3	1	15	11	41	34	-26
12	Dundee	38	7	4	8	21	24	1	5	13	16	47	33	-34

BELL'S SCOTTISH DIVISION ONE

Pos		P	Home					Away					Pts	Goal
			W	D	L	F	A	W	D	L	F	A		Diff
1	Falkirk	36	10	6	2	35	15	12	3	3	31	15	75	+36
2	St Mirren	36	10	6	2	24	11	5	9	4	17	12	60	+18
3	Clyde	36	9	4	5	17	13	7	8	3	18	16	60	+6
4	Queen of Sth	36	7	5	6	17	14	7	4	7	19	24	51	-2
5	Airdrie Utd	36	8	3	7	25	25	6	5	7	19	23	50	-4
6	Ross County	36	6	5	7	20	16	7	3	8	20	21	47	+3
7	Hamilton	36	5	5	8	13	18	7	6	5	22	18	47	-1
8	St Johnstone	36	6	6	6	18	18	6	4	8	20	21	46	-1
9	Partick	36	7	5	6	23	25	3	4	11	15	27	39	-14
10	Raith	36	3	4	11	19	33	0	3	15	7	34	16	-41

BELL'S SCOTTISH DIVISION TWO

Pos		P	Home					Away					Pts	Goal
			W	D	L	F	A	W	D	L	F	A		Diff
1	Brechin	36	12	1	5	47	25	10	5	3	34	18	72	+38
2	Stranraer	36	9	5	4	24	19	9	4	5	24	22	63	+7
3	Morton	36	13	2	3	35	14	5	6	7	25	23	62	+23
4	Stirling	36	8	5	5	29	26	6	4	8	27	29	51	+1
5	Forfar	36	7	4	7	29	20	6	4	8	22	25	47	+6
6	Alloa	36	6	7	5	39	35	6	3	9	27	33	46	-2
7	Dumbarton	36	5	7	6	22	23	6	2	10	21	31	42	-10
8	Ayr	36	6	6	6	22	23	5	3	10	17	31	42	-15
9	Arbroath	36	6	3	9	18	30	4	5	9	31	43	38	-24
10	Berwick	36	5	3	10	20	33	3	7	8	20	31	34	-24

BELL'S SCOTTISH DIVISION THREE

Pos		P	Home					Away					Pts	Goal
			W	D	L	F	A	W	D	L	F	A		Diff
1	Gretna	36	18	0	0	70	10	14	2	2	60	19	98	+101
2	Peterhead	36	11	6	1	46	17	12	3	3	35	21	78	+43
3	Cowdenbeath	36	8	4	6	24	32	6	5	7	30	29	51	-7
4	Queen's Park	36	7	5	6	24	24	6	4	8	27	26	48	+1
5	Montrose	36	7	2	9	27	29	7	2	9	20	24	46	-6
6	Elgin	36	7	5	6	24	31	5	2	11	15	30	43	-22
7	Stenhsmuir	36	5	7	6	31	25	5	5	8	27	33	42	0
8	East Fife	36	7	4	7	17	19	3	4	11	23	37	38	-16
9	Albion	36	3	4	11	20	46	5	6	7	20	32	34	-38
10	E Stirling	36	4	3	11	17	39	1	4	13	15	49	22	-56

BUNDESLIGA

Pos		Home						Away					Goal	
		P	W	D	L	F	A	W	D	L	F	A	Pts	Diff
1	B Munich	34	14	2	1	44	14	10	3	4	31	19	42	77
2	Schalke	34	11	2	4	33	24	9	1	7	23	22	10	63
3	W Bremen	34	9	4	4	33	15	9	1	7	35	22	31	59
4	Hertha Berlin	34	8	8	1	34	13	7	5	5	25	18	28	58
5	Stuttgart	34	12	2	3	34	15	5	5	7	20	25	14	58
6	B Leverkusen	34	12	3	2	42	18	4	6	7	23	26	21	57
7	B Dortmund	34	8	5	4	24	18	7	5	5	23	26	3	55
8	Hamburg	34	9	1	7	27	22	7	2	8	28	28	5	51
9	Wolfsburg	34	10	1	6	35	20	5	2	10	14	31	-2	48
10	Hannover 96	34	8	2	7	21	19	5	4	8	13	17	-2	45
11	Mainz	34	9	3	5	28	21	3	4	10	22	34	-5	43
12	Kaiserslautern	34	8	2	5	20	21	4	4	9	23	31	-9	42
13	A Bielefeld	34	7	3	7	21	21	4	4	9	16	28	-12	40
14	Nuremberg	34	4	6	7	25	25	6	2	9	30	38	-8	38
15	B M'gladbach	34	8	5	4	26	21	0	7	10	9	30	-16	36
16	Bochum (R)	34	6	5	6	30	29	3	3	11	17	39	-21	35
17	H Rostock (R)	34	4	5	8	17	31	3	4	10	14	34	-34	30
18	Freiburg (R)	34	2	6	9	18	31	1	3	13	12	44	-45	18

PRIMERA LIGA

Pos		Home						Away					Goal	
		P	W	D	L	F	A	W	D	L	F	A	Pts	Diff
1	Barcelona	38	14	4	1	40	12	11	5	3	33	17	84	+44
2	Real Madrid	38	15	1	3	43	12	10	4	5	28	20	80	+39
3	Villarreal	38	14	4	1	41	10	4	7	8	28	27	65	+32
4	Real Betis	38	12	5	2	36	22	4	9	6	26	28	62	+12
5	Espanyol	38	12	5	2	34	18	5	5	9	20	28	61	+8
6	Seville	38	10	5	4	25	19	7	4	8	19	22	60	+3
7	Valencia	38	11	5	3	31	17	3	11	5	23	22	58	+15
8	Ath Bilbao	38	11	4	4	39	24	3	5	11	20	30	51	+5
9	Deportivo	38	6	7	6	25	29	6	8	5	21	21	51	-4
10	Malaga	38	8	4	7	19	24	7	2	10	21	24	51	-8
11	Ath Madrid	38	11	6	2	28	13	2	5	12	12	21	50	+6
12	Real Zaragoza	38	11	3	5	35	25	3	5	11	17	32	50	-5
13	Getafe	38	11	4	4	23	12	1	7	11	15	34	47	-8
14	Real Sociedad	38	9	4	6	21	24	4	4	11	26	32	47	-9
15	Osasuna	38	9	6	4	28	24	3	4	12	18	41	46	-19
16	R Santander	38	8	6	5	25	23	4	2	13	16	35	44	-17
17	Real Mallorca	38	6	5	8	28	31	4	4	11	14	32	39	-21
18	Levante	38	6	6	7	19	20	3	4	12	20	38	37	-19
19	Numancia	38	4	9	6	19	23	2	2	15	11	38	29	-31
20	Albacete	38	4	7	8	17	22	2	3	14	16	34	28	-23

Pos		P	Home W	D	L	F	A	Away W	D	L	F	A	Pts	Goal Diff
1	Lyon	38	13	5	1	33	10	9	8	2	23	12	79	+34
2	Lille	38	11	6	2	31	11	7	7	5	21	18	67	+23
3	Monaco	38	11	6	2	38	21	4	12	3	14	14	63	+17
4	Rennes	38	13	4	2	35	12	2	6	11	14	30	55	+7
5	Marseille	38	9	4	6	26	19	6	6	7	21	23	55	+5
6	StEtienne	38	9	8	2	25	7	3	9	7	22	27	53	+13
7	Lens	38	10	6	3	30	15	3	7	9	15	24	52	+6
8	Auxerre	38	10	7	2	33	19	4	3	12	15	28	52	+1
9	Paris St-G	38	9	8	2	24	15	3	7	9	16	26	51	-1
10	Sochaux	38	10	3	6	25	16	3	8	8	17	25	50	+1
11	Strasbourg	38	10	5	4	29	17	2	7	10	13	26	48	-1
12	Nice	38	7	10	2	22	13	3	6	10	16	32	46	-7
13	Toulouse	38	9	4	6	20	19	3	6	10	16	24	46	-7
14	Ajaccio	38	7	10	2	24	15	3	5	11	12	25	45	-4
15	Bordeaux	38	5	11	3	24	18	3	9	7	13	23	44	-4
16	Metz	38	7	9	3	22	15	3	5	11	11	30	44	-12
17	Nantes	38	7	9	3	21	16	3	4	12	12	22	43	-5
18	Caen	38	5	8	6	15	18	5	4	10	21	42	42	-24
19	Bastia	38	10	4	5	24	19	1	4	14	8	29	41	-16
20	Istres	38	5	5	9	11	19	1	9	9	14	32	32	-26

Pos		P	Home W	D	L	F	A	Away W	D	L	F	A	Pts	Goal Diff
1	Juventus	38	15	2	2	38	13	11	6	2	29	14	86	+40
2	ACMilan	38	11	5	3	38	17	12	5	2	25	11	79	+35
3	InterMilan	38	11	7	1	34	16	7	11	1	31	21	72	+28
4	Udinese	38	8	7	4	29	18	9	4	6	27	22	62	+16
5	Sampdoria	38	10	3	6	21	13	7	7	5	21	16	61	+13
6	Palermo	38	9	7	3	28	22	3	10	6	20	22	53	+4
7	Messina	38	10	7	2	26	19	2	5	12	18	33	48	-8
8	Roma	38	6	8	5	31	26	5	4	10	24	32	45	-3
9	Livorno	38	9	5	5	28	25	2	7	10	21	35	45	-11
10	Lazio	38	6	6	7	26	24	5	5	9	22	29	44	-5
11	Lecce	38	8	8	3	40	30	2	6	11	26	43	44	-7
12	Cagliari	38	9	9	1	30	17	1	5	13	21	43	44	-9
13	Reggina	38	7	6	6	21	23	3	8	8	15	22	44	-9
14	Siena	38	5	8	6	21	27	4	8	7	23	28	43	-11
15	Chievo	38	8	5	6	20	18	3	5	11	12	31	43	-17
16	Bologna	38	6	7	6	20	17	3	8	8	13	19	42	-3
17	Fiorentina	38	7	7	5	29	22	2	8	9	13	28	42	-8
18	Parma	38	8	9	2	33	25	2	3	14	15	40	42	-17
19	Brescia	38	6	3	10	15	22	5	5	9	22	32	41	-17
20	Atalanta	38	7	6	6	21	17	1	5	13	13	28	35	-11

MATCHDAY
WHAT MAKES SATURDAY SPECIAL?

BY CHRIS GREEN

SPECIAL OFFER
£12.99
Save £2 off
RRP of £14.99
plus free p&p

Chris Green goes behind the scenes to provide a multi-faceted snapshot of modern football. From plush boardrooms to mud-spattered dressing rooms he tells the unfolding drama of a typical football Saturday via an amazing array of characters.

ORDER A COPY TODAY
call Highdown's credit / debit card orderline on
01635 578080
and quote ref MDFG05
or order online at www.highdownbooks.co.uk

HIGHDOWN, RFM HOUSE, COMPTON, NEWBURY RG20 6NL

FA PREMIER LEAGUE 2004-2005 RESULTS

	Arsenal	Aston Villa	Birmingham	Blackburn	Bolton	Charlton	Chelsea	Crystal Pal	Everton	Fulham	Liverpool	Man City	Man Utd	Middlesboro	Newcastle	Norwich	Portsmouth	Southampton	Tottenham	West Brom
Arsenal	*	3-1	3-0	3-0	2-2	4-0	2-2	5-1	7-0	2-0	3-1	1-1	2-4	5-3	1-0	4-1	3-0	2-2	1-0	1-1
Aston Villa	1-3	*	1-2	1-0	1-1	0-0	0-0	1-1	1-3	2-0	1-1	1-2	0-1	2-0	4-2	3-0	3-0	2-0	1-0	1-1
Birmingham	2-1	2-0	*	2-1	1-2	1-1	0-1	0-1	0-1	1-2	2-0	1-0	0-0	2-0	2-2	1-1	0-0	2-1	1-1	4-0
Blackburn	0-1	2-2	3-3	*	0-1	1-0	0-1	1-0	0-0	1-3	2-2	0-0	1-1	0-4	2-2	3-0	1-0	3-0	0-1	1-1
Bolton	1-0	1-2	1-1	0-1	*	1-0	0-2	1-0	3-2	3-1	1-0	0-1	2-2	0-0	2-1	1-0	0-1	1-1	3-1	1-1
Charlton	1-3	3-0	3-1	1-0	1-2	*	0-4	2-2	2-0	2-1	1-2	2-2	0-4	1-2	1-1	4-0	2-1	0-0	2-0	1-4
Chelsea	0-0	1-0	1-1	4-0	2-2	4-0	*	4-1	1-0	3-1	1-0	0-0	1-0	0-0	4-0	4-0	3-0	2-1	0-0	1-0
Crystal Pal	1-1	2-0	2-0	0-0	0-1	1-0	0-2	*	1-3	2-0	1-0	1-2	0-0	0-1	0-2	3-3	0-1	2-2	3-0	1-0
Everton	1-4	1-1	1-1	0-1	3-2	0-1	0-1	4-0	*	1-0	1-0	2-1	1-1	1-0	2-0	1-0	2-1	1-0	0-1	3-0
Fulham	0-3	1-1	2-3	0-2	2-0	0-0	1-4	3-1	2-0	*	2-4	1-1	1-1	0-2	1-3	6-0	3-1	1-0	2-0	2-1
Liverpool	2-1	2-1	0-1	0-0	1-0	2-0	1-0	3-2	2-1	3-1	*	2-1	2-1	1-1	3-1	3-0	1-1	2-1	2-2	1-0
Man City	0-1	2-0	3-0	1-1	0-1	4-0	0-1	3-1	0-1	1-1	1-0	*	0-2	1-1	1-1	1-1	2-0	3-0	0-1	3-0
Man Utd	2-0	3-1	2-0	0-0	2-0	2-0	1-3	5-2	0-0	1-0	2-1	0-2	*	1-1	2-1	2-1	2-1	1-3	0-0	1-1
Middlesboro	0-1	3-0	2-1	1-0	1-1	2-2	0-1	2-1	1-1	1-1	2-0	1-1	0-2	*	2-2	2-0	1-1	2-1	1-0	1-1
Newcastle	0-1	0-3	2-1	3-0	2-1	1-1	1-1	0-0	1-1	1-4	1-0	3-2	1-3	0-0	*	2-2	1-1	2-1	0-1	4-0
Norwich	1-4	0-0	1-0	1-1	3-2	1-0	1-3	1-1	2-3	0-1	1-2	4-3	2-0	4-4	2-1	*	2-2	4-1	0-2	3-1
Portsmouth	0-1	1-2	1-1	0-1	1-1	4-2	0-2	3-1	0-1	4-3	1-2	2-3	2-0	2-1	1-1	1-1	*	4-1	1-0	3-2
Southampton	1-1	2-3	0-0	3-2	1-2	0-0	1-3	2-2	2-2	3-3	1-1	1-3	1-2	2-2	1-2	4-3	2-1	*	1-0	1-0
Tottenham	4-5	5-1	1-0	0-0	1-1	2-3	0-2	1-1	5-2	2-0	1-1	0-0	0-1	2-0	1-0	0-0	3-1	5-1	*	1-1
West Brom	0-2	1-1	2-0	1-1	2-1	1-4	1-4	2-2	1-0	1-1	0-5	2-0	0-3	1-2	0-0	0-0	2-0	0-0	1-1	*

CHAMPIONSHIP 2004-2005 RESULTS

	Brighton	Burnley	Cardiff	Coventry	Crewe	Derby	Gillingham	Ipswich	Leeds	Leicester	Millwall	Nottm F	Plymouth	Preston	QPR	Reading	Rotherham	Sheff Utd	Stoke	Sunderland	Watford	West Ham	Wigan	Wolves
Brighton	*	0-1	1-1	1-1	1-3	2-3	1-0	1-1	1-0	1-1	1-0	0-0	0-2	1-0	2-3	0-1	1-0	1-1	0-1	2-1	2-1	2-2	2-4	0-1
Burnley	1-1	*	1-0	2-2	3-0	0-2	1-2	0-2	0-1	0-0	1-0	1-0	2-0	2-0	2-0	0-0	2-1	1-1	2-2	0-2	3-1	0-1	1-0	1-1
Cardiff	2-0	2-0	*	2-1	1-1	0-2	3-1	0-1	0-0	0-0	0-1	3-0	0-1	0-1	1-2	2-0	2-0	1-0	0-1	0-2	0-3	4-1	0-2	1-1
Coventry	2-1	0-2	2-1	*	0-1	6-2	2-2	1-2	1-2	1-1	0-1	2-0	2-1	1-1	0-2	3-2	0-1	2-3	0-0	0-1	1-0	2-1	1-0	2-2
Crewe	3-1	1-1	2-2	2-1	*	1-2	4-1	2-2	2-2	2-2	0-1	1-1	3-0	1-2	0-1	1-1	3-2	2-3	0-2	0-2	3-0	2-3	1-3	1-4
Derby	3-0	1-1	0-1	2-2	2-4	*	3-2	3-2	2-0	2-2	0-3	3-0	1-0	3-1	0-0	2-1	3-1	1-3	0-2	0-2	2-2	1-1	1-3	3-3
Gillingham	0-1	1-0	1-1	2-2	3-1	0-2	*	0-0	0-2	1-0	0-0	3-0	1-0	2-1	0-1	0-0	3-1	1-3	3-1	0-4	0-0	1-1	2-1	1-0
Ipswich	1-0	1-1	3-1	2-2	5-1	1-1	2-1	*	1-0	2-1	2-0	6-0	3-2	3-0	0-2	1-1	4-3	5-1	2-1	2-2	1-2	0-2	2-1	1-0
Leeds	1-1	1-2	1-1	3-0	0-2	1-1	1-1	1-0	*	0-2	2-0	1-1	2-1	1-0	6-1	3-1	0-0	0-4	0-0	2-2	2-2	1-0	0-2	2-1
Leicester	0-1	0-0	0-2	1-1	2-2	2-2	1-1	0-2	0-2	*	3-1	0-1	2-1	1-0	1-0	0-2	1-2	3-2	1-1	2-0	0-1	0-0	0-2	1-1
Millwall	2-0	0-0	2-2	1-0	4-3	3-1	2-0	2-2	2-0	3-1	*	1-0	3-0	2-1	0-0	0-2	1-2	1-1	1-1	2-0	0-2	2-1	0-2	1-1
Nottm F	0-1	1-0	1-0	1-4	2-2	1-1	3-1	1-1	0-0	2-0	3-1	*	3-0	2-1	2-1	1-0	2-2	1-1	0-1	1-2	0-2	2-1	1-1	1-0
Plymouth	5-1	1-1	1-1	3-0	3-0	3-2	2-1	1-1	2-4	1-1	0-0	3-2	*	0-2	2-1	2-2	2-0	3-0	0-0	2-1	1-0	2-1	1-2	1-2
Preston	3-0	1-0	3-0	3-2	1-2	1-0	1-1	1-1	1-1	3-2	0-0	3-2	1-1	*	2-1	3-0	2-0	0-1	3-0	3-2	3-1	2-1	2-2	1-1
QPR	0-0	3-0	1-0	4-1	4-0	0-2	3-1	2-4	1-1	0-0	0-0	1-0	3-2	1-2	*	0-0	1-0	0-1	1-0	1-3	3-1	1-0	1-1	1-1
Reading	3-2	0-0	2-1	1-2	2-3	0-1	3-1	1-1	1-0	0-2	2-1	1-0	0-0	3-1	1-0	*	1-0	0-0	1-0	1-0	3-0	3-1	1-1	1-2
Rotherham	0-1	0-0	2-2	1-2	2-3	1-3	3-3	0-2	1-0	0-2	1-1	0-1	0-1	1-1	0-1	1-0	*	2-2	1-1	0-1	0-1	2-2	0-2	1-2
Sheff Utd	1-2	2-1	2-1	1-1	4-0	0-1	0-0	2-0	1-2	2-0	0-1	1-1	2-0	1-1	3-2	0-1	1-0	*	0-0	1-0	1-1	1-2	0-1	3-3
Stoke	2-0	0-1	1-3	1-0	1-0	0-1	2-0	3-2	0-1	2-0	1-0	0-0	2-0	0-0	0-0	0-1	1-2	2-0	*	0-1	0-1	1-2	0-1	2-1
Sunderland	2-0	2-1	2-1	1-0	3-1	2-0	2-3	2-1	1-2	2-1	3-2	2-0	5-1	3-1	2-2	1-2	4-1	0-0	1-0	*	4-2	0-2	1-1	2-0
Watford	1-1	0-1	1-3	2-3	3-1	0-0	2-2	2-0	2-2	0-0	1-0	3-1	3-1	0-2	3-0	0-1	0-0	0-0	0-1	1-1	*	1-2	1-3	1-0
West Ham	1-1	0-1	2-1	3-0	3-1	1-0	3-1	2-2	2-0	3-1	2-1	3-2	3-0	2-1	2-1	1-2	1-0	2-0	0-1	1-1	3-2	*	1-2	2-0
Wigan	3-0	0-0	2-1	4-1	1-1	1-2	2-0	2-2	3-0	0-0	2-0	2-1	5-0	2-2	0-0	3-1	2-0	4-0	0-1	0-1	2-2	4-2	*	3-3
Wolves	1-1	2-0	2-3	0-1	1-1	2-0	2-2	2-0	0-0	1-1	1-2	2-1	1-1	1-1	1-1	4-1	2-0	4-2	1-1	1-1	0-0	4-2	3-3	*

LEAGUE 1 2004-2005 RESULTS

Home \ Away	Barnsley	Blackpool	B'mouth	Bradford	Brentford	Bristol C	Chesterfld	Colchester	Doncaster	Hartlepool	H'dersfield	Hull	Luton	MK Dons	Oldham	Peterboro	Port Vale	Sheff Wed	Stockport	Swindon	Torquay	Tranmere	Walsall	Wrexham
Barnsley	*	1-0	0-1	2-1	1-1	2-1	1-0	1-1	4-0	1-1	0-2	1-2	3-4	1-1	2-0	4-0	1-2	0-0	3-3	2-2	4-1	0-1	3-2	2-2
Blackpool	0-2	*	3-3	2-1	0-3	1-1	1-0	1-1	2-0	2-0	1-0	0-2	1-3	1-0	4-0	0-1	0-2	1-2	0-4	1-1	4-0	3-1	2-0	2-1
Bournemouth	1-3	2-3	*	2-0	4-1	2-2	0-0	0-2	5-0	1-1	3-2	0-4	0-1	4-0	0-0	0-1	4-0	1-2	2-1	2-1	3-0	1-1	2-2	2-1
Bradford	1-0	2-1	*	*	4-1	2-2	0-0	1-3	2-0	0-1	0-1	0-2	0-1	1-4	4-0	2-2	4-0	3-1	2-1	1-2	3-0	1-1	2-2	1-0
Brentford	1-1	0-3	4-2	4-1	*	1-0	2-2	1-0	4-3	2-1	0-1	0-2	0-1	1-4	1-3	2-2	0-2	3-1	3-1	2-2	2-2	1-3	1-1	1-1
Bristol C	0-0	1-1	2-1	1-0	1-2	*	2-3	0-0	2-2	0-0	1-1	2-1	2-0	5-1	2-0	1-3	2-0	3-3	5-0	2-1	1-3	4-0	1-1	1-0
Chesterfield	2-2	0-0	1-2	0-0	4-1	*	*	4-1	0-0	4-1	0-1	1-1	0-1	1-0	1-0	2-0	2-0	1-4	4-0	1-0	1-1	2-2	1-0	1-0
Colchester	0-2	0-1	3-1	0-0	0-1	0-2	1-0	*	4-1	2-0	0-1	1-2	0-1	2-2	0-0	2-1	2-1	1-3	3-2	1-0	2-1	2-2	5-0	1-0
Doncaster	4-0	2-0	1-1	1-1	0-0	1-1	0-1	1-1	*	2-0	2-1	1-0	0-1	0-0	1-1	1-3	2-0	1-3	4-0	1-0	2-1	2-0	1-0	2-4
Hartlepool	1-1	1-1	1-1	3-1	0-0	2-1	0-1	1-1	4-1	*	0-1	1-0	0-1	0-0	0-0	2-1	2-0	1-3	3-2	0-1	2-2	2-2	5-0	0-0
Huddersfield	0-2	1-0	3-2	0-1	1-1	2-2	0-0	1-1	2-1	2-0	*	2-0	3-3	5-0	1-1	2-2	1-0	3-0	3-1	3-0	4-1	0-1	1-3	0-2
Hull	2-1	2-1	1-0	2-0	2-0	1-1	1-0	2-0	3-1	2-0	4-0	*	1-1	3-1	2-1	2-1	2-1	1-1	5-3	4-0	1-1	1-3	3-1	4-6
Luton	1-3	1-0	1-0	2-0	1-1	1-1	1-0	2-2	2-1	2-0	2-1	1-0	*	1-0	2-1	2-1	1-1	1-1	3-0	1-1	1-1	6-1	3-1	1-2
MK Dons	1-1	3-1	4-0	4-2	2-0	5-0	2-1	2-0	0-1	0-1	2-1	3-0	1-2	*	1-1	2-1	1-1	2-2	2-1	3-1	1-0	1-1	1-0	2-1
Oldham	3-2	1-2	2-1	0-0	0-0	1-2	4-1	1-1	0-1	4-2	3-0	1-0	1-4	3-0	*	2-1	3-0	1-1	2-1	1-2	1-2	2-2	5-3	3-0
Peterboro	1-3	0-0	2-2	3-0	3-0	1-1	1-2	0-3	0-2	3-2	1-2	2-3	2-2	0-3	1-2	*	4-0	1-1	2-1	0-2	1-1	2-2	0-2	2-2
Port Vale	5-0	0-1	2-1	0-1	3-0	3-0	0-0	0-0	2-0	0-1	0-3	3-2	2-2	3-1	1-1	4-0	*	0-2	0-0	1-2	1-2	3-1	0-2	0-2
Sheff Wed	1-0	0-3	2-1	0-1	3-0	0-0	2-2	0-3	2-0	2-0	1-0	3-1	3-2	1-1	1-1	1-0	1-0	*	0-0	2-0	2-2	3-1	2-0	1-0
Stockport	2-2	0-1	2-2	1-2	0-1	2-3	2-2	1-2	2-4	1-0	2-3	1-3	3-1	1-2	1-2	2-1	1-0	0-2	*	2-0	2-2	1-2	0-1	2-4
Swindon	2-1	2-2	0-3	3-0	0-0	1-2	1-1	0-3	2-0	2-3	1-2	1-3	3-1	1-0	2-1	1-0	1-2	0-3	3-0	*	0-2	1-2	0-1	1-4
Torquay	0-1	2-0	1-2	0-0	2-2	0-1	1-3	1-3	1-1	1-2	2-1	0-3	1-1	2-0	2-0	2-1	1-0	2-4	1-2	3-3	*	1-2	4-1	1-0
Tranmere	1-1	3-2	1-2	1-0	0-1	1-2	3-0	1-1	1-1	2-1	3-0	2-0	1-1	2-0	2-1	0-1	3-2	1-1	1-0	2-1	1-2	*	2-1	1-1
Walsall	2-2	3-2	1-2	1-0	1-0	1-2	1-3	2-1	1-1	0-1	2-1	2-2	0-0	0-1	1-1	2-1	3-2	1-1	1-0	3-2	4-1	0-2	*	2-2
Wrexham	2-1	1-2	1-0	1-0	1-3	1-3	3-1	2-2	0-0	1-5	0-1	2-2	1-2	1-0	1-0	1-1	3-2	0-3	2-1	3-2	1-1	0-2	2-2	*

154

LEAGUE 2 2004-2005 RESULTS

	Boston	Bristol R	Bury	C'bridge	Cheltenhm	Chester	Darlington	Grimsby	Kidderminstr	Leyton O	Lincoln	Macclesf'd	Mansfield	North'pton	Notts Co	Oxford Utd	Rochdale	Rushden	Scunthorpe	Shrewsbury	Southend	Swansea	Wycombe	Yeovil
Boston	*	2-2	2-2	2-1	2-1	3-1	3-1	1-1	3-0	2-2	0-2	1-1	0-0	0-1	4-0	1-0	1-1	1-0	2-1	2-2	2-0	2-3	2-0	2-2
Bristol R	1-1	*	2-2	1-1	1-1	4-1	3-3	3-0	2-0	1-1	0-0	0-0	4-4	3-1	2-1	2-0	0-0	3-0	4-0	0-0	2-1	2-0	1-0	2-2
Bury	1-1	1-1	*	2-1	3-1	1-1	0-1	3-1	4-0	1-1	0-1	2-1	0-2	2-0	1-0	0-0	0-0	1-1	3-2	0-0	0-1	0-1	2-2	3-1
Cambridge U	0-1	1-0	1-0	*	1-0	0-0	3-1	0-2	1-3	1-1	0-1	0-1	2-2	0-1	0-2	2-1	2-0	3-1	0-1	1-0	0-2	0-1	2-1	3-5
Cheltenham	1-0	1-1	1-0	2-1	*	0-3	0-2	2-3	2-0	1-2	0-1	0-1	2-2	0-1	0-2	1-3	2-0	4-1	1-2	1-0	0-3	1-2	1-1	1-1
Chester	2-1	2-2	2-1	0-0	0-3	*	0-3	2-0	0-2	1-1	0-1	3-0	0-3	0-2	3-2	1-1	5-1	2-0	0-0	1-0	0-2	1-1	1-1	0-2
Darlington	1-0	0-1	1-2	0-3	3-1	1-0	*	0-2	2-1	3-0	0-3	3-1	2-1	1-1	3-2	1-1	0-3	2-0	1-1	3-0	4-0	2-1	1-0	2-1
Grimsby	1-1	0-0	5-1	1-1	1-1	1-0	1-0	*	2-1	2-0	2-4	3-1	2-0	1-2	3-2	1-1	0-1	0-0	1-3	3-0	4-0	2-1	1-0	1-1
Kidderminstr	0-4	1-1	2-2	1-1	2-3	0-1	1-0	0-2	*	1-2	2-1	1-3	1-3	0-2	3-2	1-3	2-1	0-0	3-2	4-1	1-3	3-1	0-2	2-3
Leyton O	0-0	4-2	1-1	2-1	0-0	2-0	0-1	1-4	2-1	*	1-1	2-0	2-0	3-2	2-0	1-0	1-1	2-2	0-1	2-0	2-2	3-1	2-3	3-1
Lincoln	2-2	2-1	1-0	2-1	0-0	1-1	1-0	0-0	3-0	3-4	*	2-0	2-0	3-2	1-2	3-0	3-0	1-3	2-0	2-0	1-1	1-0	2-3	3-1
Macclesfield	1-1	2-1	2-1	1-1	0-2	0-0	1-1	3-1	2-0	3-1	2-2	*	3-1	4-1	0-0	1-0	1-1	0-1	3-1	1-1	1-2	1-0	2-1	3-1
Mansfield	3-2	0-2	0-0	2-2	1-2	1-1	1-1	0-1	2-0	0-1	1-0	2-0	*	4-1	0-0	2-1	3-1	2-1	3-1	3-1	1-2	2-2	1-1	4-1
Northampton	2-1	2-1	2-0	2-0	2-0	0-2	1-1	3-0	2-1	3-2	3-2	4-1	3-2	*	3-1	3-0	0-0	2-0	2-0	2-0	2-0	2-1	1-4	1-1
Notts Co	2-1	1-2	0-1	2-1	1-1	1-1	1-2	2-2	0-2	1-2	1-0	0-5	2-1	0-0	*	0-1	1-1	1-0	5-1	3-0	4-0	1-2	0-1	1-2
Oxford Utd	2-0	3-2	3-1	2-1	2-1	0-1	0-2	1-2	1-3	2-2	0-1	1-1	1-0	1-2	2-1	*	0-1	1-0	1-3	3-0	2-1	1-2	2-1	2-1
Rochdale	2-0	0-0	0-3	2-1	1-2	2-2	1-2	2-0	1-1	2-0	2-0	1-1	3-2	0-0	0-3	0-1	*	0-1	3-3	3-1	2-0	0-2	1-1	2-0
Rushden & D	4-2	4-0	3-0	0-1	1-0	0-1	1-2	1-0	0-0	2-0	3-0	3-1	0-0	3-2	5-1	3-3	0-0	*	1-0	3-1	1-4	0-2	1-2	2-0
Scunthorpe	1-1	4-0	3-2	4-0	4-1	1-2	0-1	2-0	2-1	1-0	2-0	3-1	3-1	2-0	5-1	3-3	3-1	1-0	*	3-1	3-2	1-0	2-0	1-0
Shrewsbury	0-0	2-0	2-2	0-0	2-0	5-0	4-0	1-1	1-1	4-1	1-0	1-1	5-2	2-0	3-0	4-0	3-0	2-2	3-1	*	0-0	4-2	0-1	1-2
Southend	2-1	1-0	2-0	2-1	0-2	3-0	2-1	0-0	3-0	1-0	1-0	2-0	4-0	1-3	2-0	2-0	1-4	2-0	1-0	3-2	*	4-2	2-1	0-1
Swansea	3-1	1-0	1-3	3-0	1-1	4-2	1-1	2-0	3-0	3-2	3-0	1-0	2-2	2-1	4-0	4-0	3-0	2-2	4-0	1-0	1-1	*	2-2	0-2
Wycombe	1-2	1-0	1-2	2-1	1-1	1-1	1-1	2-0	3-0	1-0	1-0	2-0	1-1	0-1	1-2	1-0	0-3	1-1	2-1	1-1	0-1	2-2	*	0-1
Yeovil	2-0	4-2	0-1	2-1	4-1	4-1	1-1	2-1	2-1	1-0	3-0	1-2	5-2	1-1	1-3	6-1	2-2	3-1	4-3	4-2	3-1	1-0	1-1	*

NATIONWIDE CONFERENCE 2004-2005 RESULTS

	Accrington	Aldershot	Barnet	Burton	Canvey I	Carlisle	Crawley	Dagenham	Exeter	Farnboro	Forest G	Gravesend	Halifax	Hereford	Leigh RMI	Morcambe	Northwich	Scarboro	Stevenage	Tamworth	Woking	York
Accrington	*	3-3	4-1	3-1	1-0	1-2	4-0	0-3	0-0	2-1	2-2	1-2	1-1	2-1	2-1	2-1	5-0	2-1	4-1	2-3	0-0	2-2
Aldershot	0-0	*	2-3	3-0	2-0	0-5	1-0	4-0	2-1	3-1	1-2	1-0	0-0	0-2	2-0	3-3	2-1	2-0	0-1	4-3	4-0	2-0
Barnet	3-0	2-1	*	2-3	1-0	1-1	3-0	5-0	1-0	7-1	3-1	4-1	3-1	0-2	3-2	5-1	4-0	1-0	2-1	0-3	2-2	4-0
Burton	2-2	1-3	2-3	*	1-1	0-1	1-0	1-3	1-0	0-0	4-1	3-2	2-2	3-0	0-0	1-3	1-0	2-3	0-3	1-1	0-1	0-2
Canvey Islnd	0-2	2-2	0-1	1-1	*	0-3	2-2	4-2	2-2	1-1	2-1	1-1	0-1	0-4	3-0	0-0	2-2	1-0	3-0	3-3	2-2	4-0
Carlisle	2-0	1-1	1-3	0-1	0-3	*	1-0	1-0	0-2	7-0	0-1	2-2	1-0	3-1	3-0	3-3	1-0	2-1	1-2	2-1	2-1	6-0
Crawley	0-5	3-0	1-3	4-0	2-1	1-0	*	2-0	0-1	2-0	4-2	1-1	1-2	1-1	2-2	2-1	0-0	2-1	1-2	3-0	2-1	1-0
Dagenham & R	1-2	2-0	0-3	3-1	3-1	1-0	2-0	*	2-0	0-0	2-2	5-0	4-2	3-1	2-0	2-1	2-2	2-0	3-2	0-0	1-1	0-0
Exeter	1-2	3-1	0-3	3-1	0-1	3-2	1-0	2-3	*	2-1	2-0	3-0	2-1	4-0	5-1	1-1	2-3	3-1	2-0	2-2	0-0	1-2
Farnborough	2-1	1-2	0-0	1-3	1-3	1-2	2-3	2-1	2-1	*	1-1	0-3	3-2	0-6	0-1	1-2	0-1	0-1	2-1	2-0	1-1	4-0
Forest G.	1-0	0-0	0-2	3-2	2-2	0-3	1-1	1-4	1-1	1-1	*	1-5	0-0	1-3	1-1	0-3	1-3	4-0	4-0	1-1	1-1	1-3
Gravesend	2-2	1-3	1-3	0-2	3-2	1-3	0-0	2-1	1-1	2-2	0-0	*	0-3	1-2	4-1	1-2	2-2	2-1	2-0	3-3	3-1	0-0
Halifax	1-2	2-0	2-3	2-0	4-1	2-2	0-0	2-2	2-1	2-0	4-0	0-3	*	0-1	5-1	1-3	2-2	1-0	2-1	2-1	2-2	2-0
Hereford	0-0	2-0	0-3	0-0	1-0	0-0	1-2	0-1	1-2	3-1	2-1	1-2	0-3	*	3-0	1-1	4-0	1-1	0-0	2-3	0-3	2-2
Leigh RMI	0-6	3-3	0-3	1-4	2-1	1-6	1-2	0-1	0-1	1-2	2-0	2-0	2-1	3-4	*	0-2	0-1	2-1	3-3	3-0	2-1	2-0
Morecambe	1-2	0-0	1-1	3-0	4-0	3-3	1-2	1-0	2-2	2-1	4-0	1-0	2-1	2-1	2-1	*	3-1	1-1	0-1	1-2	0-3	1-0
Northwich	3-3	1-2	2-0	4-0	3-1	2-2	1-2	2-2	2-2	2-0	3-1	1-3	1-2	4-0	2-1	2-2	*	1-0	4-1	2-2	2-1	5-1
Scarborough	4-0	2-2	1-1	3-1	1-4	1-1	1-0	2-0	1-1	4-0	2-2	1-0	2-1	1-4	3-0	1-1	1-0	*	3-3	2-0	2-0	2-2
Stevenage	5-0	0-1	2-1	0-1	1-0	1-0	1-0	3-2	1-2	3-1	4-0	2-0	2-1	0-0	3-3	0-1	4-1	3-3	*	0-0	0-2	3-1
Tamworth	1-0	1-2	1-1	1-0	1-0	2-0	2-0	0-4	3-3	2-1	0-1	2-1	2-1	2-3	2-1	0-0	3-0	2-0	0-0	*	1-3	2-0
Woking	2-1	1-2	1-1	1-0	2-0	1-0	3-1	2-4	1-2	2-0	2-1	1-1	2-1	2-2	1-0	0-0	3-0	1-1	1-2	2-1	*	1-0
York	0-1	0-2	2-1	1-2	3-1	0-0	1-3	0-0	1-2	4-0	1-3	0-0	1-1	0-3	1-1	1-0	0-0	0-2	3-1	2-0	0-2	*

	Alfreton	Altrincham	Ashton Utd	Barrow	Bradford P	Droylsden	Gainsboro	Harrogate	Hinckley	Hucknall T	Kettering	Lancaster	Moor Green	Nuneaton	Redditch	Runcorn	Southport	Stafford	Stalybridge	Vauxhall M	Worcester	Worksop
Alfreton	*	0-2	1-2	1-1	2-1	0-1	0-1	2-0	0-2	0-2	1-2	2-3	2-2	2-0	1-2	4-0	2-1	0-1	1-0	3-1	0-0	0-0
Altrincham	1-2	*	1-2	2-0	0-0	2-2	4-1	3-0	4-1	1-1	3-3	4-0	0-2	1-0	0-0	3-3	2-1	1-0	4-1	3-1	2-0	4-1
Ashton Utd	3-1	0-1	*	1-2	0-0	1-0	1-3	3-2	0-2	0-0	0-2	2-0	1-3	2-3	2-3	5-4	0-3	1-2	2-3	0-2	1-0	2-3
Barrow	0-3	2-0	1-1	*	3-2	1-3	2-0	1-0	3-0	0-3	2-1	2-2	3-4	1-3	1-6	1-1	0-2	2-2	2-1	1-2	2-2	2-1
Bradford Pk	0-4	1-2	3-3	3-2	*	0-2	0-3	1-2	1-1	2-4	1-2	1-0	1-1	2-2	0-3	0-1	3-1	3-1	0-1	0-1	0-1	1-1
Droylsden	3-2	2-0	4-0	0-1	3-3	*	2-1	2-1	1-0	3-1	2-3	3-4	2-2	1-0	1-0	3-0	1-3	4-0	0-0	4-0	2-3	1-3
Gainsborough	1-2	0-1	1-0	2-0	2-0	1-1	*	0-0	1-1	0-1	1-1	4-2	1-1	1-2	2-1	2-3	1-0	1-1	2-2	1-2	3-0	1-1
Harrogate	2-1	1-1	5-1	2-1	2-1	2-1	5-1	*	1-1	0-0	2-1	1-1	1-2	3-1	4-2	1-0	2-5	0-1	2-0	2-1	2-0	0-0
Hinckley	1-0	2-1	3-1	1-0	4-0	3-3	3-1	0-1	*	0-3	0-1	2-2	2-1	2-3	1-2	0-0	0-0	0-2	1-1	1-4	0-4	3-1
Hucknall T	4-0	4-2	2-1	1-2	0-0	0-4	2-5	1-1	1-1	*	2-1	0-2	1-1	1-3	2-1	0-0	2-4	2-1	3-0	1-1	2-2	0-0
Kettering	1-1	0-1	0-0	2-0	1-0	0-2	0-1	0-0	3-1	2-1	*	0-2	1-2	1-0	1-0	2-1	0-5	0-1	2-0	1-1	2-1	2-1
Lancaster	0-1	1-1	2-0	2-1	0-1	0-1	2-0	0-3	2-3	3-1	1-0	*	3-1	0-2	0-0	2-1	1-1	1-0	0-1	3-1	0-2	1-0
Moor Green	0-1	2-2	2-0	1-1	1-0	1-2	2-1	2-1	2-1	2-2	1-2	0-2	*	1-3	1-0	3-0	2-3	0-1	2-2	0-2	1-2	2-0
Nuneaton	1-1	0-0	1-0	1-1	2-1	3-2	1-0	2-0	0-1	1-1	2-0	2-0	1-0	*	1-3	3-0	0-1	4-3	1-0	2-1	2-0	0-2
Redditch	1-3	0-1	3-2	3-1	3-1	1-1	0-1	0-0	3-0	1-3	2-3	0-0	3-1	1-5	*	1-0	3-2	1-0	2-3	4-1	0-4	3-2
Runcorn	1-0	2-1	2-0	1-0	2-1	1-3	1-3	2-3	3-2	1-1	2-0	2-2	2-1	0-2	0-1	*	0-2	3-3	1-1	1-1	2-2	0-1
Southport	3-1	1-2	1-2	0-0	1-0	3-0	2-1	1-1	1-1	1-0	1-3	2-2	2-1	2-3	0-1	3-1	*	0-0	2-0	2-1	2-2	1-1
Stafford	3-1	0-1	1-1	2-2	1-0	2-0	2-0	1-3	1-1	1-2	3-0	3-1	2-1	2-3	1-1	0-0	1-1	*	3-2	1-1	0-0	4-0
Stalybridge	2-3	2-1	2-1	0-0	1-4	1-3	3-2	1-1	0-2	2-0	1-2	3-1	1-0	1-1	1-0	1-0	3-5	1-0	*	2-1	1-0	2-2
Vauxhall M	2-0	2-0	0-0	0-1	1-0	1-2	1-0	1-2	1-1	1-0	0-2	2-0	4-1	0-2	1-1	1-2	0-3	0-0	1-2	*	2-2	1-1
Worcester	0-0	2-1	2-2	2-1	2-1	3-1	1-2	2-0	3-1	3-0	2-2	3-1	1-0	2-3	2-1	2-1	1-3	0-0	2-1	1-0	*	2-0
Worksop	3-2	1-1	3-1	2-1	2-1	0-2	1-3	2-0	3-1	2-1	0-3	2-0	1-0	2-3	5-3	1-1	1-2	0-0	1-1	2-3	2-0	*

	Weymouth	Weston SM	Welling	Thurrock	Sutton Utd	St Albans	Redbridge	Newport AFC	Margate	Maidenhead	Lewes	Hornchurch	Hayes	Havant & W	Grays	Eastbourne	Dorchester	Carshalton	Cambridge	Bognor	Basingstoke	B Stortford
B Stortford	0-2	2-2	4-2	0-0	3-2	2-0	2-1	3-0	3-0	2-1	1-0	3-1	0-4	1-1	1-2	2-0	2-1	2-0	3-0	2-3	1-3	*
Basingstoke	0-1	1-1	4-0	3-0	1-0	5-1	3-0	3-0	2-1	0-0	2-1	2-1	0-1	2-1	3-0	0-2	2-2	0-1	2-1	2-1	*	2-3
Bognor	2-2	3-0	6-5	3-2	0-1	4-1	4-1	0-2	2-2	1-2	1-3	2-2	1-2	7-2	1-0	1-0	2-2	1-0	1-2	*	2-1	3-1
Cambridge C	4-1	1-2	0-1	0-0	0-1	0-2	2-1	2-0	2-1	0-1	2-3	2-1	1-0	2-2	2-0	2-2	4-3	3-0	*	1-0	2-1	3-2
Carshalton	0-1	1-1	0-1	0-2	1-2	1-3	1-0	1-0	0-1	1-1	1-0	1-1	1-1	2-1	0-2	1-4	*	0-1	0-2	0-0	2-0	0-3
Dorchester	4-1	2-3	3-2	0-2	2-2	2-3	2-0	1-0	2-0	4-2	1-1	1-1	3-2	2-1	0-7	3-1	*	1-1	0-2	0-0	2-0	4-3
Eastbourne	4-2	3-0	0-1	4-0	2-2	1-1	1-2	1-0	1-1	0-0	3-1	1-2	1-0	2-1	0-6	*	3-1	1-4	1-2	4-1	2-0	1-1
Grays	2-0	2-0	4-2	2-1	5-1	2-0	4-1	1-0	5-0	1-1	4-0	1-1	1-1	3-0	*	1-1	2-2	4-0	1-2	6-0	0-1	3-0
Havant & W	1-0	3-2	2-3	0-2	2-3	1-1	1-0	1-0	3-1	2-1	2-1	4-1	1-1	3-0	0-6	2-1	4-0	4-1	0-2	0-0	5-1	0-4
Hayes	1-3	1-0	1-1	1-3	1-0	3-2	0-1	3-1	1-0	2-1	3-2	4-3	0-0	5-1	0-6	1-3	1-2	1-4	0-0	1-0	0-1	2-3
Hornchurch	2-1	3-2	0-5	0-1	3-0	1-2	5-4	1-1	1-0	6-0	3-2	*	1-1	1-5	1-2	1-1	0-1	1-3	0-1	1-1	6-0	3-1
Lewes	0-0	3-1	2-1	1-1	0-1	3-3	4-3	2-2	7-3	0-1	*	3-2	3-2	3-1	0-3	2-0	2-3	1-1	2-2	2-1	0-0	2-1
Maidenhead	2-3	0-0	2-1	0-3	2-2	2-3	2-0	0-2	2-4	*	1-0	2-2	3-2	3-1	0-6	1-0	3-1	2-1	0-1	1-5	2-1	2-2
Margate	0-1	2-0	1-2	2-1	1-1	1-0	2-3	1-1	*	2-0	1-0	1-2	0-1	3-1	1-1	2-1	1-2	0-1	0-2	1-0	2-1	1-0
Newport AFC	2-0	2-2	4-1	1-2	2-4	2-3	2-3	*	2-0	2-1	2-2	2-2	1-1	1-1	4-1	2-0	3-2	4-1	0-1	1-0	0-1	6-3
Redbridge	0-1	1-1	1-2	0-3	0-5	1-0	*	0-5	2-1	4-1	0-1	0-1	0-1	3-1	1-4	0-3	4-1	1-3	0-1	1-0	0-3	1-1
St Albans	1-0	1-1	2-5	1-2	1-2	*	2-3	0-1	3-3	1-2	2-3	4-3	0-1	3-1	0-6	0-0	1-1	3-1	0-3	4-0	2-1	2-0
Sutton Utd	0-3	1-0	1-0	1-2	*	1-2	2-3	0-0	2-0	2-2	3-5	1-2	2-4	1-1	0-6	0-0	3-2	1-2	0-3	1-0	2-1	0-0
Thurrock	2-1	3-1	1-0	*	1-2	1-2	2-3	2-2	1-2	1-2	2-0	1-1	2-1	2-1	2-4	1-0	1-2	1-4	1-2	3-1	3-1	1-0
Welling	0-1	3-1	*	1-2	3-2	1-2	1-0	3-1	1-0	2-1	2-0	1-1	2-1	0-1	2-4	0-3	1-4	1-1	2-1	1-1	3-1	1-0
Western SM	3-1	*	0-2	2-1	2-1	1-2	1-0	3-1	1-2	2-1	1-2	0-0	1-1	2-1	2-0	0-2	2-2	1-1	2-1	2-1	1-1	2-1
Weymouth	*	1-1	0-3	2-1	1-1	1-0	1-0	0-1	2-2	3-1	3-3	2-0	3-1	3-2	1-1	0-1	1-1	1-1	1-2	2-1	1-1	3-2

158

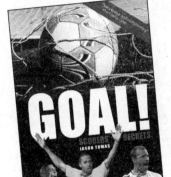

SCOTTISH PREMIER LEAGUE 2004-2005 RESULTS

	Aberdeen	Celtic	Dundee	Dundee U	D'fermline	Hearts	Hibs	Inverness	K'marnock	Livingston	Motherwell	Rangers
Aberdeen	*	0-1	1-1 1-1	1-0	2-1	0-1 2-0	0-1 3-0	0-0	3-2	2-0 2-0	2-1 1-3	0-0 1-2 1-3
Celtic	2-3 3-2 2-0	*	3-0 3-0	1-0	3-0 6-0	3-0 0-2	2-1 1-3	3-0	2-1	2-1	2-0 2-0	1-0 0-2
Dundee	1-0	2-2	*	1-0 1-2	1-2 2-1	0-1 1-1	1-4	3-1 1-1	3-1 1-0	0-0 0-1	1-2 2-1	0-2 0-2
Dundee Utd	1-1 1-2	2-3 0-3	2-2 1-2	*	1-2 0-1	2-1 1-1	1-1 1-4	2-1 1-1	3-0 0-1	1-0 1-1	0-1	1-1
Dunfermline	0-1 2-1	0-2	3-1 5-0	1-1 1-1	*	1-0 0-1	3-0	1-1 0-0	4-1	0-0	1-1 0-0	1-2 0-1
Hearts	0-0 1-0	0-2 1-2	3-0	3-2	3-0	*	1-1 2-2	1-0 0-2	3-0 3-0	0-0 3-1	0-1 0-0	1-2 0-0
Hibernian	2-1 1-2	2-2 1-3	4-4 4-0	2-0 3-2	2-1	1-1 2-2	*	2-1	0-1 3-0	2-1 0-3	1-0	0-1 0-1
Inv CT	1-3 0-1	1-3 0-2	2-1 3-2	1-1 0-1	2-0 2-0	1-1	1-2 3-0	*	0-2 1-2	2-1 0-3	1-1 1-0	1-1
Kilmarnock	0-1 0-1	2-4 0-1	3-1 1-0	5-2 3-0	1-0 2-1	1-1	3-1	2-2 0-1	*	0-2 3-1	2-0	0-1
Livingston	0-2	2-4 0-4	1-0 1-1	1-1 0-2	2-0 1-2	4-0 1-1	0-2	3-0 1-4	0-2 3-1	*	2-3 1-1	1-4
Motherwell	0-0 0-1	2-3 2-1	3-0	4-2 2-0	2-1	2-0 2-0	1-2 1-1 2-0	1-2	0-1 1-1	1-3 2-0	*	0-2 2-3
Rangers	5-0	2-0 1-2	3-0	1-1 0-1	3-0	3-2 2-1	4-1 3-0	1-1 1-0	2-0 2-1	4-0 3-0	4-1 4-1	*

SCOTTISH DIVISION ONE 2004-2005 RESULTS

	Airdrie	Clyde	Falkirk	Hamilton	Partick	Queen S	Raith	Ross C	St J'stone	St Mirren
Airdrie Utd	*	3-1 2-4	1-3 2-2	0-2 1-0	4-2 0-1	0-1 2-0	1-1 2-1	1-2 2-1	1-0 0-0	3-2 0-2
Clyde	1-2 1-0	*	0-2 0-1	2-1 0-1	2-1 1-1	2-0 0-1	2-0 1-0	1-0 1-0	1-0 1-1	0-0 0-0
Falkirk	5-0 1-0	1-1 0-0	*	1-1 1-1	2-1 3-0	4-2 1-2	4-2 2-0	2-2 1-0	3-1 3-0	0-0 1-2
Hamilton	1-3 1-1	0-1 0-1	0-1 1-0	*	0-1 1-0	1-0 1-1	2-0 1-0	1-2 0-1	1-1 0-3	2-2 0-0
Partick	3-2 1-1	0-0 1-0	1-4 2-1	0-1 1-1	*	1-0 3-1	2-0 4-1	4-0 0-0	0-4 0-4	0-3 0-0
Queen of Sth	1-0 0-0	0-1 0-1	1-3 1-1	1-1 1-2	1-0 3-1	*	1-2 0-1	0-1 1-0	0-1 2-0	2-1 0-0
Raith	0-2 0-1	2-3 3-3	0-2 3-3	2-2 0-2	0-0 2-1	1-2 0-1	*	1-2 1-4	1-0 1-2	0-3 2-0
Ross County	1-2 3-1	0-1 1-1	0-1 0-1	1-1 2-1	0-1 2-1	1-0 1-1	2-0 1-1	*	0-1 4-0	1-1 0-1
St Johnstone	1-1 1-2	3-0 0-0	1-2 0-3	3-0 0-2	0-1 2-1	1-3 0-0	1-0 2-0	1-1 0-2	*	1-0 0-0
St Mirren	1-1 1-0	0-0 0-0	2-0 0-1	1-0 0-1	2-1 1-1	2-2 3-0	1-0 3-0	3-2 1-0	2-1 1-1	*

SCOTTISH DIVISION TWO 2004-2005 RESULTS

	Alloa	Arbroath	Ayr	Berwick	Brechin	Dumbarth	Forfar	Morton	Stirling	Stranraer
Alloa	*	4-2 2-2	1-3 5-1	2-2 2-2	2-2 1-1	3-2 4-2	2-3 0-2	1-6 2-2	3-0 1-1	1-2 3-0
Arbroath	0-3 2-1	*	0-0 2-0	1-1 2-0	2-2 1-4	0-2 2-1	0-2 1-2	0-3 0-1	2-1 3-2	0-1 0-4
Ayr	4-3 1-1	1-1 2-2	*	2-1 0-1	0-1 0-1	0-1 1-1	3-3 1-0	2-0 2-1	3-2 0-3	0-1 0-0
Berwick	2-3 2-1	0-3 2-3	0-1 2-1	*	0-2 2-1	0-4 0-3	1-1 1-2	1-2 1-2	0-1 2-2	1-2 1-2
Brechin	4-0 2-3	4-1 4-3	5-0 3-0	4-1 1-1	*	4-0 0-2	2-0 0-3	2-1 3-0	0-3 5-3	4-1 2-1
Dumbarton	3-2 0-1	1-3 3-0	1-0 1-1	3-1 1-1	1-1 1-1	*	0-1 1-1	0-3 0-0	1-1 0-2	1-3 1-1
Forfar	3-1 1-1	5-0 1-1	2-3 1-0	1-1 0-2	1-0 1-3	0-2 6-0	*	0-0 2-0	0-2 4-1	0-1 1-2
Morton	2-2 2-0	2-1 2-0	0-1 2-1	2-0 4-2	0-3 0-2	3-0 0-0	2-1 4-0	*	3-0 2-0	3-1 2-0
Stirling	2-0 0-4	5-2 0-3	1-1 2-0	3-1 0-1	1-5 1-2	1-0 3-0	3-1 3-2	1-1 1-1	*	1-1 1-1
Stranraer	3-0 0-1	2-1 3-3	2-1 1-3	2-2 1-0	4-2 0-1	1-0 2-1	1-0 0-0	1-0 1-1	0-0 0-3	*

SCOTTISH DIVISION THREE 2004-2005 RESULTS

	Albion	C'beath	East Fife	Elgin	E Stirling	Gretna	Montrose	Peterhead	Queens P	Stnhsmuir
Albion	*	2-3 1-4	2-0 0-6	2-2 2-0	3-3 1-1	2-6 0-5	1-2 1-2	0-1 0-4	1-2 0-4	1-0 1-1
Cowdenbeath	2-0 1-2	*	1-1 4-2	3-1 1-1	2-1 3-2	0-8 0-1	0-0 0-0	0-4 4-0	2-1 1-0	0-6 0-2
East Fife	1-0 1-1	1-1 1-1	*	1-2 2-0	1-0 2-0	1-3 0-2	1-0 1-0	0-2 1-2	1-4 0-1	0-0 2-0
Elgin	1-0 1-1	0-4 2-0	2-1 2-1	*	1-3 0-0	1-3 2-6	1-3 2-2	0-2 2-2	1-0 1-0	1-1 4-2
E Stirling	1-1 0-2	0-2 2-1	1-1 1-0	0-1 0-3	*	8-1 1-0	1-1 1-2	1-2 1-5	0-5 3-1	1-4 3-2
Gretna	6-0 6-2	2-1 2-0	5-1 4-0	3-0 2-1	4-1 4-1	*	1-0 4-1	2-1 6-1	4-1 4-0	3-0 7-0
Montrose	1-1 0-1	3-1 1-2	2-0 2-2	2-0 2-0	5-0 3-0	2-3 0-4	*	0-1 0-2	2-4 2-0	0-2 0-3
Peterhead	4-1 2-3	3-1 1-1	2-0 0-0	2-1 3-0	5-0 3-0	1-1 4-2	3-2 4-1	*	2-2 1-1	1-1 5-0
Queen's Park	1-1 0-3	3-2 2-3	1-2 2-1	0-1 1-0	0-0 2-0	3-2 1-1	1-2 1-0	1-2 1-1	*	4-3 0-0
Stenhsmuir	3-0 1-1	2-2 1-1	5-2 1-2	0-2 4-0	6-0 3-2	0-3 1-4	1-1 0-1	1-2 1-1	1-1 0-0	*

It looks tight at the top of the pyramid

BARNET were runaway winners of last season's Conference winning the title by 12 points. Paul Fairclough's Bees were joined in League Two by Carlisle, who were promoted via the Play-Offs.

Behind Barnet, it was very tight with three points separating runners-up Hereford and seventh-placed Morecambe, who dropped from fifth to seventh on the final day off the season, missing out on a Play-Off place.

Special mention has to be made of Paul Simpson's Carlisle. It was a good effort by the Cumbrian outfit to earn promotion as their ground was out of action for over a month due to severe flooding - at one point, the pitch was under eight feet of water!

On paper, there does not seem to be an outstanding candidate for honours for the coming season and a tight League looks the likeliest scenario. The aforementioned Hereford and Morecambe must come into the reckoning as well as Stevenage, runners-up in last season's Play-Off.

Aldershot look sure to be thereabouts although they will miss the now retired Ray Warburton while local rivals Woking may find it hard to replace defensive rock Luke Oliver, who has joined Northampton.

Newly promoted Grays, Accrington and Southport, who did followers of this section a favour by winning Conference North last season, are likely to find this standard of football a considerable step-up even though last year's Trophy winners Grays ran away with the Conference South.

The two relegated sides, Kidderminster and Cambridge, may struggle to bounce straight back, particularly the latter who at the time of writing were in administration. In the circumstances, an each-way investment on last season's FA Cup heroes Exeter at a double-figure price may be pragmatic.

The Grecians finished sixth last year and hopefully most of their financial worries have been taken care of, courtesy of their two memorable encounters with Manchester United. The core of that team is still at St James Park and Alex Inglethorpe's side look well positioned to launch a title assault.

An honourable mention has to be made of Steve Burr's Northwich. Saddled with a ten-point penalty early in the season, they still finished nine points clear of the relegation places, only to be demoted on a technicality. They would be worthy winners of Conference North and look well worth backing at around 6-1. Stalybridge, who they are scheduled to meet on the first day of the new season, may provide them with most to do.

The latter failed to pull up any trees last term, finishing one place above the relegation zone, but they have made a couple of notable signings thus far, notably experienced Chris Price who captained Southport to their league title last season and are of interest at a double-figure price.

Having had my figures burned tipping Hornchurch for success in Conference South last season - Bet365 were betting without them for a time at the

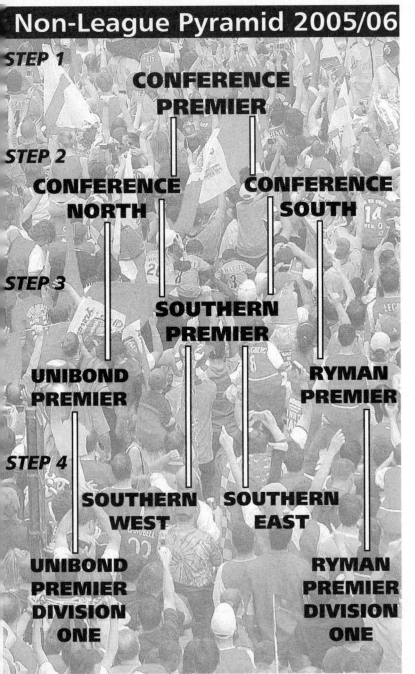

Non-League Pyramid 2005/06

STEP 1

CONFERENCE PREMIER

STEP 2

CONFERENCE NORTH

CONFERENCE SOUTH

STEP 3

SOUTHERN PREMIER

UNIBOND PREMIER

RYMAN PREMIER

STEP 4

SOUTHERN WEST

SOUTHERN EAST

UNIBOND PREMIER DIVISION ONE

RYMAN PREMIER DIVISION ONE

JUST DEVINE: Exeter skipper Sean Devine should have a decent season in the Conference

end of September and they were 1-5 chances to win the division until the company that backed them went bust in November - it may seem foolish to suggest any non-league side to win a division at a best price of less than 3-1. However, I cannot resist Weymouth in a league which appears to lack strength in depth.

Backed by millionaire owner Martyn Harrison, The Terras will be a full-time outfit this term. Manager Garry Hill, who was at Hornchurch before their demise, has brought in plenty of classy players in the close season, notably striker Wayne Purser, who Aldershot were interested in. With Kirk Jackson and Ritchie Hanlon also on the books, he has a plethora of striking talent to call upon.

As long as the money doesn't run out - and they do have the potential to attract large crowds to the Wessex Stadium - they should be a class apart. At this stage, they rate my non-league best bet.

In the Ryman Premier, it is hard to look beyond AFC Wimbledon who won Ryman Division one by nine points with a goal difference of plus 58. Manager Dave Anderson, who has just signed a new contract with

the club, has already made one useful acquisition in Matt York from Carshalton and others are sure to follow. Justin Edinburgh's Billericay may provide them with their most serious challenge.

In the Southern Premier, it may be worth chancing Salisbury. Managed by Southampton old boy Nick Holmes, they have switched leagues from the Ryman and, although they had an up-and-down season last year, it is worth remembering that they managed to beat FA Cup heroes Yeading on their own ground a couple of weeks after Premiership Newcastle were made to battle hard for success.

The Whites finished the season only losing one of their last twelve matches and are worth a small interest at a double-figure price.

Finally Telford United look worth supporting in the Unibond Premier league, again at a double-figure price.

Having been demoted three leagues after going into administration in 2004, they were promoted from Division One via the Play-Offs and look capable of further progress back up the pyramid.

164

THE CRAZY GANG

The Inside Story of Vinnie, Fash, Harry and Wimbledon FC

BY MATT ALLEN

SPECIAL OFFER
£16.99
Save £2 off
RRP of £18.99
plus free p&p

The untold story of 'The Crazy Gang' – one of the most evocative names in English football over the last 25 years. THE CRAZY GANG draws on dozens of exclusive interviews with Wimbledon's protagonists including fans, coaches, chairmen and the players themselves.

ORDER A COPY TODAY

call Highdown's credit / debit card orderline on
01635 578080
and quote ref CGFG05
or order online at www.highdownbooks.co.uk

HIGHDOWN, RFM HOUSE, COMPTON, NEWBURY RG20 6NL

x = Score draw
O = 0-0 draw
V = Void match
* = Pools panel

No	Aug 7	Aug 14	Aug 21	Aug 28	Sep 4	Sep 11	Sep 18	Sep 25	Oct 2	Oct 9	Oct 16	Oct 23	Oct 30	Nov 6	Nov 13	Nov 20	Nov 27	Dec 4	Dec 11	Dec 18	Dec 26	Jan 1	Jan 8	Jan 15	Jan 22	Jan 29	Feb 5	Feb 12	Feb 19	Feb 26	Mar 5	Mar 12	Mar 19	Mar 26	Apr 2	Apr 9	Apr 16	Apr 23	Apr 30	May 7	O	X
1																																									3	10
2																																									2	8
3																																									1	7
4																																									2	6
5																																									3	10
6																																									2	5
7																																									2	8
8																																									5	9
9																																									4	8
10																																									3	12
11																																									5	5
12																																									2	11
13																																									5	5
14																																									2	7
15																																									7	5
16																																									4	10
17																																									3	9
18																																									3	4
19																																									4	5
20																																									5	7
21																																									4	6
22																																									3	6

Top column totals:

12 4 9 6 8 9 5 7 7 9 6 6 6 5 4 6 7 5 7 8 9 5 7 7 6 6 9   **349**

3 0 1 2 1 5 2 6 4 4 3 1 5 4 3 5 4 3 1 2 0 1 5 4 4 1 3   **153**

Row		
23	3	12
24	2	5
25	9	6
26	4	14
27	3	8
28	5	9
29	3	6
30	4	13
31	5	10
32	6	5
33	5	9
34	2	11
35	2	8
36	5	8
37	3	8
38	3	10
39	5	8
40	5	9
41	3	10
42	5	8
43	2	3
44	5	9
45	1	9
46	1	8
47	6	2
48	0	10
49	3	7
	3	12
	5	9
	3	6
	8	8
	5	16
	2	12
	7	8
	4	13
	7	7
	2	4
	2	9
	4	12
	2	8
0 X		

How to read the results

Alongside each fixture are the results for the corresponding league match over the last six seasons. The most recent result (ie 2004/05) is on the right. The final figure on each fixture line is, from left to right the number of home wins draws and away wins between the two sides dating back to 1988/89.

Where Scottish clubs have met more than once in the same season each result is divided by an oblique stroke, the most recent of the matches appearing to the right.

Please note that Sky television coverage and weather conditions will cause alterations to the fixture list.

The Scottish Premier League will also spilt into top and bottom six sections later in the season. These fixtures cover the period until that split.

SATURDAY 30TH JULY 2005
BANK OF SCOTLAND SCOTTISH PREMIER LEAGUE

Dundee Utd	v	Aberdeen	3-1/1-1	3-5/1-1	1-1	1-1/0-2	3-2	1-1/1-2	10-13-07
Falkirk	v	Inv CT	0-2/2-2	2-2/2-1	1-2/0-0	1-1/2-3	2-1/2-1	-	03-04-03
Hibernian	v	Dunfermline	-	3-0	5-1/1-1	1-4/1-3	1-2	2-1	10-04-03
Kilmarnock	v	Hearts	2-2/0-1	0-3/1-1	1-0/3-3	0-1/1-0	0-2/1-1	1-1	09-07-07
Motherwell	v	Celtic	3-2/1-1	3-3	1-2/0-4	2-1/0-4	0-2/1-1	2-3	07-12-13

SUNDAY 31ST JULY 2005
BANK OF SCOTLAND SCOTTISH PREMIER LEAGUE

Rangers	v	Livingston	-	-	0-0/3-0	4-3	1-0	4-0/3-0	05-01-00

SATURDAY 6TH AUGUST 2005
COCA-COLA CHAMPIONSHIP

Crewe	v	Burnley	-	4-2	1-2	-	3-1	1-1	05-02-01
Crystal Pal	v	Luton	-	-	-	-	-	-	03-02-00
Derby	v	Brighton	-	-	-	1-0	-	3-0	03-00-00
Hull	v	QPR	-	-	-	-	-	-	00-00-00
Ipswich	v	Cardiff	-	-	-	-	1-1	3-1	01-01-00
Norwich	v	Coventry	-	-	2-0	2-0	1-1	-	04-05-01
Reading	v	Plymouth	-	-	-	-	-	0-0	02-01-00
Sheff Utd	v	Leicester	-	-	-	2-1	-	2-0	02-01-01
Southampton	v	Wolves	-	-	-	-	2-0	-	01-00-00
Stoke	v	Sheff Weds	-	-	-	3-2	-	-	01-00-00
Watford	v	Preston	-	2-3	1-1	0-1	2-0	0-2	03-01-03

168

COCA-COLA LEAGUE 1

Barnsley	v	Swindon	1-0	-	-	1-1	1-1	2-2	04-06-02
Blackpool	v	Chesterfield	2-2	1-3	1-0	1-1	1-0	1-0	06-04-03
Brentford	v	Scunthorpe	4-3	-	-	-	-	-	02-00-00
Bristol C	v	Doncaster	-	-	-	-	-	-	00-00-00
Gillingham	v	Colchester	2-1	-	-	-	-	-	02-02-03
Hartlepool	v	Bradford	-	-	-	-	-	2-1	03-00-01
Milton K	v	Bournemouth	-	-	-	-	-	1-3	00-00-01
Nottm F	v	Huddersfield	1-3	1-3	-	-	-	-	01-00-02
Oldham	v	Yeovil	-	-	-	-	-	-	00-00-00
Rotherham	v	Walsall	-	2-3	2-0	0-0	2-0	-	03-02-03
Southend	v	Port Vale	-	-	-	-	-	-	01-03-01
Swansea	v	Tranmere	-	-	-	-	-	-	01-01-00

COCA-COLA LEAGUE 2

Barnet	v	Bristol R	-	-	-	-	-	-	00-00-01
Cheltenham	v	Bury	-	-	-	-	1-2	1-0	01-00-01
Grimsby	v	Oxford Utd	-	-	-	-	-	1-1	03-02-01
Leyton O	v	Macclesfield	0-0	2-1	2-0	3-2	2-0	1-3	04-02-01
Lincoln	v	Northampton	2-2	-	-	-	0-0	3-2	06-04-01
Peterboro	v	Chester	2-1	-	-	-	-	-	05-00-00
Rushden & D	v	Darlington	-	-	2-1	2-0	-	1-2	02-00-01
Shrewsbury	v	Rochdale	2-4	0-4	1-0	3-1	-	0-2	04-01-04
Stockport	v	Mansfield	-	-	-	2-0	-	-	01-00-01
Torquay	v	Notts Co	-	-	-	-	-	-	00-00-01
Wrexham	v	Boston	-	-	-	1-1	-	-	00-01-00
Wycombe	v	Carlisle	-	-	-	-	-	-	02-00-01

BANK OF SCOTLAND SCOTTISH PREMIER LEAGUE

Aberdeen	v	Kilmarnock	2-2/5-1	1-2	2-0/1-1	0-1	3-1	3-2	11-05-05
Celtic	v	Dundee Utd	4-1/2-0	2-1	5-1/1-0	5-0/2-0	5-0/2-1/2-1	1-0	24-05-02
Dunfermline	v	Motherwell	-	1-2/1-2	5-2/3-1	1-0/3-0	1-0/3-0	1-1/0-0	09-07-06
Inv CT	v	Rangers	-	-	-	-	-	1-1	00-01-00
Livingston	v	Falkirk	1-1/0-1	4-1/3-0	-	-	-	-	04-01-03

BELL'S SCOTTISH FIRST DIVISION

Brechin	v	Hamilton	-	0-0/3-4	-	1-0/4-1	-	-	02-03-05
Dundee	v	St Mirren	-	5-0	-	-	-	-	08-01-04
Ross County	v	Clyde	2-0/2-2	0-2/2-0	4-0/2-1	1-1/1-1	0-1/0-0	0-1	04-04-03
St Johnstone	v	Queen of Sth	-	-	-	2-2/0-1	4-1/2-2	1-3/0-0	03-03-02
Stranraer	v	Airdrie Utd	-	-	-	2-0/1-2	-	-	01-00-05

BELL'S SCOTTISH SECOND DIVISION

Alloa	v	Peterhead	-	-	-	-	-	-	00-00-00
Ayr	v	Dumbarton	-	-	-	-	-	0-1	01-03-03
Morton	v	Raith	2-0/1-0	1-2/1-1	-	-	-	-	05-04-08
Gretna	v	Forfar	-	-	-	-	-	-	00-00-00
Partick	v	Stirling	1-0/1-1	3-1/1-1	-	-	-	-	04-04-04

BELL'S SCOTTISH THIRD DIVISION

Albion	v	Arbroath	-	-	-	-	-	-	02-03-11
East Fife	v	Berwick	1-2/3-1	-	-	-	3-1/2-2	-	07-06-04
E Stirling	v	Cowdenbeath	0-1/0-4	0-2/0-2	-	-	1-1/0-1	0-2/2-1	09-07-10
Elgin	v	Montrose	-	1-1/0-2	1-2/1-0	0-0/0-2	2-3/2-1	1-3/2-2	02-03-05
Queen's Park	v	Stenhsmuir	-	2-0/1-2	-	-	-	4-3/0-0	06-06-03

SUNDAY 7TH AUGUST 2005
COCA-COLA CHAMPIONSHIP

Leeds	v	Millwall	-	-	-	-	-	1-1	00-01-00

Hearts	v	Hibernian	0-3/2-1	0-0/1-1	1-1	5-1/4-4	2-0	2-1/1-2	15-11-0

MONDAY 8TH AUGUST 2005
COCA-COLA CHAMPIONSHIP

Preston	v	Derby	-	-	-	4-2	3-0	3-0	03-00-00

TUESDAY 9TH AUGUST 2005
COCA-COLA CHAMPIONSHIP

Brighton	v	Reading	-	-	3-1	0-1	-	0-1	01-00-04
Burnley	v	Sheff Utd	-	2-0	2-0	0-1	3-2	1-1	04-01-01
Cardiff	v	Leeds	-	-	-	-	-	0-0	00-01-00
Leicester	v	Stoke	-	-	-	0-0	-	1-1	02-03-01
Luton	v	Southampton	-	-	-	-	-	-	02-01-01
Millwall	v	Coventry	-	-	3-2	2-0	2-1	1-1	05-01-00
Norwich	v	Crewe	2-1	1-1	2-2	-	1-0	-	03-02-01
Plymouth	v	Watford	-	-	-	-	-	1-0	02-03-02
QPR	v	Ipswich	3-1	-	-	-	-	2-4	02-03-03
Sheff Weds	v	Hull	-	-	-	-	-	2-4	01-00-01
Wolves	v	Crystal Pal	2-1	1-3	0-1	4-0	-	-	03-01-04

COCA-COLA LEAGUE 1

Bournemouth	v	Hartlepool	-	-	-	2-1	2-2	-	02-02-01
Bradford	v	Southend	-	-	-	-	-	-	01-01-00
Colchester	v	Swansea	-	3-0	-	-	-	-	02-00-01
Doncaster	v	Milton K	-	-	-	-	-	3-0	01-00-00
Huddersfield	v	Bristol C	-	-	1-0	1-2	-	2-2	02-02-02
Port Vale	v	Gillingham	-	-	-	-	-	-	01-00-00
Scunthorpe	v	Barnsley	-	-	-	-	-	-	00-00-00
Swindon	v	Oldham	-	3-0	0-2	0-1	1-2	1-0	05-02-04
Tranmere	v	Blackpool	-	-	4-0	2-1	1-1	0-0	03-02-00
Walsall	v	Nottm F	0-2	-	2-0	2-1	4-1	-	03-00-01
Yeovil	v	Rotherham	-	-	-	-	-	-	00-00-00

COCA-COLA LEAGUE 2

Bristol R	v	Grimsby	-	-	-	-	-	3-0	01-00-03
Bury	v	Leyton O	-	-	-	0-1	1-1	0-0	04-02-01
Carlisle	v	Peterboro	1-1	-	-	-	-	-	01-05-00
Chester	v	Lincoln	1-3	-	-	-	-	0-1	03-01-02
Darlington	v	Stockport	-	-	-	-	-	-	01-00-02
Macclesfield	v	Cheltenham	1-2	2-1	1-0	-	1-2	0-2	04-02-03
Mansfield	v	Rushden & D	-	-	1-4	-	-	0-0	00-01-01
Northampton	v	Barnet	1-0	-	-	-	-	-	02-03-01
Notts Co	v	Wrexham	2-1	1-0	2-2	-	0-1	-	03-03-01
Rochdale	v	Wycombe	-	-	-	-	-	1-1	00-02-00

WEDNESDAY 10TH AUGUST 2005
COCA-COLA LEAGUE 1

Chesterfield	v	Brentford	1-0	-	0-1	0-2	1-2	3-1	02-03-04

COCA-COLA LEAGUE 2

Boston	v	Shrewsbury	-	-	-	6-0	-	2-2	01-01-00
Oxford Utd	v	Torquay	-	-	1-1	2-2	1-0	-	01-02-00

FRIDAY 12TH AUGUST 2005
COCA-COLA CHAMPIONSHIP

Cardiff	v	Watford	-	-	-	-	3-0	0-3	01-00-01

Sponsored by Stan James

Tranmere	v	Oldham	-	-	2-2	1-2	2-1	2-0	04-02-01

SATURDAY 13TH AUGUST 2005

FA BARCLAYCARD PREMIER LEAGUE

Aston Villa	v	Bolton	-	-	3-2	2-0	1-1	1-1	03-02-01
Everton	v	Man Utd	1-1	1-3	0-2	1-2	3-4	1-0	03-03-11
Fulham	v	Birmingham	0-0	0-1	-	0-1	0-0	2-3	00-03-05
Man City	v	WBA	2-1	-	0-0	1-2	-	1-1	03-03-01
Middlesbro	v	Liverpool	1-0	1-0	1-2	1-0	0-0	2-0	05-02-04
Portsmouth	v	Tottenham	-	-	-	-	2-0	1-0	02-00-00
Sunderland	v	Charlton	-	3-2	2-2	1-3	-	-	02-04-03
West Ham	v	Blackburn	-	-	2-0	2-1	-	-	07-02-01

COCA-COLA CHAMPIONSHIP

Brighton	v	Crewe	-	-	-	-	-	1-3	00-01-02
Burnley	v	Coventry	-	-	1-0	3-1	1-2	2-2	02-01-01
Leicester	v	Ipswich	-	2-1	1-1	1-2	-	2-2	02-03-05
Luton	v	Leeds	-	-	-	-	-	-	01-00-01
Millwall	v	Stoke	1-0	2-0	-	3-1	1-1	0-1	05-02-02
Norwich	v	Crystal Pal	0-1	0-0	2-1	2-0	2-1	1-1	06-05-03
Plymouth	v	Derby	-	-	-	-	-	0-2	00-01-01
Preston	v	Reading	2-2	-	-	1-0	2-1	3-0	07-02-01
QPR	v	Sheff Utd	3-1	1-3	-	-	-	0-1	05-01-04
Sheff Weds	v	Southampton	0-1	-	-	-	-	-	04-05-02
Wolves	v	Hull	-	-	-	-	-	-	00-01-01

COCA-COLA LEAGUE 1

Bournemouth	v	Bristol C	2-3	4-0	1-3	-	0-0	2-2	02-03-03
Bradford	v	Milton K	3-0	-	3-3	3-5	2-3	1-4	01-01-03
Chesterfield	v	Rotherham	-	-	-	-	-	-	01-02-00
Colchester	v	Barnsley	-	-	-	1-1	1-1	0-2	00-02-01
Doncaster	v	Hartlepool	-	-	-	-	-	2-0	05-03-00
Huddersfield	v	Swansea	-	-	-	-	3-0	-	04-02-02
Scunthorpe	v	Gillingham	1-4	-	-	-	-	-	03-04-01
Swindon	v	Nottm F	0-0	-	-	-	-	-	00-02-00
Walsall	v	Southend	-	-	-	-	-	-	01-00-00
Yeovil	v	Blackpool	-	-	-	-	-	-	00-00-00

COCA-COLA LEAGUE 2

Boston	v	Stockport	-	-	-	-	-	-	00-00-00
Bristol R	v	Peterboro	-	1-2	-	-	-	-	03-01-01
Bury	v	Shrewsbury	-	-	-	4-3	-	0-0	03-04-01
Carlisle	v	Barnet	3-1	0-2	-	-	-	1-3	04-00-04
Chester	v	Grimsby	-	-	-	-	-	2-1	01-00-01
Darlington	v	Leyton O	3-1	1-1	3-0	2-2	2-1	3-0	06-04-02
Macclesfield	v	Rushden & D	-	-	0-0	0-1	-	-	01-01-01
Mansfield	v	Torquay	4-3	0-0	2-0	-	2-1	-	06-03-01
Northampton	v	Wrexham	-	2-2	4-1	-	-	-	02-02-03
Notts Co	v	Lincoln	-	-	-	-	-	1-0	01-00-02
Oxford Utd	v	Wycombe	0-0	1-2	-	-	-	2-1	01-01-03
Rochdale	v	Cheltenham	0-0	1-1	2-2	-	0-0	1-2	00-04-01

BANK OF SCOTLAND SCOTTISH PREMIER LEAGUE

Celtic	v	Falkirk	-	-	-	-	-	-	07-00-01
Dundee Utd	v	Hearts	0-2/0-1	0-4/1-1	0-2	0-3	2-1/0-2	1-1/2-1	09-11-10
Dunfermline	v	Inv CT	4-0/1-0	-	-	-	-	1-1/0-0	02-02-00
Hibernian	v	Livingston	-	-	0-3	1-0/2-2	0-2/3-1	2-1/0-3	03-01-03
Kilmarnock	v	Motherwell	0-1/0-2	3-2/1-2	2-0/1-4	0-3/1-0	2-0	2-0	09-03-10

BELL'S SCOTTISH FIRST DIVISION

Airdrie Utd	v	Ross County	-	5-1/2-2	1-1/0-2	-	-	1-2/2-1	02-02-02
Clyde	v	Dundee	-	-	-	-	-	-	01-00-01
Hamilton	v	St Johnstone	-	-	-	-	-	1-1/0-3	03-02-03
Queen of Sth	v	Brechin	-	-	-	1-0/2-2	-	-	04-05-04
St Mirren	v	Stranraer	-	-	-	-	-	-	04-00-00

BELL'S SCOTTISH SECOND DIVISION

Dumbarton	v	Alloa	-	-	-	-	1-0/3-1	0-1/3-2	03-04-04
Forfar	v	Ayr	-	-	-	-	-	2-3/1-0	05-02-04
Peterhead	v	Partick	-	-	-	-	-	-	00-00-00
Raith	v	Gretna	-	-	-	-	-	-	00-00-00
Stirling	v	Morton	-	-	-	2-0/0-3	-	1-1/1-1	05-05-06

BELL'S SCOTTISH THIRD DIVISION

Arbroath	v	East Fife	-	-	-	-	0-1/0-0	-	04-03-06
Berwick	v	E Stirling	1-0/3-0	-	-	-	-	-	07-03-05
Cowdenb'th	v	Queen's Park	0-2/2-3	-	-	-	0-1/5-1	2-1	06-06-11
Montrose	v	Albion	2-1/1-2	0-2/0-1	1-2/2-0	0-1/1-1	1-0/3-1	1-1/0-1	12-03-11
Stenhsmuir	v	Elgin	-	-	-	-	-	0-2/4-0	01-00-01

NATIONWIDE CONFERENCE

Accrington	v	Canvey Islnd	-	-	-	-	-	1-0	01-00-00
Aldershot	v	Tamworth	-	-	-	-	1-1	4-3	01-01-00
Burton	v	Grays	-	-	-	-	-	-	00-00-00
Dagenham & R	v	Southport	-	0-1	1-1	0-3	-	-	01-02-03
Forest G	v	Cambridge U	-	-	-	-	-	-	00-00-00
Gravesend	v	Exeter	-	-	-	-	3-2	1-1	01-01-00
Hereford	v	Scarborough	4-4	1-1	6-0	0-1	2-1	1-0	06-06-03
Kidderminstr	v	Woking	3-2	-	-	-	-	-	05-01-02
Morecambe	v	Halifax	-	-	-	2-0	2-0	2-1	04-01-01
Stevenage	v	Altrincham	1-1	-	-	-	-	-	02-02-00
York	v	Crawley	-	-	-	-	-	3-1	01-00-00

SUNDAY 14TH AUGUST 2005
FA BARCLAYCARD PREMIER LEAGUE

Arsenal	v	Newcastle	0-0	5-0	1-3	1-0	3-2	1-0	09-01-03
Wigan	v	Chelsea	-	-	-	-	-	-	00-00-00

BANK OF SCOTLAND SCOTTISH PREMIER LEAGUE

Aberdeen	v	Rangers	1-5/1-1	1-2	0-3/0-1	2-2	2-3/1-1	0-0/1-2	07-11-15

MONDAY 15TH AUGUST 2005
COCA-COLA LEAGUE 1

Port Vale	v	Brentford	-	1-1	2-1	1-0	1-0	0-1	05-01-01

TUESDAY 16TH AUGUST 2005
NATIONWIDE CONFERENCE

Altrincham	v	Accrington	-	5-2	3-1	1-1	-	-	04-01-00
Cambridge U	v	Hereford	-	-	-	-	-	-	01-01-02
Canvey Islnd	v	Aldershot	2-1	1-1	1-3	0-1	-	2-2	01-02-02
Crawley	v	Dagenham & R	-	-	-	-	-	2-0	01-00-00
Exeter	v	Kidderminstr	-	2-1	2-1	2-5	-	-	02-00-01
Grays	v	Gravesend	-	2-1	2-0	-	-	-	02-00-00
Halifax	v	Burton	-	-	-	0-1	1-4	2-0	01-00-02
Scarborough	v	Morecambe	0-2	2-2	0-2	1-0	1-0	1-1	02-02-02
Southport	v	York	-	-	-	-	-	-	00-00-00
Tamworth	v	Forest G	-	-	-	-	1-0	4-0	02-00-01
Woking	v	Stevenage	0-2	1-1	1-1	1-5	1-1	1-2	04-03-04

SATURDAY 20TH AUGUST 2005

FA BARCLAYCARD PREMIER LEAGUE

Birmingham	v	Man City	0-1	-	1-2	0-2	2-1	1-0	04-00-04
Blackburn	v	Fulham	2-0	1-2	3-0	2-1	0-2	-	03-00-02
Charlton	v	Wigan	-	-	-	-	-	-	00-00-00
Liverpool	v	Sunderland	1-1	1-1	1-0	0-0	-	-	02-04-00
Man Utd	v	Aston Villa	3-0	2-0	1-0	1-1	4-0	3-1	11-06-00
Newcastle	v	West Ham	2-2	2-1	3-1	4-0	-	-	08-03-03
Tottenham	v	Middlesbro	2-3	0-0	2-1	0-3	0-0	2-0	04-04-03
WBA	v	Portsmouth	3-2	2-0	5-0	-	-	-	06-03-03

COCA-COLA CHAMPIONSHIP

Coventry	v	QPR	-				-	1-2	02-02-05
Crewe	v	Leicester	-	-	-	-	-	2-2	00-01-00
Crystal Pal	v	Plymouth	-	-	-	-	-	-	01-00-00
Derby	v	Cardiff	-	-	-	-	2-2	0-1	00-01-01
Hull	v	Brighton	2-0	0-2	-	-	-	-	04-04-04
Ipswich	v	Sheff Weds	-	-	-	2-1	-	-	01-00-04
Leeds	v	Wolves	-	-	-	-	4-1	1-1	02-01-00
Reading	v	Millwall	2-0	3-4	-	2-0	1-0	2-1	05-01-02
Sheff Utd	v	Preston	-	3-2	2-2	1-0	2-0	1-1	04-02-00
Southampton	v	Norwich	-	-	-	-	-	-	03-03-01
Stoke	v	Luton	2-1	1-3	-	-	-	-	03-01-02
Watford	v	Burnley	-	0-1	1-2	2-1	1-1	0-1	03-02-03

COCA-COLA LEAGUE 1

Barnsley	v	Yeovil	-		-	-	-	-	00-00-00
Blackpool	v	Swindon	-	-	1-0	0-0	2-2	1-1	01-04-00
Brentford	v	Tranmere	-	-	4-0	1-2	2-2	1-0	02-01-04
Bristol C	v	Port Vale	-	1-1	1-1	2-0	0-1	2-0	04-04-02
Gillingham	v	Bournemouth	4-1	-	-	-	-	-	03-01-00
Hartlepool	v	Walsall	-	-	-	-	-	-	01-01-00
Milton K	v	Colchester	-	-	-	-	-	2-0	01-00-00
Nottm F	v	Scunthorpe	-	-	-	-	-	-	00-00-00
Oldham	v	Chesterfield	1-2	-	1-1	4-0	2-0	4-1	05-01-01
Rotherham	v	Bradford	-	-	1-1	3-2	1-2	-	05-01-02
Southend	v	Huddersfield	-	-	-	-	1-2	-	00-01-04
Swansea	v	Doncaster	-	-	-	-	1-1	-	01-02-00

COCA-COLA LEAGUE 2

Barnet	v	Macclesfield	2-1	0-2	-	-	-	-	03-01-02
Cheltenham	v	Boston	-	-	-	-	1-0	1-0	04-02-00
Grimsby	v	Darlington	-	-	-	-	-	0-1	00-01-01
Leyton O	v	Rochdale	0-0	1-1	4-2	0-1	2-1	2-1	08-02-01
Lincoln	v	Oxford Utd	-	-	1-0	0-1	0-1	3-0	02-00-02
Peterboro	v	Mansfield	1-0	-	-	0-0	-	-	02-02-00
Rushden & D	v	Chester	-	2-0	-	-	-	0-1	01-00-01
Shrewsbury	v	Northampton	1-0	-	-	-	-	2-0	04-00-01
Stockport	v	Notts Co	-	-	-	0-0	2-2	-	01-03-00
Torquay	v	Bristol R	-	-	2-1	2-1	2-1	-	03-00-00
Wrexham	v	Carlisle	-	-	-	6-1	-	-	07-01-00
Wycombe	v	Bury	3-0	2-1	0-2	-	-	1-2	03-00-03

BANK OF SCOTLAND SCOTTISH PREMIER LEAGUE

Falkirk	v	Hibernian	-	-	-	-	-	-	04-04-02
Hearts	v	Aberdeen	3-0/3-0	3-0	1-0/3-1	0-0	2-0/1-0	0-0/1-0	17-07-08
Inv CT	v	Kilmarnock	-	-	-	-	-	0-2	00-00-01
Livingston	v	Dunfermline	0-1/1-0	-	0-0/4-1	1-1	0-0/0-0	2-0/1-1	04-05-03
Motherwell	v	Dundee Utd	2-2/1-3	2-1	0-0/2-0	1-2/2-2	3-1/0-1	4-2/2-0	14-06-11
Rangers	v	Celtic	4-2/4-0	5-1/0-3	0-2/1-1	3-2/1-2	0-1/1-2	2-0/1-2	15-10-09

BELL'S SCOTTISH FIRST DIVISION

Home		Away							Record
Brechin	v	Airdrie Utd	-	-	-	1-5/0-1	-	-	00-01-05
Dundee	v	Queen of Sth	-	-	-	-	-	-	00-00-00
Ross County	v	Hamilton	2-1/0-1	-	-	-	-	1-1/2-1	02-01-01
St Johnstone	v	St Mirren	-	2-0/2-2	-	2-0/1-1	1-0/1-3	1-0	10-04-03
Stranraer	v	Clyde	2-2/2-1	-	-	-	-	-	04-07-00

BELL'S SCOTTISH SECOND DIVISION

Home		Away							Record
Alloa	v	Raith	-	0-1/1-2	-	-	-	-	01-00-03
Ayr	v	Peterhead	-	-	-	-	-	-	00-00-00
Morton	v	Forfar	-	-	1-3/1-4	-	1-1/1-1	2-1/4-0	03-06-03
Gretna	v	Stirling	-	-	-	0-2/0-0	0-1/1-0	-	01-01-02
Partick	v	Dumbarton	-	-	-	-	-	-	00-00-00

BELL'S SCOTTISH THIRD DIVISION

Home		Away							Record
Albion	v	Stenhsmuir	-	-	-	-	-	1-0/1-1	02-04-05
East Fife	v	Montrose	0-0/2-0	3-1/1-0	1-2/2-0	2-0/2-0	-	1-0/1-0	12-04-04
E Stirling	v	Arbroath	-	-	-	-	-	-	05-05-07
Elgin	v	Cowdenbeath	-	2-3/0-2	-	-	0-4/0-0	0-4/2-0	01-01-04
Queen's Park	v	Berwick	1-4/0-1	1-0/0-2	-	-	-	-	08-04-05

NATIONWIDE CONFERENCE

Home		Away							Record
Altrincham	v	Forest G	1-1	-	-	-	-	-	00-01-00
Cambridge U	v	Accrington	-	-	-	-	-	-	00-00-00
Canvey Islnd	v	Gravesend	4-1	1-1	0-2	-	-	1-1	01-02-01
Crawley	v	Hereford	-	-	-	-	-	1-1	00-01-00
Exeter	v	Morecambe	-	-	-	-	4-0	1-1	01-01-00
Grays	v	York	-	-	-	-	-	-	00-00-00
Halifax	v	Aldershot	-	-	-	-	1-2	2-0	01-00-01
Scarborough	v	Kidderminstr	0-0	-	-	-	-	-	00-01-00
Southport	v	Stevenage	2-1	2-2	0-0	3-2	-	-	04-04-01
Tamworth	v	Dagenham & R	-	-	-	-	2-0	0-4	01-00-01
Woking	v	Burton	-	-	-	2-2	1-0	1-0	02-01-00

SUNDAY 21ST AUGUST 2005
FA BARCLAYCARD PREMIER LEAGUE

Home		Away							Record
Bolton	v	Everton	-	-	2-2	1-2	2-0	-	01-03-01
Chelsea	v	Arsenal	2-3	2-2	1-1	1-1	1-2	0-0	04-07-05

TUESDAY 23RD AUGUST 2005
FA BARCLAYCARD PREMIER LEAGUE

Home		Away							Record
Arsenal	v	Fulham	-	-	4-1	2-1	0-0	2-0	03-01-00
Birmingham	v	Middlesbro	-	-	-	3-0	3-1	2-0	04-01-00
Bolton	v	Newcastle	-	-	0-4	4-3	1-0	2-1	04-00-02
Charlton	v	Liverpool	-	0-4	0-2	2-0	3-2	1-2	03-00-05
Portsmouth	v	Aston Villa	-	-	-	-	2-1	1-2	01-00-01
Sunderland	v	Man City	-	1-0	-	0-3	-	-	02-01-02

WEDNESDAY 24TH AUGUST 2005
FA BARCLAYCARD PREMIER LEAGUE

Home		Away							Record
Blackburn	v	Tottenham	-	-	2-1	1-2	1-0	0-1	05-01-05
Chelsea	v	WBA	-	-	-	2-0	-	1-0	02-01-00
Everton	v	West Ham	1-0	1-1	5-0	0-0	-	-	09-02-01
Man Utd	v	Wigan	-	-	-	-	-	-	00-00-00

FRIDAY 26TH AUGUST 2005
COCA-COLA CHAMPIONSHIP

Home		Away							Record
QPR	v	Sheff Weds	-	1-2	-	-	3-0	-	05-01-03

COCA-COLA LEAGUE 1

Scunthorpe	v	Southend	-	1-1	2-0	4-1	1-1	3-2	03-04-00

SATURDAY 27TH AUGUST 2005

FA BARCLAYCARD PREMIER LEAGUE

Aston Villa	v	Blackburn	-	-	2-0	3-0	0-2	1-0	05-01-05
Fulham	v	Everton	-	-	2-0	2-0	2-1	-	03-00-00
Liverpool	v	Arsenal	2-0	4-0	1-2	2-2	1-2	2-1	09-03-05
Man City	v	Portsmouth	4-2	-	3-1	-	1-1	-	03-03-00
Tottenham	v	Chelsea	0-1	0-3	2-3	0-0	0-1	0-2	00-06-10
WBA	v	Birmingham	0-3	1-1	1-0	1-1	-	2-0	05-03-04
West Ham	v	Bolton	-	-	2-1	1-1	-	-	03-01-00
Wigan	v	Sunderland	-	-	-	-	0-0	0-1	00-01-01

COCA-COLA CHAMPIONSHIP

Burnley	v	Derby	-	-	-	2-0	1-0	0-2	03-00-01
Cardiff	v	Wolves	-	-	-	-	-	1-1	00-02-00
Crystal Pal	v	Stoke	-	-	-	1-0	6-3	-	05-01-00
Leicester	v	Luton	-	-	-	-	-	-	02-01-00
Millwall	v	Ipswich	-	-	-	1-1	0-0	3-1	02-03-01
Norwich	v	Leeds	-	-	-	-	-	-	04-01-00
Plymouth	v	Hull	0-1	1-1	1-0	-	-	-	05-03-02
Preston	v	Brighton	-	-	-	2-2	-	3-0	02-01-00
Sheff Utd	v	Coventry	-	-	0-1	0-0	2-1	1-1	01-04-03
Southampton	v	Crewe	-	-	-	-	-	-	00-00-00
Watford	v	Reading	-	-	-	0-3	1-0	0-1	02-01-02

COCA-COLA LEAGUE 1

Barnsley	v	Brentford	-	-	-	1-0	0-2	0-0	02-01-01
Bradford	v	Bournemouth	-	-	-	-	-	-	04-01-03
Bristol C	v	Milton K	-	-	-	-	-	4-1	01-00-00
Chesterfield	v	Tranmere	-	-	0-2	1-0	2-2	2-2	01-02-01
Colchester	v	Oldham	0-1	1-1	2-1	0-1	2-1	0-0	02-03-02
Gillingham	v	Nottm F	-	1-3	3-1	1-4	2-1	2-1	03-00-02
Huddersfield	v	Hartlepool	-	-	-	-	-	0-2	02-01-01
Port Vale	v	Doncaster	-	-	-	-	-	2-0	01-00-00
Rotherham	v	Blackpool	-	-	-	-	-	-	03-01-03
Swindon	v	Yeovil	-	-	-	-	-	-	00-00-00
Walsall	v	Swansea	-	5-1	-	-	-	-	02-00-01

COCA-COLA LEAGUE 2

Barnet	v	Grimsby	-	-	-	-	-	-	00-00-00
Boston	v	Mansfield	-	-	-	-	1-2	0-0	00-01-01
Bury	v	Wrexham	0-2	1-4	2-2	0-3	-	-	01-02-03
Carlisle	v	Northampton	0-1	-	-	-	1-1	-	05-01-03
Cheltenham	v	Leyton O	2-0	1-1	1-1	-	1-0	1-2	02-02-01
Chester	v	Darlington	1-2	-	-	-	-	0-3	04-01-03
Notts Co	v	Bristol R	0-2	1-1	-	-	-	1-2	05-03-02
Oxford Utd	v	Stockport	-	-	-	-	-	-	04-00-00
Peterboro	v	Torquay	0-2	-	-	-	-	1-1	03-03-02
Rochdale	v	Macclesfield	0-1	2-2	1-1	3-1	1-2	3-0	03-02-02
Rushden & D	v	Lincoln	-	-	0-0	1-0	-	1-4	01-01-01
Shrewsbury	v	Wycombe	-	-	-	-	-	0-1	01-03-01

BANK OF SCOTLAND SCOTTISH PREMIER LEAGUE

Aberdeen	v	Falkirk	-	-	-	-	-	-	03-05-00
Dundee Utd	v	Inv CT	-	-	-	-	-	2-1/1-1	01-01-00
Hearts	v	Motherwell	1-1/0-0	3-0/3-0	3-1	4-2/2-1	0-0/3-2	0-1	18-10-04
Kilmarnock	v	Livingston	-	-	1-5/1-1	2-0	0-3/4-2	1-3	07-01-04
Rangers	v	Hibernian	2-0/5-2	1-0/4-0	2-2/1-1	2-1	5-2/3-0	4-1/3-0	25-04-02

BELL'S SCOTTISH FIRST DIVISION

Airdrie Utd	v	St Johnstone	-	-	-	-	-	1-0/0-0	02-06-07
Clyde	v	Queen of Sth	3-0/3-1	-	-	2-1/2-2	3-1/2-0	2-0/0-1	15-04-04
Hamilton	v	Dundee	-	-	-	-	-	-	03-01-08
Ross County	v	Stranraer	1-1/3-1	-	-	-	-	-	01-01-00
St Mirren	v	Brechin	-	-	-	-	0-0/3-3	-	01-03-00

BELL'S SCOTTISH SECOND DIVISION

Dumbarton	v	Morton	-	-	-	-	1-0/3-0	0-3/3-0	08-00-04
Forfar	v	Peterhead	-	-	-	-	-	-	00-00-00
Gretna	v	Ayr	-	-	-	-	-	-	00-00-00
Partick	v	Raith	-	-	2-1/1-0	-	-	2-0/4-1	06-04-06
Stirling	v	Alloa	0-1/1-1	-	-	-	-	2-0/0-4	04-02-03

BELL'S SCOTTISH THIRD DIVISION

Berwick	v	Elgin	-	-	-	-	-	-	00-00-00
East Fife	v	Cowdenbeath	2-3/1-1	0-2/1-2	-	-	-	1-1/1-1	04-05-04
Montrose	v	Arbroath	-	-	-	-	-	-	08-04-02
Queen's Park	v	Albion	2-0/0-1	-	1-2/0-3	2-4/1-1	1-1/0-1	1-1/0-3	08-13-07
Stenhsmuir	v	E Stirling	-	-	-	-	-	6-0/3-2	09-03-01

NATIONWIDE CONFERENCE

Accrington	v	Exeter	-	-	-	-	1-2	0-0	00-01-01
Aldershot	v	Altrincham	-	-	-	-	-	-	00-00-00
Burton	v	Canvey Islnd	-	-	-	-	-	1-1	00-01-00
Dagenham & R	v	Scarborough	-	1-0	4-2	1-0	1-0	0-3	04-00-01
Forest G	v	Halifax	-	-	-	0-2	1-2	0-0	00-01-02
Gravesend	v	Cambridge U	-	-	-	-	-	-	00-00-00
Hereford	v	Grays	-	-	-	-	-	-	00-00-00
Kidderminstr	v	Southport	5-0	-	-	-	-	-	04-01-02
Morecambe	v	Crawley	-	-	-	-	-	1-2	00-00-01
Stevenage	v	Tamworth	-	-	-	-	3-1	2-0	02-00-00
York	v	Woking	-	-	-	-	-	0-2	00-00-01

SUNDAY 28TH AUGUST 2005
FA BARCLAYCARD PREMIER LEAGUE

Middlesbro	v	Charlton	-	0-0	0-0	1-1	0-0	2-2	05-06-01
Newcastle	v	Man Utd	3-0	1-1	4-3	2-6	1-2	1-3	03-04-06

BANK OF SCOTLAND SCOTTISH PREMIER LEAGUE

Dunfermline	v	Celtic	-	1-2/0-3	0-4	1-4/1-4	0-0/1-4	0-2	01-06-13

MONDAY 29TH AUGUST 2005
COCA-COLA CHAMPIONSHIP

Brighton	v	Plymouth	1-1	2-0	-	-	2-1	0-2	07-03-02
Coventry	v	Southampton	0-1	1-1	-	-	-	-	06-04-03
Crewe	v	Sheff Utd	1-0	1-0	2-2	-	0-1	2-3	03-01-03
Derby	v	Watford	2-0	-	-	3-0	3-2	2-2	04-03-02
Hull	v	Leicester	-	-	-	-	-	-	01-02-00
Ipswich	v	Preston	-	-	-	3-0	2-0	3-0	03-00-00
Luton	v	Millwall	0-2	0-1	-	-	-	-	02-03-06
Reading	v	Burnley	0-0	-	-	3-0	2-2	0-0	03-05-00
Stoke	v	Norwich	-	-	-	1-1	1-1	-	01-03-01

COCA-COLA LEAGUE 1

Blackpool	v	Bradford	-	-	-	-	-	2-1	03-01-01
Bournemouth	v	Walsall	-	2-2	-	-	-	2-2	02-03-02
Brentford	v	Gillingham	1-2	-	-	-	-	-	03-00-01
Doncaster	v	Huddersfield	-	-	-	-	1-1	2-1	01-01-00

Sponsored by Stan James

Hartlepool	v	Scunthorpe	-	1-0	3-2	2-2	-	-	05-01-05
Milton K	v	Port Vale	-	-	-	-	-	1-1	00-01-00
Oldham	v	Rotherham	-	2-3	-	-	-	-	00-00-01
Southend	v	Colchester	-	-	-	-	-	-	00-00-01
Swansea	v	Barnsley	-	-	-	-	-	-	00-00-00
Tranmere	v	Swindon	3-1	-	0-0	0-1	1-0	2-1	07-03-01
Yeovil	v	Chesterfield	-	-	-	-	-	-	00-00-00

COCA-COLA LEAGUE 2

Darlington	v	Rochdale	4-1	1-2	1-0	0-1	1-0	0-3	07-02-06
Grimsby	v	Rushden & D	-	-	-	-	1-0	0-0	01-01-00
Leyton O	v	Shrewsbury	1-2	2-0	2-4	0-2	-	4-1	07-00-04
Lincoln	v	Carlisle	5-0	1-1	3-1	0-1	2-0	-	06-04-03
Macclesfield	v	Bury	-	-	-	0-0	1-0	2-1	02-01-00
Mansfield	v	Notts Co	-	-	-	3-2	-	3-1	02-01-02
Northampton	v	Boston	-	-	-	-	2-0	2-1	02-00-00
Stockport	v	Peterboro	-	-	-	2-1	2-2	1-0	04-04-02
Torquay	v	Chester	2-2	-	-	-	-	-	02-03-02
Wrexham	v	Barnet	-	-	-	-	-	-	02-00-01
Wycombe	v	Cheltenham	-	-	-	1-1	-	1-1	01-03-02

NATIONWIDE CONFERENCE

Altrincham	v	Morecambe	2-2	-	-	-	-	-	01-01-01
Cambridge U	v	Kidderminstr	-	-	-	0-2	0-0	1-3	00-01-02
Canvey Islnd	v	Dagenham & R	3-1	-	-	-	-	4-2	02-00-00
Crawley	v	Stevenage	-	-	-	-	-	1-2	00-00-01
Exeter	v	Forest G	-	-	-	-	2-2	2-0	01-01-00
Grays	v	Aldershot	-	1-1	3-1	0-0	-	-	01-02-00
Halifax	v	York	0-2	1-3	1-1	-	-	2-0	02-04-03
Scarborough	v	Accrington	-	-	-	-	2-1	4-0	02-00-00
Southport	v	Burton	-	-	-	2-2	-	-	00-01-00
Tamworth	v	Hereford	-	-	-	-	1-3	2-2	00-01-01
Woking	v	Gravesend	-	-	-	2-3	3-2	2-0	02-00-01

TUESDAY 30TH AUGUST 2005
COCA-COLA CHAMPIONSHIP

Leeds	v	Crystal Pal	-	-	-	-	-	-	01-02-03
Sheff Weds	v	Cardiff	-	-	-	-	-	-	00-00-00
Wolves	v	QPR	3-2	1-1	-	-	-	2-1	03-02-01

COCA-COLA LEAGUE 1

Nottm F	v	Bristol C	-	-	-	-	-	-	00-01-00

COCA-COLA LEAGUE 2

Bristol R	v	Oxford Utd	1-0	6-2	1-1	0-2	1-1	2-0	07-02-02

SATURDAY 3RD SEPTEMBER 2005
COCA-COLA LEAGUE 1

Bournemouth	v	Tranmere	-	-	0-2	-	1-5	1-1	01-01-02
Bradford	v	Chesterfield	-	-	-	-	-	2-3	01-00-01
Bristol C	v	Colchester	1-1	1-1	3-1	1-2	1-0	0-0	02-03-01
Doncaster	v	Blackpool	-	-	-	-	-	2-0	02-00-01
Gillingham	v	Barnsley	-	0-0	3-0	-	-	-	01-01-00
Hartlepool	v	Yeovil	-	-	-	-	-	-	00-00-00
Huddersfield	v	Scunthorpe	-	-	-	-	3-2	-	01-00-00
Milton K	v	Swansea	-	-	-	-	-	-	00-00-00
Nottm F	v	Brentford	-	-	-	-	-	-	00-00-00
Port Vale	v	Rotherham	-	0-2	-	-	-	-	02-00-01
Southend	v	Oldham	-	-	-	-	-	-	01-03-00
Walsall	v	Swindon	0-0	1-0	-	-	-	3-2	02-03-00

COCA-COLA LEAGUE 2

Home	v	Away							Record
Bury	v	Carlisle	-	-	-	1-1	1-3	-	03-01-01
Cheltenham	v	Barnet	1-2	4-3	-	-	-	-	02-00-03
Chester	v	Mansfield	5-0	-	-	-	-	0-3	04-03-04
Darlington	v	Notts Co	-	-	-	-	-	1-2	00-00-02
Grimsby	v	Stockport	0-1	1-1	3-1	-	1-1	-	04-02-01
Leyton O	v	Bristol R	-	-	3-1	1-2	1-1	4-2	03-01-03
Lincoln	v	Wrexham	-	-	-	1-1	-	-	03-04-00
Macclesfield	v	Boston	-	-	-	2-0	0-0	1-1	03-03-02
Rochdale	v	Torquay	1-1	2-1	2-0	0-2	1-0	-	09-03-03
Rushden & D	v	Peterboro	-	-	-	-	0-1	-	00-00-01
Shrewsbury	v	Oxford Utd	-	-	1-0	1-2	-	3-0	03-02-01
Wycombe	v	Northampton	-	1-0	2-1	1-1	-	0-1	03-02-02

NATIONWIDE CONFERENCE

Home	v	Away							Record
Accrington	v	Woking	-	-	-	-	3-3	0-0	00-02-00
Aldershot	v	Crawley	-	-	-	-	-	1-0	01-00-00
Burton	v	Scarborough	-	-	-	1-1	2-0	2-3	01-01-01
Dagenham & R	v	Exeter	-	-	-	-	0-2	2-3	00-00-02
Forest G	v	Grays	-	-	-	-	-	-	00-00-00
Gravesend	v	Southport	-	-	-	1-3	-	-	00-00-01
Hereford	v	Altrincham	2-2	-	-	-	-	-	00-01-00
Kidderminstr	v	Canvey Islnd	-	-	-	-	-	-	00-00-00
Morecambe	v	Tamworth	-	-	-	-	4-0	3-0	02-00-00
Stevenage	v	Halifax	-	-	-	0-1	1-0	2-1	05-00-02
York	v	Cambridge U	-	-	-	3-1	2-0	-	05-00-01

SATURDAY 10TH SEPTEMBER 2005

FA BARCLAYCARD PREMIER LEAGUE

Home	v	Away							Record
Birmingham	v	Charlton	1-0	-	-	1-1	1-2	1-1	03-04-02
Chelsea	v	Sunderland	4-0	2-4	4-0	3-0	-	-	05-01-01
Everton	v	Portsmouth	-	-	-	-	1-0	2-1	02-00-00
Man Utd	v	Man City	-	1-1	-	1-1	3-1	0-0	06-05-00
Middlesbro	v	Arsenal	2-1	0-1	0-4	0-2	0-4	0-1	02-00-09
Newcastle	v	Fulham	-	-	1-1	2-0	3-1	1-4	02-01-01
Tottenham	v	Liverpool	1-0	2-1	1-0	2-3	2-1	1-1	07-04-06
WBA	v	Wigan	-	-	-	-	2-1	-	02-01-00

COCA-COLA CHAMPIONSHIP

Home	v	Away							Record
Burnley	v	Cardiff	2-1	-	-	-	1-1	1-0	05-01-00
Coventry	v	Reading	-	-	-	2-0	1-2	3-2	02-00-01
Crystal Pal	v	Hull	-	-	-	-	-	-	01-00-00
Leeds	v	Brighton	-	-	-	-	-	1-1	02-01-00
Leicester	v	Sheff Weds	3-0	-	-	1-1	-	-	02-02-03
Luton	v	Wolves	-	-	-	-	-	-	00-02-02
Millwall	v	Preston	0-2	-	2-1	2-1	0-1	2-1	04-01-03
Norwich	v	Plymouth	-	-	-	-	-	-	00-00-00
Sheff Utd	v	Ipswich	2-2	-	-	0-0	1-1	0-2	02-05-04
Southampton	v	QPR	-	-	-	-	-	-	04-00-04
Stoke	v	Watford	-	-	-	1-2	3-1	-	05-01-01

COCA-COLA LEAGUE 1

Home	v	Away							Record
Barnsley	v	Nottm F	1-0	3-4	2-1	-	-	-	03-00-01
Blackpool	v	Hartlepool	-	1-2	-	-	4-0	2-2	03-02-01
Brentford	v	Milton K	-	-	-	-	-	1-0	01-00-00
Chesterfield	v	Bournemouth	0-1	-	2-1	-	1-1	2-3	03-03-02
Colchester	v	Doncaster	-	-	-	-	-	4-1	06-01-00
Oldham	v	Huddersfield	-	-	1-1	4-0	-	2-1	03-01-01
Rotherham	v	Gillingham	-	-	3-2	1-1	1-1	1-3	01-03-02
Scunthorpe	v	Port Vale	-	-	-	-	-	-	00-00-00

Sponsored by Stan James

Swansea	v	Bristol C	-	2-2	-	-	-	-	01-02-01
Swindon	v	Southend	-	-	-	-	-	-	02-02-00
Tranmere	v	Bradford	-	-	-	-	-	4-5	03-00-02
Yeovil	v	Walsall	-	-	-	-	-	-	00-00-00

COCA-COLA LEAGUE 2

Barnet	v	Leyton O	2-2	1-2	-	-	-	-	03-02-02
Boston	v	Rochdale	-	-	-	3-1	2-0	-	02-00-00
Bristol R	v	Lincoln	-	-	1-2	2-0	3-1	0-0	03-01-01
Carlisle	v	Macclesfield	0-1	1-0	3-2	1-0	0-1	-	03-00-02
Mansfield	v	Darlington	1-2	3-2	4-2	-	3-1	1-1	05-02-04
Northampton	v	Bury	-	2-1	1-0	-	3-2	2-0	07-00-03
Notts Co	v	Chester	-	-	-	-	-	1-1	00-03-01
Oxford Utd	v	Rushden & D	-	-	3-2	3-0	-	0-0	02-01-00
Peterboro	v	Grimsby	-	-	-	-	0-0	-	01-02-02
Stockport	v	Wycombe	-	-	-	2-1	2-0	-	04-01-00
Torquay	v	Shrewsbury	3-1	0-0	2-1	2-1	-	-	05-02-02
Wrexham	v	Cheltenham	-	-	-	-	-	-	00-00-00

BANK OF SCOTLAND SCOTTISH PREMIER LEAGUE

Celtic	v	Aberdeen	7-0/5-1	6-0	2-0/1-0	7-0	4-0/1-2	2-3/3-2	22-04-06
Falkirk	v	Rangers	-	-	-	-	-	-	00-00-08
Hibernian	v	Dundee Utd	3-2/1-0	3-0/1-0	0-1	2-1/1-1	2-2	2-0/3-2	17-06-05
Inv CT	v	Motherwell	-	-	-	-	-	1-1/1-0	01-01-00
Kilmarnock	v	Dunfermline	-	2-1/2-1	0-0	2-2/1-1	1-1	1-0/2-1	07-08-02
Livingston	v	Hearts	-	-	2-1/2-0	1-1/1-1	2-3	1-2	02-02-02

BELL'S SCOTTISH FIRST DIVISION

Brechin	v	Clyde	-	-	-	-	1-3/2-5	-	06-01-08
Dundee	v	Airdrie Utd	-	-	-	-	-	-	05-03-03
Queen of Sth	v	St Mirren	-	.	-	3-0/0-2	1-2/1-0	2-1/0-0	03-01-02
St Johnstone	v	Ross County	-	-	-	1-1/2-0	1-1/1-1	1-1/0-2	01-04-01
Stranraer	v	Hamilton	0-2/2-2	-	2-1/3-2	1-2/0-0	-	-	04-03-05

BELL'S SCOTTISH SECOND DIVISION

Alloa	v	Forfar	-	-	1-2/2-1	-	1-1/4-0	2-3/0-2	03-03-10
Ayr	v	Partick	-	-	0-2/1-1	-	-	-	01-04-05
Morton	v	Gretna	-	-	-	2-2/5-0	-	-	01-01-00
Peterhead	v	Dumbarton	-	2-0/0-1	0-3/4-0	-	-	-	02-00-02
Raith	v	Stirling	-	-	-	-	-	-	03-01-02

BELL'S SCOTTISH THIRD DIVISION

Albion	v	East Fife	1-3/3-1	0-1/1-2	3-0/2-1	1-5/0-0	-	2-0/0-6	07-02-09
Arbroath	v	Stenhsmuir	0-3/2-2	3-0/5-0	-	-	2-1/1-1	-	09-03-03
Cowdenb'th	v	Berwick	1-1/1-3	-	2-1/1-1	1-2/0-1	-	-	06-04-08
E Stirling	v	Montrose	2-0/1-0	1-2/0-1	0-1/2-1	1-1/0-3	1-1/1-4	1-1/1-2	09-05-13
Elgin	v	Queen's Park	-	-	2-0/0-1	2-2/0-0	2-2/1-3	1-0/1-0	03-03-02

NATIONWIDE CONFERENCE

Altrincham	v	Dagenham & R	-	-	-	-	-	-	02-00-02
Burton	v	Accrington	-	-	3-1	-	1-1	2-2	01-02-00
Crawley	v	Canvey Islnd	-	-	-	-	-	2-1	01-00-00
Exeter	v	Cambridge U	-	-	-	1-2	-	-	03-00-06
Forest G	v	York	-	-	-	-	-	1-1	00-01-00
Grays	v	Kidderminstr	-	-	-	-	-	-	00-00-00
Halifax	v	Tamworth	-	-	-	-	1-2	3-3	00-01-01
Morecambe	v	Aldershot	-	-	-	-	2-0	0-0	01-01-00
Scarborough	v	Gravesend	-	-	-	3-2	2-0	1-0	03-00-00
Stevenage	v	Hereford	0-3	2-1	3-1	0-2	0-2	0-1	03-00-05
Woking	v	Southport	0-0	1-2	2-0	1-1	-	-	04-03-03

Sponsored by Stan James

SUNDAY 11TH SEPTEMBER 2005
FA BARCLAYCARD PREMIER LEAGUE

Bolton	v	Blackburn	3-1	1-4	1-1	1-1	2-2	0-1	03-03-02

COCA-COLA CHAMPIONSHIP

Crewe	v	Derby	-	-	-	-	3-0	1-2	01-00-01

MONDAY 12TH SEPTEMBER 2005
FA BARCLAYCARD PREMIER LEAGUE

West Ham	v	Aston Villa	1-1	1-1	1-1	2-2	-	-	03-07-02

TUESDAY 13TH SEPTEMBER 2005
COCA-COLA CHAMPIONSHIP

Brighton	v	Sheff Utd	-	-	-	2-4	-	1-1	00-02-01
Cardiff	v	Leicester	-	-	-	-	-	0-0	00-01-00
Hull	v	Stoke	-	-	-	-	-	-	01-01-02
Ipswich	v	Southampton	-	3-1	1-3	-	-	-	03-01-01
Plymouth	v	Crewe	-	-	-	1-3	-	3-0	03-00-01
Preston	v	Burnley	0-0	2-1	2-3	3-1	5-3	1-0	06-02-02
QPR	v	Luton	-	-	-	2-0	1-1	-	03-03-00
Reading	v	Crystal Pal	-	-	-	2-1	0-3	-	01-00-03
Sheff Weds	v	Leeds	0-3	-	-	-	-	-	01-04-04
Watford	v	Norwich	-	4-1	2-1	2-1	1-2	-	03-01-02
Wolves	v	Millwall	-	-	1-0	3-0	-	1-2	05-03-01

WEDNESDAY 14TH SEPTEMBER 2005
COCA-COLA CHAMPIONSHIP

Derby	v	Coventry	0-0	1-0	-	1-0	1-3	2-2	06-04-01

FRIDAY 16TH SEPTEMBER 2005
COCA-COLA CHAMPIONSHIP

Preston	v	Stoke	2-1	-	-	4-3	1-0	3-0	05-01-02

SATURDAY 17TH SEPTEMBER 2005
FA BARCLAYCARD PREMIER LEAGUE

Aston Villa	v	Tottenham	1-1	2-0	1-1	0-1	1-0	1-0	11-05-01
Charlton	v	Chelsea	-	2-0	2-1	2-3	4-2	0-4	04-00-03
Fulham	v	West Ham	-	-	0-1	0-1	-	-	00-00-02
Man City	v	Bolton	2-0	-	-	2-0	6-2	0-1	04-00-02
Portsmouth	v	Birmingham	2-2	1-1	1-1	-	3-1	1-1	03-06-03
Sunderland	v	WBA	-	-	-	1-2	0-1	-	03-04-02
Wigan	v	Middlesbro	-	-	-	-	-	-	00-00-00

COCA-COLA CHAMPIONSHIP

Brighton	v	Coventry	-	-	-	0-0	-	1-1	00-02-00
Cardiff	v	Crystal Pal	-	-	-	-	0-2	-	00-00-01
Hull	v	Luton	-	-	0-4	-	-	3-0	01-00-01
Ipswich	v	Norwich	0-2	-	-	1-1	0-2	-	05-01-04
Plymouth	v	Burnley	-	-	-	-	-	1-0	02-02-01
QPR	v	Leeds	-	-	-	-	-	1-1	04-01-02
Reading	v	Crewe	-	-	-	-	1-1	4-0	02-03-00
Sheff Weds	v	Millwall	-	-	1-1	0-1	-	-	02-02-01
Watford	v	Sheff Utd	-	4-1	0-3	2-0	0-2	0-0	03-03-03
Wolves	v	Leicester	-	-	-	1-1	4-3	1-1	05-03-01

COCA-COLA LEAGUE 1

Bournemouth	v	Swindon	-	3-0	0-0	-	2-2	2-1	02-03-02

180

Bradford	v	Yeovil	-	-	-	-	-	-	00-00-00
Bristol C	v	Blackpool	5-2	-	2-1	2-0	2-1	1-1	06-02-02
Doncaster	v	Scunthorpe	-	-	-	-	1-0	-	03-03-05
Gillingham	v	Oldham	2-1	-	-	-	-	-	03-00-00
Hartlepool	v	Swansea	0-1	-	7-1	4-0	-	-	04-01-04
Huddersfield	v	Brentford	-	-	1-1	0-2	-	-1-1	03-02-04
Milton K	v	Barnsley	-	1-1	0-1	-	-	1-1	01-02-01
Nottm F	v	Rotherham	-	-	2-0	3-2	2-2	2-2	02-02-00
Port Vale	v	Colchester	-	3-1	3-1	1-0	4-3	0-0	04-01-00
Southend	v	Tranmere	-	-	-	-	-	-	02-03-02
Walsall	v	Chesterfield	-	-	-	-	-	3-0	05-03-02

COCA-COLA LEAGUE 2

Bury	v	Boston	-	-	-	0-0	1-3	1-1	00-02-01
Cheltenham	v	Carlisle	3-1	1-0	2-0	-	2-1	-	04-00-00
Chester	v	Bristol R	-	-	-	-	-	2-2	00-03-01
Darlington	v	Oxford Utd	-	-	1-0	0-1	2-0	1-1	02-01-01
Grimsby	v	Torquay	-	-	-	-	-	-	01-01-00
Leyton O	v	Wrexham	-	-	-	0-1	-	-	00-02-02
Lincoln	v	Peterboro	1-2	-	-	-	-	-	02-01-02
Macclesfield	v	Northampton	1-0	-	-	-	0-4	1-3	01-00-03
Rochdale	v	Mansfield	2-1	1-0	3-1	-	3-0	1-1	06-04-02
Rushden & D	v	Stockport	-	-	-	-	2-2	-	00-01-00
Shrewsbury	v	Notts Co	-	-	-	-	-	1-1	01-02-02
Wycombe	v	Barnet	-	-	-	-	-	-	01-00-02

BANK OF SCOTLAND SCOTTISH PREMIER LEAGUE

Dundee Utd	v	Livingston	-	-	0-0	2-3/0-1	2-0	1-0/1-1	02-02-02
Dunfermline	v	Aberdeen	-	0-0/3-2	1-0/0-0	3-0	2-2	0-1/2-1	05-09-06
Hibernian	v	Celtic	0-2/2-1	0-0/2-5	1-4/1-1	0-1	1-2/0-4	2-2/1-3	05-08-18
Inv CT	v	Hearts	-	-	-	-	-	1-1	00-01-00
Motherwell	v	Falkirk	-	-	-	-	-	-	05-02-01
Rangers	v	Kilmarnock	2-1/1-0	0-3/5-1	3-1/5-0	6-1/4-0	4-0/2-0	2-0/2-1	19-01-04

BELL'S SCOTTISH FIRST DIVISION

Hamilton	v	Airdrie Utd	-	-	-	1-0/2-1	2-1/0-1	1-3/1-1	08-04-07
Ross County	v	Brechin	-	-	-	-	4-0/2-1	-	03-01-02
St Johnstone	v	Dundee	0-1/2-1	0-0/2-3	0-2/0-1	-	-	-	05-06-07
St Mirren	v	Clyde	-	-	4-1/2-2	1-4/1-2	2-1/2-3	0-0/0-0	03-04-03
Stranraer	v	Queen of Sth	1-0/1-2	3-2/2-0	2-2/1-2	-	-	-	09-04-07

BELL'S SCOTTISH SECOND DIVISION

Forfar	v	Dumbarton	5-0/4-3	-	-	2-0/0-1	3-1/1-0	0-2/6-0	06-00-02
Morton	v	Alloa	-	2-0/1-1	1-1/0-0	-	2-2/2-1	2-2/2-0	05-05-00
Gretna	v	Partick	-	-	-	-	-	-	00-00-00
Raith	v	Ayr	5-1/2-0	1-3/1-4	1-1/3-3	-	1-1/2-1	-	09-08-05
Stirling	v	Peterhead	-	-	2-1/0-2	1-0/2-1	3-1/0-2	-	04-00-02

BELL'S SCOTTISH THIRD DIVISION

Berwick	v	Arbroath	-	2-1/1-0	-	-	3-0/1-3	0-3/2-3	09-03-05
Cowdenb'th	v	Montrose	1-1/2-1	2-0/2-1	-	-	3-3/0-0	0-0/0-0	07-07-07
Elgin	v	Albion	-	1-2/1-0	2-0/0-0	0-1/1-2	1-5/1-2	1-0/1-1	03-02-05
Queen's Park	v	E Stirling	2-1/0-1	-	2-3/1-0	0-2/3-4	3-0/1-0	0-0/2-0	15-06-08
Stenhsmuir	v	East Fife	-	-	-	-	3-0/0-1	5-2/1-2	06-06-07

NATIONWIDE CONFERENCE

Accrington	v	Crawley	-	-	-	-	-	4-0	01-00-00
Aldershot	v	Stevenage	-	-	-	-	2-0	0-1	01-00-01
Cambridge U	v	Woking	-	-	-	-	-	-	00-00-00
Canvey Islnd	v	Scarborough	-	-	-	-	-	1-0	01-00-00

Dagenham & R v	Burton	-	-	-	1-2	0-2	3-1	01-00-02
Gravesend v	Halifax	-	-	-	1-0	1-0	0-3	02-00-01
Hereford v	Morecambe	1-1	2-2	0-2	1-2	3-0	1-1	03-03-02
Kidderminstr v	Forest G	3-3	-	-	-	-	-	00-02-00
Southport v	Exeter	-	-	-	-	-	-	00-00-00
Tamworth v	Grays	-	-	-	-	-	-	00-00-00
York v	Altrincham	-	-	-	-	-	-	00-00-00

SUNDAY 18TH SEPTEMBER 2005
FA BARCLAYCARD PREMIER LEAGUE

Blackburn v	Newcastle	-	-	2-2	5-2	1-1	2-2	08-04-01
Liverpool v	Man Utd	2-3	2-0	3-1	1-2	1-2	0-1	07-03-07

COCA-COLA CHAMPIONSHIP

Derby v	Southampton	2-0	2-2	1-0	-	-	-	05-03-01

MONDAY 19TH SEPTEMBER 2005
FA BARCLAYCARD PREMIER LEAGUE

Arsenal v	Everton	4-1	4-1	4-3	2-1	2-1	-	14-01-01

TUESDAY 20TH SEPTEMBER 2005
NATIONWIDE CONFERENCE

Accrington v	Aldershot	-	-	-	-	4-2	3-3	01-01-00
Altrincham v	Scarborough	2-1	-	-	-	-	-	01-00-00
Burton v	Morecambe	-	-	-	1-4	0-1	1-3	00-00-03
Forest G v	Crawley	-	-	-	-	-	1-1	01-01-00
Grays v	Cambridge U	-	-	-	-	-	-	00-00-00
Hereford v	Gravesend	-	-	-	3-0	3-3	1-0	02-01-00
Kidderminstr v	Halifax	-	2-1	2-0	-	-	-	06-00-01
Southport v	Tamworth	-	-	-	-	-	-	00-00-00
Stevenage v	Exeter	-	-	-	-	2-2	3-2	01-01-00
Woking v	Canvey Islnd	-	-	-	-	-	1-0	01-00-00
York v	Dagenham & R	-	-	-	-	-	0-0	00-01-00

FRIDAY 23RD SEPTEMBER 2005
COCA-COLA CHAMPIONSHIP

Luton v	Sheff Weds	-	-	-	-	3-2	1-1	02-02-01

SATURDAY 24TH SEPTEMBER 2005
FA BARCLAYCARD PREMIER LEAGUE

Birmingham v	Liverpool	-	-	-	2-1	0-3	2-0	02-00-01
Bolton v	Portsmouth	3-0	2-0	-	-	1-0	0-1	05-02-01
Chelsea v	Aston Villa	1-0	1-0	1-3	2-0	1-0	1-0	09-02-05
Everton v	Wigan	-	-	-	-	-	-	00-00-00
Man Utd v	Blackburn	-	-	2-1	3-1	2-1	0-0	08-03-00
Newcastle v	Man City	-	0-1	-	2-0	3-0	4-3	05-01-01
WBA v	Charlton	2-0	-	-	0-1	-	0-1	05-00-04
West Ham v	Arsenal	2-1	1-2	1-1	2-2	-	-	01-04-07

COCA-COLA CHAMPIONSHIP

Burnley v	Brighton	-	-	-	1-3	-	1-1	02-01-02
Coventry v	Hull	-	-	-	-	-	-	00-00-00
Crewe v	Watford	-	2-0	1-0	-	0-1	3-0	03-00-03
Crystal Pal v	Preston	-	0-2	2-0	2-0	1-1	-	02-01-01
Leeds v	Ipswich	-	1-2	2-0	-	-	1-1	03-03-02
Leicester v	QPR	-	-	-	-	-	1-0	01-01-00
Millwall v	Cardiff	2-0	-	-	-	0-0	2-2	01-02-00

Sponsored by Stan James

Norwich	v	Reading	-	-	-	0-1	2-1	-	01-03-01
Sheff Utd	v	Derby	-	-	-	2-0	1-1	0-1	03-01-02
Southampton	v	Plymouth	-	-	-	-	-	-	00-00-00
Stoke	v	Wolves	-	-	-	0-2	-	2-1	05-02-01

COCA-COLA LEAGUE 1

Barnsley	v	Doncaster	-	-	-	-	-	1-3	00-00-01
Blackpool	v	Milton K	-	-	-	-	-	1-0	01-00-00
Brentford	v	Bristol C	2-1	2-1	2-2	1-0	1-2	1-0	06-03-03
Chesterfield	v	Hartlepool	-	0-0	-	-	1-2	0-1	02-01-03
Colchester	v	Huddersfield	-	-	3-3	2-0	-	0-0	01-02-00
Oldham	v	Bournemouth	1-0	2-1	3-3	-	1-1	1-2	05-02-02
Rotherham	v	Southend	0-0	-	-	-	-	-	00-02-01
Scunthorpe	v	Walsall	-	-	-	-	-	-	03-01-01
Swansea	v	Nottm F	-	-	-	-	-	-	00-00-00
Swindon	v	Bradford	-	-	-	-	-	1-0	05-01-01
Tranmere	v	Gillingham	-	3-2	-	-	-	-	01-00-00
Yeovil	v	Port Vale	-	-	-	-	-	-	00-00-00

COCA-COLA LEAGUE 2

Barnet	v	Rochdale	1-0	3-0	-	-	-	-	07-00-02
Boston	v	Grimsby	-	-	-	-	-	1-1	00-01-00
Bristol R	v	Darlington	-	-	1-0	2-1	0-3	3-3	02-01-01
Carlisle	v	Leyton O	2-1	1-0	6-1	3-0	0-1	-	06-01-01
Mansfield	v	Wycombe	-	-	-	0-0	-	1-4	01-01-01
Northampton	v	Cheltenham	3-2	-	-	1-2	1-0	1-1	02-01-01
Notts Co	v	Rushden & D	-	-	-	-	1-3	1-1	00-01-01
Oxford Utd	v	Bury	1-1	1-0	-	2-1	1-1	3-1	03-03-01
Peterboro	v	Shrewsbury	4-1	-	-	-	-	-	02-05-00
Stockport	v	Chester	-	-	-	-	-	-	01-01-01
Torquay	v	Lincoln	5-2	1-1	2-0	0-0	1-0	-	08-02-04
Wrexham	v	Macclesfield	-	-	-	1-3	-	-	01-00-01

BANK OF SCOTLAND SCOTTISH PREMIER LEAGUE

Aberdeen	v	Livingston	-	-	0-3/3-0	0-0/1-0	0-3/1-2	2-0/2-0	04-01-03
Celtic	v	Inv CT	-	-	-	-	-	3-0	01-00-00
Dunfermline	v	Dundee Utd	-	1-0/3-1	1-1	4-1	2-0/1-1	1-1/1-1	08-10-04
Hearts	v	Rangers	0-4/1-2	0-1/1-4	2-2/0-2	0-4/0-2	0-4/1-1	0-0/1-2	06-07-21
Kilmarnock	v	Falkirk	-	-	-	-	-	-	03-04-01
Motherwell	v	Hibernian	2-2/2-0	1-3	1-3/4-0	0-2/2-1	0-1	1-2/1-1	09-12-09

BELL'S SCOTTISH FIRST DIVISION

Airdrie Utd	v	St Mirren	0-2/0-1	-	0-0/2-3	-	-	3-2/0-2	06-05-09
Brechin	v	Stranraer	-	-	-	3-1/3-1	-	4-1/2-1	06-05-03
Clyde	v	St Johnstone	-	-	-	1-2/2-1	2-0/2-3	1-0/1-1	04-01-04
Dundee	v	Ross County	-	-	-	-	-	-	00-00-00
Queen of Sth	v	Hamilton	3-2/1-1	-	0-1/3-1	-	-	1-1/1-2	03-03-02

BELL'S SCOTTISH SECOND DIVISION

Alloa	v	Gretna	-	-	-	-	-	-	00-00-00
Ayr	v	Morton	3-0/3-2	1-1/3-0	-	-	-	2-0/2-1	13-04-04
Dumbarton	v	Stirling	-	-	4-1/2-0	-	-	1-1/0-2	04-05-05
Partick	v	Forfar	-	1-1/4-0	-	-	-	-	06-04-01
Peterhead	v	Raith	-	-	-	-	-	-	00-00-00

BELL'S SCOTTISH THIRD DIVISION

Albion	v	Berwick	0-3/0-0	-	-	-	-	-	05-04-05
Arbroath	v	Cowdenbeath	-	-	-	-	-	-	06-03-06

East Fife	v	Queen's Park	0-0/0-0	-	1-4/0-3	1-1/1-0	-	1-4/0-1	06-07-04
E Stirling	v	Elgin	-	0-2/1-0	2-1/0-3	1-2/2-2	3-1/2-1	0-1/0-3	04-01-05
Montrose	v	Stenhsmuir	-	-	-	-	-	0-2/0-3	02-02-09

NATIONWIDE CONFERENCE

Aldershot	v	York	-	-	-	-	-	2-0	01-00-00
Cambridge U	v	Altrincham	-	-	-	-	-	-	00-00-00
Canvey Islnd	v	Southport	-	-	-	-	-	-	00-00-00
Crawley	v	Grays	-	-	-	-	-	-	00-00-00
Dagenham & R	v	Accrington	-	-	-	-	0-1	0-5	00-00-02
Exeter	v	Burton	-	-	-	-	2-0	3-1	02-00-00
Gravesend	v	Kidderminstr	-	-	-	-	-	-	00-00-00
Halifax	v	Hereford	-	-	-	1-0	1-2	0-1	02-02-05
Morecambe	v	Stevenage	3-3	1-2	0-3	3-1	2-1	1-3	03-02-05
Scarborough	v	Forest G	5-0	1-0	1-1	3-0	2-2	0-0	03-03-00
Tamworth	v	Woking	-	-	-	-	2-0	1-3	01-00-01

SUNDAY 25TH SEPTEMBER 2005
FA BARCLAYCARD PREMIER LEAGUE

Middlesbro	v	Sunderland	1-1	0-0	2-0	3-0	-	-	06-03-01

MONDAY 26TH SEPTEMBER 2005
FA BARCLAYCARD PREMIER LEAGUE

Tottenham	v	Fulham	-	-	4-0	1-1	0-3	2-0	02-01-01

TUESDAY 27TH SEPTEMBER 2005
COCA-COLA CHAMPIONSHIP

Burnley	v	Ipswich	-	-	-	1-1	4-2	0-2	01-01-01
Crewe	v	Wolves	1-0	2-0	1-4	-	-	1-4	02-01-03
Crystal Pal	v	Sheff Weds	-	4-1	4-1	0-0	-	-	04-04-00
Leeds	v	Derby	0-0	0-0	3-0	-	-	1-0	05-03-00
Leicester	v	Brighton	-	-	-	2-0	-	0-1	05-00-01
Luton	v	Preston	0-2	-	-	-	-	-	01-01-02
Millwall	v	QPR	-	-	-	-	-	0-0	01-01-01
Norwich	v	Hull	-	-	-	-	-	-	00-00-00
Sheff Utd	v	Plymouth	-	-	-	-	-	2-1	02-00-00
Stoke	v	Cardiff	2-1	-	1-1	-	2-3	1-3	01-01-02

COCA-COLA LEAGUE 1

Bournemouth	v	Swansea	-	2-0	-	3-0	-	-	06-00-02
Bradford	v	Colchester	-	-	-	-	-	2-2	00-01-00
Bristol C	v	Barnsley	-	-	-	2-0	2-1	0-0	05-02-02
Doncaster	v	Swindon	-	-	-	-	-	1-1	00-01-00
Gillingham	v	Chesterfield	1-0	-	-	-	-	-	04-02-05
Hartlepool	v	Rotherham	1-2	-	-	-	-	-	01-03-02
Huddersfield	v	Tranmere	1-0	3-0	2-1	1-2	-	1-3	07-01-03
Milton K	v	Scunthorpe	-	-	-	-	-	-	00-00-00
Nottm F	v	Blackpool	-	-	-	-	-	-	00-00-00
Port Vale	v	Oldham	-	0-0	3-2	1-1	1-0	3-1	07-02-01
Southend	v	Yeovil	-	-	-	-	0-2	-	00-00-01
Walsall	v	Brentford	-	3-2	-	-	-	0-1	03-01-02

COCA-COLA LEAGUE 2

Bury	v	Bristol R	0-0	1-0	-	0-1	0-0	1-1	02-05-01
Cheltenham	v	Peterboro	2-1	-	-	1-1	-	-	01-01-00
Chester	v	Carlisle	0-1	-	-	-	-	-	01-02-01
Darlington	v	Boston	-	-	-	2-3	3-0	1-0	03-00-01
Grimsby	v	Notts Co	-	-	-	-	2-0	3-2	03-02-00

eyton O	v	Torquay	0-2	0-2	1-2	2-0	0-0	-	07-01-03
incoln	v	Stockport	-	-	-	-	-	-	00-02-01
lacclesfield	v	Mansfield	5-2	0-1	0-1	-	1-1	3-1	03-01-02
tochdale	v	Oxford Utd	-	-	1-1	2-1	1-2	-	01-01-01
ushden & D	v	Northampton	-	-	-	-	-	3-2	01-00-00
hrewsbury	v	Barnet	1-1	3-2	-	-	0-1	-	03-01-02
Vycombe	v	Wrexham	0-1	1-1	5-2	-	1-1	-	03-05-01

NATIONWIDE CONFERENCE

ldershot	v	Hereford	-	-	-	-	1-2	0-2	00-00-02
Cambridge U	v	Burton	-	-	-	-	-	-	00-00-00
Canvey Islnd	v	Stevenage	-	-	-	-	-	3-0	01-00-00
Crawley	v	Kidderminstr	-	-	-	-	-	-	00-00-00
Dagenham & R	v	Grays	-	-	-	-	-	-	01-00-00
Exeter	v	Woking	-	-	-	-	1-2	0-0	00-01-01
Gravesend	v	Forest G	-	-	-	1-1	1-1	0-0	00-03-00
Halifax	v	Altrincham	-	-	-	-	-	-	00-04-00
Morecambe	v	Accrington	-	-	-	-	1-0	1-2	05-00-01
Scarborough	v	Southport	3-0	1-1	2-0	2-2	-	-	02-02-00
Tamworth	v	York	-	-	-	-	-	1-0	01-00-00

WEDNESDAY 28TH SEPTEMBER 2005
COCA-COLA CHAMPIONSHIP

Coventry	v	Watford	4-0	-	0-2	0-1	0-0	1-0	02-01-02
Southampton	v	Reading	-	-	-	-	-	-	00-00-00

FRIDAY 30TH SEPTEMBER 2005
COCA-COLA CHAMPIONSHIP

Wolves	v	Burnley	-	1-0	3-0	3-0	-	2-0	05-00-00

SATURDAY 1ST OCTOBER 2005
FA BARCLAYCARD PREMIER LEAGUE

Aston Villa	v	Middlesbro	1-0	1-1	0-0	1-0	0-2	2-0	06-04-01
Blackburn	v	WBA	2-1	1-0	-	1-1	-	1-1	03-02-02
Charlton	v	Tottenham	-	1-0	3-1	0-1	2-4	2-0	03-01-04
Fulham	v	Man Utd	-	-	2-3	1-1	1-1	1-1	00-03-01
Man City	v	Everton	-	5-0	-	3-1	5-1	0-1	07-00-04
Portsmouth	v	Newcastle	-	-	-	-	1-1	1-1	02-03-01
Sunderland	v	West Ham	1-0	1-1	1-0	0-1	2-0	0-2	04-03-02
Wigan	v	Bolton	-	-	-	-	-	-	02-02-01

COCA-COLA CHAMPIONSHIP

Brighton	v	Norwich	-	-	-	0-2	-	-	00-00-01
Cardiff	v	Luton	1-3	-	-	0-0	-	-	00-01-01
Derby	v	Leicester	3-0	2-0	2-3	1-1	-	1-2	06-01-05
Hull	v	Millwall	-	-	-	-	-	-	00-01-00
Ipswich	v	Crewe	2-1	-	-	-	6-4	-	03-00-01
Plymouth	v	Stoke	-	-	-	-	-	0-0	02-02-00
Preston	v	Southampton	-	-	-	-	-	-	00-00-00
Reading	v	Sheff Utd	-	-	-	0-2	2-1	0-0	03-01-04
Sheff Weds	v	Coventry	0-0	-	2-1	5-1	-	-	04-06-03
Watford	v	Leeds	1-2	-	-	-	-	1-2	01-01-02

COCA-COLA LEAGUE 1

Barnsley	v	Oldham	-	-	-	2-2	1-1	2-2	04-04-01
Brentford	v	Rotherham	-	0-3	-	-	-	-	03-02-03
Bristol C	v	Hartlepool	-	-	-	-	1-1	0-0	00-02-00
Colchester	v	Chesterfield	1-0	-	1-2	2-0	1-0	1-0	07-00-03
Doncaster	v	Bradford	-	-	-	-	-	1-1	00-01-00

Gillingham	v	Southend	-	-	-	-	-	-	01-01-0
Huddersfield	v	Bournemouth	-	-	1-0	-	-	3-2	03-02-0:
Milton K	v	Swindon	-	-	-	-	-	1-1	01-01-0
Nottm F	v	Tranmere	1-1	3-1	-	-	-	-	02-02-0
Port Vale	v	Walsall	1-2	0-2	-	-	-	2-0	01-00-0:
Scunthorpe	v	Yeovil	-	-	-	-	3-0	1-0	02-00-0
Swansea	v	Blackpool	-	-	-	-	-	-	02-02-0:

COCA-COLA LEAGUE 2

Barnet	v	Oxford Utd	-	-	-	-	-	-	00-00-0(
Boston	v	Peterboro	-	-	-	-	-	-	00-00-0
Bury	v	Lincoln	-	-	-	2-0	2-1	0-1	05-00-0:
Carlisle	v	Bristol R	-	-	1-0	0-0	0-2	-	02-01-0:
Cheltenham	v	Torquay	2-0	2-0	2-2	-	1-3	-	02-01-0
Leyton O	v	Mansfield	1-3	2-1	2-0	-	3-1	-	08-02-0
Macclesfield	v	Notts Co	-	-	-	-	-	1-2	01-00-0:
Northampton	v	Darlington	0-3	-	-	-	1-0	1-1	04-02-0:
Rochdale	v	Rushden & D	-	-	0-0	0-1	-	2-0	01-01-0
Shrewsbury	v	Grimsby	-	-	-	-	-	1-1	00-01-0
Wrexham	v	Stockport	-	-	-	-	0-0	2-1	03-01-0:
Wycombe	v	Chester	-	-	-	-	-	4-2	03-00-0

BANK OF SCOTLAND SCOTTISH PREMIER LEAGUE

Aberdeen	v	Motherwell	1-1/2-1	3-3	4-2/1-0	1-1	0-3/0-2	2-1/1-3	15-11-06
Dundee Utd	v	Kilmarnock	0-0/2-2	0-1	0-2/0-2	1-2/2-2	1-1/4-1	3-0	03-09-08
Falkirk	v	Hearts	-	-	-	-	-	-	05-00-0:
Hibernian	v	Inv CT	-	-	-	-	-	2-1	01-00-0
Livingston	v	Celtic	-	-	0-0/1-3	0-2	0-2	2-4/0-4	00-01-0:
Rangers	v	Dunfermline	-	4-1/2-0	4-0	3-0/6-1	4-0/4-1	3-0	18-02-00

BELL'S SCOTTISH FIRST DIVISION

Airdrie Utd	v	Clyde	-	1-3/1-0	1-2/2-2	-	-	3-1/2-4	05-05-0:
Brechin	v	Dundee	-	-	-	-	-	-	00-00-01
Hamilton	v	St Mirren	-	-	-	-	-	2-2/0-0	04-11-01
Ross County	v	Queen of Sth	1-1/2-0	-	-	2-0/0-3	1-0/1-2	1-0/1-1	04-02-02
Stranraer	v	St Johnstone	-	-	-	-	-	-	00-01-01

BELL'S SCOTTISH SECOND DIVISION

Alloa	v	Partick	1-0/1-1	-	-	-	-	-	03-01-01
Morton	v	Peterhead	-	-	-	1-0/1-0	-	-	02-00-00
Gretna	v	Dumbarton	-	-	-	-	-	-	00-00-00
Raith	v	Forfar	-	-	-	5-1/0-1	-	-	06-00-03
Stirling	v	Ayr	-	-	-	-	-	1-1/2-0	04-06-02

BELL'S SCOTTISH THIRD DIVISION

Berwick	v	Montrose	0-0/2-1	-	-	-	-	-	07-06-03
Cowdenb'th	v	Stenhsmuir	-	-	1-1/2-4	1-0/3-3	-	0-6/0-2	04-05-07
E Stirling	v	Albion	4-3/3-1	1-1/1-0	1-2/1-2	0-3/0-4	3-4/1-8	1-1/0-2	10-05-15
Elgin	v	East Fife	-	1-3/1-3	1-1/2-0	1-1/0-1	-	2-1/2-1	03-02-03
Queen's Park	v	Arbroath	-	0-0/1-1	-	-	-	-	09-05-05

NATIONWIDE CONFERENCE

Accrington	v	Gravesend	-	-	-	-	3-3	1-2	00-01-01
Altrincham	v	Crawley	-	-	-	-	-	-	00-00-00
Burton	v	Aldershot	-	-	-	-	1-4	1-3	00-00-02
Forest G	v	Morecambe	1-2	0-0	3-1	1-0	1-2	0-3	02-02-03
Grays	v	Halifax	-	-	-	-	-	-	00-00-00
Hereford	v	Canvey Islnd	-	-	-	-	-	1-0	01-00-00

186

Kidderminstr	v	Tamworth	-	-	-	-	-	-	00-00-00
Southport	v	Cambridge U	-	-	-	-	-	-	00-00-00
Stevenage	v	Dagenham & R	-	0-2	1-3	2-0	0-2	1-0	04-00-03
Woking	v	Scarborough	0-2	1-1	1-2	2-1	2-1	1-1	02-02-02
York	v	Exeter	0-0	0-3	2-3	0-2	-	1-2	03-01-04

SUNDAY 2ND OCTOBER 2005
FA BARCLAYCARD PREMIER LEAGUE

Arsenal	v	Birmingham	-	-	-	2-0	0-0	3-0	02-01-00
Liverpool	v	Chelsea	1-0	2-2	1-0	1-0	1-2	0-1	11-02-03

MONDAY 3RD OCTOBER 2005
COCA-COLA CHAMPIONSHIP

QPR	v	Crystal Pal	0-1	1-1	-	-	-	-	03-01-05

SATURDAY 8TH OCTOBER 2005
COCA-COLA LEAGUE 1

Blackpool	v	Colchester	1-1	-	2-1	3-1	0-0	1-1	03-03-00
Bournemouth	v	Doncaster	-	-	-	-	-	5-0	01-00-00
Chesterfield	v	Bristol C	0-2	-	2-1	2-0	1-1	2-2	04-04-01
Hartlepool	v	Gillingham	-	-	-	-	-	-	02-01-01
Oldham	v	Brentford	3-0	3-0	3-2	2-1	1-1	0-2	04-02-01
Rotherham	v	Barnsley	-	-	1-1	-	-	-	00-01-00
Swindon	v	Port Vale	2-1	0-1	3-0	1-2	0-0	1-0	07-03-03
Tranmere	v	Scunthorpe	-	-	-	-	-	-	01-00-00
Walsall	v	Milton K	-	-	2-1	2-0	1-0	0-0	03-01-00
Yeovil	v	Swansea	-	-	-	-	2-0	1-0	02-00-00

COCA-COLA LEAGUE 2

Bristol R	v	Northampton	-	0-1	-	-	1-2	3-1	02-02-03
Chester	v	Rochdale	0-2	-	-	-	-	0-0	02-03-02
Darlington	v	Macclesfield	3-0	1-1	0-1	0-0	0-1	3-1	03-03-02
Grimsby	v	Wycombe	-	-	-	-	3-1	0-0	01-02-00
Lincoln	v	Cheltenham	1-2	1-0	0-1	-	0-0	0-0	01-02-02
Mansfield	v	Shrewsbury	4-0	1-0	2-1	-	-	1-1	07-02-00
Notts Co	v	Boston	-	-	-	-	-	2-1	01-00-00
Oxford Utd	v	Carlisle	-	-	1-1	0-0	2-1	-	02-02-00
Peterboro	v	Wrexham	-	1-0	2-3	-	6-1	2-2	06-02-02
Rushden & D	v	Bury	-	-	-	0-1	-	3-0	01-00-01
Stockport	v	Leyton O	-	-	-	-	-	-	03-02-00
Torquay	v	Barnet	0-1	2-1	-	-	-	-	01-03-04

NATIONWIDE CONFERENCE

Accrington	v	Hereford	-	-	-	-	2-0	2-1	02-00-00
Burton	v	Stevenage	-	-	-	1-2	1-1	0-3	00-01-02
Cambridge U	v	Tamworth	-	-	-	-	-	-	00-00-00
Canvey Islnd	v	Altrincham	-	-	-	-	-	-	00-00-00
Dagenham & R	v	Aldershot	3-1	-	-	-	2-3	3-0	02-00-02
Exeter	v	Halifax	1-0	0-0	0-0	-	1-1	2-1	05-03-00
Gravesend	v	York	-	-	-	-	-	4-0	01-00-00
Kidderminstr	v	Morecambe	2-1	-	-	-	-	-	03-01-01
Scarborough	v	Crawley	-	-	-	-	-	2-2	00-01-00
Southport	v	Forest G	2-1	1-1	5-1	2-2	-	-	02-03-00
Woking	v	Grays	-	-	-	-	-	-	01-01-00

SUNDAY 9TH OCTOBER 2005
COCA-COLA LEAGUE 1

Southend	v	Nottm F	-	-	-	-	-	-	00-01-00

MONDAY 10TH OCTOBER 2005
COCA-COLA LEAGUE 1

Bradford	v	Huddersfield	-	-	-	-	2-0	02-04-03

SATURDAY 15TH OCTOBER 2005
FA BARCLAYCARD PREMIER LEAGUE

Birmingham	v	Aston Villa	-	-	3-0	0-0	2-0	02-01-00
Chelsea	v	Bolton	-	5-1	1-0	1-2	2-2	04-01-01
Liverpool	v	Blackburn	-	4-3	1-1	4-0	0-0	06-04-01
Middlesbro	v	Portsmouth	-	-	-	0-0	1-1	03-03-02
Sunderland	v	Man Utd	2-2	0-1	1-3	1-1	-	02-02-02
Tottenham	v	Everton	3-2	3-2	1-1	4-3	3-0	5-2	11-06-00
WBA	v	Arsenal	-	-	-	1-2	-	00-00-01
Wigan	v	Newcastle	-	-	-	-	-	00-00-00

COCA-COLA CHAMPIONSHIP

Brighton	v	Cardiff	-	1-0	1-0	-	-	1-1	03-02-03
Burnley	v	Leeds	-	-	-	-	-	0-1	00-00-01
Coventry	v	Crystal Pal	-	-	2-0	1-0	2-1	-	05-02-02
Crewe	v	Luton	-	-	-	0-1	-	-	00-01-01
Derby	v	Stoke	-	-	-	2-0	0-3	3-1	05-00-01
Norwich	v	Millwall	-	-	0-0	3-1	3-1	-	02-04-00
Plymouth	v	Sheff Weds	-	-	-	-	2-0	-	01-01-00
Preston	v	QPR	-	5-0	-	-	-	2-1	02-00-00
Sheff Utd	v	Wolves	3-0	1-0	2-2	3-3	-	3-3	06-05-01
Southampton	v	Hull	-	-	-	-	-	-	00-00-00
Watford	v	Leicester	1-1	-	-	1-2	-	2-2	03-03-04

COCA-COLA LEAGUE 1

Barnsley	v	Blackpool	-	-	-	2-1	3-0	1-0	03-00-00
Brentford	v	Swindon	-	0-1	2-0	3-1	0-2	2-1	03-01-03
Bristol C	v	Tranmere	-	-	2-0	2-0	2-0	4-0	05-02-03
Colchester	v	Bournemouth	3-1	3-1	1-2	-	1-0	3-1	05-00-01
Doncaster	v	Southend	-	-	-	-	2-0	-	01-00-01
Gillingham	v	Yeovil	-	-	-	-	-	-	00-00-00
Huddersfield	v	Walsall	1-1	-	-	-	-	3-1	02-01-00
Milton K	v	Chesterfield	-	-	-	-	-	1-1	00-01-00
Nottm F	v	Hartlepool	-	-	-	-	-	-	00-00-00
Port Vale	v	Bradford	-	-	-	-	-	0-1	01-04-02
Scunthorpe	v	Rotherham	-	-	-	-	-	-	02-02-00
Swansea	v	Oldham	-	1-2	-	-	-	-	00-00-01

COCA-COLA LEAGUE 2

Barnet	v	Chester	2-0	-	3-1	0-3	0-0	-	03-03-02
Boston	v	Bristol R	-	-	-	0-0	1-0	2-2	01-02-00
Bury	v	Darlington	-	-	-	2-2	1-1	0-1	03-04-01
Carlisle	v	Mansfield	0-2	2-1	0-1	-	0-2	-	02-03-04
Cheltenham	v	Grimsby	-	-	-	-	-	2-3	00-00-01
Leyton O	v	Lincoln	2-3	1-0	5-0	1-1	0-2	1-1	05-02-03
Macclesfield	v	Peterboro	1-1	-	-	-	-	-	00-02-00
Northampton	v	Oxford Utd	-	0-1	-	-	2-1	1-0	02-00-01
Rochdale	v	Notts Co	-	-	-	-	-	0-3	00-00-02
Shrewsbury	v	Stockport	-	-	-	-	-	-	01-01-02
Wrexham	v	Torquay	-	-	-	2-1	-	1-1	04-02-00
Wycombe	v	Rushden & D	-	-	-	-	0-2	1-1	00-01-01

BANK OF SCOTLAND SCOTTISH PREMIER LEAGUE

Celtic	v	Hearts	4-0/2-3	6-1/1-0	2-0/2-0	4-2/1-0	5-0/2-2	3-0/0-2	20-10-04
Dundee Utd	v	Rangers	0-4/0-2	1-1	1-6/0-1	0-3/1-4	1-3/2-0/3-3	1-1	05-08-18

Dunfermline	v	Falkirk	1-1/2-2	-	-	-	-	-	03-03-01
Hibernian	v	Kilmarnock	0-3/2-2	1-1/1-1	2-2/2-2	2-0	3-1/3-0	0-1/3-0	08-08-05
Inv CT	v	Aberdeen	-	-	-	-	-	1-3/0-1	00-00-02
Motherwell	v	Livingston	-	-	0-0/1-2	1-5/6-2	1-1	2-0	02-02-02

BELL'S SCOTTISH FIRST DIVISION

Clyde	v	Hamilton	2-1/1-0	-	-	-	-	2-1/1-3	04-02-05
Dundee	v	Stranraer	-	-	-	-	-	-	02-00-00
Queen of Sth	v	Airdrie Utd	-	-	-	-	-	1-0/0-0	01-01-01
St Johnstone	v	Brechin	-	-	-	-	3-1/2-2	-	01-01-00
St Mirren	v	Ross County	-	-	1-0/1-1	1-1/1-0	1-1/2-0	3-2	04-03-00

BELL'S SCOTTISH SECOND DIVISION

Ayr	v	Alloa	-	3-1/4-1	-	3-1/0-1	-	4-3/1-1	05-01-01
Dumbarton	v	Raith	-	-	-	0-3/4-1	-	-	01-00-03
Forfar	v	Stirling	-	1-0/3-1	-	-	-	0-2/4-1	03-03-04
Partick	v	Morton	-	-	-	-	-	-	02-03-05
Peterhead	v	Gretna	-	-	-	1-1/1-0	2-0/2-1	1-1/4-2	04-02-00

BELL'S SCOTTISH THIRD DIVISION

Albion	v	Cowdenbeath	1-4/0-3	1-0/0-0	-	-	1-2/2-4	2-3/1-4	09-02-14
Arbroath	v	Elgin	-	-	-	-	-	-	00-00-00
East Fife	v	E Stirling	1-0/3-1	3-1/4-1	0-4/1-0	4-1/3-0	-	1-0/2-0	10-07-02
Montrose	v	Queen's Park	2-1/0-2	-	3-1/3-1	1-0/1-1	0-0/1-1	2-4/2-0	12-07-06
Stenhsmuir	v	Berwick	-	2-0/0-2	3-0/1-3	2-0/1-0	0-3/3-1	-	09-08-08

NATIONWIDE CONFERENCE

Aldershot	v	Kidderminstr	-	-	-	-	-	-	00-00-00
Altrincham	v	Southport	3-0	-	-	-	1-0	2-1	04-02-01
Crawley	v	Exeter	-	-	-	-	-	0-1	00-00-01
Forest G	v	Woking	0-0	0-0	2-1	3-2	2-2	1-3	02-03-02
Grays	v	Scarborough	-	-	-	-	-	-	00-00-00
Halifax	v	Cambridge U	-	-	-	-	-	-	00-03-00
Hereford	v	Burton	-	-	-	4-0	1-2	0-0	01-01-01
Morecambe	v	Dagenham & R	-	2-3	1-1	2-1	3-2	1-0	03-02-01
Stevenage	v	Accrington	-	-	-	-	2-1	5-0	02-00-00
Tamworth	v	Gravesend	-	-	-	-	1-3	2-1	01-00-01
York	v	Canvey Islnd	-	-	-	-	-	0-0	00-01-00

SUNDAY 16TH OCTOBER 2005
FA BARCLAYCARD PREMIER LEAGUE

Man City	v	West Ham	-	1-0	-	0-1	-	-	04-01-01

COCA-COLA CHAMPIONSHIP

Reading	v	Ipswich	-	-	-	3-1	1-1	1-1	02-02-02

MONDAY 17TH OCTOBER 2005
FA BARCLAYCARD PREMIER LEAGUE

Charlton	v	Fulham	1-0	-	1-1	0-1	3-1	2-1	03-01-01

TUESDAY 18TH OCTOBER 2005
COCA-COLA CHAMPIONSHIP

Cardiff	v	Preston	0-4	-	-	-	2-2	0-1	01-02-03
Crystal Pal	v	Brighton	-	-	-	5-0	-	-	02-00-00
Hull	v	Reading	-	-	-	-	-	-	00-01-02
Ipswich	v	Coventry	-	2-0	-	2-1	1-1	3-2	04-02-01
Leeds	v	Southampton	1-0	2-0	2-0	1-1	0-0	-	07-06-01
Leicester	v	Burnley	-	-	-	0-1	-	0-0	00-01-01
Luton	v	Norwich	-	-	-	-	-	-	03-00-02
Millwall	v	Sheff Utd	-	-	2-0	1-0	2-0	1-2	05-00-01

QPR	v	Plymouth	-	-	-	2-2	3-0	3-2	02-01-00
Sheff Weds	v	Watford	2-2	2-3	2-1	2-2	-	-	02-02-01
Stoke	v	Crewe	-	-	-	-	1-1	1-0	02-01-01
Wolves	v	Derby	-	-	-	1-1	-	2-0	02-02-03

FRIDAY 21ST OCTOBER 2005
COCA-COLA CHAMPIONSHIP

Leeds	v	Sheff Utd	-	-	-	-	-	0-4	05-00-01

SATURDAY 22ND OCTOBER 2005
FA BARCLAYCARD PREMIER LEAGUE

Arsenal	v	Man City	-	5-0	-	2-1	2-1	1-1	08-03-00
Aston Villa	v	Wigan	-	-	-	-	-	-	00-00-00
Blackburn	v	Birmingham	1-0	2-1	-	1-1	1-1	3-3	03-03-00
Bolton	v	WBA	1-1	0-1	-	1-1	-	1-1	04-04-02
Fulham	v	Liverpool	-	-	0-2	3-2	1-2	2-4	01-00-03
Man Utd	v	Tottenham	3-1	2-0	4-0	1-0	3-0	0-0	13-03-01
Portsmouth	v	Charlton	0-2	-	-	-	1-2	4-2	04-01-06
West Ham	v	Middlesbro	0-1	1-0	1-0	1-0	-	-	06-02-02

COCA-COLA CHAMPIONSHIP

Cardiff	v	Crewe	-	-	-	2-1	3-0	1-1	02-04-01
Crystal Pal	v	Burnley	-	0-1	1-2	1-1	0-0	-	00-02-02
Hull	v	Derby	-	-	-	-	-	-	00-00-00
Ipswich	v	Watford	-	-	-	4-2	4-1	1-2	06-01-02
Leicester	v	Coventry	1-0	1-3	-	2-1	-	3-0	04-02-02
Luton	v	Plymouth	-	-	2-0	1-0	1-1	-	03-02-00
Millwall	v	Southampton	-	-	-	-	-	-	00-02-00
QPR	v	Norwich	2-2	2-3	-	-	-	-	05-04-03
Sheff Weds	v	Brighton	-	-	-	1-1	2-1	-	01-02-00
Stoke	v	Reading	2-1	0-0	2-0	1-0	3-0	0-1	06-03-05
Wolves	v	Preston	-	0-1	2-3	4-0	-	2-2	02-01-02

COCA-COLA LEAGUE 1

Blackpool	v	Brentford	0-1	-	1-3	1-0	1-1	2-1	05-02-05
Bournemouth	v	Port Vale	-	1-1	0-0	-	2-1	4-0	05-02-00
Bradford	v	Gillingham	-	-	5-1	1-3	0-1	-	01-00-02
Chesterfield	v	Huddersfield	-	-	1-1	1-0	-	2-1	02-02-00
Hartlepool	v	Milton K	-	-	-	-	-	5-0	01-00-00
Oldham	v	Bristol C	1-1	0-0	0-1	1-0	1-1	0-0	03-04-02
Rotherham	v	Swansea	1-1	4-2	-	-	-	-	03-06-01
Southend	v	Barnsley	-	-	-	-	-	-	03-01-02
Swindon	v	Scunthorpe	-	-	-	-	-	-	00-00-00
Tranmere	v	Colchester	-	-	0-0	1-1	1-1	1-1	00-05-00
Walsall	v	Doncaster	-	-	-	-	-	1-1	03-01-02
Yeovil	v	Nottm F	-	-	-	-	-	-	00-00-00

COCA-COLA LEAGUE 2

Bristol R	v	Wrexham	3-1	4-0	-	0-3	-	-	06-01-02
Chester	v	Bury	-	-	-	-	-	2-1	05-01-01
Darlington	v	Cheltenham	1-0	1-0	0-2	-	2-1	-	04-00-01
Grimsby	v	Leyton O	-	-	-	-	-	2-0	01-02-00
Lincoln	v	Wycombe	-	-	-	-	-	2-3	00-00-03
Mansfield	v	Barnet	0-1	4-1	-	-	-	-	04-01-03
Notts Co	v	Carlisle	-	-	-	-	-	-	01-00-00
Oxford Utd	v	Boston	-	-	-	2-1	0-0	2-0	02-01-00
Peterboro	v	Rochdale	3-3	-	-	-	-	-	03-02-01
Rushden & D	v	Shrewsbury	-	-	3-0	5-1	-	0-0	02-01-00
Stockport	v	Northampton	-	-	-	4-0	-	-	02-00-00
Torquay	v	Macclesfield	3-2	2-0	1-2	2-2	4-1	-	04-01-01

BANK OF SCOTLAND SCOTTISH PREMIER LEAGUE

berdeen	v	Hibernian	2-2/4-0	0-2/1-0	2-0	0-1	3-1/0-1	0-1/3-0	15-06-09
alkirk	v	Dundee Utd	-						01-01-04
earts	v	Dunfermline	-	2-0/7-1	1-1/2-0	2-0/3-0	1-0/2-1	3-0	16-03-02
ilmarnock	v	Celtic	0-1/1-1	0-1/1-0	0-1/0-2	1-1/0-4	0-5/0-1	2-4/0-1	04-08-12
ivingston	v	Inv CT	2-2/1-1	3-1/4-1	-	-	-	3-0/1-4	05-04-03
angers	v	Motherwell	4-1/6-2	2-0	3-0/3-0	3-0/2-0	1-0/4-0	4-1	28-01-03

BELL'S SCOTTISH FIRST DIVISION

irdrie Utd	v	Stranraer	-	-	-	2-1/3-3	-	-	05-01-00
lyde	v	Ross County	3-1/0-0	2-2/2-0	3-0/0-0	2-1/1-0	2-2/1-0	1-0/1-0	08-04-00
amilton	v	Brechin	-	4-1/1-0	-	1-2/2-2	-	-	07-01-01
ueen of Sth	v	St Johnstone	-	-	-	0-0/1-2	1-1/1-1	0-1	00-04-02
t Mirren	v	Dundee	-	2-1/2-1	-	-	-	-	07-03-04

BELL'S SCOTTISH SECOND DIVISION

umbarton	v	Ayr	-	-	-	-	-	1-0/1-1	02-04-02
orfar	v	Gretna	-	-	-	-	-	-	00-00-00
eterhead	v	Alloa	-	-	-	-	-	-	00-00-00
aith	v	Morton	3-1/3-0	0-1/0-0	-	-	-	-	09-04-03
tirling	v	Partick	3-1/0-2	1-1/0-3	-	-	-	-	04-04-04

BELL'S SCOTTISH THIRD DIVISION

rbroath	v	Albion	-	-	-	-	-	-	07-03-04
erwick	v	East Fife	0-1/0-1	-	-	-	0-2/1-1	-	03-04-10
owdenb'th	v	E Stirling	1-2/0-0	3-0/1-3	-	-	2-1/2-0	2-1/3-2	16-03-06
ontrose	v	Elgin	-	0-0/2-1	0-2/1-0	1-0/2-0	3-3/4-3	2-0/2-0	07-02-01
tenhsmuir	v	Queen's Park	-	1-1/2-0	-	-	-	1-1/0-0	06-06-03

SUNDAY 23RD OCTOBER 2005
FA BARCLAYCARD PREMIER LEAGUE

Everton	v	Chelsea	1-1	2-1	0-0	1-3	0-1	0-1	04-06-06
Newcastle	v	Sunderland	1-2	1-2	1-1	2-0	-	-	03-03-02

TUESDAY 25TH OCTOBER 2005
BELL'S SCOTTISH FIRST DIVISION

Brechin	v	Queen of Sth	-	-	-	-	0-1/2-1	-	04-03-05
Ross County	v	Airdrie Utd	-	1-1/3-4	0-1/4-1	-	-	1-2/3-1	02-01-03
St Johnstone	v	Hamilton	-	-	-	-	-	3-0/0-2	05-01-01
Stranraer	v	St Mirren	-	-	-	-	-	-	00-01-03

BELL'S SCOTTISH SECOND DIVISION

Alloa	v	Dumbarton	-	-	-	-	1-2/3-0	3-2/4-2	06-00-04
Morton	v	Stirling	-	-	-	5-1/2-2	-	3-0/2-0	07-06-03
Gretna	v	Raith	-	-	-	-	-	-	00-00-00
Partick	v	Peterhead	-	-	-	-	-	-	00-00-00

BELL'S SCOTTISH THIRD DIVISION

Albion	v	Montrose	1-3/0-2	3-2/2-1	0-0/0-0	1-1/3-0	0-1/3-0	1-2/1-2	09-06-11
East Fife	v	Arbroath	-	-	-	-	0-1/1-2	-	04-02-07
E Stirling	v	Berwick	0-3/0-1	-	-	-	-	-	07-03-05
Elgin	v	Stenhsmuir	-	-	-	-	-	1-1	00-01-00
Queen's Park	v	Cowdenbeath	1-0/3-1	-	-	-	0-0/1-2	3-2/2-3	12-03-08

WEDNESDAY 26TH OCTOBER 2005
BANK OF SCOTLAND SCOTTISH PREMIER LEAGUE

Aberdeen	v	Dundee Utd	1-2/3-1	4-1/1-2	2-1/4-0	1-2/3-0	0-1/3-0	1-0	15-06-10
Celtic	v	Motherwell	0-1/4-0	1-0/1-0	2-0	3-1	3-0/1-1	2-0/2-0	18-08-06
Dunfermline	v	Hibernian	-	1-1/2-1	1-0	1-1	0-0/1-1	1-1/1-4	04-12-02

Hearts	v	Kilmarnock	2-2/0-0	0-2/3-0	2-0	1-1/3-0	2-1	3-0/3-0	13-07-0
Inv CT	v	Falkirk	2-3/0-3	2-3/1-1	1-2/3-2	1-2/3-4	1-2/0-0	-	01-02-0
Livingston	v	Rangers	-	-	0-2/2-1	0-2/1-2	0-0/1-1	1-4	01-02-0

BELL'S SCOTTISH FIRST DIVISION

Dundee	v	Clyde	-	-	-	-	-	-	01-00-0

BELL'S SCOTTISH SECOND DIVISION

Ayr	v	Forfar	-	-	-	-	-	3-3/1-0	04-05-0

FRIDAY 28TH OCTOBER 2005
COCA-COLA CHAMPIONSHIP

Burnley	v	Hull	-	-	-	-	-	-	03-00-0

SATURDAY 29TH OCTOBER 2005
FA BARCLAYCARD PREMIER LEAGUE

Birmingham	v	Everton	-	-	-	1-1	3-0	0-1	01-01-01
Charlton	v	Bolton	2-1	-	1-2	1-1	1-2	1-2	02-02-04
Chelsea	v	Blackburn	-	-	0-0	1-2	2-2	4-0	01-05-06
Liverpool	v	West Ham	1-0	3-0	2-1	2-0	-	-	09-03-06
Middlesbro	v	Man Utd	3-4	0-2	0-1	3-1	0-1	0-2	02-02-07
Sunderland	v	Portsmouth	-	-	-	-	-	-	05-03-01
Tottenham	v	Arsenal	2-1	1-1	1-1	1-1	2-2	4-5	05-08-04
Wigan	v	Fulham	-	-	-	-	-	-	04-03-03

COCA-COLA CHAMPIONSHIP

Brighton	v	Ipswich	-	-	-	1-1	-	-	02-02-01
Coventry	v	Luton	-	-	-	-	-	-	04-00-00
Crewe	v	Crystal Pal	2-0	1-1	0-0	-	2-3	-	01-02-02
Derby	v	QPR	-	-	-	-	-	0-0	01-02-01
Norwich	v	Sheff Weds	-	1-0	2-0	3-0	-	-	06-03-00
Preston	v	Leicester	-	-	-	2-0	-	1-1	01-01-00
Reading	v	Leeds	-	-	-	-	-	1-1	00-01-00
Sheff Utd	v	Cardiff	-	-	-	-	5-3	2-1	02-00-01
Southampton	v	Stoke	-	-	-	-	-	-	00-00-00
Watford	v	Wolves	-	3-2	1-1	1-1	-	1-1	06-04-02

COCA-COLA LEAGUE 1

Barnsley	v	Walsall	3-2	-	4-1	-	-	3-2	04-00-00
Brentford	v	Bournemouth	0-2	3-2	1-0	-	1-0	2-1	07-03-02
Bristol C	v	Southend	-	-	-	-	-	-	02-02-02
Colchester	v	Yeovil	-	-	-	-	-	-	01-00-01
Doncaster	v	Tranmere	-	-	-	-	-	0-0	00-02-00
Gillingham	v	Blackpool	1-3	-	-	-	-	-	03-02-02
Huddersfield	v	Swindon	4-0	-	2-0	2-3	-	-	02-02-02
Milton K	v	Rotherham	-	-	1-0	2-1	1-2	-	02-00-01
Nottm F	v	Bradford	-	-	1-0	3-0	2-1	-	03-01-00
Port Vale	v	Hartlepool	-	-	-	-	2-5	0-1	02-00-02
Scunthorpe	v	Oldham	1-2	-	-	-	-	-	00-00-00
Swansea	v	Chesterfield	-	-	-	-	-	-	02-00-00

COCA-COLA LEAGUE 2

Barnet	v	Rushden & D	-	-	-	-	-	-	00-00-00
Boston	v	Torquay	-	-	-	2-1	4-0	-	02-00-00
Bury	v	Notts Co	1-3	1-1	0-4	-	-	1-0	03-02-02
Carlisle	v	Stockport	-	-	-	-	-	-	02-01-01
Cheltenham	v	Mansfield	1-0	2-2	2-3	3-1	4-2	2-0	04-01-01
Leyton O	v	Oxford Utd	-	-	3-0	1-2	1-0	0-0	02-02-01
Macclesfield	v	Bristol R	-	-	2-1	2-1	2-1	2-1	04-00-01
Northampton	v	Grimsby	-	-	-	-	-	0-1	01-00-01
Rochdale	v	Lincoln	1-1	3-1	2-2	0-1	0-3	3-1	07-06-03

192

Shrewsbury	v	Chester	0-1	-	-	-	0-0	5-0	06-03-01
Wrexham	v	Darlington	-	-	-	0-0	-	-	00-04-00
Wycombe	v	Peterboro	-	2-0	3-0	3-2	1-2	-	05-01-01

BANK OF SCOTLAND SCOTTISH PREMIER LEAGUE

Dundee Utd	v	Celtic	2-1/0-1	1-2/0-4	0-4	0-2	1-5	0-3/2-3	08-05-16
Falkirk	v	Livingston	0-2/2-3	3-2/1-0	-	-	-	-	04-03-02
Hibernian	v	Hearts	1-1/3-1	6-2/0-0	2-1/1-2	1-2	1-0/1-1	1-1/2-2	09-12-10
Kilmarnock	v	Aberdeen	2-0/1-0	1-0/0-0	3-1	2-2/2-0	1-3/3-1/4-0	0-1/0-1	14-05-05
Motherwell	v	Dunfermline	-	0-1/1-1	1-0	2-1	2-2/1-0	2-1	08-06-05
Rangers	v	Inv CT	-	-	-	-	-	1-0/1-1	01-01-00

BELL'S SCOTTISH FIRST DIVISION

Airdrie Utd	v	Dundee	-	-	-	-	-	-	02-05-05
Clyde	v	Brechin	-	-	-	-	2-1/0-0	-	05-07-02
Hamilton	v	Stranraer	2-1/2-0	-	0-1/2-0	1-5/1-2	-	-	08-00-04
Ross County	v	St Johnstone	-	-	-	0-0/2-3	0-3/2-0	0-1/4-0	02-01-03
St Mirren	v	Queen of Sth	-	-	-	2-1/2-2	1-2/3-1	2-2/3-0	03-02-01

BELL'S SCOTTISH SECOND DIVISION

Dumbarton	v	Peterhead	-	1-3/2-2	0-3/3-0	-	-	-	01-01-02
Forfar	v	Alloa	-	-	0-1/4-1	-	1-1/2-0	3-1	08-05-03
Gretna	v	Morton	-	-	-	1-1/0-1	-	-	00-01-01
Partick	v	Ayr	-	-	2-1/2-1	-	-	-	07-02-02
Stirling	v	Raith	-	-	-	-	-	-	02-01-03

BELL'S SCOTTISH THIRD DIVISION

Berwick	v	Cowdenbeath	0-2/0-0	-	2-5/1-0	2-1/1-2	-	-	07-03-07
East Fife	v	Albion	1-4/2-1	0-0/2-1	0-0/2-3	0-4/1-1	-	1-0	07-05-04
Montrose	v	E Stirling	1-2/0-0	0-1/1-1	2-0/2-0	2-2/5-4	5-1/1-0	4-1/4-1	16-07-05
Queen's Park	v	Elgin	-	-	0-0/3-0	1-2/3-2	5-2/4-0	0-1	04-01-02
Stenhsmuir	v	Arbroath	1-3/3-0	3-1/0-1	-	-	1-0/0-3	-	10-01-04

NATIONWIDE CONFERENCE

Accrington	v	York	-	-	-	-	-	2-2	00-01-00
Burton	v	Altrincham	-	-	1-1	-	-	-	00-01-00
Cambridge U	v	Crawley	-	-	-	-	-	-	00-00-00
Canvey Islnd	v	Morecambe	-	-	-	-	-	0-0	00-01-00
Dagenham & R	v	Forest G	-	3-1	1-1	3-1	5-2	2-2	03-02-00
Exeter	v	Tamworth	-	-	-	-	3-2	2-2	01-01-00
Gravesend	v	Stevenage	-	-	-	2-1	2-3	2-1	02-00-01
Kidderminstr	v	Hereford	1-1	-	-	-	-	-	01-01-01
Scarborough	v	Aldershot	-	-	-	-	1-0	2-2	01-01-00
Southport	v	Grays	-	-	-	-	-	-	00-00-00
Woking	v	Halifax	-	-	-	2-1	2-2	2-1	03-03-02

SUNDAY 30TH OCTOBER 2005
FA BARCLAYCARD PREMIER LEAGUE

WBA	v	Newcastle	-	-	-	2-2	-	0-0	00-03-01

COCA-COLA CHAMPIONSHIP

Plymouth	v	Millwall	-	-	-	-	-	0-0	03-02-00

MONDAY 31ST OCTOBER 2005
FA BARCLAYCARD PREMIER LEAGUE

Man City	v	Aston Villa	-	1-3	-	3-1	4-1	2-0	07-02-02

TUESDAY 1ST NOVEMBER 2005
COCA-COLA CHAMPIONSHIP

Brighton	v	Wolves	-	-	-	4-1	-	0-1	01-03-01

Burnley	v	Millwall	4-3	-	0-0	2-2	1-1	1-0	04-03-02
Crewe	v	Leeds	-	-	-	-	-	2-2	00-01-00
Norwich	v	Cardiff	-	-	-	-	4-1	-	01-00-00
Plymouth	v	Leicester	-	-	-	-	-	-	02-02-00
Preston	v	Hull	-	-	-	-	-	-	01-00-01
Reading	v	Sheff Weds	-	-	-	2-1	-	-	01-00-00
Sheff Utd	v	Luton	-	-	-	-	-	-	02-01-01
Watford	v	QPR	-	3-1	-	-	-	3-0	03-00-00

WEDNESDAY 2ND NOVEMBER 2005
COCA-COLA CHAMPIONSHIP

Coventry	v	Stoke	-	-	-	0-1	4-2	0-0	01-01-01
Derby	v	Ipswich	-	1-1	1-3	1-4	2-2	3-2	02-03-02
Southampton	v	Crystal Pal	-	-	-	-	-	2-2	04-02-01

SATURDAY 5TH NOVEMBER 2005
FA BARCLAYCARD PREMIER LEAGUE

Arsenal	v	Sunderland	4-1	2-2	3-0	3-1	-	-	05-01-00
Aston Villa	v	Liverpool	0-0	0-3	1-2	0-1	0-0	1-1	06-06-05
Blackburn	v	Charlton	1-1	-	4-1	1-0	0-1	1-0	04-02-02
Everton	v	Middlesbro	0-2	2-2	2-0	2-1	1-1	1-0	06-03-02
Fulham	v	Man City	0-0	-	-	0-1	2-2	1-1	01-03-01
Newcastle	v	Birmingham	-	-	-	1-0	0-1	2-1	02-01-01
Portsmouth	v	Wigan	-	-	-	-	-	-	00-00-00
West Ham	v	WBA	-	-	-	0-1	3-4	-	01-00-03

COCA-COLA CHAMPIONSHIP

Cardiff	v	Coventry	-	-	-	-	0-1	2-1	01-00-01
Crystal Pal	v	Sheff Utd	1-1	0-1	0-1	2-2	1-2	-	04-03-04
Hull	v	Watford	-	-	-	-	-	-	00-02-01
Ipswich	v	Plymouth	-	-	-	-	-	3-2	04-01-00
Leeds	v	Preston	-	-	-	-	-	1-0	01-00-00
Leicester	v	Southampton	2-1	1-0	0-4	-	2-2	-	05-02-01
Luton	v	Burnley	2-1	-	-	-	-	-	02-00-03
Millwall	v	Crewe	-	-	2-0	-	1-1	4-3	03-01-00
QPR	v	Reading	-	-	0-0	-	-	0-0	00-03-01
Sheff Weds	v	Derby	0-2	-	-	1-3	-	-	01-02-04
Stoke	v	Brighton	-	-	3-1	1-0	-	2-0	04-02-00
Wolves	v	Norwich	1-0	4-0	0-0	1-0	-	-	05-02-01

BANK OF SCOTLAND SCOTTISH PREMIER LEAGUE

Falkirk	v	Celtic	-	-	-	-	-	-	01-02-05
Hearts	v	Dundee Utd	3-0/1-2	3-1	1-2/1-2	2-0/2-1	3-0/3-1	3-2	20-05-05
Inv CT	v	Dunfermline	1-1/1-2	-	-	-	-	2-0/2-0	02-01-01
Livingston	v	Hibernian	-	-	1-0/0-3	1-2/1-2	1-0/4-1	0-2	03-00-04
Motherwell	v	Kilmarnock	0-4/2-0	1-2	2-2/2-0	0-1	2-1/1-0	0-1/1-1	10-05-07
Rangers	v	Aberdeen	3-0/5-0	3-1/1-0	2-0/2-0	2-0/2-1	3-0	5-0	24-06-02

BELL'S SCOTTISH FIRST DIVISION

Brechin	v	St Mirren	-	-	-	-	1-1/2-0	-	01-01-02
Dundee	v	Hamilton	-	-	-	-	-	-	07-02-02
Queen of Sth	v	Clyde	1-1/3-0	-	-	2-1/1-1	4-1/1-2	0-1/0-1	09-04-09
St Johnstone	v	Airdrie Utd	-	-	-	-	-	1-1/1-2	08-05-02
Stranraer	v	Ross County	0-0/0-2	-	-	-	-	-	00-01-01

BELL'S SCOTTISH SECOND DIVISION

Alloa	v	Stirling	4-4/1-0	-	-	-	-	1-1/3-0	05-03-01
Ayr	v	Gretna	-	-	-	-	-	-	00-00-00

Morton	v	Dumbarton	-	-	-	-	2-2/3-2	3-0/0-0	07-03-02
Peterhead	v	Forfar	-	-	-	-	-	-	00-00-00
Raith	v	Partick	-	-	1-2/2-0	-	-	0-0/2-1	07-06-04

BELL'S SCOTTISH THIRD DIVISION

Albion	v	Queen's Park	2-4/0-3	-	2-1/2-0	0-2/2-1	3-1/3-1	0-4/1-2	13-05-09
Arbroath	v	Montrose	-	-	-	-	-	-	04-04-05
Cowdenb'th	v	East Fife	4-0/1-0	1-0/3-2	-	-	-	1-1/4-2	07-04-03
E Stirling	v	Stenhsmuir	-	-	-	-	-	3-2/1-4	03-04-06
Elgin	v	Berwick	-	-	-	-	-	-	00-00-00

SUNDAY 6TH NOVEMBER 2005
FA BARCLAYCARD PREMIER LEAGUE

Man Utd	v	Chelsea	3-2	3-3	0-3	2-1	1-1	-	03-08-04

MONDAY 7TH NOVEMBER 2005
FA BARCLAYCARD PREMIER LEAGUE

Bolton	v	Tottenham	-	-	1-1	1-0	2-0	3-1	03-02-01

FRIDAY 11TH NOVEMBER 2005
COCA-COLA LEAGUE 1

Swindon	v	Bristol C	-	1-1	1-2	1-1	1-1	0-0	04-04-03

SATURDAY 12TH NOVEMBER 2005
COCA-COLA LEAGUE 1

Bournemouth	v	Nottm F	-	-	-	-	-	-	00-00-00
Bradford	v	Barnsley	-	-	4-0	-	-	1-0	03-02-01
Chesterfield	v	Port Vale	-	-	1-1	2-1	1-0	1-0	03-01-01
Hartlepool	v	Brentford	-	-	-	-	1-2	3-1	02-00-03
Oldham	v	Doncaster	-	-	-	-	-	1-2	00-00-01
Rotherham	v	Colchester	-	3-2	-	-	-	-	03-00-00
Southend	v	Swansea	2-1	-	4-2	0-2	1-1	4-2	05-01-02
Tranmere	v	Milton K	-	0-4	-	-	-	2-0	01-00-01
Walsall	v	Gillingham	-	-	1-1	1-0	2-1	-	07-03-01
Yeovil	v	Huddersfield	-	-	-	-	2-1	-	01-00-00

COCA-COLA LEAGUE 2

Bristol R	v	Rochdale	-	-	0-2	1-2	0-0	0-0	00-02-02
Chester	v	Northampton	0-2	-	-	-	-	-	04-00-02
Darlington	v	Wycombe	-	-	-	-	-	1-0	01-01-01
Grimsby	v	Macclesfield	-	-	-	-	-	0-0	00-01-00
Lincoln	v	Shrewsbury	1-2	2-2	1-2	1-1	-	2-0	02-02-04
Mansfield	v	Bury	-	-	-	-	5-3	0-0	02-03-03
Notts Co	v	Cheltenham	-	-	-	1-0	-	0-0	01-01-00
Oxford Utd	v	Wrexham	1-4	3-4	-	0-2	-	-	00-02-03
Peterboro	v	Leyton O	2-1	-	-	-	-	-	03-01-02
Rushden & D	v	Boston	-	0-0	-	1-0	-	4-2	02-01-00
Torquay	v	Carlisle	4-1	4-2	2-1	2-3	4-1	-	06-03-04

BELL'S SCOTTISH FIRST DIVISION

Airdrie Utd	v	Hamilton	-	-	-	0-0/2-2	3-0/1-1	0-2/1-0	11-05-03
Brechin	v	Ross County	-	-	-	-	4-2/1-0	-	03-01-02
Clyde	v	St Mirren	-	-	1-1/3-1	2-3/3-2	2-0/2-2	0-0/0-0	04-04-02
Dundee	v	St Johnstone	1-2/1-1	1-1	1-1/1-0	-	-	-	04-06-07
Queen of Sth	v	Stranraer	0-5/0-0	1-4/2-3	1-0/3-1	-	-	-	07-05-07

BELL'S SCOTTISH SECOND DIVISION

Alloa	v	Morton	-	2-1/0-3	1-1/4-0	-	0-1/3-3	1-6/2-2	02-04-03

Ayr	v	Raith	0-1/0-1	4-2/2-0	1-1/3-1	-	1-0/1-0	-	11-08-04
Dumbarton	v	Forfar	3-3/0-0	-	-	1-2/1-2	2-1/1-1	0-1/1-1	01-04-03
Partick	v	Gretna	-	-	-	-	-	-	00-00-00
Peterhead	v	Stirling	-	-	3-3/5-1	1-0/6-0	2-2/0-0	-	03-03-00

BELL'S SCOTTISH THIRD DIVISION

Albion	v	Elgin	-	1-1/0-1	4-4/2-2	1-1/1-1	1-2/1-2	2-2/2-0	01-06-03
Arbroath	v	Berwick	-	0-2/2-0	-	-	1-0/1-2	1-1/2-0	08-02-07
East Fife	v	Stenhsmuir	-	-	-	-	3-2/1-0	0-0/2-0	10-04-05
E Stirling	v	Queen's Park	1-1/0-1	-	0-1/3-1	0-4/0-2	1-2/2-4	0-5/3-1	13-06-10
Montrose	v	Cowdenbeath	0-1/1-3	1-2/0-1	-	-	1-3/1-1	3-1/1-2	08-04-11

NATIONWIDE CONFERENCE

Aldershot	v	Gravesend	2-1	1-0	1-2	-	2-2	1-0	04-01-01
Altrincham	v	Exeter	-	-	-	-	-	-	00-00-00
Crawley	v	Southport	-	-	-	-	-	-	00-00-00
Forest G	v	Canvey Islnd	-	-	-	-	-	2-2	00-01-00
Grays	v	Accrington	-	-	-	-	-	-	00-00-00
Halifax	v	Dagenham & R	-	-	-	3-3	3-0	2-2	02-03-01
Hereford	v	Woking	2-4	0-1	2-2	5-0	0-1	2-2	02-02-04
Morecambe	v	Cambridge U	-	-	-	-	-	-	00-00-00
Stevenage	v	Kidderminstr	0-2	-	-	-	-	-	03-01-02
Tamworth	v	Scarborough	-	-	-	-	0-0	1-0	01-01-00
York	v	Burton	-	-	-	-	-	1-2	00-00-01

SUNDAY 13TH NOVEMBER 2005

COCA-COLA LEAGUE 1

| Blackpool | v | Scunthorpe | 0-2 | 6-0 | - | - | - | - | 03-00-01 |

COCA-COLA LEAGUE 2

| Stockport | v | Barnet | - | - | - | - | - | - | 01-00-00 |

FRIDAY 18TH NOVEMBER 2005

| Derby | v | Wolves | - | - | - | 1-4 | - | 3-3 | 01-03-03 |

SATURDAY 19TH NOVEMBER 2005

FA BARCLAYCARD PREMIER LEAGUE

Charlton	v	Man Utd	-	3-3	0-2	1-3	0-2	-	02-01-04
Chelsea	v	Newcastle	1-0	3-1	1-1	3-0	5-0	4-0	08-04-00
Liverpool	v	Portsmouth	-	-	-	-	3-0	1-1	01-01-00
Man City	v	Blackburn	2-0	-	-	2-2	1-1	1-1	03-04-02
Sunderland	v	Aston Villa	2-1	1-1	1-1	1-0	-	-	03-02-01
Tottenham	v	West Ham	0-0	1-0	1-1	3-2	-	-	07-02-03
WBA	v	Everton	-	-	-	1-2	-	1-0	01-00-01
Wigan	v	Arsenal	-	-	-	-	-	-	00-00-00

COCA-COLA CHAMPIONSHIP

Burnley	v	Leicester	-	-	-	1-2	-	0-0	00-01-01
Coventry	v	Ipswich	-	0-1	-	2-4	1-1	1-2	02-02-03
Crewe	v	Stoke	-	-	-	-	2-0	0-2	02-00-02
Norwich	v	Luton	-	-	-	-	-	-	02-01-02
Plymouth	v	QPR	-	-	-	0-1	2-0	2-1	02-00-01
Preston	v	Cardiff	0-0	-	-	-	2-2	3-0	03-03-00
Reading	v	Hull	-	-	-	-	-	-	00-01-02
Sheff Utd	v	Millwall	-	-	3-2	3-1	2-1	-	04-01-00
Southampton	v	Leeds	0-3	1-0	0-1	3-2	2-1	-	05-02-07
Watford	v	Sheff Weds	1-0	1-3	3-1	1-0	-	-	03-01-01

COCA-COLA LEAGUE 1

| Barnsley | v | Rotherham | - | - | 1-1 | - | - | - | 00-01-00 |

rentford	v	Oldham	2-0	1-1	2-2	0-0	2-1	2-0	04-03-00
ristol C	v	Chesterfield	3-0	-	3-0	4-0	4-0	2-3	08-00-01
olchester	v	Blackpool	1-1	-	1-1	0-2	1-1	0-1	00-04-02
oncaster	v	Bournemouth	-	-	-	-	-	1-1	00-01-00
illingham	v	Hartlepool	-	-	-	-	-	-	02-02-00
uddersfield	v	Bradford	-	-	-	-	-	0-1	02-03-04
ilton K	v	Walsall	-	-	2-2	3-2	0-1	1-1	01-02-01
ottm F	v	Southend	-	-	-	-	-	-	01-00-00
ort Vale	v	Swindon	2-0	3-0	0-2	1-1	3-3	1-0	06-04-03
cunthorpe	v	Tranmere	-	-	-	-	-	-	00-00-01
wansea	v	Yeovil	-	-	-	-	3-2	0-2	01-00-01

COCA-COLA LEAGUE 2

arnet	v	Torquay	1-2	2-3	-	-	-	-	04-02-02
oston	v	Notts Co	-	-	-	-	-	4-0	01-00-00
ury	v	Rushden & D	-	-	-	0-1	-	1-1	00-01-01
arlisle	v	Oxford Utd	-	-	2-1	1-0	2-0	-	03-00-01
heltenham	v	Lincoln	0-2	2-1	2-1	-	3-2	1-0	04-00-01
eyton O	v	Stockport	-	-	-	-	-	-	01-02-02
acclesfield	v	Darlington	2-1	1-1	1-1	1-0	0-1	1-0	04-03-01
orthampton	v	Bristol R	-	2-1	-	-	2-0	2-1	04-01-02
ochdale	v	Chester	2-1	-	-	-	-	2-2	03-02-02
hrewsbury	v	Mansfield	1-2	2-1	3-0	-	-	0-2	04-01-04
rexham	v	Peterboro	-	2-1	1-2	-	2-0	1-1	04-05-01
ycombe	v	Grimsby	-	-	-	-	4-1	2-0	02-01-00

BANK OF SCOTLAND SCOTTISH PREMIER LEAGUE

berdeen	v	Hearts	3-1/1-2	1-1/1-0	3-2/2-3	1-1/0-1	0-1	0-1	14-07-11
eltic	v	Rangers	1-1/0-1	6-2/1-0	2-1/1-1	3-3/1-0	3-0/1-0	1-0/0-2	13-07-14
undee Utd	v	Motherwell	0-2/1-2	1-1/2-0/1-0	1-1/1-0	1-1/2-1	0-2/1-0	0-1	11-15-06
unfermline	v	Livingston	3-0/4-1	-	1-2/1-0	2-1/2-0	2-2	0-0	07-03-02
ibernian	v	Falkirk	-	-	-	-	-	-	05-03-02
ilmarnock	v	Inv CT	-	-	-	-	-	2-2/0-1	00-01-01

BELL'S SCOTTISH FIRST DIVISION

amilton	v	Queen of Sth	0-3/1-1	-	1-1/3-1	-	-	1-0/1-1	03-04-01
oss County	v	Dundee	-	-	-	-	-	-	00-00-00
St Johnstone	v	Clyde	-	-	-	0-1/1-2	3-0/1-3	3-0/0-0	03-03-03
St Mirren	v	Airdrie Utd	5-0/3-1	-	0-0/2-1	-	-	1-1/1-0	08-02-10
Stranraer	v	Brechin	-	-	-	3-1/2-3	-	4-2/0-1	04-02-08

NATIONWIDE CONFERENCE

Accrington	v	Forest G	-	-	-	-	4-1	2-2	01-01-00
Burton	v	Crawley	3-0	2-1	-	-	-	1-0	10-02-02
Cambridge U	v	Aldershot	-	-	-	-	-	-	00-00-00
Canvey Islnd	v	Tamworth	-	-	-	-	-	3-3	00-01-00
Dagenham & R	v	Hereford	-	2-1	1-0	1-0	0-9	3-1	04-00-01
Exeter	v	Grays	-	-	-	-	-	-	00-00-00
Gravesend	v	Altrincham	-	-	-	-	-	-	00-00-00
Kidderminstr	v	York	-	3-1	4-1	1-2	4-1	-	03-00-01
Scarborough	v	Stevenage	1-3	2-2	1-1	1-2	2-2	3-3	00-04-02
Southport	v	Halifax	-	-	-	2-0	-	-	03-03-00
Woking	v	Morecambe	0-0	3-1	1-3	0-6	4-1	0-0	03-02-05

SUNDAY 20TH NOVEMBER 2005
FA BARCLAYCARD PREMIER LEAGUE

Middlesbro	v	Fulham	-	-	2-1	2-2	2-1	1-1	02-02-00

COCA-COLA CHAMPIONSHIP

Brighton	v	Crystal Pal	-	-	-	0-0	-	-	01-01-00

MONDAY 21ST NOVEMBER 2005
FA BARCLAYCARD PREMIER LEAGUE

Birmingham	v	Bolton	2-1	1-1	-	3-1	2-0	1-2	07-02-0

TUESDAY 22ND NOVEMBER 2005
COCA-COLA CHAMPIONSHIP

Cardiff	v	Brighton	-	1-1	1-1	-	-	2-0	04-04-0
Crystal Pal	v	Coventry	-	-	1-3	1-1	1-1	-	01-03-0
Hull	v	Southampton	-	-	-	-	-	-	00-00-0
Ipswich	v	Reading	-	-	-	3-1	1-1	1-1	03-02-0
Leeds	v	Burnley	-	-	-	-	-	1-2	00-00-0
Leicester	v	Watford	1-0	-	-	2-0	-	0-1	04-04-0
Luton	v	Crewe	-	-	-	0-4	-	-	01-00-0
Millwall	v	Norwich	-	-	4-0	0-2	0-0	-	02-01-0
QPR	v	Preston	-	0-0	-	-	-	1-2	00-01-0
Sheff Weds	v	Plymouth	-	-	-	-	1-3	-	01-00-0
Stoke	v	Derby	-	-	-	1-3	2-1	1-0	03-02-0
Wolves	v	Sheff Utd	1-0	0-0	1-0	1-3	-	-	04-04-0

SATURDAY 26TH NOVEMBER 2005
FA BARCLAYCARD PREMIER LEAGUE

Arsenal	v	Blackburn	-	-	3-3	1-2	1-0	3-0	04-04-03
Aston Villa	v	Charlton	-	2-1	1-0	2-0	2-1	0-0	04-02-02
Fulham	v	Bolton	1-1	1-1	3-0	4-1	2-1	2-0	04-05-02
Man City	v	Liverpool	-	1-1	-	0-3	2-2	1-0	03-05-03
Middlesbro	v	WBA	-	-	-	3-0	-	4-0	06-01-00
Portsmouth	v	Chelsea	-	-	-	-	0-2	0-2	00-00-03
Sunderland	v	Birmingham	-	-	-	0-1	-	-	03-02-02
Wigan	v	Tottenham	-	-	-	-	-	-	00-00-00

COCA-COLA CHAMPIONSHIP

Brighton	v	Derby	-	-	-	1-0	-	2-3	01-00-02
Burnley	v	Crewe	-	1-0	3-3	-	1-0	3-0	05-02-01
Cardiff	v	Ipswich	-	-	-	-	2-3	0-1	00-00-02
Coventry	v	Norwich	-	-	2-1	1-1	0-2	-	06-03-01
Leicester	v	Sheff Utd	-	-	-	0-0	-	3-2	01-01-02
Luton	v	Crystal Pal	-	-	-	-	-	-	01-03-01
Millwall	v	Leeds	-	-	-	-	-	1-1	00-01-00
Plymouth	v	Reading	-	-	-	-	-	2-2	01-02-00
Preston	v	Watford	-	3-2	1-1	1-1	2-1	2-1	04-03-00
QPR	v	Hull	-	-	-	-	-	-	00-00-00
Sheff Weds	v	Stoke	-	-	-	0-0	-	-	00-01-00
Wolves	v	Southampton	-	-	-	-	1-4	-	00-00-01

COCA-COLA LEAGUE 1

Bournemouth	v	Milton K	-	-	-	-	-	0-1	00-00-01
Bradford	v	Hartlepool	-	-	-	-	-	1-2	01-01-02
Chesterfield	v	Blackpool	0-0	2-1	2-1	1-0	1-0	1-0	06-05-02
Colchester	v	Gillingham	2-1	-	-	-	-	-	03-03-01
Doncaster	v	Bristol C	-	-	-	-	-	1-1	00-01-00
Huddersfield	v	Nottm F	2-1	1-1	-	-	-	-	01-01-01
Port Vale	v	Southend	-	-	-	-	-	-	04-01-00
Scunthorpe	v	Brentford	0-0	-	-	-	-	-	00-02-00
Swindon	v	Barnsley	1-2	-	-	3-1	1-1	2-1	05-04-03
Tranmere	v	Swansea	-	-	-	-	-	-	02-00-00
Walsall	v	Rotherham	-	1-1	3-2	3-4	3-2	-	03-03-02
Yeovil	v	Oldham	-	-	-	-	-	-	00-00-00

Sponsored by Stan James

COCA-COLA LEAGUE 2

Boston	v	Wrexham	-	-	-	3-3	-	-	00-01-00
Bristol R	v	Barnet	-	-	-	-	-	-	01-00-00
Bury	v	Cheltenham	-	-	-	-	1-1	3-1	01-01-00
Carlisle	v	Wycombe	-	-	-	-	-	-	01-02-00
Chester	v	Peterboro	0-1	-	-	-	-	-	01-02-02
Darlington	v	Rushden & D	-	-	0-0	2-2	-	2-0	01-02-00
Macclesfield	v	Leyton O	1-0	0-2	2-1	3-1	1-0	3-1	06-00-01
Mansfield	v	Stockport	-	-	-	4-2	-	-	02-00-00
Northampton	v	Lincoln	1-0	-	-	-	1-1	1-0	04-06-01
Notts Co	v	Torquay	-	-	-	-	-	-	01-00-00
Oxford Utd	v	Grimsby	-	-	-	-	-	1-2	01-02-03
Rochdale	v	Shrewsbury	2-1	1-7	1-0	1-1	-	1-1	05-02-02

BANK OF SCOTLAND SCOTTISH PREMIER LEAGUE

Celtic	v	Dunfermline	-	3-1	3-1/5-0/5-0	2-1/1-0	5-0/1-2	3-0/6-0	19-00-04
Falkirk	v	Aberdeen	-	-	-	-	-	-	01-02-05
Hibernian	v	Rangers	0-1/2-2	1-0/0-0	0-3	2-4/0-2	0-1	0-1	05-06-18
Inv CT	v	Dundee Utd	-	-	-	-	-	1-1	00-01-00
Livingston	v	Kilmarnock	-	-	0-1	0-1/0-4	1-2/1-1	0-2/3-1	03-03-09
Motherwell	v	Hearts	2-1/0-2	2-0	2-0/1-2	6-1	1-1/1-1	2-0/2-0	10-08-14

BELL'S SCOTTISH FIRST DIVISION

Clyde	v	Airdrie Utd	-	4-1/1-1	0-3/0-1	-	-	1-2/1-0	03-02-07
Dundee	v	Brechin	-	-	-	-	-	-	00-00-02
Queen of Sth	v	Ross County	0-2/0-3	-	-	2-0/1-0	1-0/1-1	0-1/1-0	04-01-03
St Johnstone	v	Stranraer	-	-	-	-	-	-	02-00-00
St Mirren	v	Hamilton	-	-	-	-	-	1-0/0-1	09-01-06

BELL'S SCOTTISH SECOND DIVISION

Forfar	v	Partick	-	0-1/2-2	-	-	-	-	03-02-05
Morton	v	Ayr	0-0/1-2	1-1/0-6	-	-	-	0-1/2-1	06-04-10
Gretna	v	Alloa	-	-	-	-	-	-	00-00-00
Raith	v	Peterhead	-	-	-	-	-	-	00-00-00
Stirling	v	Dumbarton	-	-	4-5/2-1	-	-	1-0/3-0	08-03-04

BELL'S SCOTTISH THIRD DIVISION

Berwick	v	Albion	1-1/2-1	-	-	-	-	-	07-06-00
Cowdenb'th	v	Arbroath	-	-	-	-	-	-	05-07-04
Elgin	v	E Stirling	-	1-2/4-2	2-1/2-2	3-1/3-0	3-1/3-0	1-3/0-0	06-02-02
Queen's Park	v	East Fife	0-1/1-0	-	1-2/2-0	0-0/1-2	-	1-2/2-1	08-02-07
Stenhsmuir	v	Montrose	-	-	-	-	-	1-1/0-1	07-01-06

NATIONWIDE CONFERENCE

Accrington	v	Southport	-	-	-	-	-	-	00-02-00
Aldershot	v	Forest G	-	-	-	-	3-0	1-2	01-00-01
Altrincham	v	Tamworth	-	-	-	-	-	-	00-00-00
Burton	v	Kidderminstr	-	-	-	-	-	-	00-00-00
Canvey Islnd	v	Cambridge U	-	-	-	-	-	-	00-00-00
Crawley	v	Gravesend	-	-	-	-	-	1-1	02-02-03
Dagenham & R	v	Woking	-	1-2	3-1	1-1	1-0	1-1	03-03-03
Hereford	v	Exeter	-	-	-	-	1-1	1-2	03-02-02
Morecambe	v	York	-	-	-	-	-	2-1	01-00-00
Scarborough	v	Halifax	-	-	-	0-1	1-0	3-1	07-00-02
Stevenage	v	Grays	-	-	-	-	-	-	02-00-00

SUNDAY 27TH NOVEMBER 2005
FA BARCLAYCARD PREMIER LEAGUE

Everton	v	Newcastle	0-2	1-1	1-3	2-1	2-2	-	05-03-04
West Ham	v	Man Utd	2-4	2-2	3-5	1-1	-	-	01-07-04

SATURDAY 3RD DECEMBER 2005

FA BARCLAYCARD PREMIER LEAGUE

Blackburn	v	Everton	-	-	1-0	0-1	2-1	0-0	05-02-0(
Bolton	v	Arsenal	-	-	0-2	2-2	1-1	1-0	02-02-0:
Chelsea	v	Middlesbro	1-1	2-1	2-2	1-0	0-0	2-0	07-03-0(
Liverpool	v	Wigan	-	-	-	-	-	-	00-00-0(
Man Utd	v	Portsmouth	-	-	-	-	3-0	2-1	02-00-0(
Newcastle	v	Aston Villa	0-1	3-0	3-0	1-1	1-1	0-3	08-02-0:
Tottenham	v	Sunderland	3-1	2-1	2-1	4-1	-	-	05-01-0(
WBA	v	Fulham	0-0	1-3	-	1-0	-	1-1	02-02-0:

COCA-COLA CHAMPIONSHIP

Coventry	v	Plymouth	-	-	-	-	-	2-1	01-00-0C
Crewe	v	Preston	-	1-3	2-1	-	2-1	1-2	05-01-0⊄
Crystal Pal	v	Millwall	-	-	1-3	1-0	0-1	-	03-00-03
Derby	v	Norwich	-	-	-	2-1	0-4	-	02-01-03
Hull	v	Cardiff	-	2-0	-	-	-	-	03-01-02
Ipswich	v	Wolves	1-0	-	-	2-4	-	2-1	05-02-03
Leeds	v	Leicester	2-1	3-1	2-2	-	3-2	0-2	06-02-03
Reading	v	Luton	1-2	4-1	-	-	-	-	03-01-01
Sheff Utd	v	Sheff Weds	-	1-1	0-0	3-1	-	-	02-04-00
Southampton	v	Burnley	-	-	-	-	-	-	00-00-00
Stoke	v	QPR	-	-	0-1	-	-	0-1	01-01-02
Watford	v	Brighton	-	-	-	1-0	-	1-1	02-02-02

BANK OF SCOTLAND SCOTTISH PREMIER LEAGUE

Aberdeen	v	Celtic	0-5/0-6	1-1/0-1	2-0/0-1	0-4/1-1	1-3	0-1	06-13-13
Dundee Utd	v	Hibernian	3-1/0-0	0-1	3-1/1-2/2-1	1-1/1-2	1-2/0-0	1-4	10-11-08
Dunfermline	v	Kilmarnock	-	1-0	0-2/2-0	0-2/2-2	2-3/2-1	4-1	09-04-05
Hearts	v	Livingston	-	-	1-3/2-3	2-1	3-1/1-1	0-0/3-1	03-02-02
Motherwell	v	Inv CT	-	-	-	-	-	1-2	00-00-01
Rangers	v	Falkirk	-	-	-	-	-	-	05-03-00

BELL'S SCOTTISH FIRST DIVISION

Airdrie Utd	v	Queen of Sth	-	-	-	-	-	0-1/2-0	03-00-01
Brechin	v	St Johnstone	-	-	-	-	0-1/0-2	-	00-00-02
Hamilton	v	Clyde	2-3/1-1	-	-	-	-	0-1/0-1	06-01-04
Ross County	v	St Mirren	-	-	0-1/4-1	4-0/2-0	2-0/1-0	1-1/0-1	05-01-02
Stranraer	v	Dundee	-	-	-	-	-	-	00-00-02

BELL'S SCOTTISH SECOND DIVISION

Alloa	v	Ayr	-	1-1/0-2	-	0-1/2-3	-	1-3/5-1	01-03-04
Morton	v	Partick	-	-	-	-	-	-	06-03-02
Gretna	v	Peterhead	-	-	-	1-4/1-1	3-2/3-2	2-1/6-1	04-01-01
Raith	v	Dumbarton	-	-	-	1-0/2-1	-	-	04-00-00
Stirling	v	Forfar	-	3-3/1-0	-	-	-	3-1/3-2	07-02-01

BELL'S SCOTTISH THIRD DIVISION

Berwick	v	Stenhsmuir	-	4-1/1-0	1-1/2-1	2-2/0-0	2-1/3-0	-	13-06-06
Cowdenb'th	v	Albion	0-0/5-0	5-0/1-0	-	-	1-4/1-1	2-0/1-2	09-08-06
E Stirling	v	East Fife	0-2/1-0	2-5/1-0	2-1/1-2	1-4/0-4	-	1-1/1-0	09-02-08
Elgin	v	Arbroath	-	-	-	-	-	-	00-00-00
Queen's Park	v	Montrose	2-1/1-1	-	2-2/0-1	0-1/1-1	1-1/1-1	1-2/1-0	09-09-08

NATIONWIDE CONFERENCE

Cambridge U	v	Scarborough	-	-	-	-	-	-	03-01-02
Exeter	v	Canvey Islnd	-	-	-	-	-	0-1	00-00-01
Forest G	v	Burton	-	-	-	2-0	1-1	3-2	02-01-01
Gravesend	v	Morecambe	-	-	-	3-2	6-0	1-2	02-00-01

Sponsored by Stan James

Grays	v	Altrincham	-	-	-	-	-	-	00-00-00
Halifax	v	Crawley	-	-	-	-	-	1-0	01-00-00
Kidderminstr	v	Dagenham & R	-	-	-	-	-	-	02-01-01
Southport	v	Hereford	0-1	1-1	1-1	1-2	-	-	00-04-02
Tamworth	v	Accrington	-	-	-	-	1-1	1-0	01-01-00
Woking	v	Aldershot	-	-	-	-	2-2	1-2	00-01-01
York	v	Stevenage	-	-	-	-	-	3-1	01-00-00

SUNDAY 4TH DECEMBER 2005
FA BARCLAYCARD PREMIER LEAGUE

Charlton	v	Man City	0-1	4-0	-	2-2	0-3	2-2	02-04-02

MONDAY 5TH DECEMBER 2005
FA BARCLAYCARD PREMIER LEAGUE

Birmingham	v	West Ham	-	-	-	2-2	-	00-01-01

TUESDAY 6TH DECEMBER 2005
COCA-COLA LEAGUE 1

Barnsley	v	Tranmere	3-0	1-1	-	1-1	2-0	0-0	06-06-00
Blackpool	v	Bournemouth	0-0	-	4-3	-	1-2	3-3	06-04-01
Brentford	v	Yeovil	-	-	-	-	-	-	00-00-00
Bristol C	v	Bradford	-	-	-	-	-	0-0	01-01-01
Gillingham	v	Doncaster	-	-	-	-	-	-	05-02-00
Hartlepool	v	Colchester	-	-	-	-	0-0	2-1	06-01-01
Milton K	v	Huddersfield	-	1-1	-	-	-	2-1	01-01-00
Nottm F	v	Port Vale	2-0	-	-	-	-	-	02-00-00
Oldham	v	Walsall	-	0-0	-	-	-	5-3	02-02-01
Rotherham	v	Swindon	-	4-3	-	-	-	-	01-00-01
Southend	v	Chesterfield	-	3-2	-	-	-	-	02-00-02
Swansea	v	Scunthorpe	-	-	2-2	1-1	4-2	2-1	03-03-01

COCA-COLA LEAGUE 2

Barnet	v	Bury	-	-	-	-	-	-	01-02-00
Cheltenham	v	Oxford Utd	-	-	2-0	-	0-0	0-1	01-01-01
Grimsby	v	Rochdale	-	-	-	-	-	0-1	00-00-03
Leyton O	v	Chester	1-2	-	-	-	-	2-0	06-02-03
Lincoln	v	Macclesfield	1-1	1-2	1-0	3-0	3-2	2-0	05-02-01
Peterboro	v	Notts Co	-	1-0	0-1	1-0	5-2	-	04-01-04
Rushden & D	v	Carlisle	-	-	3-1	1-1	-	-	01-01-00
Shrewsbury	v	Darlington	0-1	1-0	3-0	2-2	-	4-0	05-02-03
Stockport	v	Bristol R	-	-	-	-	-	-	03-00-01
Torquay	v	Northampton	1-2	-	-	-	3-1	-	05-01-02
Wrexham	v	Mansfield	-	-	-	-	-	-	01-00-00
Wycombe	v	Boston	-	-	-	-	-	1-2	04-01-01

SATURDAY 10TH DECEMBER 2005
FA BARCLAYCARD PREMIER LEAGUE

Birmingham	v	Fulham	2-2	1-3	-	0-0	2-2	1-2	02-04-02
Blackburn	v	West Ham	-	-	7-1	2-2	-	-	08-01-01
Bolton	v	Aston Villa	-	-	3-2	1-0	2-2	1-2	02-01-03
Charlton	v	Sunderland	-	0-1	2-2	1-1	-	-	01-05-03
Chelsea	v	Wigan	-	-	-	-	-	-	00-00-00
Liverpool	v	Middlesbro	0-0	0-0	2-0	1-1	2-0	-	07-03-00
Newcastle	v	Arsenal	4-2	0-0	0-2	1-1	0-0	0-1	04-04-05
WBA	v	Man City	0-2	-	4-0	1-2	-	2-0	03-00-04

COCA-COLA CHAMPIONSHIP

Coventry	v	Millwall	-	-	0-1	2-3	4-0	0-1	02-01-03

Crewe	v	Norwich	1-0	0-0	1-0	-	1-3	-	04-01-01
Crystal Pal	v	Wolves	1-1	0-2	0-2	4-2	-	-	03-02-03
Derby	v	Preston	-	-	-	0-2	5-1	-	01-00-01
Hull	v	Sheff Weds	-	-	-	-	-	-	00-00-01
Ipswich	v	QPR	1-4	-	-	-	-	0-2	02-02-04
Leeds	v	Cardiff	-	-	-	-	-	1-1	00-01-00
Reading	v	Brighton	-	-	0-0	1-2	-	3-2	03-01-01
Sheff Utd	v	Burnley	-	2-0	3-0	4-2	1-0	2-1	06-00-00
Southampton	v	Luton	-	-	-	-	-	-	03-00-01
Stoke	v	Leicester	-	-	-	0-1	-	3-2	03-01-02
Watford	v	Plymouth	-	-	-	-	-	3-1	04-01-02

COCA-COLA LEAGUE 1

Barnsley	v	Scunthorpe	-	-	-	-	-	-	00-00-00
Blackpool	v	Tranmere	-	-	1-1	3-0	2-1	0-1	02-01-02
Brentford	v	Chesterfield	1-1	-	0-0	2-1	1-1	2-2	03-05-01
Bristol C	v	Huddersfield	-	-	1-1	1-0	-	3-3	02-03-01
Gillingham	v	Port Vale	-	-	-	-	-	-	01-00-00
Hartlepool	v	Bournemouth	-	-	-	0-0	2-1	3-2	03-02-01
Milton K	v	Doncaster	-	-	-	-	-	0-1	00-00-01
Nottm F	v	Walsall	4-1	-	2-3	1-1	3-3	-	01-02-01
Oldham	v	Swindon	-	1-0	2-0	4-0	0-1	1-2	06-03-02
Rotherham	v	Yeovil	-	-	-	-	-	-	00-00-00
Southend	v	Bradford	-	-	-	-	-	-	00-02-00
Swansea	v	Colchester	-	0-2	-	-	-	-	00-01-02

COCA-COLA LEAGUE 2

Barnet	v	Northampton	2-1	-	-	-	-	-	04-01-01
Cheltenham	v	Macclesfield	1-1	1-1	4-1	-	3-2	-	03-03-02
Grimsby	v	Bristol R	-	-	-	-	-	0-0	01-01-02
Leyton O	v	Bury	-	-	-	1-2	2-0	1-1	03-01-03
Lincoln	v	Chester	4-1	-	-	-	-	1-1	01-03-02
Peterboro	v	Carlisle	0-2	-	-	-	-	-	02-01-03
Rushden & D	v	Mansfield	-	-	3-1	-	-	0-0	01-01-00
Shrewsbury	v	Boston	-	-	-	1-2	-	0-0	00-01-01
Stockport	v	Darlington	-	-	-	-	-	-	02-01-00
Torquay	v	Oxford Utd	-	-	3-3	2-3	3-0	-	01-01-01
Wrexham	v	Notts Co	2-3	1-1	2-1	-	0-1	-	02-03-02
Wycombe	v	Rochdale	-	-	-	-	-	0-3	00-01-01

BANK OF SCOTLAND SCOTTISH PREMIER LEAGUE

Aberdeen	v	Dunfermline	-	0-0/1-0	3-2/1-0	3-1/1-0	1-2/2-0	2-1	15-03-03
Celtic	v	Hibernian	4-0/1-1	3-0/1-1	3-0	1-0/3-2	6-0	2-1	18-09-02
Falkirk	v	Motherwell	-	-	-	-	-	-	02-02-04
Hearts	v	Inv CT	-	-	-	-	-	1-0/0-2	01-00-01
Kilmarnock	v	Rangers	1-1/0-2	2-4/1-2	2-2	1-1/0-1	2-3	0-1	01-05-15
Livingston	v	Dundee Utd	-	-	2-0/1-1	3-0/1-2	0-0/2-3	1-1/0-2	02-03-03

BELL'S SCOTTISH FIRST DIVISION

Brechin	v	Hamilton	-	0-0/3-4	-	1-0/4-1	-	-	02-03-05
Dundee	v	St Mirren	-	5-0	-	-	-	-	08-01-04
Ross County	v	Clyde	2-0/2-2	0-2/2-0	4-0/2-1	1-1/1-1	0-1/0-0	0-1	04-04-03
St Johnstone	v	Queen of Sth	-	-	-	2-2/0-1	4-1/2-2	1-3/0-0	03-03-02
Stranraer	v	Airdrie Utd	-	-	-	2-0/1-2	-	-	01-00-05

NATIONWIDE CONFERENCE

Accrington	v	Kidderminstr	-	-	-	-	-	-	00-00-00
Aldershot	v	Southport	-	-	-	-	-	-	00-00-00
Altrincham	v	Woking	1-1	-	-	-	-	-	02-02-02
Burton	v	Gravesend	-	-	-	1-1	3-0	3-2	05-02-02

202

Canvey Islnd v	Halifax	-	-	-	-	-	0-1	00-00-01
Crawley v	Tamworth	3-0	0-2	1-2	1-0	-	3-0	05-00-02
Dagenham & R v	Cambridge U	-	-	-	-	-	-	00-00-00
Hereford v	York	-	-	-	-	-	2-0	03-01-02
Morecambe v	Grays	-	-	-	-	-	-	00-00-00
Scarborough v	Exeter	-	-	-	-	2-3	1-1	03-02-04
Stevenage v	Forest G	1-1	3-1	4-1	0-0	2-1	2-2	03-04-00

SUNDAY 11TH DECEMBER 2005
FA BARCLAYCARD PREMIER LEAGUE

Man Utd v	Everton	5-1	1-0	4-1	3-0	3-2	0-0	11-03-03

MONDAY 12TH DECEMBER 2005
FA BARCLAYCARD PREMIER LEAGUE

Tottenham v	Portsmouth	-	-	-	-	4-3	3-1	02-00-00

SATURDAY 17TH DECEMBER 2005
FA BARCLAYCARD PREMIER LEAGUE

Aston Villa v	Man Utd	0-1	0-1	1-1	0-1	0-2	0-1	03-05-09
Everton v	Bolton	-	-	3-1	0-0	1-2	3-2	04-01-01
Fulham v	Blackburn	2-2	2-1	2-0	0-4	3-4	0-2	02-01-03
Man City v	Birmingham	1-0	-	3-0	1-0	0-0	3-0	05-02-01
Portsmouth v	WBA	2-0	0-1	1-2	-	-	3-2	04-03-06
Sunderland v	Liverpool	0-2	1-1	0-1	2-1	-	-	01-01-04
West Ham v	Newcastle	2-1	1-0	3-0	2-2	-	-	06-05-03
Wigan v	Charlton	-	-	-	-	-	-	00-00-00

COCA-COLA CHAMPIONSHIP

Brighton v	Hull	3-0	3-0	-	-	-	-	09-03-00
Burnley v	Watford	-	2-0	1-0	4-7	2-3	3-1	05-01-02
Cardiff v	Derby	-	-	-	-	4-1	0-2	01-00-01
Leicester v	Crewe	-	-	-	-	-	1-1	00-01-00
Luton v	Stoke	2-1	1-2	-	-	-	-	02-00-04
Millwall v	Reading	5-0	2-0	-	0-2	0-1	1-0	04-02-02
Norwich v	Southampton	-	-	-	-	-	2-1	04-03-01
Plymouth v	Crystal Pal	-	-	-	-	-	-	00-00-01
Preston v	Sheff Utd	-	3-0	3-0	2-0	3-3	0-1	04-01-01
QPR v	Coventry	-	-	-	-	-	4-1	05-04-00
Sheff Weds v	Ipswich	-	-	-	0-1	-	-	02-02-01
Wolves v	Leeds	-	-	-	-	3-1	0-0	02-01-00

COCA-COLA LEAGUE 1

Bournemouth v	Gillingham	0-1	-	-	-	-	-	01-02-01
Bradford v	Rotherham	-	-	3-1	4-2	0-2	-	05-00-03
Chesterfield v	Oldham	0-1	-	4-2	0-1	1-1	-	02-01-03
Colchester v	Milton K	-	-	-	-	-	0-1	00-00-01
Doncaster v	Swansea	-	-	-	-	3-1	-	01-00-02
Huddersfield v	Southend	-	-	-	-	1-0	-	03-01-01
Port Vale v	Bristol C	-	1-2	1-0	2-3	2-1	3-0	06-01-03
Scunthorpe v	Nottm F	-	-	-	-	-	-	00-00-00
Swindon v	Blackpool	-	-	1-0	1-1	2-2	2-2	01-04-00
Tranmere v	Brentford	-	-	1-0	3-1	4-1	1-0	06-01-00
Walsall v	Hartlepool	-	-	-	-	-	2-1	02-00-01
Yeovil v	Barnsley	-	-	-	-	-	-	00-00-00

COCA-COLA LEAGUE 2

Boston v	Cheltenham	-	-	-	-	3-1	2-1	04-02-00
Bristol R v	Torquay	-	-	1-0	1-1	2-2	-	01-02-00
Bury v	Wycombe	2-0	1-1	1-1	-	-	2-2	02-03-01

Home		Away							Record
Carlisle	v	Wrexham	-	-	-	1-2	-	-	02-01-05
Chester	v	Rushden & D	-	1-2	-	-	-	3-1	01-00-01
Darlington	v	Grimsby	-	-	-	-	-	1-0	01-01-00
Macclesfield	v	Barnet	2-0	3-0	-	-	-	-	03-02-01
Mansfield	v	Peterboro	3-1	-	-	1-5	-	-	03-00-01
Northampton	v	Shrewsbury	3-0	-	-	-	-	2-0	03-01-01
Notts Co	v	Stockport	-	-	-	3-2	4-1	-	03-00-01
Oxford Utd	v	Lincoln	-	-	2-1	1-0	0-0	0-1	02-01-01
Rochdale	v	Leyton O	1-4	3-1	3-0	1-0	3-0	2-0	08-00-03

BANK OF SCOTLAND SCOTTISH PREMIER LEAGUE

Home		Away							Record
Dundee Utd	v	Dunfermline	-	3-2/1-0	3-2/0-2	1-2/3-0	1-0/3-2	1-2	13-06-04
Falkirk	v	Kilmarnock	-	-	-	-	-	-	03-02-01
Hibernian	v	Motherwell	2-2/2-2	2-0/1-1	1-1/4-0	3-1/1-0	0-2/3-3	1-0	15-13-03
Inv CT	v	Celtic	-	-	-	-	1-3/0-2	-	00-00-02
Livingston	v	Aberdeen	-	-	2-2/0-0	1-2/1-2	1-1/2-0	0-2	01-03-03
Rangers	v	Hearts	1-0/1-0	1-0/2-0	3-1/2-0	2-0/1-0	2-1/0-1	3-2	25-06-02

BELL'S SCOTTISH FIRST DIVISION

Home		Away							Record
Airdrie Utd	v	Brechin	-	-	-	2-4/3-0	-	-	03-00-02
Clyde	v	Stranraer	0-0/1-1	-	-	-	-	-	03-06-02
Hamilton	v	Ross County	1-0/0-3	-	-	-	-	1-2/0-1	01-00-03
Queen of Sth	v	Dundee	-	-	-	-	-	-	00-00-00
St Mirren	v	St Johnstone	-	0-1/1-0	-	0-2/1-3	1-1/1-1	2-1/1-1	03-08-07

BELL'S SCOTTISH SECOND DIVISION

Home		Away							Record
Ayr	v	Stirling	-	-	-	-	-	3-2/0-3	06-02-04
Dumbarton	v	Gretna	-	-	-	-	-	-	00-00-00
Forfar	v	Raith	-	-	-	1-2/4-2	-	-	03-02-03
Partick	v	Alloa	2-2/0-1	-	-	-	-	-	03-02-01
Peterhead	v	Morton	-	-	-	4-2/3-1	-	-	02-00-00

BELL'S SCOTTISH THIRD DIVISION

Home		Away							Record
Albion	v	E Stirling	1-1/0-1	2-1/2-2	0-4/5-1	6-0/3-1	5-0/5-1	3-3/1-1	14-08-07
Arbroath	v	Queen's Park	-	2-2/2-0	-	-	-	-	08-11-00
East Fife	v	Elgin	-	1-1/1-1	3-0/0-1	4-0/5-0	-	2-0/1-2	04-02-02
Montrose	v	Berwick	1-2/2-3	-	-	-	-	-	03-02-10
Stenhsmuir	v	Cowdenbeath	-	-	0-3/0-1	4-1/1-1	-	2-2	04-05-05

SUNDAY 18TH DECEMBER 2005
FA BARCLAYCARD PREMIER LEAGUE

Home		Away							Record
Middlesbro	v	Tottenham	2-1	1-1	1-1	5-1	1-0	-	04-04-02
Arsenal	v	Chelsea	2-1	1-1	2-1	3-2	2-1	2-2	11-04-01

MONDAY 26TH DECEMBER 2005
FA BARCLAYCARD PREMIER LEAGUE

Home		Away							Record
Aston Villa	v	Everton	3-0	2-1	0-0	3-2	0-0	1-3	10-06-01
Charlton	v	Arsenal	-	1-0	0-3	0-3	1-1	1-3	01-02-05
Chelsea	v	Fulham	-	-	3-2	1-1	2-1	3-1	03-01-00
Liverpool	v	Newcastle	2-1	3-0	3-0	2-2	1-1	3-1	09-02-02
Man Utd	v	WBA	-	-	-	1-0	-	-	01-00-00
Middlesbro	v	Blackburn	-	-	1-3	1-0	0-1	1-0	06-01-04
Portsmouth	v	West Ham	-	-	-	-	-	-	00-00-03
Sunderland	v	Bolton	-	-	1-0	0-2	-	-	03-01-01
Tottenham	v	Birmingham	-	-	-	2-1	4-1	1-0	03-00-00
Wigan	v	Man City	-	-	-	-	-	-	00-00-01

COCA-COLA CHAMPIONSHIP

Home		Away							Record
Brighton	v	QPR	-	-	2-1	-	2-1	2-3	02-00-01

Sponsored by Stan James

Burnley	v	Stoke	1-0	-	-	2-1	0-1	2-2	02-02-03
Cardiff	v	Plymouth	-	4-1	-	1-1	-	0-1	02-01-04
Crewe	v	Hull	-	-	-	-	-	-	02-00-00
Derby	v	Luton	-	-	-	-	-	-	02-03-02
Ipswich	v	Crystal Pal	1-0	-	-	1-2	1-3	-	04-01-04
Leeds	v	Coventry	3-0	1-0	-	-	-	3-0	09-02-01
Leicester	v	Millwall	-	-	-	4-1	-	3-1	05-01-01
Preston	v	Sheff Weds	-	2-0	4-2	2-2	-	-	02-01-00
Sheff Utd	v	Norwich	0-0	1-1	2-1	0-1	1-0	-	06-03-04
Watford	v	Southampton	3-2	-	-	-	-	-	01-00-00
Wolves	v	Reading	-	-	-	0-1	-	4-1	04-01-02

COCA-COLA LEAGUE 1

Barnsley	v	Hartlepool	-	-	-	-	2-2	0-0	00-02-00
Brentford	v	Swansea	-	0-0	-	-	-	-	04-05-00
Gillingham	v	Bristol C	3-0	-	-	-	-	-	03-00-01
Nottm F	v	Doncaster	-	-	-	-	-	-	00-00-00
Oldham	v	Bradford	-	-	-	-	-	-	00-02-01
Port Vale	v	Blackpool	-	-	1-1	1-0	2-1	0-3	05-01-01
Rotherham	v	Huddersfield	-	-	-	-	-	-	01-02-02
Scunthorpe	v	Chesterfield	0-0	1-1	-	-	-	-	02-03-03
Southend	v	Milton K	-	-	-	-	-	-	00-00-00
Swindon	v	Colchester	-	0-0	1-0	2-2	2-0	0-3	02-02-01
Walsall	v	Tranmere	1-2	-	-	-	-	0-2	01-00-02
Yeovil	v	Bournemouth	-	-	-	-	-	-	00-00-00

COCA-COLA LEAGUE 2

Barnet	v	Peterboro	0-2	-	-	-	-	-	01-00-02
Bristol R	v	Shrewsbury	-	-	0-0	0-0	-	0-0	04-03-00
Bury	v	Grimsby	-	-	-	-	-	3-1	03-00-00
Carlisle	v	Darlington	1-1	0-2	1-3	2-2	1-1	-	03-05-04
Cheltenham	v	Chester	1-0	-	-	-	-	0-0	01-01-00
Leyton O	v	Rushden & D	-	-	2-1	0-0	-	2-2	01-02-00
Lincoln	v	Boston	-	-	-	1-1	1-1	2-2	00-03-00
Macclesfield	v	Stockport	-	-	-	-	-	-	00-00-00
Northampton	v	Mansfield	1-0	-	-	2-0	0-3	2-1	06-01-04
Oxford Utd	v	Notts Co	2-3	2-3	-	-	-	2-1	02-03-02
Torquay	v	Wycombe	-	-	-	-	-	-	00-01-00
Wrexham	v	Rochdale	-	-	-	2-5	-	-	04-01-01

BANK OF SCOTLAND SCOTTISH PREMIER LEAGUE

Celtic	v	Livingston	-	-	3-2/5-1	2-0/2-1	5-1/5-1	2-1	07-00-00
Dunfermline	v	Rangers	-	0-0	1-4/2-4/1-1	0-6/1-3	2-0/2-3	1-2/0-1	01-04-17
Hearts	v	Falkirk	-	-	-	-	-	-	05-02-01
Inv CT	v	Hibernian	-	-	-	-	-	1-2/3-0	01-00-01
Kilmarnock	v	Dundee Utd	1-1/1-0	1-0/0-0	2-0/2-2	1-2	0-2	5-2/3-0	09-05-06
Motherwell	v	Aberdeen	5-6/1-0	1-1/0-1/0-2	3-2	1-2/0-1/2-3	1-0	0-0/0-1	07-13-14

BELL'S SCOTTISH FIRST DIVISION

Brechin	v	Clyde	-	-	-	-	1-3/2-5	-	06-01-08
Dundee	v	Airdrie Utd	-	-	-	-	-	-	05-03-03
Queen of Sth	v	St Mirren	-	-	-	3-0/0-2	1-2/1-0	2-1/0-0	03-01-02
St Johnstone	v	Ross County	-	-	-	1-1/2-0	1-1/1-1	1-1/0-2	01-04-01
Stranraer	v	Hamilton	0-2/2-2	-	2-1/3-2	1-2/0-0	-	-	04-03-05

BELL'S SCOTTISH SECOND DIVISION

Alloa	v	Peterhead	-	-	-	-	-	-	00-00-00
Ayr	v	Dumbarton	-	-	-	-	-	0-1	01-03-03
Morton	v	Raith	2-0/1-0	1-2/1-1	-	-	-	-	05-04-08
Gretna	v	Forfar	-	-	-	-	-	-	00-00-00
Partick	v	Stirling	1-0/1-1	3-1/1-1	-	-	-	-	04-04-04

BELL'S SCOTTISH THIRD DIVISION

Albion	v	Arbroath	-	-	-	-	-	-	02-03-11
East Fife	v	Berwick	1-2/3-1	-	-	-	3-1/2-2	-	07-06-04
E Stirling	v	Cowdenbeath	0-1/0-4	0-2/0-2	-	-	1-1/0-1	0-2/2-1	09-07-10
Elgin	v	Montrose	-	1-1/0-2	1-2/1-0	0-0/0-2	2-3/2-1	1-3/2-2	02-03-05
Queen's Park	v	Stenhsmuir	-	2-0/1-2	-	-	-	4-3/0-0	06-06-03

NATIONWIDE CONFERENCE

Cambridge U	v	Stevenage	-	-	-	-	-	-	00-00-00
Exeter	v	Aldershot	-	-	-	-	2-1	3-1	02-00-00
Forest G	v	Hereford	0-1	1-1	1-1	1-3	1-7	1-3	01-02-04
Gravesend	v	Dagenham & R	1-2	-	-	1-2	1-2	2-1	02-01-03
Grays	v	Canvey Islnd	-	0-3	0-1	1-2	1-1	-	00-01-03
Halifax	v	Accrington	-	-	-	-	1-1	1-2	00-01-01
Kidderminstr	v	Altrincham	1-1	-	-	-	-	-	01-04-05
Southport	v	Morecambe	1-1	1-2	1-1	2-3	-	-	02-08-03
Tamworth	v	Burton	1-1	2-3	-	-	1-1	0-2	00-03-03
Woking	v	Crawley	-	-	-	-	-	2-0	01-00-00
York	v	Scarborough	-	-	-	-	-	0-2	03-01-02

WEDNESDAY 28TH DECEMBER 2005

FA BARCLAYCARD PREMIER LEAGUE

Arsenal	v	Portsmouth	-	-	-	-	1-1	3-0	01-01-00
Birmingham	v	Man Utd	-	-	-	0-1	1-2	0-0	00-01-02
Blackburn	v	Sunderland	-	-	0-3	0-0	-	-	01-04-01
Bolton	v	Middlesbro	-	-	1-0	2-1	2-0	0-0	05-02-00
Everton	v	Liverpool	0-0	2-3	1-3	1-2	0-3	1-0	05-06-06
Fulham	v	Aston Villa	-	-	0-0	2-1	1-2	1-1	01-02-01
Man City	v	Chelsea	-	1-2	-	0-3	0-1	1-0	02-03-07
Newcastle	v	Charlton	-	0-1	3-0	2-1	3-1	1-1	03-03-04
WBA	v	Tottenham	-	-	-	2-3	-	1-1	00-01-01
West Ham	v	Wigan	-	-	-	-	4-0	1-3	01-00-01

COCA-COLA CHAMPIONSHIP

Coventry	v	Crewe	-	-	1-0	-	2-0	0-1	02-00-01
Crystal Pal	v	Derby	-	-	-	0-1	1-1	-	02-04-01
Hull	v	Ipswich	-	-	-	-	-	-	01-02-00
Luton	v	Brighton	-	-	-	-	2-0	-	01-00-00
Millwall	v	Watford	-	-	1-0	4-0	1-2	0-2	05-01-06
Norwich	v	Burnley	-	2-3	2-1	2-0	2-0	-	03-00-01
Plymouth	v	Preston	-	-	-	-	-	0-2	03-00-02
QPR	v	Cardiff	-	-	2-1	0-4	-	1-0	02-00-01
Reading	v	Leicester	-	-	-	1-3	-	0-0	00-02-01
Sheff Weds	v	Wolves	-	0-1	2-2	0-4	-	-	00-02-02
Southampton	v	Sheff Utd	-	-	-	-	-	-	02-01-01
Stoke	v	Leeds	-	-	-	-	-	0-1	00-01-02

COCA-COLA LEAGUE 1

Blackpool	v	Oldham	1-2	-	0-2	0-0	1-1	2-0	02-03-02
Bournemouth	v	Barnsley	-	-	-	-	2-2	1-3	02-01-01
Bradford	v	Walsall	-	-	2-0	1-2	1-1	1-1	03-02-01
Bristol C	v	Rotherham	-	0-1	-	-	-	-	01-01-02
Chesterfield	v	Swindon	-	-	4-0	2-4	3-0	1-0	03-00-02
Colchester	v	Scunthorpe	0-1	-	-	-	-	-	05-02-02
Doncaster	v	Brentford	-	-	-	-	-	0-0	00-01-00
Hartlepool	v	Southend	1-2	1-0	5-1	2-1	-	-	03-01-02
Huddersfield	v	Port Vale	2-2	-	2-1	2-2	-	2-1	03-04-04
Milton K	v	Nottm F	-	2-1	1-0	2-3	0-1	-	08-01-04
Swansea	v	Gillingham	-	-	-	-	-	-	01-00-00
Tranmere	v	Yeovil	-	-	-	-	-	-	00-00-00

COCA-COLA LEAGUE 2

Boston	v	Carlisle	-	-	-	0-0	1-0	-	01-01-00
Chester	v	Wrexham	-	-	-	-	-	-	00-01-00
Darlington	v	Barnet	4-0	1-0	-	-	-	-	03-01-05
Grimsby	v	Lincoln	-	-	-	-	-	2-4	02-00-01
Mansfield	v	Bristol R	-	-	2-0	-	0-0	0-2	02-01-02
Notts Co	v	Northampton	-	2-0	0-3	2-1	-	0-0	04-01-02
Peterboro	v	Oxford Utd	-	4-2	-	-	-	-	02-02-01
Rochdale	v	Bury	-	-	-	1-2	0-0	0-3	01-02-04
Rushden & D	v	Cheltenham	-	-	1-0	-	-	1-0	04-00-02
Shrewsbury	v	Macclesfield	0-1	2-2	1-1	2-3	-	0-1	01-02-03
Stockport	v	Torquay	-	-	-	-	-	0-2	02-02-01
Wycombe	v	Leyton O	-	-	-	-	-	-	01-00-00

SATURDAY 31ST DECEMBER 2005
FA BARCLAYCARD PREMIER LEAGUE

Aston Villa	v	Arsenal	1-1	0-0	1-2	1-1	0-2	1-3	05-06-06
Charlton	v	West Ham	-	1-1	4-4	4-2	-	-	02-05-00
Chelsea	v	Birmingham	-	-	-	3-0	0-0	1-1	02-02-00
Liverpool	v	WBA	-	-	-	2-0	-	3-0	02-00-00
Man Utd	v	Bolton	-	-	1-2	0-1	4-0	2-0	03-01-02
Middlesbro	v	Man City	-	1-1	-	3-1	2-1	3-2	06-01-00
Portsmouth	v	Fulham	0-1	1-1	-	-	1-1	4-3	01-02-01
Sunderland	v	Everton	2-1	2-0	1-0	0-1	-	-	04-01-01
Tottenham	v	Newcastle	3-1	4-2	1-3	0-1	1-0	1-0	08-01-04
Wigan	v	Blackburn	-	-	-	-	-	-	00-00-00

COCA-COLA CHAMPIONSHIP

Brighton	v	Millwall	-	-	-	1-0	-	1-0	02-01-01
Burnley	v	Sheff Weds	-	1-0	1-2	2-7	-	-	01-00-02
Cardiff	v	Southampton	-	-	-	-	-	-	00-00-00
Crewe	v	QPR	2-1	2-2	-	2-0	-	0-2	02-01-03
Derby	v	Reading	-	-	-	3-0	2-3	2-1	03-00-02
Ipswich	v	Luton	-	-	-	-	-	-	00-00-01
Leeds	v	Hull	-	-	-	-	-	-	02-00-00
Leicester	v	Norwich	-	-	-	1-1	-	-	02-01-00
Preston	v	Coventry	-	-	4-0	2-2	4-2	3-2	03-01-00
Sheff Utd	v	Stoke	-	-	-	2-1	0-1	0-0	04-03-01
Watford	v	Crystal Pal	-	2-2	1-0	3-3	1-5	-	02-03-03
Wolves	v	Plymouth	-	-	-	-	-	1-1	03-01-00

COCA-COLA LEAGUE 1

Barnsley	v	Huddersfield	4-2	3-1	-	0-1	-	4-2	06-00-01
Brentford	v	Colchester	0-0	1-0	4-1	1-1	3-2	1-0	04-02-00
Gillingham	v	Milton K	-	0-0	0-0	3-3	1-2	-	00-03-01
Nottm F	v	Chesterfield	-	-	-	-	-	-	00-00-00
Oldham	v	Hartlepool	-	-	-	-	0-2	3-2	01-00-01
Port Vale	v	Tranmere	1-0	-	1-1	1-4	2-1	3-1	05-04-02
Rotherham	v	Doncaster	-	-	-	-	-	-	03-00-00
Scunthorpe	v	Bradford	-	-	-	-	-	-	00-00-00
Southend	v	Bournemouth	-	-	-	0-1	-	-	02-00-01
Swindon	v	Swansea	-	1-1	-	-	-	-	01-01-00
Walsall	v	Blackpool	-	-	-	-	-	3-2	05-03-00
Yeovil	v	Bristol C	-	-	-	-	-	-	00-00-00

COCA-COLA LEAGUE 2

Barnet	v	Boston	-	-	0-1	-	-	-	01-01-02
Bristol R	v	Wycombe	1-0	1-2	-	-	-	-	04-00-03
Bury	v	Stockport	-	-	-	-	-	-	00-03-01
Carlisle	v	Rochdale	1-2	1-2	1-2	0-2	3-2	-	05-02-07

Cheltenham	v	Shrewsbury	0-1	1-1	1-0	-	-	1-1	01-02-0
Leyton O	v	Notts Co	-	-	-	-	-	2-0	01-01-0
Lincoln	v	Darlington	1-0	2-2	1-1	1-1	1-1	-	06-05-0
Macclesfield	v	Chester	1-1	-	-	-	-	1-2	01-01-01
Northampton	v	Peterboro	0-1	0-0	2-1	0-1	-	-	01-01-0
Oxford Utd	v	Mansfield	-	-	3-2	-	1-1	1-0	02-01-0
Torquay	v	Rushden & D	-	-	1-1	1-1	-	-	00-02-0
Wrexham	v	Grimsby	-	-	-	-	3-0	-	01-01-0

BANK OF SCOTLAND SCOTTISH PREMIER LEAGUE

Aberdeen	v	Inv CT	-	-	-	-	-	0-0	00-01-0
Falkirk	v	Dunfermline	1-3/1-1	-	-	-	-	-	05-01-0
Hearts	v	Celtic	1-2/1-0	2-4/0-3	0-1/1-4	1-4/2-1	0-1/1-1	0-2	08-05-21
Kilmarnock	v	Hibernian	0-2/1-0	0-1/1-1	0-0/1-0	2-1/6-2	0-2/2-0	3-1	09-06-06
Livingston	v	Motherwell	-	-	3-1	3-2/1-0	1-0/3-1	2-3/1-1	05-01-0
Rangers	v	Dundee Utd	4-1/3-0	3-0/0-2	3-2	3-0	2-1	1-1/0-1	19-03-07

BELL'S SCOTTISH FIRST DIVISION

Airdrie Utd	v	St Johnstone	-	-	-	-	-	1-0/0-0	02-06-07
Clyde	v	Queen of Sth	3-0/3-1	-	-	2-1/2-2	3-1/2-0	2-0/0-1	15-04-04
Hamilton	v	Dundee	-	-	-	-	-	-	03-01-08
Ross County	v	Stranraer	1-1/3-1	-	-	-	-	-	01-01-00
St Mirren	v	Brechin	-	-	-	-	0-0/3-3	-	01-03-00

BELL'S SCOTTISH SECOND DIVISION

Dumbarton	v	Partick	-	-	-	-	-	-	00-00-00
Forfar	v	Morton	-	-	2-1/2-1	-	2-3/2-1	2-0/0-0	05-03-05
Peterhead	v	Ayr	-	-	-	-	-	-	00-00-00
Raith	v	Alloa	-	1-2/2-1	-	-	-	-	01-01-01
Stirling	v	Gretna	-	-	-	0-1/1-0	0-1/0-1	-	01-00-03

BELL'S SCOTTISH THIRD DIVISION

Arbroath	v	E Stirling	-	-	-	-	-	-	06-07-04
Berwick	v	Queen's Park	1-2/1-1	1-1/1-0	-	-	-	-	06-05-06
Cowdenb'th	v	Elgin	-	3-1/1-0	-	-	3-2/2-0	3-1/1-1	05-01-00
Montrose	v	East Fife	1-2/1-1	0-1/1-1	2-1/0-1	0-5/0-2	-	2-1	03-04-11
Stenhsmuir	v	Albion	-	-	-	-	-	3-0/1-1	06-03-03

NATIONWIDE CONFERENCE

Cambridge U	v	Canvey Islnd	-	-	-	-	-	-	00-00-00
Exeter	v	Hereford	-	-	-	-	0-1	4-0	03-02-02
Forest G	v	Aldershot	-	-	-	-	3-1	0-0	01-01-00
Gravesend	v	Crawley	-	-	-	-	-	0-0	02-02-03
Grays	v	Stevenage	-	-	-	-	-	-	01-00-01
Halifax	v	Scarborough	-	-	-	2-1	1-0	2-1	04-00-05
Kidderminstr	v	Burton	-	-	-	-	-	-	00-00-00
Southport	v	Accrington	-	-	-	-	-	-	00-02-00
Tamworth	v	Altrincham	-	-	-	-	-	-	00-00-00
Woking	v	Dagenham & R	-	4-4	0-2	0-0	0-0	2-4	00-05-04
York	v	Morecambe	-	-	-	-	-	1-0	01-00-00

MONDAY 2ND JANUARY 2006
FA BARCLAYCARD PREMIER LEAGUE

Birmingham	v	Wigan	-	-	-	-	-	-	00-03-00
Blackburn	v	Portsmouth	1-1	3-1	-	-	1-2	1-0	04-03-01
Bolton	v	Liverpool	-	-	2-1	2-3	2-2	1-0	02-02-02
Everton	v	Charlton	-	3-0	0-3	1-0	0-1	0-1	05-00-03
Fulham	v	Sunderland	-	-	2-0	1-0	-	-	02-00-00
Man City	v	Tottenham	-	0-1	-	2-3	0-0	0-1	03-03-05
Newcastle	v	Middlesbro	2-1	1-2	3-0	2-0	2-1	0-0	07-04-02

WBA	v	Aston Villa	-	-	-	0-0	-	1-1	00-02-00
West Ham	v	Chelsea	0-0	0-2	2-1	1-0	-	-	05-03-03

COCA-COLA CHAMPIONSHIP

Coventry	v	Wolves	-	-	0-1	0-2	-	2-2	00-01-02
Crystal Pal	v	Leicester	-	-	-	0-0	-	-	03-01-02
Hull	v	Sheff Utd	-	-	-	-	-	-	00-01-00
Luton	v	Watford	-	-	-	-	-	-	02-03-01
Millwall	v	Derby	-	-	-	3-0	0-0	3-1	05-03-02
Norwich	v	Preston	-	1-2	3-0	2-0	3-2	-	03-00-01
Plymouth	v	Leeds	-	-	-	-	-	0-1	01-01-01
QPR	v	Burnley	-	0-1	-	-	-	3-0	01-00-01
Reading	v	Cardiff	0-1	-	1-2	-	2-1	2-1	03-01-03
Sheff Weds	v	Crewe	-	0-0	1-0	-	-	-	01-01-00
Southampton	v	Brighton	-	-	-	-	-	-	00-00-00
Stoke	v	Ipswich	-	-	-	2-1	2-0	3-2	04-03-01

COCA-COLA LEAGUE 1

Blackpool	v	Southend	-	2-2	-	-	-	-	02-01-00
Bournemouth	v	Scunthorpe	1-1	-	-	2-1	-	-	01-01-00
Bradford	v	Brentford	-	-	-	-	-	4-1	04-00-02
Bristol C	v	Walsall	-	1-3	-	-	-	0-1	03-00-03
Chesterfield	v	Barnsley	-	-	-	1-0	0-2	2-2	01-01-01
Colchester	v	Nottm F	-	-	-	-	-	-	00-00-00
Doncaster	v	Yeovil	0-3	2-0	1-2	0-4	0-1	-	01-00-05
Hartlepool	v	Swindon	-	-	-	-	2-0	3-0	02-00-00
Huddersfield	v	Gillingham	-	2-3	-	-	-	-	00-01-01
Milton K	v	Oldham	-	-	-	-	-	1-1	03-01-00
Swansea	v	Port Vale	-	0-1	-	-	-	-	01-01-02
Tranmere	v	Rotherham	-	-	-	-	-	-	01-01-01

COCA-COLA LEAGUE 2

Boston	v	Leyton O	-	-	-	0-1	3-0	2-2	01-01-01
Chester	v	Oxford Utd	-	-	-	-	-	1-3	01-00-01
Darlington	v	Torquay	1-1	2-0	1-3	1-1	1-1	-	05-04-06
Grimsby	v	Carlisle	-	-	-	-	-	-	02-01-00
Mansfield	v	Lincoln	5-2	2-3	2-1	-	1-2	2-2	04-04-03
Notts Co	v	Barnet	-	-	-	-	-	-	01-00-00
Peterboro	v	Bury	-	1-1	2-1	-	-	-	01-02-01
Rochdale	v	Northampton	0-3	-	-	-	1-1	1-0	03-04-03
Rushden & D	v	Bristol R	-	-	3-1	2-1	-	0-0	02-01-00
Shrewsbury	v	Wrexham	-	-	-	1-2	-	-	00-02-03
Stockport	v	Cheltenham	-	-	-	1-1	-	-	00-01-00
Wycombe	v	Macclesfield	-	-	-	-	-	1-1	01-04-02

BELL'S SCOTTISH FIRST DIVISION

Hamilton	v	Airdrie Utd	-	-	-	1-0/2-1	2-1/0-1	1-3/1-1	08-04-07
Ross County	v	Brechin	-	-	-	-	4-0/2-1	-	03-01-02
St Johnstone	v	Dundee	0-1/2-1	0-0/2-3	0-2/0-1	-	-	-	05-06-07
St Mirren	v	Clyde	-	-	4-1/2-2	1-4/1-2	2-1/2-3	0-0/0-0	03-04-03
Stranraer	v	Queen of Sth	1-0/1-2	3-2/2-0	2-2/1-2	-	-	-	09-04-07

BELL'S SCOTTISH SECOND DIVISION

Dumbarton	v	Morton	-	-	-	-	1-0/3-0	0-3/3-0	08-00-04
Forfar	v	Peterhead	-	-	-	-	-	-	00-00-00
Gretna	v	Ayr	-	-	-	-	-	-	00-00-00
Partick	v	Raith	-	-	2-1/1-0	-	-	2-0/4-1	06-04-06
Stirling	v	Alloa	0-1/1-1	-	-	-	-	2-0/0-4	04-02-03

BELL'S SCOTTISH THIRD DIVISION

Berwick	v	Elgin	-	-	-	-	-	-	00-00-00

Sponsored by Stan James

East Fife	v	Cowdenbeath	2-3/1-1	0-2/1-2	-	-	-	1-1/1-1	04-05-0
Montrose	v	Arbroath	-	-	-	-	-		08-04-0
Queen's Park	v	Albion	2-0/0-1	-	1-2/0-3	2-4/1-1	1-1/0-1	1-1/0-3	08-13-0
Stenhsmuir	v	E Stirling	-	-	-	-	-	6-0/3-2	09-03-0

NATIONWIDE CONFERENCE

Accrington	v	Halifax	-	-	-	-	2-1	1-1	01-01-0
Aldershot	v	Exeter	-	-	-	-	2-1	2-1	02-00-0
Altrincham	v	Kidderminstr	0-0	-	-	-	-	-	03-04-0
Burton	v	Tamworth	1-1	3-1	-	-	0-1	1-1	02-03-0
Canvey Islnd	v	Grays	-	1-0	1-2	2-0	1-1		02-01-0
Crawley	v	Woking	-	-	-	-	-	2-1	01-00-0
Dagenham & R	v	Gravesend	2-1	-	-	4-0	0-4	5-0	04-01-0
Hereford	v	Forest G	1-0	3-1	0-0	1-1	5-1	2-1	05-02-0
Morecambe	v	Southport	3-3	1-3	2-2	3-0	-	-	06-03-0
Scarborough	v	York	-	-	-	-	-	5-1	03-02-0
Stevenage	v	Cambridge U	-	-	-	-	-	-	00-00-0

TUESDAY 3RD JANUARY 2006
FA BARCLAYCARD PREMIER LEAGUE

Arsenal	v	Man Utd	1-2	1-0	3-1	2-2	1-1	2-4	08-05-04

SATURDAY 7TH JANUARY 2006
COCA-COLA LEAGUE 1

Barnsley	v	Gillingham	-	3-1	4-1	-	-	-	02-00-00
Blackpool	v	Doncaster	-	-	-	-	-	1-1	02-01-00
Brentford	v	Nottm F	-	-	-	-	-	-	00-00-00
Chesterfield	v	Bradford	-	-	-	-	-	0-0	01-01-00
Colchester	v	Bristol C	3-4	4-0	0-0	2-2	2-1	0-2	02-02-02
Oldham	v	Southend	-	-	-	-	-	-	01-01-02
Rotherham	v	Port Vale	-	3-2	-	-	-	-	02-00-01
Scunthorpe	v	Huddersfield	-	-	-	-	6-2	-	01-00-00
Swansea	v	Milton K	-	-	-	-	-	-	00-00-00
Swindon	v	Walsall	1-1	1-4	-	-	-	1-2	01-02-02
Tranmere	v	Bournemouth	-	-	0-0	-	1-1	2-0	02-02-00
Yeovil	v	Hartlepool	-	-	-	-	-	-	00-00-00

COCA-COLA LEAGUE 2

Barnet	v	Cheltenham	3-2	2-2	-	-	-	-	04-01-00
Boston	v	Macclesfield	-	-	-	2-1	3-1	1-1	05-02-01
Bristol R	v	Leyton O	-	-	5-3	1-2	1-1	1-1	02-04-01
Carlisle	v	Bury	-	-	-	1-2	2-1	-	03-00-02
Mansfield	v	Chester	2-1	-	-	-	-	0-0	07-01-03
Northampton	v	Wycombe	-	2-2	4-1	0-5	-	1-1	02-04-01
Notts Co	v	Darlington	-	-	-	-	-	1-1	00-02-00
Oxford Utd	v	Shrewsbury	-	-	0-1	2-2	-	2-0	03-02-01
Peterboro	v	Rushden & D	-	-	-	-	3-1	-	01-00-00
Stockport	v	Grimsby	2-1	1-1	3-3	-	2-1	-	04-02-01
Torquay	v	Rochdale	1-0	1-0	3-0	2-2	1-3	-	09-03-03
Wrexham	v	Lincoln	-	-	-	0-2	-	-	03-02-02

NATIONWIDE CONFERENCE

Altrincham	v	Stevenage	0-1	-	-	-	-	-	00-00-04
Cambridge U	v	Forest G	-	-	-	-	-	-	00-00-00
Canvey Islnd	v	Accrington	-	-	-	-	-	-	00-00-01
Crawley	v	York	-	-	-	-	-	0-2	00-00-01
Exeter	v	Gravesend	-	-	-	-	-	1-0	01-00-01
Grays	v	Burton	-	-	-	-	0-1	3-0	01-00-01
Halifax	v	Morecambe	-	-	-	1-0	1-0	1-3	03-02-01

210

carborough	v	Hereford	3-0	2-4	3-2	2-1	3-3	0-0	06-05-04
outhport	v	Dagenham & R	-	0-1	2-2	2-3	-	-	01-03-02
amworth	v	Aldershot	-	-	-	-	3-3	1-2	00-01-01
oking	v	Kidderminstr	1-0	-	-	-	-	-	04-02-02

SATURDAY 14TH JANUARY 2006
FA BARCLAYCARD PREMIER LEAGUE

rsenal	v	Middlesbro	5-1	0-3	2-1	2-0	4-1	5-3	07-03-01
ston Villa	v	West Ham	2-2	2-2	2-1	4-1	-	-	05-05-02
ackburn	v	Bolton	3-1	1-1	1-1	0-0	3-4	0-1	03-03-02
harlton	v	Birmingham	1-0	-	-	0-2	1-1	3-1	05-03-01
ulham	v	Newcastle	-	-	3-1	2-1	2-3	-	02-00-01
iverpool	v	Tottenham	2-0	3-1	1-0	2-1	0-0	2-2	11-05-01
an City	v	Man Utd	-	0-1	-	3-1	4-1	0-2	03-03-05
ortsmouth	v	Everton	-	-	-	-	1-2	0-1	00-00-02

COCA-COLA CHAMPIONSHIP

righton	v	Leeds	-	-	-	-	-	1-0	02-01-00
ardiff	v	Burnley	1-2	-	-	-	2-0	2-0	04-00-02
erby	v	Crewe	-	-	-	-	0-0	2-4	00-01-01
ull	v	Crystal Pal	-	-	-	-	-	-	00-00-01
swich	v	Sheff Utd	1-1	-	-	3-2	3-0	5-1	06-05-00
lymouth	v	Norwich	-	-	-	-	-	-	00-00-00
reston	v	Millwall	3-2	-	1-0	2-1	1-2	1-1	05-01-02
QPR	v	Southampton	-	-	-	-	-	-	04-02-02
Reading	v	Coventry	-	-	-	1-2	1-2	1-2	00-00-03
heff Weds	v	Leicester	4-0	-	-	0-0	-	-	04-02-01
Watford	v	Stoke	-	-	-	1-2	1-3	0-1	02-02-04
Wolves	v	Luton	-	-	-	-	-	-	01-01-02

COCA-COLA LEAGUE 1

Bournemouth	v	Rotherham	-	0-1	-	-	-	-	02-04-01
Bradford	v	Swansea	-	-	-	-	-	-	02-01-03
Bristol C	v	Scunthorpe	2-1	-	-	-	-	-	01-00-00
Doncaster	v	Chesterfield	-	-	-	-	-	0-1	02-01-04
Gillingham	v	Swindon	-	-	-	-	-	-	00-00-00
Hartlepool	v	Tranmere	-	-	-	-	0-0	0-1	00-02-01
Huddersfield	v	Blackpool	-	-	2-4	0-0	-	1-0	03-04-01
Milton K	v	Yeovil	-	-	-	-	-	-	00-00-00
Nottm F	v	Oldham	-	-	-	-	-	-	02-00-00
Port Vale	v	Barnsley	2-2	-	-	0-0	3-1	5-0	06-03-02
Southend	v	Brentford	-	-	-	-	-	-	02-01-02
Walsall	v	Colchester	-	0-1	-	-	-	2-1	02-01-03

COCA-COLA LEAGUE 2

Bury	v	Torquay	-	-	-	0-1	2-1	-	04-02-01
Cheltenham	v	Bristol R	-	-	0-0	-	1-2	1-1	00-02-01
Chester	v	Boston	-	2-2	1-2	-	-	2-1	01-01-01
Darlington	v	Peterboro	2-0	-	-	-	-	-	03-01-02
Grimsby	v	Mansfield	-	-	-	-	-	2-0	02-00-00
Leyton O	v	Northampton	0-0	-	-	-	1-1	3-2	03-03-00
Lincoln	v	Barnet	0-0	2-1	-	-	-	-	04-01-03
Macclesfield	v	Oxford Utd	-	-	0-1	2-1	2-1	1-0	03-00-01
Rochdale	v	Stockport	-	-	-	-	-	-	01-02-00
Rushden & D	v	Wrexham	-	-	-	2-2	2-3	-	00-01-01
Shrewsbury	v	Carlisle	4-1	0-1	1-0	2-3	-	-	03-02-03
Wycombe	v	Notts Co	2-0	3-1	3-0	3-1	1-1	1-2	05-03-01

BANK OF SCOTLAND SCOTTISH PREMIER LEAGUE

Celtic	v	Kilmarnock	5-1/4-2	2-1/6-0	1-0	5-0/2-0	5-1	2-1	16-05-00
Dundee Utd	v	Falkirk	-	-	-	-	-	-	06-00-00

Dunfermline	v	Hearts	-	1-0	0-1/1-1	3-1/0-1	2-1/0-0	1-0/1-1	08-05-0
Hibernian	v	Aberdeen	2-0/1-0	0-2	2-0/3-4	1-2/2-0/3-1	1-1/0-1	2-1	12-07-1
Inv CT	v	Livingston	2-0/4-1	2-2/2-3	-	-	-	2-0	05-03-0
Motherwell	v	Rangers	1-5/2-0	0-1/1-2	2-2	1-0	1-1/0-1	0-2/2-3	09-05-1

BELL'S SCOTTISH FIRST DIVISION

Airdrie Utd	v	St Mirren	0-2/0-1	-	0-0/2-3	-	-	3-2/0-2	06-05-0
Brechin	v	Stranraer	-	-	-	3-1/3-1	-	4-1/2-1	06-05-0
Clyde	v	St Johnstone	-	-	-	1-2/2-1	2-0/2-3	1-0/1-1	04-01-0
Dundee	v	Ross County	-	-	-	-	-	-	00-00-0
Queen of Sth	v	Hamilton	3-2/1-1	-	0-1/3-1	-	-	1-1/1-2	03-03-0

BELL'S SCOTTISH SECOND DIVISION

Alloa	v	Forfar	-	-	1-2/2-1	-	1-1/4-0	2-3/0-2	03-03-1
Ayr	v	Partick	-	-	0-2/1-1	-	-	-	01-04-0
Morton	v	Gretna	-	-	-	2-2/5-0	-	-	01-01-0
Peterhead	v	Dumbarton	-	2-0/0-1	0-3/4-0	-	-	-	02-00-0
Raith	v	Stirling	-	-	-	-	-	-	03-01-0

BELL'S SCOTTISH THIRD DIVISION

Albion	v	East Fife	1-3/3-1	0-1/1-2	3-0/2-1	1-5/0-0	-	2-0/0-6	07-02-0
Arbroath	v	Stenhsmuir	0-3/2-2	3-0/5-0	-	-	2-1/1-1	-	09-03-0
Cowdenb'th	v	Berwick	1-1/1-3	-	2-1/1-1	1-2/0-1	-	-	06-04-0
E Stirling	v	Montrose	2-0/1-0	1-2/0-1	0-1/2-1	1-1/0-3	1-1/1-4	1-1/1-2	09-05-1
Elgin	v	Queen's Park	-	-	2-0/0-1	2-2/0-0	2-2/1-3	1-0/1-0	03-03-0

MONDAY 15TH JANUARY 2006
FA BARCLAYCARD PREMIER LEAGUE

Sunderland	v	Chelsea	4-1	1-0	0-0	1-2	-	-	04-01-0
Wigan	v	WBA	-	-	-	-	1-0	-	02-00-0

SATURDAY 21ST JANUARY 2006
FA BARCLAYCARD PREMIER LEAGUE

Birmingham	v	Portsmouth	1-0	0-0	1-1	-	2-0	0-0	05-04-03
Bolton	v	Man City	0-1	-	-	2-0	1-3	0-1	02-01-03
Chelsea	v	Charlton	-	0-1	0-1	4-1	1-0	-	04-00-02
Everton	v	Arsenal	0-1	2-0	0-1	2-1	1-1	1-4	04-06-07
Man Utd	v	Liverpool	1-1	0-1	0-1	4-0	0-1	2-1	07-06-04
Middlesbro	v	Wigan	-	-	-	-	-	-	00-00-00
Newcastle	v	Blackburn	-	-	2-1	5-1	0-1	3-0	07-05-01
Tottenham	v	Aston Villa	2-4	0-0	0-0	1-0	2-1	-	07-04-05
WBA	v	Sunderland	-	-	-	2-2	0-0	-	01-05-03
West Ham	v	Fulham	-	-	0-2	1-1	-	-	00-01-01

COCA-COLA CHAMPIONSHIP

Burnley	v	Preston	0-3	3-0	2-1	2-0	1-1	2-0	05-02-03
Coventry	v	Derby	2-0	2-0	-	3-0	2-0	-	07-01-02
Crewe	v	Plymouth	-	-	-	0-1	-	3-0	02-01-01
Crystal Pal	v	Reading	-	-	-	0-1	2-2	-	01-01-02
Leeds	v	Sheff Weds	2-0	-	-	-	-	-	04-02-03
Leicester	v	Cardiff	-	-	-	-	-	1-1	00-01-00
Luton	v	QPR	-	-	-	0-0	1-1	-	00-04-02
Millwall	v	Wolves	-	-	1-0	1-1	-	1-2	06-01-02
Norwich	v	Watford	-	2-1	3-1	4-0	1-2	-	03-01-02
Sheff Utd	v	Brighton	-	-	-	2-1	-	1-2	02-00-01
Southampton	v	Ipswich	-	0-3	3-3	-	-	-	02-01-02
Stoke	v	Hull	-	-	-	-	-	-	02-01-01

COCA-COLA LEAGUE 1

Barnsley	v	Milton K	-	0-1	1-1	-	-	1-1	01-02-01

Home		Away	1	2	3	4	5	6	Ref
ackpool	v	Bristol C	1-2	-	5-1	0-0	1-0	1-1	04-04-02
rentford	v	Huddersfield	-	-	3-0	1-0	-	0-1	05-01-03
hesterfield	v	Walsall	-	-	-	-	-	1-0	04-03-03
olchester	v	Port Vale	-	0-1	2-0	4-1	1-4	2-1	03-00-02
ldham	v	Gillingham	1-3	-	-	-	-	-	01-00-02
otherham	v	Nottm F	-	-	1-2	2-2	1-1	0-0	00-03-01
cunthorpe	v	Doncaster	-		-	-	2-2	-	03-04-04
wansea	v	Hartlepool	2-1	-	0-1	2-2	-	-	03-04-02
windon	v	Bournemouth	-	1-1	0-0	-	2-1	0-3	02-03-02
ranmere	v	Southend	-		-	-	-	-	04-02-01
eovil	v	Bradford	-		-	-	-	-	00-00-00

COCA-COLA LEAGUE 2

Home		Away	1	2	3	4	5	6	Ref
arnet	v	Wycombe	-		-			-	03-00-00
oston	v	Bury				1-1	1-0	2-2	01-02-00
ristol R	v	Chester	-					4-1	04-00-00
arlisle	v	Cheltenham	1-1	1-1	0-0		1-1	-	00-04-00
Mansfield	v	Rochdale	0-0	1-0	3-1		1-0	1-0	07-04-01
orthampton	v	Macclesfield	2-0				0-0	1-0	02-01-01
lotts Co	v	Shrewsbury	-					3-0	02-02-01
xford Utd	v	Darlington	-		1-2	1-1	3-1	1-2	01-01-02
eterboro	v	Lincoln	2-2						03-02-00
tockport	v	Rushden & D	-				2-1		01-00-00
orquay	v	Grimsby							00-01-01
Vrexham	v	Leyton O	-			0-0			02-01-01

BANK OF SCOTLAND SCOTTISH PREMIER LEAGUE

Home		Away	1	2	3	4	5	6	Ref
Dundee Utd	v	Aberdeen	3-1/1-1	3-5/1-1	1-1	1-1/0-2	3-2	1-1/1-2	10-13-07
Falkirk	v	Inv CT	0-2/2-2	2-2/2-1	1-2/0-0	1-1/2-3	2-1/2-1	-	03-04-03
Hibernian	v	Dunfermline	-	3-0	5-1/1-1	1-4/1-3	1-2	2-1	10-04-03
Kilmarnock	v	Hearts	2-2/0-1	0-3/1-1	1-0/3-3	0-1/1-0	0-2/1-1	1-1	09-07-07
Motherwell	v	Celtic	3-2/1-1	3-3	1-2/0-4	2-1/0-4	0-2/1-1	2-3	07-12-13
Rangers	v	Livingston	-	-	0-0/3-0	4-3	1-0	4-0/3-0	05-01-00

BELL'S SCOTTISH FIRST DIVISION

Home		Away	1	2	3	4	5	6	Ref
Airdrie Utd	v	Clyde	-	1-3/1-0	1-2/2-2	-	-	3-1/2-4	05-05-03
Brechin	v	Dundee	-					-	00-00-01
Hamilton	v	St Mirren	-					2-2/0-0	04-11-01
Ross County	v	Queen of Sth	1-1/2-0	-		2-0/0-3	1-0/1-2	1-0/1-1	04-02-02
Stranraer	v	St Johnstone	-					-	00-01-01

BELL'S SCOTTISH SECOND DIVISION

Home		Away	1	2	3	4	5	6	Ref
Forfar	v	Dumbarton	5-0/4-3	-		2-0/0-1	3-1/1-0	0-2/6-0	06-00-02
Morton	v	Alloa	-	2-0/1-1	1-1/0-0	-	2-2/2-1	2-2/2-0	05-05-00
Gretna	v	Partick	-				-	-	00-00-00
Raith	v	Ayr	5-1/2-0	1-3/1-4	1-1/3-3		1-1/2-1	-	09-08-05
Stirling	v	Peterhead	-		2-1/0-2	1-0/2-1	3-1/0-2	-	04-00-02

BELL'S SCOTTISH THIRD DIVISION

Home		Away	1	2	3	4	5	6	Ref
Berwick	v	Arbroath	-	2-1/1-0	-	-	3-0/1-3	0-3/2-3	09-03-05
Cowdenb'th	v	Montrose	1-1/2-1	2-0/2-1	-	-	3-3/0-0	0-0/0-0	07-07-07
Elgin	v	Albion	-	1-2/1-0	2-0/0-0	0-1/1-2	1-5/1-2	1-0/1-1	03-02-05
Queen's Park	v	E Stirling	2-1/0-1	-	2-3/1-0	0-2/3-4	3-0/1-0	0-0/2-0	15-06-08
Stenhsmuir	v	East Fife	-				3-0/0-1	5-2/1-2	06-06-07

NATIONWIDE CONFERENCE

Home		Away	1	2	3	4	5	6	Ref
Accrington	v	Cambridge U	-	-		-	-	-	00-00-00
Aldershot	v	Halifax	-	-	-	-	3-1	0-0	01-01-00
Burton	v	Woking	-	-		0-2	2-0	0-1	01-00-02
Dagenham & R	v	Tamworth	-	-	-		0-0	0-0	00-02-00

Forest G	v	Altrincham	1-1	-	-	-	-	-	00-01-0
Gravesend	v	Canvey Islnd	0-1	1-2	0-1	-	-	3-2	01-00-0
Hereford	v	Crawley	-	-	-	-	-	0-0	00-01-0
Kidderminstr	v.	Scarborough	2-0	-	-	-	-	-	01-00-0
Morecambe	v	Exeter	-	-	-	-	0-3	2-2	00-01-0
Stevenage	v	Southport	1-1	1-3	2-1	3-0	-	-	04-02-0:
York	v	Grays	-	-	-	-	-	-	00-00-0

TUESDAY 24TH JANUARY 2006
NATIONWIDE CONFERENCE

Accrington	v	Altrincham	-	2-1	0-0	3-1	-	-	02-02-0
Aldershot	v	Canvey Islnd	3-1	1-0	1-3	1-0	-	2-0	04-00-0
Burton	v	Halifax	-	-	-	2-2	2-2	2-2	00-03-0(
Dagenham & R	v	Crawley	-	-	-	-	-	1-0	01-00-0(
Forest G	v	Tamworth	-	-	-	-	2-1	1-1	02-01-0
Gravesend	v	Grays	-	0-1	2-0	-	-	-	01-00-0
Hereford	v	Cambridge U	-	-	-	-	-	-	02-00-0:
Kidderminstr	v	Exeter	-	0-0	3-1	4-3	-	-	02-01-0(
Morecambe	v	Scarborough	0-1	4-4	2-0	3-1	2-1	2-1	04-01-0
Stevenage	v	Woking	0-1	0-3	1-4	1-1	1-1	0-2	02-03-0€
York	v	Southport	-	-	-	-	-	-	00-00-0(

SATURDAY 28TH JANUARY 2006
COCA-COLA LEAGUE 1

Bournemouth	v	Chesterfield	1-1	-	3-1	-	2-2	0-0	04-04-0(
Bradford	v	Tranmere	-	-	-	-	-	1-1	02-01-02
Bristol C	v	Swansea	-	3-1	-	-	-	-	03-00-01
Doncaster	v	Colchester	-	-	-	-	-	1-1	05-02-02
Gillingham	v	Rotherham	-	-	2-1	1-1	2-0	3-1	05-01-00
Hartlepool	v	Blackpool	-	3-1	-	-	1-1	1-1	03-02-01
Huddersfield	v	Oldham	-	-	0-0	1-1	-	2-1	02-03-00
Milton K	v	Brentford	-	-	-	-	-	0-0	00-01-00
Nottm F	v	Barnsley	3-0	1-0	0-0	-	-	-	03-01-00
Port Vale	v	Scunthorpe	-	-	-	-	-	-	00-00-00
Southend	v	Swindon	-	-	-	-	-	-	02-01-01
Walsall	v	Yeovil	-	-	-	-	-	-	00-00-00

COCA-COLA LEAGUE 2

Bury	v	Northampton	-	1-0	2-1	-	1-0	2-0	06-02-02
Cheltenham	v	Wrexham	-	-	-	-	-	-	00-00-00
Chester	v	Notts Co	-	-	-	-	-	3-2	02-01-01
Darlington	v	Mansfield	0-0	2-1	0-1	-	1-0	2-1	05-04-02
Grimsby	v	Peterboro	-	-	-	-	1-1	-	01-02-02
Leyton O	v	Barnet	0-0	3-1	-	-	-	-	03-03-01
Lincoln	v	Bristol R	-	-	0-1	2-1	3-1	1-1	03-01-01
Macclesfield	v	Carlisle	2-1	1-0	1-1	2-2	1-1	-	02-03-00
Rochdale	v	Boston	-	-	-	1-0	1-0	2-0	03-00-00
Rushden & D	v	Oxford Utd	-	-	2-1	0-2	-	3-3	01-01-01
Shrewsbury	v	Torquay	1-2	1-1	0-1	2-3	-	-	01-02-06
Wycombe	v	Stockport	-	-	-	1-4	1-0	-	02-01-02

BANK OF SCOTLAND SCOTTISH PREMIER LEAGUE

Aberdeen	v	Kilmarnock	2-2/5-1	1-2	2-0/1-1	0-1	3-1	3-2	11-05-05
Celtic	v	Dundee Utd	4-1/2-0	2-1	5-1/1-0	5-0/2-0	5-0/2-1/2-1	1-0	24-05-02
Dunfermline	v	Motherwell	-	1-2/1-2	5-2/3-1	1-0/3-0	1-0/3-0	1-1/0-0	09-07-06
Hearts	v	Hibernian	0-3/2-1	0-0/1-1	1-1	5-1/4-4	2-0	2-1/1-2	15-11-04
Inv CT	v	Rangers	-	-	-	-	-	1-1	00-01-00
Livingston	v	Falkirk	1-1/0-1	4-1/3-0	-	-	-	-	04-01-03

BELL'S SCOTTISH FIRST DIVISION

Clyde	v	Hamilton	2-1/1-0	-	-	-	-	2-1/1-3	04-02-05

214

Dundee	v	Stranraer	-	-	-	-	-	-	02-00-00
Queen of Sth	v	Airdrie Utd	-	-	-	-	-	1-0/0-0	01-01-01
St Johnstone	v	Brechin	-	-	-	-	3-1/2-2	-	01-01-00
St Mirren	v	Ross County	-	-	1-0/1-1	1-1/1-0	1-1/2-0	3-2	04-03-00

BELL'S SCOTTISH SECOND DIVISION

Alloa	v	Gretna	-	-	-	-	-	-	00-00-00
Ayr	v	Morton	3-0/3-2	1-1/3-0	-	-	-	2-0/2-1	13-04-04
Dumbarton	v	Stirling	-	-	4-1/2-0	-	-	1-1/0-2	04-05-05
Partick	v	Forfar	-	1-1/4-0	-	-	-	-	06-04-01
Peterhead	v	Raith	-	-	-	-	-	-	00-00-00

BELL'S SCOTTISH THIRD DIVISION

Albion	v	Berwick	0-3/0-0	-	-	-	-	-	05-04-05
Arbroath	v	Cowdenbeath	-	-	-	-	-	-	06-03-06
East Fife	v	Queen's Park	0-0/0-0	-	1-4/0-3	1-1/1-0	-	1-4/0-1	06-07-04
E Stirling	v	Elgin	-	0-2/1-0	2-1/0-3	1-2/2-2	3-1/2-1	0-1/0-3	04-01-05
Montrose	v	Stenhsmuir	-	-	-	-	-	0-2/0-3	02-02-09

NATIONWIDE CONFERENCE

Altrincham	v	Aldershot	-	-	-	-	-	-	00-00-00
Cambridge U	v	Gravesend	-	-	-	-	-	-	00-00-00
Canvey Islnd	v	Burton	-	-	-	-	-	2-2	00-01-00
Crawley	v	Morecambe	-	-	-	-	-	2-1	01-00-00
Exeter	v	Accrington	-	-	-	-	3-2	1-2	01-00-01
Grays	v	Hereford	-	-	-	-	-	-	00-00-00
Halifax	v	Forest G	-	-	-	1-1	0-1	4-0	01-01-01
Scarborough	v	Dagenham & R	-	0-1	0-0	0-1	0-0	2-0	01-02-02
Southport	v	Kidderminstr	0-1	-	-	-	-	-	02-02-03
Tamworth	v	Stevenage	-	-	-	-	1-2	0-0	00-01-01
Woking	v	York	-	-	-	-	-	1-0	01-00-00

TUESDAY 31ST JANUARY 2006
FA BARCLAYCARD PREMIER LEAGUE

Arsenal	v	West Ham	2-1	3-0	2-0	3-1	-	-	09-00-03
Charlton	v	WBA	0-0	-	-	1-0	-	1-4	05-03-01
Liverpool	v	Birmingham	-	-	-	2-2	3-1	0-1	01-01-01
Portsmouth	v	Bolton	0-0	1-2	-	-	4-0	-	01-03-03
Sunderland	v	Middlesbro	1-1	1-0	0-1	1-3	-	-	04-02-04
Wigan	v	Everton	-	-	-	-	-	-	00-00-00

COCA-COLA CHAMPIONSHIP

Brighton	v	Burnley	-	-	-	2-2	-	0-1	02-02-01
Cardiff	v	Millwall	1-1	-	-	-	1-3	0-1	00-01-02
Hull	v	Coventry	-	-	-	-	-	-	00-00-00
Ipswich	v	Leeds	-	1-2	1-2	-	-	1-0	03-02-03
Plymouth	v	Southampton	-	-	-	-	-	-	00-00-00
Preston	v	Crystal Pal	-	2-0	2-1	1-2	4-1	-	03-00-01
QPR	v	Leicester	-	-	-	-	-	3-2	02-00-00
Reading	v	Norwich	-	-	-	0-2	0-1	-	01-00-04
Sheff Weds	v	Luton	-	-	-	-	0-0	0-0	02-03-00
Watford	v	Crewe	-	3-0	0-1	-	2-1	3-1	04-00-02
Wolves	v	Stoke	-	-	-	0-0	-	1-1	02-05-01

WEDNESDAY 1ST FEBRUARY 2006
FA BARCLAYCARD PREMIER LEAGUE

Aston Villa	v	Chelsea	0-0	1-1	1-1	2-1	3-2	0-0	06-05-05
Blackburn	v	Man Utd	-	-	2-2	1-0	1-0	1-1	03-04-04
Fulham	v	Tottenham	-	-	0-2	3-2	2-1	2-0	03-00-01

Man City	v	Newcastle	-	0-1	-	1-0	1-0	1-1	03-03-01

COCA-COLA CHAMPIONSHIP

Derby	v	Sheff Utd	-	-	-	2-1	2-0	0-1	03-01-02

SATURDAY 4TH FEBRUARY 2006
FA BARCLAYCARD PREMIER LEAGUE

Birmingham	v	Arsenal	-	-	-	0-4	0-3	-	00-00-02
Bolton	v	Wigan	-	-	-	-	-	-	03-02-00
Chelsea	v	Liverpool	2-0	3-0	4-0	2-1	0-1	1-0	10-04-02
Everton	v	Man City	-	3-1	-	2-2	0-0	2-1	05-04-02
Man Utd	v	Fulham	-	-	3-2	3-0	1-3	1-0	03-00-01
Middlesbro	v	Aston Villa	0-4	1-1	2-1	2-5	1-2	3-0	03-03-05
Newcastle	v	Portsmouth	-	-	-	-	3-0	1-1	05-01-00
Tottenham	v	Charlton	-	0-0	0-1	2-2	0-1	2-3	01-04-03
WBA	v	Blackburn	2-2	1-0	-	0-2	-	1-1	03-03-01
West Ham	v	Sunderland	1-1	0-2	3-0	2-0	3-2	-	06-01-01

COCA-COLA CHAMPIONSHIP

Burnley	v	Plymouth	-	-	-	-	-	-	03-01-00
Coventry	v	Brighton	-	-	-	0-0	-	2-1	01-01-00
Crewe	v	Reading	-	-	-	-	1-0	1-1	03-02-00
Crystal Pal	v	Cardiff	-	-	-	-	2-1	-	01-00-00
Leeds	v	QPR	-	-	-	-	-	6-1	03-02-02
Leicester	v	Wolves	-	-	-	1-0	0-0	1-1	04-05-00
Luton	v	Hull	-	-	0-1	-	-	1-0	01-00-01
Millwall	v	Sheff Weds	-	-	1-2	3-0	-	-	04-00-01
Norwich	v	Ipswich	0-0	-	-	0-2	3-1	-	06-02-02
Sheff Utd	v	Watford	-	0-1	0-2	1-2	2-2	1-1	03-03-03
Southampton	v	Derby	3-3	1-0	2-0	-	-	-	04-02-03
Stoke	v	Preston	2-1	-	-	2-1	1-1	0-0	04-02-02

COCA-COLA LEAGUE 1

Barnsley	v	Bristol C	-	-	-	1-4	0-1	2-1	05-01-03
Blackpool	v	Nottm F	-	-	-	-	-	-	00-00-00
Brentford	v	Walsall	-	2-1	-	-	-	1-0	05-01-00
Chesterfield	v	Gillingham	0-0	-	-	-	-	-	05-06-00
Colchester	v	Bradford	-	-	-	-	0-0	-	00-01-00
Oldham	v	Port Vale	-	4-1	2-0	1-1	2-1	3-0	08-02-00
Rotherham	v	Hartlepool	3-0	-	-	-	-	-	05-01-00
Scunthorpe	v	Milton K	-	-	-	-	-	-	00-00-00
Swansea	v	Bournemouth	-	0-3	-	2-0	-	-	04-02-02
Swindon	v	Doncaster	-	-	-	-	-	1-1	00-01-00
Tranmere	v	Huddersfield	1-0	2-0	1-0	2-1	-	3-0	09-01-01
Yeovil	v	Southend	-	-	-	-	4-0	3-1	02-00-00

COCA-COLA LEAGUE 2

Barnet	v	Shrewsbury	1-1	3-0	-	-	0-1	-	01-04-01
Boston	v	Darlington	-	-	-	1-0	1-0	3-1	03-00-01
Bristol R	v	Bury	0-0	2-0	-	2-1	1-2	2-2	04-02-02
Carlisle	v	Chester	4-1	-	-	-	-	-	03-01-00
Mansfield	v	Macclesfield	1-0	4-4	4-0	-	3-2	0-1	04-01-01
Northampton	v	Rushden & D	-	-	-	-	-	1-0	01-00-00
Notts Co	v	Grimsby	-	-	-	-	3-1	2-2	03-01-01
Oxford Utd	v	Rochdale	-	-	1-2	2-0	2-0	0-1	02-00-02
Peterboro	v	Cheltenham	1-0	-	-	4-1	-	-	02-00-00
Stockport	v	Lincoln	-	-	-	-	-	-	02-01-00
Torquay	v	Leyton O	0-0	1-2	1-1	2-2	2-1	-	04-06-01
Wrexham	v	Wycombe	1-3	0-0	0-0	-	0-0	-	04-03-02

BELL'S SCOTTISH SECOND DIVISION

loa	v	Partick	1-0/1-1	-	-	-	-	-	03-01-01
orton	v	Peterhead	-	-	-	1-0/1-0	-	-	02-00-00
retna	v	Dumbarton	-	-	-	-	-	-	00-00-00
aith	v	Forfar	-	-	-	5-1/0-1	-	-	06-00-03
tirling	v	Ayr	-	-	-	-	-	1-1/2-0	04-06-02

BELL'S SCOTTISH THIRD DIVISION

erwick	v	Montrose	0-0/2-1	-	-	-	-	-	07-06-03
owdenb'th	v	Stenhsmuir	-	-	1-1/2-4	1-0/3-3	-	0-6/0-2	04-05-07
Stirling	v	Albion	4-3/3-1	1-1/1-0	1-2/1-2	0-3/0-4	3-4/1-8	1-1/0-2	10-05-15
lgin	v	East Fife	-	1-3/1-3	1-1/2-0	1-1/0-1	-	2-1/2-1	03-02-03
Queen's Park	v	Arbroath	-	0-0/1-1	-	-	-	-	09-05-05

NATIONWIDE CONFERENCE

Aldershot	v	Accrington	-	-	-	-	2-1	0-0	01-01-00
Cambridge U	v	Grays	-	-	-	-	-	-	00-00-00
Canvey Islnd	v	Woking	-	-	-	-	-	2-2	00-01-00
Crawley	v	Forest G	-	-	-	-	-	4-2	01-01-00
Dagenham & R	v	York	-	-	-	-	-	0-3	00-00-01
Exeter	v	Stevenage	-	-	-	-	1-0	2-0	02-00-00
Gravesend	v	Hereford	-	-	-	3-0	2-5	1-2	01-00-02
Halifax	v	Kidderminstr	-	3-2	1-0	-	-	-	04-00-03
Morecambe	v	Burton	-	-	-	5-0	2-1	3-0	03-00-00
Scarborough	v	Altrincham	1-0	-	-	-	-	-	01-00-00
Tamworth	v	Southport	-	-	-	-	-	-	00-00-00

TUESDAY 7TH FEBRUARY 2006
BANK OF SCOTLAND SCOTTISH PREMIER LEAGUE

Dundee Utd	v	Hearts	0-2/0-1	0-4/1-1	0-2	0-3	2-1/0-2	1-1/2-1	09-11-10

WEDNESDAY 8TH FEBRUARY 2006
BANK OF SCOTLAND SCOTTISH PREMIER LEAGUE

Aberdeen	v	Rangers	1-5/1-1	1-2	0-3/0-1	2-2	2-3/1-1	0-0/1-2	07-11-15
Celtic	v	Falkirk	-	-	-	-	-	-	07-00-01
Dunfermline	v	Inv CT	4-0/1-0	-	-	-	-	1-1/0-0	02-02-00
Hibernian	v	Livingston	-	-	0-3	1-0/2-2	0-2/3-1	2-1/0-3	03-01-03
Kilmarnock	v	Motherwell	0-1/0-2	3-2/1-2	2-0/1-4	0-3/1-0	2-0	2-0	09-03-10

SATURDAY 11TH FEBRUARY 2006
FA BARCLAYCARD PREMIER LEAGUE

Arsenal	v	Bolton	-	-	1-1	2-1	2-1	2-2	04-02-00
Aston Villa	v	Newcastle	0-1	1-1	1-1	0-1	0-0	4-2	03-05-05
Everton	v	Blackburn	-	-	1-2	2-1	0-1	0-1	04-01-06
Fulham	v	WBA	1-0	0-0	-	3-0	-	1-0	03-03-00
Man City	v	Charlton	1-1	1-4	-	0-1	1-1	4-0	02-03-03
Middlesbro	v	Chelsea	0-1	1-0	0-2	1-1	1-2	0-1	03-03-04
Portsmouth	v	Man Utd	-	-	-	-	1-0	2-0	02-00-00
Sunderland	v	Tottenham	2-1	2-3	1-2	2-0	-	-	02-01-03
West Ham	v	Birmingham	-	-	-	1-2	-	-	01-00-01
Wigan	v	Liverpool	-	-	-	-	-	-	00-00-00

COCA-COLA CHAMPIONSHIP

Brighton	v	Leicester	-	-	-	0-1	-	1-1	02-02-02
Cardiff	v	Stoke	1-2	-	2-0	-	3-1	0-1	02-00-02
Derby	v	Leeds	0-1	1-1	0-1	-	-	2-0	01-03-04
Hull	v	Norwich	-	-	-	-	-	-	00-00-00
Ipswich	v	Burnley	-	-	-	2-2	6-1	1-1	01-02-00
Plymouth	v	Sheff Utd	-	-	-	-	-	3-0	01-01-00
Preston	v	Luton	1-0	-	-	-	-	-	04-00-00

QPR	v	Millwall	-	-	-	-	-	1-1	00-02-0
Reading	v	Southampton	-	-	-	-	-	-	00-00-0
Sheff Weds	v	Crystal Pal	-	4-1	1-3	0-0	-	-	04-02-0
Watford	v	Coventry	1-0	-	3-0	5-2	1-1	2-3	03-01-0
Wolves	v	Crewe	2-0	0-0	0-1	-	-	1-1	03-02-0

COCA-COLA LEAGUE 1

Bournemouth	v	Oldham	3-0	1-1	3-2	-	1-0	4-0	06-03-0
Bradford	v	Swindon	-	-	-	-	-	1-2	02-04-0
Bristol C	v	Brentford	1-0	1-2	0-2	0-0	3-1	4-1	05-03-0
Doncaster	v	Barnsley	-	-	-	-	-	4-0	01-00-0
Gillingham	v	Tranmere	-	2-1	-	-	-	-	01-00-0
Hartlepool	v	Chesterfield	-	1-2	-	-	2-0	3-2	04-00-0
Huddersfield	v	Colchester	-	-	2-1	1-1	-	2-2	01-02-0
Milton K	v	Blackpool	-	-	-	-	-	3-1	01-00-0
Nottm F	v	Swansea	-	-	-	-	-	-	00-00-0
Port Vale	v	Yeovil	-	-	-	-	-	-	00-00-0
Southend	v	Rotherham	1-2	-	-	-	-	-	02-00-0
Walsall	v	Scunthorpe	-	-	-	-	-	-	04-01-0

COCA-COLA LEAGUE 2

Bury	v	Oxford Utd	1-2	3-1	-	1-1	0-4	0-0	03-02-0
Cheltenham	v	Northampton	2-1	-	-	1-1	4-3	1-0	03-01-0
Chester	v	Stockport	-	-	-	-	-	-	02-00-0
Darlington	v	Bristol R	-	-	1-0	1-0	0-4	0-1	02-00-0
Grimsby	v	Boston	-	-	-	-	-	1-1	00-01-0
Leyton O	v	Carlisle	0-1	1-0	0-0	2-1	1-1	-	05-02-0
Lincoln	v	Torquay	2-1	1-2	0-0	1-1	1-3	-	05-05-04
Macclesfield	v	Wrexham	-	-	-	0-1	-	-	00-00-0
Rochdale	v	Barnet	1-1	0-0	-	-	-	-	02-05-02
Rushden & D	v	Notts Co	-	-	-	-	2-1	5-1	02-00-00
Shrewsbury	v	Peterboro	0-1	-	-	-	-	-	02-04-01
Wycombe	v	Mansfield	-	-	-	3-3	-	1-1	01-02-0

BANK OF SCOTLAND SCOTTISH PREMIER LEAGUE

Falkirk	v	Hibernian	-	-	-	-	-	-	04-04-02
Hearts	v	Aberdeen	3-0/3-0	3-0	1-0/3-1	0-0	2-0/1-0	0-0/1-0	17-07-08
Inv CT	v	Kilmarnock	-	-	-	-	-	0-2	00-00-01
Livingston	v	Dunfermline	0-1/1-0	-	0-0/4-1	1-1	0-0/0-0	2-0/1-1	04-05-03
Motherwell	v	Dundee Utd	2-2/1-3	2-1	0-0/2-0	1-2/2-2	3-1/0-1	4-2/2-0	14-06-11
Rangers	v	Celtic	4-2/4-0	5-1/0-3	0-2/1-1	3-2/1-2	0-1/1-2	2-0/1-2	15-10-09

BELL'S SCOTTISH FIRST DIVISION

Brechin	v	Airdrie Utd	-	-	-	1-5/0-1	-	-	00-01-05
Dundee	v	Queen of Sth	-	-	-	-	-	-	00-00-00
Ross County	v	Hamilton	2-1/0-1	-	-	-	-	1-1/2-1	02-01-01
St Johnstone	v	St Mirren	-	2-0/2-2	-	2-0/1-1	1-0/1-3	1-0	10-04-03
Stranraer	v	Clyde	2-2/2-1	-	-	-	-	-	04-07-00

BELL'S SCOTTISH SECOND DIVISION

Ayr	v	Alloa	-	3-1/4-1	-	3-1/0-1	-	4-3/1-1	05-01-01
Dumbarton	v	Raith	-	-	-	0-3/4-1	-	-	01-00-03
Forfar	v	Stirling	-	1-0/3-1	-	-	-	0-2/4-1	03-03-04
Partick	v	Morton	-	-	-	-	-	-	02-03-05
Peterhead	v	Gretna	-	-	-	1-1/1-0	2-0/2-1	1-1/4-2	04-02-00

BELL'S SCOTTISH THIRD DIVISION

Albion	v	Cowdenbeath	1-4/0-3	1-0/0-0	-	-	1-2/2-4	2-3/1-4	09-02-14
Arbroath	v	Elgin	-	-	-	-	-	-	00-00-00
East Fife	v	E Stirling	1-0/3-1	3-1/4-1	0-4/1-0	4-1/3-0	-	1-0/2-0	10-07-02
Montrose	v	Queen's Park	2-1/0-2	-	3-1/3-1	1-0/1-1	0-0/1-1	2-4/2-0	12-07-06

218

Stenhsmuir	v	Berwick	-	2-0/0-2	3-0/1-3	2-0/1-0	0-3/3-1	-	09-08-08

NATIONWIDE CONFERENCE

Accrington	v	Dagenham & R	-	-	-		2-3	0-3	00-00-02
Altrincham	v	Cambridge U	-	-	-	-	-	-	00-00-00
Burton	v	Exeter	-	-	-	-	3-4	1-0	01-00-01
Forest G	v	Scarborough	0-1	2-3	2-2	0-0	4-0	0-1	01-02-03
Grays	v	Crawley	-	-	-	-	-		00-00-00
Hereford	v	Halifax				1-1	7-1	2-3	04-02-03
Kidderminstr	v	Gravesend	-	-	-	-	-		00-00-00
Southport	v	Canvey Islnd	-	-	-	-	-		00-00-00
Stevenage	v	Morecambe	1-2	1-1	3-1	1-1	0-1	0-1	03-03-04
Woking	v	Tamworth	-	-	-	-	4-0	2-1	02-00-00
York	v	Aldershot					-	0-2	00-00-01

TUESDAY 14TH FEBRUARY 2006

COCA-COLA CHAMPIONSHIP

Burnley	v	Wolves	-	1-2	2-3	2-1	-	1-1	01-01-03
Crewe	v	Ipswich	1-2	-	-	-	1-0	2-2	01-02-02
Crystal Pal	v	QPR	3-0	1-1	-	-	-	-	02-06-01
Leeds	v	Watford	3-1	-	-	-		2-2	02-01-01
Leicester	v	Derby	0-1	2-1	0-3	3-1		1-0	05-02-05
Luton	v	Cardiff	1-0	-	-	2-0	-	-	02-00-00
Millwall	v	Hull	-	-	-	-	-	-	00-01-00
Norwich	v	Brighton	-	-	-	0-1	-		00-00-01
Sheff Utd	v	Reading	-	-	-	1-3	1-2	0-1	03-02-03
Stoke	v	Plymouth	-	-	-	-		2-0	02-02-00

COCA-COLA LEAGUE 1

Barnsley	v	Port Vale	3-1	-	-	2-1	0-0	1-2	04-04-03
Blackpool	v	Huddersfield	-	-	1-2	1-1	-	1-1	02-04-02
Brentford	v	Southend	-	-	-	-		-	03-01-01
Colchester	v	Walsall	-	0-2	-	-	-	5-0	04-00-02
Oldham	v	Nottm F	-	-	-	-	-		02-00-00
Rotherham	v	Bournemouth	-	3-1	-	-	-	-	04-01-02
Scunthorpe	v	Bristol C	1-2	-	-	-	-	-	00-00-01
Swansea	v	Bradford	-	-	-	-	-	-	02-03-01
Swindon	v	Gillingham	-	-	-	-	-	-	00-00-00
Tranmere	v	Hartlepool	-	-	-	-	0-0	2-1	02-01-00
Yeovil	v	Milton K	-	-	-	-	-	-	00-00-00

COCA-COLA LEAGUE 2

Barnet	v	Lincoln	5-3	4-3	-	-		-	06-02-00
Bristol R	v	Cheltenham	-	-	1-2	-	2-0	1-1	01-01-01
Carlisle	v	Shrewsbury	1-1	1-0	0-1	1-2	-	-	04-02-02
Mansfield	v	Grimsby	-	-	-	-		2-0	01-01-00
Northampton	v	Leyton O	2-1	-	-	-	1-0	2-2	02-01-03
Notts Co	v	Wycombe	2-1	0-2	0-1	1-1	1-1	0-1	03-02-04
Peterboro	v	Darlington	4-2	-	-	-	-	-	01-04-01
Stockport	v	Rochdale	-	-	-	-	-		03-00-00
Torquay	v	Bury	-	-	-	1-1	3-1	-	01-03-03
Wrexham	v	Rushden & D	-	-	-	3-0	1-1	-	01-01-00

WEDNESDAY 15TH FEBRUARY 2006

COCA-COLA CHAMPIONSHIP

Coventry	v	Sheff Weds	4-1	-	2-0	1-1	-	-	07-04-02
Southampton	v	Preston	-	-	-	-	-	-	00-00-00

COCA-COLA LEAGUE 1

Chesterfield	v	Doncaster	-	-	-	-		0-0	02-04-01

COCA-COLA LEAGUE 2

Boston	v	Chester	-	0-0	0-1	-	-	3-1	01-01-01
Oxford Utd	v	Macclesfield	-	-	0-2	0-1	3-1	1-1	01-01-02

SATURDAY 18TH FEBRUARY 2006
COCA-COLA CHAMPIONSHIP

Brighton	v	Watford	-	-	-	4-0	-	2-1	05-00-01
Burnley	v	Southampton	-	-	-	-	-	-	00-00-00
Cardiff	v	Hull	-	2-0	-	-	-	-	03-01-02
Leicester	v	Leeds	2-1	3-1	0-2	-	4-0	-	06-00-04
Luton	v	Reading	3-1	1-1	-	-	-	-	01-02-02
Millwall	v	Crystal Pal	-	-	3-0	3-2	1-1	-	03-01-02
Norwich	v	Derby	-	-	-	1-0	2-1	-	06-00-00
Plymouth	v	Coventry	-	-	-	-	-	1-1	00-01-00
Preston	v	Crewe	-	2-1	2-2	-	0-0	1-0	04-03-01
QPR	v	Stoke	-	-	1-0	-	-	1-0	02-02-00
Sheff Weds	v	Sheff Utd	-	1-2	0-0	2-0	-	-	02-02-02
Wolves	v	Ipswich	2-1	-	-	1-1	-	2-0	04-05-01

COCA-COLA LEAGUE 1

Bournemouth	v	Blackpool	2-0	-	0-1	-	1-2	2-3	05-02-04
Bradford	v	Bristol C	-	-	-	-	-	4-1	03-00-00
Chesterfield	v	Southend	-	1-1	-	-	-	-	02-02-00
Colchester	v	Hartlepool	-	-	-	-	1-2	1-1	03-01-04
Doncaster	v	Gillingham	-	-	-	-	-	-	01-04-02
Huddersfield	v	Milton K	-	0-2	-	-	-	3-1	01-00-01
Port Vale	v	Nottm F	0-2	-	-	-	-	-	00-00-00
Scunthorpe	v	Swansea	-	-	2-2	2-0	2-2	1-0	04-02-01
Swindon	v	Rotherham	-	2-1	-	-	-	-	02-00-00
Tranmere	v	Barnsley	2-2	2-3	-	1-0	2-0	1-1	06-03-03
Walsall	v	Oldham	-	3-2	-	-	-	0-1	02-02-01
Yeovil	v	Brentford	-	-	-	-	-	-	00-00-00

COCA-COLA LEAGUE 2

Boston	v	Wycombe	-	-	-	-	-	2-0	02-01-03
Bristol R	v	Stockport	-	-	-	-	-	-	00-03-01
Bury	v	Barnet	-	-	-	-	-	-	01-02-00
Carlisle	v	Rushden & D	-	-	3-0	1-2	-	-	01-00-01
Chester	v	Leyton O	1-5	-	-	-	-	1-1	04-03-04
Darlington	v	Shrewsbury	2-2	3-0	3-3	5-1	-	3-0	05-03-02
Macclesfield	v	Lincoln	1-1	2-0	0-1	0-1	0-0	2-1	03-03-02
Mansfield	v	Wrexham	-	-	-	-	-	-	01-00-00
Northampton	v	Torquay	3-0	-	-	-	0-1	-	02-02-04
Notts Co	v	Peterboro	-	3-3	1-0	2-2	0-1	-	04-04-01
Oxford Utd	v	Cheltenham	-	-	3-0	-	1-0	1-0	03-00-00
Rochdale	v	Grimsby	-	-	-	-	-	2-0	01-00-02

BANK OF SCOTLAND SCOTTISH PREMIER LEAGUE

Aberdeen	v	Falkirk	-	-	-	-	-	-	03-05-00
Dundee Utd	v	Inv CT	-	-	-	-	-	2-1/1-1	01-01-00
Dunfermline	v	Celtic	-	1-2/0-3	0-4	1-4/1-4	0-0/1-4	0-2	06-13
Hearts	v	Motherwell	1-1/0-0	3-0/3-0	3-1	4-2/2-1	0-0/3-2	0-1	18-10-04
Kilmarnock	v	Livingston	-	-	1-5/1-1	2-0	0-3/4-2	1-3	07-01-04
Rangers	v	Hibernian	2-0/5-2	1-0/4-0	2-2/1-1	2-1	5-2/3-0	4-1/3-0	25-04-02

BELL'S SCOTTISH FIRST DIVISION

Airdrie Utd	v	Ross County	-	5-1/2-2	1-1/0-2	-	-	1-2/2-1	02-02-02
Clyde	v	Dundee	-	-	-	-	-	-	01-00-01
Hamilton	v	St Johnstone	-	-	-	-	-	1-1/0-3	03-02-03

220

Queen of Sth	v	Brechin	-	-	-	-	1-0/2-2	-	04-05-04
St Mirren	v	Stranraer	-	-	-	-	-	-	04-00-00

BELL'S SCOTTISH SECOND DIVISION

Dumbarton	v	Alloa	-	-	-	-	1-0/3-1	0-1/3-2	03-04-04
Forfar	v	Ayr	-	-	-	-	-	2-3/1-0	05-02-04
Peterhead	v	Partick	-	-	-	-	-	-	00-00-00
Raith	v	Gretna	-	-	-	-	-	-	00-00-00
Stirling	v	Morton	-	-	-	2-0/0-3	-	1-1/1-1	05-05-06

BELL'S SCOTTISH THIRD DIVISION

Arbroath	v	East Fife	-	-	-	-	0-1/0-0	-	04-03-06
Berwick	v	E Stirling	1-0/3-0	-	-	-	-	-	07-03-05
Cowdenb'th	v	Queen's Park	0-2/2-3	-	-	-	0-1/5-1	2-1	06-06-11
Montrose	v	Albion	2-1/1-2	0-2/0-1	1-2/2-0	0-1/1-1	1-0/3-1	1-1/0-1	12-03-11
Stenhsmuir	v	Elgin	-	-	-	-	-	0-2/4-0	01-00-01

NATIONWIDE CONFERENCE

Aldershot	v	Burton	-	-	-	-	3-1	3-0	02-00-00
Cambridge U	v	Southport	-	-	-	-	-	-	00-00-00
Canvey Islnd	v	Hereford	-	-	-	-	-	0-4	00-00-01
Crawley	v	Altrincham	-	-	-	-	-	-	00-00-00
Dagenham & R	v	Stevenage	-	3-0	1-0	3-2	1-2	3-1	04-00-03
Exeter	v	York	2-1	3-1	2-1	0-1	-	0-1	05-00-03
Gravesend	v	Accrington	-	-	-	-	0-0	2-2	00-02-00
Halifax	v	Grays	-	-	-	-	-	-	00-00-00
Morecambe	v	Forest G	1-1	0-2	2-0	4-0	4-0	3-1	05-01-01
Scarborough	v	Woking	3-2	3-2	1-0	1-1	2-2	2-0	04-02-00
Tamworth	v	Kidderminstr	-	-	-	-	-	-	00-00-00

TUESDAY 21ST FEBRUARY 2006
NATIONWIDE CONFERENCE

Accrington	v	Morecambe	-	-	-	-	1-0	2-1	04-01-01
Altrincham	v	Halifax	-	-	-	-	-	-	03-01-00
Burton	v	Cambridge U	-	-	-	-	-	-	00-00-00
Forest G	v	Gravesend	-	-	-	2-1	1-2	1-5	01-00-02
Grays	v	Dagenham & R	-	-	-	-	-	-	00-00-01
Hereford	v	Aldershot	-	-	-	-	4-3	2-0	02-00-00
Kidderminstr	v	Crawley	-	-	-	-	-	-	00-00-00
Southport	v	Scarborough	2-2	3-1	1-0	1-1	-	-	02-02-00
Stevenage	v	Canvey Islnd	-	-	-	-	-	1-4	00-00-01
Woking	v	Exeter	-	-	-	-	1-0	3-3	01-01-00
York	v	Tamworth	-	-	-	-	-	2-0	01-00-00

SATURDAY 25TH FEBRUARY 2006
FA BARCLAYCARD PREMIER LEAGUE

Birmingham	v	Sunderland	-	-	-	2-0	-	-	03-02-02
Blackburn	v	Arsenal	-	-	2-3	2-0	0-2	0-1	03-02-06
Bolton	v	Fulham	3-1	0-2	0-0	0-0	0-2	3-1	05-03-03
Charlton	v	Aston Villa	-	3-3	1-2	3-0	1-2	3-0	02-02-04
Chelsea	v	Portsmouth	-	-	-	-	3-0	3-0	02-01-00
Liverpool	v	Man City	-	3-2	-	1-2	2-1	2-1	07-03-01
Man Utd	v	West Ham	7-1	3-1	0-1	3-0	-	-	11-00-01
Newcastle	v	Everton	1-1	0-1	6-2	2-1	4-2	1-1	09-02-02
Tottenham	v	Wigan	-	-	-	-	-	-	00-00-00
WBA	v	Middlesbro	-	-	-	1-0	-	1-2	02-02-03

COCA-COLA CHAMPIONSHIP

Coventry	v	Burnley	-	-	0-2	0-1	4-0	0-2	01-00-03

Crewe	v	Brighton	-	-	-	-	3-1		03-00-00
Crystal Pal	v	Norwich	1-0	1-1	3-2	2-0	1-0	3-3	07-02-05
Derby	v	Plymouth	-	-	-	-	-	1-0	02-00-00
Hull	v	Wolves	-	-	-	-	-	-	01-00-01
Ipswich	v	Leicester	-	2-0	2-0	6-1	-	2-1	08-02-00
Leeds	v	Luton	-	-	-	-	-	-	02-00-00
Reading	v	Preston	2-2	-	-	5-1	3-2	3-1	06-04-00
Sheff Utd	v	QPR	1-1	1-1	-	-	-	3-2	03-06-01
Southampton	v	Sheff Weds	2-0	-	-	-	-	-	02-03-06
Stoke	v	Millwall	3-1	3-2	-	0-1	0-0	1-0	06-01-02
Watford	v	Cardiff	-	-	-	-	2-1	0-0	01-01-00

COCA-COLA LEAGUE 1

Barnsley	v	Colchester	-	-	-	1-1	1-0	-	01-01-00
Blackpool	v	Yeovil	-	-	-	-	-	-	00-00-00
Brentford	v	Port Vale	-	1-1	2-0	1-1	3-2	1-0	04-02-01
Bristol C	v	Bournemouth	3-1	3-3	1-0	-	2-0	0-2	04-02-02
Gillingham	v	Scunthorpe	3-1	-	-	-	-	-	03-04-01
Hartlepool	v	Doncaster	-	-	-	-	-	2-1	04-01-03
Milton K	v	Bradford	3-2	-	1-2	2-2	2-1	1-2	02-01-02
Nottm F	v	Swindon	3-1	-	-	-	-	-	02-00-00
Oldham	v	Tranmere	-	-	1-1	2-0	1-1	2-2	01-04-02
Rotherham	v	Chesterfield	-	-	-	-	-	-	00-01-02
Southend	v	Walsall	-	-	-	-	-	-	00-00-01
Swansea	v	Huddersfield	-	-	-	-	2-0	-	05-01-02

COCA-COLA LEAGUE 2

Barnet	v	Carlisle	3-0	0-1	-	-	-	1-1	04-02-02
Cheltenham	v	Rochdale	0-2	0-2	1-1	-	0-2	2-0	01-01-03
Grimsby	v	Chester	-	-	-	-	-	1-0	02-00-00
Leyton O	v	Darlington	2-1	1-0	0-0	2-1	1-0	1-0	09-03-00
Lincoln	v	Notts Co	-	-	-	-	-	1-2	00-00-03
Peterboro	v	Bristol R	-	2-2	-	-	-	-	00-04-01
Rushden & D	v	Macclesfield	-	-	2-0	3-0	-	0-2	02-01-01
Shrewsbury	v	Bury	-	-	-	4-1	-	2-2	04-04-00
Stockport	v	Boston	-	-	-	-	-	-	00-00-00
Torquay	v	Mansfield	4-0	2-2	0-0	-	1-0	-	05-04-01
Wrexham	v	Northampton	-	3-0	3-2	-	-	-	04-01-02
Wycombe	v	Oxford Utd	0-1	3-1	-	-	-	1-1	02-01-02

BELL'S SCOTTISH SECOND DIVISION

Alloa	v	Raith	-	0-1/1-2	-	-	-	-	01-00-03
Ayr	v	Peterhead	-	-	-	-	-	-	00-00-00
Morton	v	Forfar	-	-	1-3/1-4	-	1-1/1-1	2-1/4-0	03-06-03
Gretna	v	Stirling	-	-	-	0-2/0-0	0-1/1-0	-	01-01-02
Partick	v	Dumbarton	-	-	-	-	-	-	00-00-00

BELL'S SCOTTISH THIRD DIVISION

Albion	v	Stenhsmuir	-	-	-	-	-	1-0/1-1	02-04-05
East Fife	v	Montrose	0-0/2-0	3-1/1-0	1-2/2-0	2-0/2-0	-	1-0/1-0	12-04-04
E Stirling	v	Arbroath	-	-	-	-	-	-	05-05-07
Elgin	v	Cowdenbeath	-	2-3/0-2	-	-	0-4/0-0	0-4/2-0	01-01-04
Queen's Park	v	Berwick	1-4/0-1	1-0/0-2	-	-	-	-	08-04-05

NATIONWIDE CONFERENCE

Accrington	v	Burton	-	-	3-3	-	3-1	3-1	02-01-00
Aldershot	v	Morecambe	-	-	-	-	2-2	3-3	00-02-00
Cambridge U	v	Exeter	-	-	-	2-1	-	-	07-02-00
Canvey Islnd	v	Crawley	-	-	-	-	-	2-2	00-01-00
Dagenham & R	v	Altrincham	-	-	-	-	-	-	02-01-01

Gravesend	v	Scarborough	-	-	-	5-2	1-1	4-0	02-01-00
Hereford	v	Stevenage	1-2	1-1	1-1	2-2	1-0	0-1	01-03-04
Kidderminstr	v	Grays	-	-	-	-	-	-	00-00-00
Southport	v	Woking	4-1	0-1	2-0	5-1	-	-	06-03-01
Tamworth	v	Halifax	-	-	-	-	2-0	2-1	02-00-00
York	v	Forest G	-	-	-	-	-	1-3	00-00-01

SATURDAY 4TH MARCH 2006
FA BARCLAYCARD PREMIER LEAGUE

Aston Villa	v	Portsmouth	-	-	-	-	2-1	3-0	02-00-00
Fulham	v	Arsenal	-	-	1-3	0-1	0-1	0-3	00-00-04
Liverpool	v	Charlton	-	3-0	2-0	2-1	0-1	2-0	06-01-01
Man City	v	Sunderland	-	4-2	-	3-0	-	-	03-01-01
Middlesbro	v	Birmingham	-	-	-	1-0	5-3	2-1	04-01-00
Newcastle	v	Bolton	-	-	3-2	1-0	0-0	2-1	05-01-00
Tottenham	v	Blackburn	-	-	1-0	0-4	1-0	-	05-01-04
WBA	v	Chelsea	-	-	-	0-2	-	1-4	00-00-03
West Ham	v	Everton	0-4	0-2	1-0	0-1	-	-	03-03-06
Wigan	v	Man Utd	-	-	-	-	-	-	00-00-00

COCA-COLA CHAMPIONSHIP

Burnley	v	Reading	3-0	-	-	2-5	3-0	0-0	02-03-03
Cardiff	v	Sheff Weds	-	-	-	-	-	-	00-00-00
Crystal Pal	v	Leeds	-	-	-	-	-	-	02-02-02
Leicester	v	Hull	-	-	-	-	-	-	01-00-02
Millwall	v	Luton	1-0	1-0	-	-	-	-	05-03-03
Norwich	v	Stoke	-	-	-	2-2	1-0	-	02-02-01
Plymouth	v	Brighton	3-3	0-2	-	-	3-3	5-1	05-04-03
Preston	v	Ipswich	-	-	-	0-0	1-1	1-1	00-03-00
QPR	v	Wolves	1-1	2-2	-	-	-	1-1	00-05-01
Sheff Utd	v	Crewe	1-1	1-0	1-0	-	2-0	4-0	06-01-00
Southampton	v	Coventry	0-0	1-2	-	-	-	-	05-06-02
Watford	v	Derby	0-0	-	-	2-0	2-1	2-2	03-04-02

COCA-COLA LEAGUE 1

Barnsley	v	Swansea	-	-	-	-	-	-	00-00-00
Bradford	v	Blackpool	-	-	-	-	-	2-1	04-00-01
Bristol C	v	Nottm F	-	-	-	-	-	-	00-00-00
Chesterfield	v	Yeovil	-	-	-	-	-	-	00-00-01
Colchester	v	Southend	-	-	-	-	-	-	02-01-01
Gillingham	v	Brentford	2-0	-	-	-	-	-	02-00-00
Huddersfield	v	Doncaster	-	-	-	-	3-1	3-1	02-00-00
Port Vale	v	Milton K	-	-	-	-	-	3-2	01-00-00
Rotherham	v	Oldham	-	3-0	-	-	-	-	01-00-00
Scunthorpe	v	Hartlepool	-	3-0	1-0	4-0	-	-	07-03-01
Swindon	v	Tranmere	3-1	-	2-2	1-1	2-0	2-1	07-03-01
Walsall	v	Bournemouth	-	1-1	-	-	-	1-2	03-03-01

COCA-COLA LEAGUE 2

Barnet	v	Wrexham	-	-	-	-	-	-	02-00-01
Boston	v	Northampton	-	-	-	-	1-1	0-1	00-01-01
Bury	v	Macclesfield	-	-	-	2-1	2-0	2-1	03-00-00
Carlisle	v	Lincoln	1-0	1-1	2-2	1-4	0-2	-	04-04-05
Cheltenham	v	Wycombe	-	-	-	0-0	-	1-1	02-03-01
Chester	v	Torquay	2-1	-	-	-	-	-	04-02-01
Notts Co	v	Mansfield	-	-	-	2-2	-	0-1	03-01-01
Oxford Utd	v	Bristol R	0-5	0-1	0-0	0-1	0-0	3-2	03-04-04
Peterboro	v	Stockport	-	-	-	2-0	1-2	2-1	05-01-04
Rochdale	v	Darlington	0-0	1-1	3-1	1-1	4-2	1-1	06-08-01
Rushden & D	v	Grimsby	-	-	-	-	3-1	1-0	02-00-00
Shrewsbury	v	Leyton O	1-0	1-1	1-0	2-1	-	4-1	07-02-02

BANK OF SCOTLAND SCOTTISH PREMIER LEAGUE

Celtic	v	Aberdeen	7-0/5-1	6-0	2-0/1-0	7-0	4-0/1-2	2-3/3-2	22-04-06
Falkirk	v	Rangers	-	-	-	-	-	-	00-00-08
Hibernian	v	Dundee Utd	3-2/1-0	3-0/1-0	0-1	2-1/1-1	2-2	2-0/3-2	17-06-05
Inv CT	v	Motherwell	-	-	-	-	-	1-1/1-0	01-01-00
Kilmarnock	v	Dunfermline	-	2-1/2-1	0-0	2-2/1-1	1-1	1-0/2-1	07-08-02
Livingston	v	Hearts	-	-	2-1/2-0	1-1/1-1	2-3	1-2	02-02-02

BELL'S SCOTTISH FIRST DIVISION

Brechin	v	St Mirren	-	-	-	-	1-1/2-0	-	01-01-02
Dundee	v	Hamilton	-	-	-	-	-	-	07-02-02
Queen of Sth	v	Clyde	1-1/3-0	-	-	2-1/1-1	4-1/1-2	0-1/0-1	09-04-09
St Johnstone	v	Airdrie Utd	-	-	-	-	-	1-1/1-2	08-05-02
Stranraer	v	Ross County	0-0/0-2	-	-	-	-	-	00-01-01

BELL'S SCOTTISH SECOND DIVISION

Alloa	v	Stirling	4-4/1-0	-	-	-	-	1-1/3-0	05-03-01
Ayr	v	Gretna	-	-	-	-	-	-	00-00-00
Morton	v	Dumbarton	-	-	-	-	2-2/3-2	3-0/0-0	07-03-02
Peterhead	v	Forfar	-	-	-	-	-	-	00-00-00
Raith	v	Partick	-	-	1-2/2-0	-	-	0-0/2-1	07-06-04

BELL'S SCOTTISH THIRD DIVISION

Albion	v	Queen's Park	2-4/0-3	-	2-1/2-0	0-2/2-1	3-1/3-1	0-4/1-2	13-05-09
Arbroath	v	Montrose	-	-	-	-	-	-	04-04-05
Cowdenb'th	v	East Fife	4-0/1-0	1-0/3-2	-	-	-	1-1/4-2	07-04-03
E Stirling	v	Stenhsmuir	-	-	-	-	-	3-2/1-4	03-04-06
Elgin	v	Berwick	-	-	-	-	-	-	00-00-00

NATIONWIDE CONFERENCE

Altrincham	v	York	-	-	-	-	-	-	00-00-00
Burton	v	Dagenham & R	-	-	-	0-0	0-0	1-3	00-02-01
Crawley	v	Accrington	-	-	-	-	-	2-0	01-00-00
Exeter	v	Southport	-	-	-	-	-	-	00-00-00
Forest G	v	Kidderminstr	3-2	-	-	-	-	-	02-00-00
Grays	v	Tamworth	-	-	-	-	-	-	00-00-00
Halifax	v	Gravesend	-	-	-	2-1	1-0	1-0	03-00-00
Morecambe	v	Hereford	3-2	1-1	2-2	3-1	2-2	2-1	04-03-01
Scarborough	v	Canvey Islnd	-	-	-	-	-	1-1	00-01-00
Stevenage	v	Aldershot	-	-	-	-	0-1	0-1	00-00-02
Woking	v	Cambridge U	-	-	-	-	-	-	00-00-00

SATURDAY 11TH MARCH 2006
FA BARCLAYCARD PREMIER LEAGUE

Arsenal	v	Liverpool	0-1	2-0	1-1	1-1	4-2	-	05-06-05
Birmingham	v	WBA	1-1	2-1	0-1	1-0	-	4-0	06-02-04
Blackburn	v	Aston Villa	-	-	3-0	0-0	0-2	2-2	06-03-02
Bolton	v	West Ham	-	-	1-0	1-0	-	-	02-01-01
Charlton	v	Middlesbro	-	1-0	0-0	1-0	1-0	1-2	05-03-04
Chelsea	v	Tottenham	1-0	3-0	4-0	1-1	4-2	0-0	10-05-01
Everton	v	Fulham	-	-	2-1	2-0	3-1	1-0	04-00-00
Man Utd	v	Newcastle	5-1	2-0	3-1	5-3	0-0	2-1	08-05-00
Portsmouth	v	Man City	2-2	-	2-1	-	4-2	1-3	03-01-03
Sunderland	v	Wigan	-	-	-	-	1-1	1-1	00-02-00

COCA-COLA CHAMPIONSHIP

Brighton	v	Preston	-	-	-	0-2	-	1-0	02-00-00
Coventry	v	Sheff Utd	-	-	1-0	2-1	0-1	1-2	03-02-03
Crewe	v	Southampton	-	-	-	-	-	-	00-00-00
Derby	v	Burnley	-	-	-	1-2	2-0	1-1	02-01-01

224

Home	v	Away							Date
Hull	v	Plymouth	0-1	1-1	0-0	-	-	-	05-04-01
Ipswich	v	Millwall	-	-	-	4-1	1-3	2-0	02-02-02
Leeds	v	Norwich	-	-	-	-	-	-	03-01-01
Luton	v	Leicester	-	-	-	-	-	-	01-01-01
Reading	v	Watford	-	-	-	1-0	2-1	3-0	04-01-00
Sheff Weds	v	QPR	-	5-2	-	-	1-3	-	05-00-04
Stoke	v	Crystal Pal	-	-	-	1-1	0-1	-	01-02-03
Wolves	v	Cardiff	-	-	-	-	-	2-3	01-00-01

COCA-COLA LEAGUE 1

Home	v	Away							Date
Blackpool	v	Rotherham	-	-	-	-	-	-	03-01-03
Bournemouth	v	Bradford	-	-	-	-	-	2-0	05-02-02
Brentford	v	Barnsley	-	-	-	1-2	2-1	1-1	02-01-01
Doncaster	v	Port Vale	-	-	-	-	-	2-0	01-00-00
Hartlepool	v	Huddersfield	-	-	-	-	-	0-1	01-01-02
Milton K	v	Bristol C	-	-	-	-	-	1-2	00-00-01
Nottm F	v	Gillingham	-	0-1	2-2	4-1	0-0	-	01-02-01
Oldham	v	Colchester	1-2	1-1	4-1	2-0	0-0	1-1	03-03-01
Southend	v	Scunthorpe	-	1-0	2-0	1-2	4-2	0-0	03-02-02
Swansea	v	Walsall	-	3-1	-	-	-	-	03-00-00
Tranmere	v	Chesterfield	-	-	0-0	2-1	2-3	1-0	02-01-01
Yeovil	v	Swindon	-	-	-	-	-	-	00-00-00

COCA-COLA LEAGUE 2

Home	v	Away							Date
Bristol R	v	Notts Co	0-1	0-0	-	-	-	2-1	04-04-02
Darlington	v	Chester	3-1	-	-	-	-	1-0	04-02-02
Grimsby	v	Barnet	-	-	-	-	-	-	00-00-00
Leyton O	v	Cheltenham	1-0	0-0	0-2	-	1-4	2-3	01-01-03
Lincoln	v	Rushden & D	-	-	2-4	1-2	-	1-3	00-00-03
Macclesfield	v	Rochdale	1-2	0-0	0-1	3-2	2-1	3-0	04-01-02
Mansfield	v	Boston	-	-	-	-	2-1	-	01-00-00
Northampton	v	Carlisle	0-0	-	-	-	2-0	-	04-05-00
Stockport	v	Oxford Utd	-	-	-	-	-	-	03-00-01
Torquay	v	Peterboro	2-1	-	-	-	-	2-1	03-02-01
Wrexham	v	Bury	1-0	0-1	1-0	2-2	-	-	03-02-01
Wycombe	v	Shrewsbury	-	-	-	-	-	1-1	03-02-00

BANK OF SCOTLAND SCOTTISH PREMIER LEAGUE

Home	v	Away							Date
Dundee Utd	v	Livingston	-	-	0-0	2-3/0-1	2-0	1-0/1-1	02-02-02
Dunfermline	v	Aberdeen	-	0-0/3-2	1-0/0-0	3-0	2-2	0-1/2-1	05-09-06
Hibernian	v	Celtic	0-2/2-1	0-0/2-5	1-4/1-1	0-1	1-2/0-4	2-2/1-3	05-08-18
Inv CT	v	Hearts	-	-	-	-	-	1-1	00-01-00
Motherwell	v	Falkirk	-	-	-	-	-	-	05-02-01
Rangers	v	Kilmarnock	2-1/1-0	0-3/5-1	3-1/5-0	6-1/4-0	4-0/2-0	2-0/2-1	19-01-04

BELL'S SCOTTISH FIRST DIVISION

Home	v	Away							Date
Airdrie Utd	v	Dundee	-	-	-	-	-	-	02-05-05
Clyde	v	Brechin	-	-	-	-	2-1/0-0	-	05-07-02
Hamilton	v	Stranraer	2-1/2-0	-	0-1/2-0	1-5/1-2	-	-	08-00-04
Ross County	v	St Johnstone	-	-	-	0-0/2-3	0-3/2-0	0-1/4-0	02-01-03
St Mirren	v	Queen of Sth	-	-	-	2-1/2-2	1-2/3-1	2-2/3-0	03-02-01

BELL'S SCOTTISH SECOND DIVISION

Home	v	Away							Date
Dumbarton	v	Peterhead	-	1-3/2-2	0-3/3-0	-	-	-	01-01-02
Forfar	v	Alloa	-	-	0-1/4-1	-	1-1/2-0	3-1	08-05-03
Gretna	v	Morton	-	-	-	1-1/0-1	-	-	00-01-01
Partick	v	Ayr	-	-	2-1/2-1	-	-	-	07-02-02
Stirling	v	Raith	-	-	-	-	-	-	02-01-03

BELL'S SCOTTISH THIRD DIVISION

Home	v	Away							Date
Berwick	v	Cowdenbeath	0-2/0-0	-	2-5/1-0	2-1/1-2	-	-	07-03-07
East Fife	v	Albion	1-4/2-1	0-0/2-1	0-0/2-3	0-4/1-1	-	1-0	07-05-04

Montrose	v	E Stirling	1-2/0-0	0-1/1-1	2-0/2-0	2-2/5-4	5-1/1-0	4-1/4-1	16-07-05
Queen's Park	v	Elgin	-	-	0-0/3-0	1-2/3-2	5-2/4-0	0-1	04-01-02
Stenhsmuir	v	Arbroath	1-3/3-0	3-1/0-1	-	-	1-0/0-3	-	10-01-04

NATIONWIDE CONFERENCE

Aldershot	v	Dagenham & R	1-0	-	-	-	2-1	4-0	04-00-00
Altrincham	v	Canvey Islnd	-	-	-	-	-	-	00-00-00
Crawley	v	Scarborough	-	-	-	-	-	2-1	01-00-00
Forest G	v	Southport	1-0	2-0	2-1	0-2	-	-	04-00-01
Grays	v	Woking	-	-	-	-	-	-	00-01-01
Halifax	v	Exeter	1-0	3-1	1-1	-	2-0	2-1	04-02-02
Hereford	v	Accrington	-	-	-	-	1-0	0-0	01-01-00
Morecambe	v	Kidderminstr	0-1	-	-	-	-	-	03-00-02
Stevenage	v	Burton	-	-	-	0-1	1-0	0-1	01-00-02
Tamworth	v	Cambridge U	-	-	-	-	-	-	00-00-00
York	v	Gravesend	-	-	-	-	-	0-0	00-01-00

SATURDAY 18TH MARCH 2006
FA BARCLAYCARD PREMIER LEAGUE

Arsenal	v	Charlton	-	5-3	2-4	2-0	2-1	4-0	05-02-01
Birmingham	v	Tottenham	-	-	-	1-1	1-0	1-1	01-02-00
Blackburn	v	Middlesbro	-	-	0-1	1-0	2-2	0-4	04-04-03
Bolton	v	Sunderland	-	-	0-2	1-1	-	-	01-02-02
Everton	v	Aston Villa	0-0	0-1	3-2	2-1	2-0	1-1	06-06-05
Fulham	v	Chelsea	-	-	1-1	0-0	0-1	1-4	00-02-02
Man City	v	Wigan	-	-	-	-	-	-	01-00-00
Newcastle	v	Liverpool	2-2	2-1	0-2	1-0	1-1	1-0	05-05-03
WBA	v	Man Utd	-	-	-	1-3	-	0-3	00-00-02
West Ham	v	Portsmouth	-	-	-	-	-	-	02-01-00

COCA-COLA CHAMPIONSHIP

Coventry	v	Leeds	3-4	0-0	-	-	-	1-2	02-07-03
Crystal Pal	v	Ipswich	2-2	-	-	1-1	3-4	-	04-04-01
Hull	v	Crewe	-	-	-	-	-	-	01-00-01
Luton	v	Derby	-	-	-	-	-	-	04-01-02
Millwall	v	Leicester	-	-	-	2-2	-	2-0	04-03-00
Norwich	v	Sheff Utd	2-1	4-2	2-1	2-3	1-0	-	07-04-02
Plymouth	v	Cardiff	-	2-1	-	2-2	-	1-1	01-05-01
QPR	v	Brighton	-	-	0-0	-	2-1	0-0	01-02-00
Reading	v	Wolves	-	-	-	0-1	-	-	03-01-02
Sheff Weds	v	Preston	-	1-3	1-2	0-1	-	-	00-00-03
Southampton	v	Watford	2-0	-	-	-	-	-	01-00-00
Stoke	v	Burnley	2-2	-	-	0-1	1-2	0-1	01-02-04

COCA-COLA LEAGUE 1

Blackpool	v	Port Vale	-	-	4-0	3-2	2-1	0-2	04-00-03
Bournemouth	v	Yeovil	-	-	-	-	-	-	00-00-00
Bradford	v	Oldham	-	-	-	-	-	1-3	01-01-02
Bristol C	v	Gillingham	0-1	-	-	-	-	-	01-00-03
Chesterfield	v	Scunthorpe	1-1	1-0	-	-	-	-	03-03-02
Colchester	v	Swindon	-	0-1	1-3	1-0	0-1	0-1	01-00-04
Doncaster	v	Nottm F	-	-	-	-	-	-	00-00-00
Hartlepool	v	Barnsley	-	-	-	-	1-2	1-1	00-01-01
Huddersfield	v	Rotherham	-	-	-	-	-	-	04-01-00
Milton K	v	Southend	-	-	-	-	-	-	00-00-00
Swansea	v	Brentford	-	6-0	-	-	-	-	04-04-01
Tranmere	v	Walsall	1-1	-	-	-	-	2-1	02-01-00

COCA-COLA LEAGUE 2

Boston	v	Lincoln	-	-	-	2-0	0-1	0-2	01-00-02

Chester	v	Cheltenham	2-1	-	-	-	-	0-3	01-00-01
Darlington	v	Carlisle	3-1	1-0	2-2	2-0	2-0	-	06-03-03
Grimsby	v	Bury	-	-	-	-	-	5-1	01-01-01
Mansfield	v	Northampton	0-0	-	-	2-1	1-2	4-1	05-04-02
Notts Co	v	Oxford Utd	0-1	2-1	-	-	-	0-1	03-02-02
Peterboro	v	Barnet	1-2	-	-	-	-	-	02-00-01
Rochdale	v	Wrexham	-	-	-	2-2	-	-	02-02-02
Rushden & D	v	Leyton O	-	-	1-0	2-0	-	2-0	03-00-00
Shrewsbury	v	Bristol R	-	-	0-1	2-5	-	2-0	03-01-03
Stockport	v	Macclesfield	-	-	-	-	-	-	00-00-00
Wycombe	v	Torquay	-	-	-	-	-	-	00-01-00

BANK OF SCOTLAND SCOTTISH PREMIER LEAGUE

Aberdeen	v	Livingston	-	-	0-3/3-0	0-0/1-0	0-3/1-2	2-0/2-0	04-01-03
Celtic	v	Inv CT	-	-	-	-	-	3-0	01-00-00
Dunfermline	v	Dundee Utd	-	1-0/3-1	1-1	4-1	2-0/1-1	1-1/1-1	08-10-04
Hearts	v	Rangers	0-4/1-2	0-1/1-4	2-2/0-2	0-4/0-2	0-4/1-1	0-0/1-2	06-07-21
Kilmarnock	v	Falkirk	-	-	-	-	-	-	03-04-01
Motherwell	v	Hibernian	2-2/2-0	1-3	1-3/4-0	0-2/2-1	0-1	1-2/1-1	09-12-09

BELL'S SCOTTISH FIRST DIVISION

Airdrie Utd	v	Hamilton	-	-	-	0-0/2-2	3-0/1-1	0-2/1-0	11-05-03
Brechin	v	Ross County	-	-	-	-	4-2/1-0	-	03-01-02
Clyde	v	St Mirren	-	-	1-1/3-1	2-3/3-2	2-0/2-2	0-0/0-0	04-04-02
Dundee	v	St Johnstone	1-2/1-1	1-1	1-1/1-0	-	-	-	04-06-07
Queen of Sth	v	Stranraer	0-5/0-0	1-4/2-3	1-0/3-1	-	-	-	07-05-07

BELL'S SCOTTISH SECOND DIVISION

Alloa	v	Morton	-	2-1/0-3	1-1/4-0	-	0-1/3-3	1-6/2-2	02-04-03
Ayr	v	Raith	0-1/0-1	4-2/2-0	1-1/3-1	-	1-0/1-0	-	11-08-04
Dumbarton	v	Forfar	3-3/0-0	-	-	1-2/1-2	2-1/1-1	0-1/1-1	01-04-03
Partick	v	Gretna	-	-	-	-	-	-	00-00-00
Peterhead	v	Stirling	-	-	3-3/5-1	1-0/6-0	2-2/0-0	-	03-03-00

BELL'S SCOTTISH THIRD DIVISION

Albion	v	Elgin	-	1-1/0-1	4-4/2-2	1-1/1-1	1-2/1-2	2-2/2-0	01-06-03
Arbroath	v	Berwick	-	0-2/2-0	-	-	1-0/1-2	1-1/2-0	08-02-07
East Fife	v	Stenhsmuir	-	-	-	-	3-2/1-0	0-0/2-0	10-04-05
E Stirling	v	Queen's Park	1-1/0-1	-	0-1/3-1	0-4/0-2	1-2/2-4	0-5/3-1	13-06-10
Montrose	v	Cowdenbeath	0-1/1-3	1-2/0-1	-	-	1-3/1-1	3-1/1-2	08-04-11

NATIONWIDE CONFERENCE

Accrington	v	Stevenage	-	-	-	-	2-1	4-1	02-00-00
Burton	v	Hereford	-	-	-	2-0	4-1	3-0	03-00-00
Cambridge U	v	Halifax	-	-	-	-	-	-	03-00-00
Canvey Islnd	v	York	-	-	-	-	-	4-0	01-00-00
Dagenham & R	v	Morecambe	-	3-2	3-2	1-1	1-3	2-1	03-02-01
Exeter	v	Crawley	-	-	-	-	-	3-2	01-00-00
Gravesend	v	Tamworth	-	-	-	-	2-0	2-0	02-00-00
Kidderminstr	v	Aldershot	-	-	-	-	-	-	00-00-00
Scarborough	v	Grays	-	-	-	-	-	-	00-00-00
Southport	v	Altrincham	2-0	-	-	-	2-2	2-1	03-01-03
Woking	v	Forest G	2-1	2-0	3-4	1-0	1-1	0-1	03-02-02

SATURDAY 25TH MARCH 2006
FA BARCLAYCARD PREMIER LEAGUE

Aston Villa	v	Fulham	-	-	2-0	3-1	3-0	2-0	04-00-00
Charlton	v	Newcastle	-	2-0	1-1	0-2	0-0	1-1	03-05-02
Chelsea	v	Man City	-	2-1	-	5-0	1-0	0-0	04-06-02

Liverpool	v	Everton	0-1	3-1	1-1	0-0	0-0	2-1	08-07-02
Man Utd	v	Birmingham	-	-	-	2-0	3-0	2-0	03-00-00
Middlesbro	v	Bolton	-	-	1-1	2-0	2-0	1-1	03-02-02
Portsmouth	v	Arsenal	-	-	-	-	1-1	0-1	00-01-01
Sunderland	v	Blackburn	-	-	1-0	0-0	-	-	02-03-01
Tottenham	v	WBA	-	-	-	3-1	-	1-1	01-01-00
Wigan	v	West Ham	-	-	-	-	1-1	1-2	00-01-01

COCA-COLA CHAMPIONSHIP

Brighton	v	Luton	-	-	-	-	2-0	-	01-00-00
Burnley	v	Norwich	-	2-0	1-1	2-0	3-5	-	02-01-01
Cardiff	v	QPR	-	-	1-1	1-2	-	-	00-01-01
Crewe	v	Coventry	-	-	1-6	-	3-1	-	01-00-01
Derby	v	Crystal Pal	-	-	-	0-1	2-1	-	04-01-02
Ipswich	v	Hull	-	-	-	-	-	-	01-01-01
Leeds	v	Stoke	-	-	-	-	-	0-0	02-01-00
Leicester	v	Reading	-	-	-	2-1	-	0-2	01-01-01
Preston	v	Plymouth	-	-	-	-	-	1-1	01-02-02
Sheff Utd	v	Southampton	-	-	-	-	-	-	02-01-01
Watford	v	Millwall	-	-	1-4	0-0	3-1	1-0	05-01-06
Wolves	v	Sheff Weds	-	1-1	0-0	2-2	-	-	01-03-00

COCA-COLA LEAGUE 1

Barnsley	v	Bournemouth	-	-	-	-	1-1	0-1	01-01-02
Brentford	v	Doncaster	-	-	-	-	-	4-3	01-00-00
Gillingham	v	Swansea	-	-	-	-	-	-	00-00-01
Nottm F	v	Milton K	-	1-2	0-0	2-0	6-0	-	06-03-04
Oldham	v	Blackpool	1-1	-	2-1	1-1	2-3	1-2	02-02-03
Port Vale	v	Huddersfield	1-2	-	1-1	5-1	-	0-3	07-02-02
Rotherham	v	Bristol C	-	1-1	-	-	-	-	00-02-02
Scunthorpe	v	Colchester	0-0	-	-	-	-	-	05-02-02
Southend	v	Hartlepool	2-1	2-1	0-0	0-1	-	-	03-02-01
Swindon	v	Chesterfield	-	-	2-1	3-0	2-0	-	03-01-00
Walsall	v	Bradford	-	-	2-2	0-1	1-0	1-1	02-02-02
Yeovil	v	Tranmere	-	-	-	-	-	-	00-00-00

COCA-COLA LEAGUE 2

Barnet	v	Darlington	1-0	3-0	-	-	-	-	04-03-02
Bristol R	v	Mansfield	-	-	0-1	-	1-3	4-4	00-03-02
Bury	v	Rochdale	-	-	-	1-1	1-2	0-0	00-04-03
Carlisle	v	Boston	-	-	-	4-2	2-1	-	02-00-00
Cheltenham	v	Rushden & D	-	-	1-1	-	-	4-1	04-01-01
Leyton O	v	Wycombe	-	-	-	-	-	1-2	00-00-02
Lincoln	v	Grimsby	-	-	-	-	-	0-0	00-03-00
Macclesfield	v	Shrewsbury	4-2	2-1	2-1	1-2	-	2-1	05-00-01
Northampton	v	Notts Co	-	1-0	0-2	2-0	-	0-0	02-03-02
Oxford Utd	v	Peterboro	-	0-1	-	-	-	-	03-00-02
Torquay	v	Stockport	-	-	-	-	-	1-2	03-01-01
Wrexham	v	Chester	-	-	-	-	-	-	00-01-00

BANK OF SCOTLAND SCOTTISH PREMIER LEAGUE

Aberdeen	v	Motherwell	1-1/2-1	3-3	4-2/1-0	1-1	0-3/0-2	2-1/1-3	15-11-06
Dundee Utd	v	Kilmarnock	0-0/2-2	0-1	0-2/0-2	1-2/2-2	1-1/4-1	3-0	03-09-08
Falkirk	v	Hearts	-	-	-	-	-	-	05-00-03
Hibernian	v	Inv CT	-	-	-	-	-	2-1	01-00-00
Livingston	v	Celtic	-	-	0-0/1-3	0-2	0-2	2-4/0-4	00-01-05
Rangers	v	Dunfermline	-	4-1/2-0	4-0	3-0/6-1	4-0/4-1	3-0	18-02-00

BELL'S SCOTTISH FIRST DIVISION

Hamilton	v	Queen of Sth	0-3/1-1	-	1-1/3-1	-	-	1-0/1-1	03-04-01
Ross County	v	Dundee	-	-	-	-	-	-	00-00-00

228

St Johnstone	v	Clyde	-	-	-	0-1/1-2	3-0/1-3	3-0/0-0	03-03-03
St Mirren	v	Airdrie Utd	5-0/3-1	-	0-0/2-1	-	-	1-1/1-0	08-02-10
Stranraer	v	Brechin	-	-	-	3-1/2-3	-	4-2/0-1	04-02-08

BELL'S SCOTTISH SECOND DIVISION

Forfar	v	Partick	-	0-1/2-2	-	-	-	-	03-02-05
Morton	v	Ayr	0-0/1-2	1-1/0-6	-	-	-	0-1/2-1	06-04-10
Gretna	v	Alloa	-	-	-	-	-	-	00-00-00
Raith	v	Peterhead	-	-	-	-	-	-	00-00-00
Stirling	v	Dumbarton	-	-	4-5/2-1	-	-	1-0/3-0	08-03-04

BELL'S SCOTTISH THIRD DIVISION

Berwick	v	Albion	1-1/2-1	-	-	-	-	-	07-06-00
Cowdenb'th	v	Arbroath	-	-	-	-	-	-	05-07-04
Elgin	v	E Stirling	-	1-2/4-2	2-1/2-2	3-1/3-0	3-1/3-0	1-3/0-0	06-02-02
Queen's Park	v	East Fife	0-1/1-0	-	1-2/2-0	0-0/1-2	-	1-2/2-1	08-02-07
Stenhsmuir	v	Montrose	-	-	-	-	-	1-1/0-1	07-01-06

NATIONWIDE CONFERENCE

Aldershot	v	Scarborough	-	-	-	-	1-2	2-0	01-00-01
Altrincham	v	Burton	-	-	0-2	-	-	-	00-00-01
Crawley	v	Cambridge U	-	-	-	-	-	-	00-00-00
Forest G	v	Dagenham & R	-	4-4	2-4	5-2	1-3	1-4	01-01-03
Grays	v	Southport	-	-	-	-	-	-	00-00-00
Halifax	v	Woking	-	-	--	1-1	2-2	3-1	03-03-02
Hereford	v	Kidderminstr	1-1	-	-	-	-	-	01-01-01
Morecambe	v	Canvey Islnd	-	-	-	-	-	4-0	01-00-00
Stevenage	v	Gravesend	-	-	-	1-0	2-2	2-0	02-01-00
Tamworth	v	Exeter	-	-	-	-	2-1	1-2	01-00-01
York	v	Accrington	-	-	-	-	-	0-1	00-00-01

SATURDAY 1ST APRIL 2006
FA BARCLAYCARD PREMIER LEAGUE

Arsenal	v	Aston Villa	3-1	1-0	3-2	3-1	2-0	3-1	09-04-04
Birmingham	v	Chelsea	-	-	-	1-3	0-0	0-1	00-01-03
Blackburn	v	Wigan	-	-	-	-	-	-	00-00-00
Bolton	v	Man Utd	-	-	0-4	1-1	1-2	2-2	00-03-03
Everton	v	Sunderland	5-0	2-2	1-0	2-1	-	-	04-01-01
Fulham	v	Portsmouth	1-0	3-1	-	-	2-0	3-1	04-00-00
Man City	v	Middlesbro	-	1-1	-	0-0	0-1	-	01-02-03
Newcastle	v	Tottenham	2-1	2-0	0-2	2-1	4-0	0-1	06-04-03
WBA	v	Liverpool	-	-	-	0-6	-	0-5	00-00-02
West Ham	v	Charlton	-	5-0	2-0	0-2	-	-	03-00-04

COCA-COLA CHAMPIONSHIP

Coventry	v	Preston	-	-	2-2	1-2	4-1	1-1	01-02-01
Crystal Pal	v	Watford	-	1-0	0-2	0-1	1-0	-	03-01-04
Hull	v	Leeds	-	-	-	-	-	-	00-00-02
Luton	v	Ipswich	-	-	-	-	-	-	00-00-01
Millwall	v	Brighton	-	-	-	1-0	-	2-0	03-00-01
Norwich	v	Leicester	-	-	-	0-0	-	-	01-01-01
Plymouth	v	Wolves	-	-	-	-	-	1-2	02-00-02
QPR	v	Crewe	1-0	1-0	-	0-0	-	1-2	03-01-02
Reading	v	Derby	-	-	-	2-1	3-1	0-1	04-00-01
Sheff Weds	v	Burnley	-	2-0	0-2	1-3	-	-	01-00-02
Southampton	v	Cardiff	-	-	-	-	-	-	00-00-00
Stoke	v	Sheff Utd	-	-	-	0-0	2-2	2-0	01-05-02

COCA-COLA LEAGUE 1

Blackpool	v	Walsall	-	-	-	-	-	2-0	05-00-03
Bournemouth	v	Southend	-	-	-	1-0	-	-	03-00-00

Bradford	v	Scunthorpe	-	-	-	-	-	-	00-00-00
Bristol C	v	Yeovil	-	-	-	-	-	-	00-00-00
Chesterfield	v	Nottm F	-	-	-	-	-	-	00-00-00
Colchester	v	Brentford	0-3	3-1	1-1	0-1	1-1	0-1	01-02-03
Doncaster	v	Rotherham	-	-	-	-	-	-	01-01-01
Hartlepool	v	Oldham	-	-	-	-	0-0	2-1	01-01-00
Huddersfield	v	Barnsley	2-1	1-1	-	1-0	-	0-2	03-02-02
Milton K	v	Gillingham	-	4-4	3-1	0-1	1-2	-	01-01-02
Swansea	v	Swindon	-	0-0	-	-	-	-	00-01-01
Tranmere	v	Port Vale	2-1	-	3-1	1-0	1-0	-	07-02-01

COCA-COLA LEAGUE 2

Boston	v	Barnet	-	-	1-1	-	-	-	01-01-02
Chester	v	Macclesfield	1-2	-	-	-	-	1-0	01-01-01
Darlington	v	Lincoln	2-0	3-0	2-1	0-0	0-0	0-3	07-05-02
Grimsby	v	Wrexham	-	-	-	-	1-3	-	01-01-02
Mansfield	v	Oxford Utd	-	-	2-1	-	3-1	1-3	02-00-01
Notts Co	v	Leyton O	-	-	-	-	-	1-2	02-00-01
Peterboro	v	Northampton	1-0	1-2	2-0	0-0	-	-	03-01-01
Rochdale	v	Carlisle	3-2	6-0	1-1	0-1	2-0	-	04-06-02
Rushden & D	v	Torquay	-	-	0-0	3-0	-	-	01-01-00
Shrewsbury	v	Cheltenham	0-2	1-0	2-1	-	-	2-0	03-00-01
Stockport	v	Bury	-	-	-	-	-	-	02-02-00
Wycombe	v	Bristol R	1-1	0-1	-	-	-	1-0	03-04-01

BANK OF SCOTLAND SCOTTISH PREMIER LEAGUE

Celtic	v	Hearts	4-0/2-3	6-1/1-0	2-0/2-0	4-2/1-0	5-0/2-2	3-0/0-2	20-10-04
Dundee Utd	v	Rangers	0-4/0-2	1-1	1-6/0-1	0-3/1-4	1-3/2-0/3-3	1-1	05-08-18
Dunfermline	v	Falkirk	1-1/2-2	-	-	-	-	-	03-03-01
Hibernian	v	Kilmarnock	0-3/2-2	1-1/1-1	2-2/2-2	2-0	3-1/3-0	0-1/3-0	08-08-05
Inv CT	v	Aberdeen	-	-	-	-	-	1-3/0-1	00-00-02
Motherwell	v	Livingston	-	-	0-0/1-2	1-5/6-2	1-1	2-0	02-02-02

BELL'S SCOTTISH FIRST DIVISION

Clyde	v	Airdrie Utd	-	4-1/1-1	0-3/0-1	-	-	1-2/1-0	03-02-07
Dundee	v	Brechin	-	-	-	-	-	-	00-00-02
Queen of Sth	v	Ross County	0-2/0-3	-	2-0/1-0	1-0/1-1	0-1/1-0	04-01-03
St Johnstone	v	Stranraer	-	-	-	-	-	-	02-00-00
St Mirren	v	Hamilton	-	-	-	-	-	1-0/0-1	09-01-06

BELL'S SCOTTISH SECOND DIVISION

Ayr	v	Stirling	-	-	-	-	-	3-2/0-3	06-02-04
Dumbarton	v	Gretna	-	-	-	-	-	-	00-00-00
Forfar	v	Raith	-	-	-	1-2/4-2	-	-	03-02-03
Partick	v	Alloa	2-2/0-1	-	-	-	-	-	03-02-01
Peterhead	v	Morton	-	-	-	4-2/3-1	-	-	02-00-00

BELL'S SCOTTISH THIRD DIVISION

Albion	v	E Stirling	1-1/0-1	2-1/2-2	0-4/5-1	6-0/3-1	5-0/5-1	3-3/1-1	14-08-07
Arbroath	v	Queen's Park	-	2-2/2-0	-	-	-	-	08-11-00
East Fife	v	Elgin	-	1-1/1-1	3-0/0-1	4-0/5-0	-	2-0/1-2	04-02-02
Montrose	v	Berwick	1-2/2-3	-	-	-	-	-	03-02-10
Stenhsmuir	v	Cowdenbeath	-	-	0-3/0-1	4-1/1-1	-	2-2	04-05-05

NATIONWIDE CONFERENCE

Accrington	v	Grays	-	-	-	-	-	-	00-00-00
Burton	v	York	-	-	-	-	-	0-2	00-00-01
Cambridge U	v	Morecambe	-	-	-	-	-	-	00-00-00
Canvey Islnd	v	Forest G	-	-	-	-	-	2-1	01-00-00
Dagenham & R	v	Halifax	-	-	-	0-0	0-1	4-2	02-02-02

230

Exeter	v	Altrincham	-	-	-	-	-	-	00-00-00
Gravesend	v	Aldershot	1-1	2-0	2-1	-	1-3	1-3	03-01-02
Kidderminstr	v	Stevenage	3-1	-	-	-	-	-	03-00-03
Scarborough	v	Tamworth	-	-	-	-	0-1	2-2	00-01-01
Southport	v	Crawley	-	-	-	-	-	-	00-00-00
Woking	v	Hereford	0-2	0-3	1-0	1-2	0-1	1-1	02-01-05

SATURDAY 8TH APRIL 2006
FA BARCLAYCARD PREMIER LEAGUE

Aston Villa	v	WBA	-	-	-	2-1	-	1-1	01-01-00
Charlton	v	Everton	-	1-0	1-2	2-1	2-2	2-0	03-01-04
Chelsea	v	West Ham	0-0	4-2	5-1	2-3	-	-	06-01-04
Liverpool	v	Bolton	-	-	1-1	2-0	3-1	1-0	05-01-00
Man Utd	v	Arsenal	1-1	6-1	0-1	2-0	0-0	2-0	08-06-03
Middlesbro	v	Newcastle	2-2	1-3	1-4	1-0	0-1	2-2	04-04-05
Portsmouth	v	Blackburn	1-2	2-2	-	-	1-2	0-1	01-03-04
Sunderland	v	Fulham	-	-	1-1	0-3	-	-	00-01-01
Tottenham	v	Man City	-	0-0	-	0-2	1-1	2-1	06-03-02
Wigan	v	Birmingham	-	-	-	-	-	-	02-01-00

COCA-COLA CHAMPIONSHIP

Brighton	v	Southampton	-	-	-	-	-	-	00-00-00
Burnley	v	QPR	-	2-1	-	-	-	2-0	02-00-00
Cardiff	v	Reading	1-0	-	2-2	-	2-3	2-0	04-01-02
Crewe	v	Sheff Weds	-	1-0	0-2	-	-	-	01-00-01
Derby	v	Millwall	-	-	-	1-2	2-0	0-3	03-02-05
Ipswich	v	Stoke	-	-	-	0-0	1-0	1-0	04-03-01
Leeds	v	Plymouth	-	-	-	-	-	2-1	03-00-00
Leicester	v	Crystal Pal	-	-	-	1-0	-	-	01-03-02
Preston	v	Norwich	-	1-0	4-0	1-2	0-0	-	02-01-01
Sheff Utd	v	Hull	-	-	-	-	-	-	00-01-00
Watford	v	Luton	-	-	-	-	-	-	00-05-01
Wolves	v	Coventry	-	-	3-1	0-2	-	0-1	01-00-02

COCA-COLA LEAGUE 1

Barnsley	v	Chesterfield	-	-	-	2-1	0-1	1-0	02-00-01
Brentford	v	Bradford	-	-	-	-	-	1-2	04-00-02
Gillingham	v	Huddersfield	-	2-1	-	-	-	-	01-00-01
Nottm F	v	Colchester	-	-	-	-	-	-	00-00-00
Oldham	v	Milton K	-	-	-	-	-	3-0	02-01-01
Port Vale	v	Swansea	-	1-0	-	-	-	-	04-00-00
Rotherham	v	Tranmere	-	-	-	-	-	-	00-03-00
Scunthorpe	v	Bournemouth	3-1	-	-	0-2	-	-	01-00-01
Southend	v	Blackpool	-	0-3	-	-	-	-	02-00-01
Swindon	v	Hartlepool	-	-	-	-	1-1	3-0	01-01-00
Walsall	v	Bristol C	-	0-0	-	-	-	1-2	02-02-02
Yeovil	v	Doncaster	1-3	2-0	1-1	1-1	0-1	-	01-03-02

COCA-COLA LEAGUE 2

Barnet	v	Notts Co	-	-	-	-	-	-	00-00-01
Bristol R	v	Rushden & D	-	-	0-3	1-2	-	3-0	01-00-02
Bury	v	Peterboro	-	2-1	2-0	-	-	-	04-00-00
Carlisle	v	Grimsby	-	-	-	-	-	-	01-01-01
Cheltenham	v	Stockport	-	-	-	0-2	-	-	00-00-01
Leyton O	v	Boston	-	-	-	3-2	1-3	0-0	01-01-01
Lincoln	v	Mansfield	3-0	0-2	1-4	-	4-1	2-0	06-01-04
Macclesfield	v	Wycombe	-	-	-	-	-	2-1	03-02-02
Northampton	v	Rochdale	0-1	-	-	-	3-1	5-1	05-02-03
Oxford Utd	v	Chester	-	-	-	-	-	-	01-00-00
Torquay	v	Darlington	1-0	2-1	2-1	3-1	2-2	-	10-03-02
Wrexham	v	Shrewsbury	-	-	-	3-3	-	-	02-02-01

BANK OF SCOTLAND SCOTTISH PREMIER LEAGUE

Aberdeen	v	Hibernian	2-2/4-0	0-2/1-0	2-0	0-1	3-1/0-1	0-1/3-0	15-06-09
Falkirk	v	Dundee Utd	-	-	-	-	-	-	01-01-04
Hearts	v	Dunfermline	-	2-0/7-1	1-1/2-0	2-0/3-0	1-0/2-1	3-0	16-03-02
Kilmarnock	v	Celtic	0-1/1-1	0-1/1-0	0-1/0-2	1-1/0-4	0-5/0-1	2-4/0-1	04-08-12
Livingston	v	Inv CT	2-2/1-1	3-1/4-1	-	-		3-0/1-4	05-04-03
Rangers	v	Motherwell	4-1/6-2	2-0	3-0/3-0	3-0/2-0	1-0/4-0	4-1	28-01-03

BELL'S SCOTTISH FIRST DIVISION

Airdrie Utd	v	Queen of Sth	-	-	-	-	-	0-1/2-0	03-00-01
Brechin	v	St Johnstone	-	-	-	-	0-1/0-2	-	00-00-02
Hamilton	v	Clyde	2-3/1-1	-	-	-	-	0-1/0-1	06-01-04
Ross County	v	St Mirren	-	-	0-1/4-1	4-0/2-0	2-0/1-0	1-1/0-1	05-01-02
Stranraer	v	Dundee	-	-	-	-	-	-	00-00-02

BELL'S SCOTTISH SECOND DIVISION

Alloa	v	Ayr	-	1-1/0-2	-	0-1/2-3	-	1-3/5-1	01-03-04
Morton	v	Partick	-	-	-	-	-	-	06-03-02
Gretna	v	Peterhead	-	-	-	1-4/1-1	3-2/3-2	2-1/6-1	04-01-01
Raith	v	Dumbarton	-	-	-	1-0/2-1	-	-	04-00-00
Stirling	v	Forfar	-	3-3/1-0	-	-	-	3-1/3-2	07-02-01

BELL'S SCOTTISH THIRD DIVISION

Berwick	v	Stenhsmuir	-	4-1/1-0	1-1/2-1	2-2/0-0	2-1/3-0	-	13-06-06
Cowdenb'th	v	Albion	0-0/5-0	5-0/1-0	-	-	1-4/1-1	2-0/1-2	09-08-06
E Stirling	v	East Fife	0-2/1-0	2-5/1-0	2-1/1-2	1-4/0-4	-	1-1/1-0	09-02-08
Elgin	v	Arbroath	-	-	-	-	-	-	00-00-00
Queen's Park	v	Montrose	2-1/1-1	-	2-2/0-1	0-1/1-1	1-1/1-1	1-2/1-0	09-09-08

NATIONWIDE CONFERENCE

Aldershot	v	Cambridge U	-	-	-	-	-	-	00-00-00
Altrincham	v	Gravesend	-	-	-	-	-	-	00-00-00
Crawley	v	Burton	1-4	2-2	-	-	-	4-0	01-08-05
Forest G	v	Accrington	-	-	-	-	2-1	1-0	02-00-00
Grays	v	Exeter	-	-	-	-	-	-	00-00-00
Halifax	v	Southport	-	-	-	3-4	-	-	03-02-01
Hereford	v	Dagenham & R	-	0-1	1-0	2-1	1-1	0-1	02-01-02
Morecambe	v	Woking	1-0	3-0	3-1	5-0	2-1	2-1	06-00-04
Stevenage	v	Scarborough	0-1	1-1	2-0	1-1	2-2	1-0	02-03-01
Tamworth	v	Canvey Islnd	-	-	-	-	-	1-0	01-00-00
York	v	Kidderminstr	-	1-0	0-1	0-0	1-0	-	02-01-01

SATURDAY 15TH APRIL 2006
FA BARCLAYCARD PREMIER LEAGUE

Arsenal	v	WBA	-	-	-	5-2	-	1-1	01-01-00
Aston Villa	v	Birmingham	-	-	-	0-2	2-2	1-2	00-01-02
Blackburn	v	Liverpool	-	-	1-1	2-2	1-3	2-2	04-04-03
Bolton	v	Chelsea	-	-	2-2	1-1	0-2	-	02-02-01
Everton	v	Tottenham	2-2	0-0	1-1	2-2	3-1	0-1	05-07-05
Fulham	v	Charlton	2-1	-	0-0	1-0	2-0	0-0	03-02-00
Man Utd	v	Sunderland	4-0	3-0	4-1	2-1	-	-	06-00-00
Newcastle	v	Wigan	-	-	-	-	-	-	00-00-00
Portsmouth	v	Middlesbro	-	-	-	-	5-1	2-1	05-02-01
West Ham	v	Man City	-	4-1	-	0-0	-	-	04-01-01

COCA-COLA CHAMPIONSHIP

Cardiff	v	Sheff Utd	-	-	-	-	2-1	1-0	02-01-00
Crystal Pal	v	Crewe	1-1	1-0	4-1	-	1-3	-	02-02-01
Hull	v	Burnley	-	-	-	-	-	-	01-00-02
Ipswich	v	Brighton	-	-	-	2-2	-	1-0	03-01-02
Leeds	v	Reading	-	-	-	-	-	3-1	01-00-00

eicester	v	Preston	-	-	-	2-1	-	1-1	01-01-00
uton	v	Coventry	-	-	-	-	-	-	03-01-00
4illwall	v	Plymouth	-	-	-	-	-	3-0	03-02-00
1PR	v	Derby	-	-	-	-	-	0-2	00-01-03
heff Weds	v	Norwich	-	3-2	0-5	2-2	-	-	03-04-02
toke	v	Southampton	-	-	-	-	-	-	00-00-00
Volves	v	Watford	-	2-2	1-0	0-0	-	0-0	04-08-00

COCA-COLA LEAGUE 1

lackpool	v	Swansea	-	-	-	-	-	-	02-04-00
ournemouth	v	Huddersfield	-	-	2-3	-	-	2-2	01-03-03
radford	v	Doncaster	-	-	-	-	-	2-0	01-00-00
hesterfield	v	Colchester	0-1	-	3-6	0-4	1-2	2-1	03-03-04
4artlepool	v	Bristol C	-	-	-	-	1-2	2-1	01-00-01
Idham	v	Barnsley	-	-	-	2-1	1-1	3-2	05-02-02
4otherham	v	Brentford	-	2-1	-	-	-	-	04-01-03
outhend	v	Gillingham	-	-	-	-	-	-	02-01-00
windon	v	Milton K	-	-	-	-	-	2-1	01-00-01
ranmere	v	Nottm F	3-0	2-2	-	-	-	-	01-02-01
Valsall	v	Port Vale	0-0	2-1	-	-	-	3-2	02-01-00
eovil	v	Scunthorpe	-	-	-	-	2-1	4-3	02-00-00

COCA-COLA LEAGUE 2

3ristol R	v	Carlisle	-	-	0-0	1-2	1-0	-	02-02-01
hester	v	Wycombe	-	-	-	-	-	0-2	01-00-02
)arlington	v	Northampton	0-1	-	-	-	1-2	1-1	03-02-04
3rimsby	v	Shrewsbury	-	-	-	-	-	0-1	01-00-01
incoln	v	Bury	-	-	-	1-1	2-1	1-0	02-03-02
4ansfield	v	Leyton O	1-1	2-0	3-2	-	1-1	0-1	04-05-03
4otts Co	v	Macclesfield	-	-	-	-	-	0-5	02-02-01
)xford Utd	v	Barnet	-	-	-	-	-	-	00-00-00
'eterboro	v	Boston	-	-	-	-	-	-	00-00-00
4ushden & D	v	Rochdale	-	-	1-1	3-3	-	0-0	00-03-00
5tockport	v	Wrexham	-	-	-	-	0-1	-	02-02-04
Torquay	v	Cheltenham	1-1	1-2	0-1	-	3-1	-	01-01-02

BELL'S SCOTTISH FIRST DIVISION

Airdrie Utd	v	Stranraer	-	-	-	2-1/3-3	-	-	05-01-00
Clyde	v	Ross County	3-1/0-0	2-2/2-0	3-0/0-0	2-1/1-0	2-2/1-0	1-0/1-0	08-04-00
4amilton	v	Brechin	-	4-1/1-0	-	1-2/2-2	-	-	07-01-01
Queen of Sth	v	St Johnstone	-	-	-	0-0/1-2	1-1/1-1	0-1	00-04-02
St Mirren	v	Dundee	-	2-1/2-1	-	-	-	-	07-03-04

BELL'S SCOTTISH SECOND DIVISION

Dumbarton	v	Ayr	-	-	-	-	-	1-0/1-1	02-04-02
Forfar	v	Gretna	-	-	-	-	-	-	00-00-00
Peterhead	v	Alloa	-	-	-	-	-	-	00-00-00
Raith	v	Morton	3-1/3-0	0-1/0-0	-	-	-	-	09-04-03
Stirling	v	Partick	3-1/0-2	1-1/0-3	-	-	-	-	04-04-04

BELL'S SCOTTISH THIRD DIVISION

Arbroath	v	Albion	-	-	-	-	-	-	07-03-04
Berwick	v	East Fife	0-1/0-1	-	-	-	0-2/1-1	-	03-04-10
Cowdenb'th	v	E Stirling	1-2/0-0	3-0/1-3	-	-	2-1/2-0	2-1/3-2	16-03-06
Montrose	v	Elgin	-	0-0/2-1	0-2/1-0	1-0/2-0	3-3/4-3	2-0/2-0	07-02-01
Stenhsmuir	v	Queen's Park	-	1-1/2-0	-	-	-	1-1/0-0	06-06-03

NATIONWIDE CONFERENCE

Altrincham	v	Hereford	2-1	-	-	-	-	-	01-00-00
Cambridge U	v	York	-	-	-	3-0	2-0	-	03-02-01

Canvey Islnd v	Kidderminstr	-	-	-	-	-	-	00-00-0
Crawley v	Aldershot	-	-	-	-	-	1-0	01-00-0
Exeter v	Dagenham & R	-	-	-	-	1-1	1-1	00-02-0
Grays v	Forest G	-	-	-	-	-	-	00-00-0
Halifax v	Stevenage	-	-	-	1-0	2-1	2-1	05-00-0
Scarborough v	Burton	-	-	-	4-1	1-2	1-1	01-01-0
Southport v	Gravesend	-	-	-	1-1	-	-	00-01-0
Tamworth v	Morecambe	-	-	-	-	2-3	0-0	00-01-0
Woking v	Accrington	-	-	-	-	2-2	2-1	01-01-0

MONDAY 17TH APRIL 2006
FA BARCLAYCARD PREMIER LEAGUE

Birmingham v	Blackburn	1-0	0-2	-	0-1	0-4	-	02-00-0
Charlton v	Portsmouth	1-1	-	-	-	1-1	2-1	08-02-0
Chelsea v	Everton	1-1	2-1	3-0	4-1	0-0	1-0	09-05-0
Liverpool v	Fulham	-	-	0-0	2-0	0-0	3-1	02-02-0
Man City v	Arsenal	-	0-4	-	1-5	1-2	0-1	01-02-0
Middlesbro v	West Ham	2-0	2-1	2-0	2-2	-	-	07-02-0
Sunderland v	Newcastle	2-2	1-1	0-1	0-1	-	-	00-04-0
Tottenham v	Man Utd	3-1	3-1	3-5	0-2	1-2	0-1	04-03-1
WBA v	Bolton	4-4	0-2	-	1-1	-	2-1	03-05-0
Wigan v	Aston Villa	-	-	-	-	-	-	00-00-0

COCA-COLA CHAMPIONSHIP

Brighton v	Sheff Weds	-	-	-	1-1	2-0	-	01-01-0
Burnley v	Crystal Pal	-	1-2	1-0	0-0	2-3	-	01-01-0
Coventry v	Leicester	0-1	1-0	-	1-2	-	1-1	02-03-0
Crewe v	Cardiff	-	-	-	1-1	0-1	2-2	01-05-0
Derby v	Hull	-	-	-	-	-	-	00-00-0
Norwich v	QPR	2-1	1-0	-	-	-	-	07-03-0
Plymouth v	Luton	-	-	2-1	2-1	2-1	-	03-01-0
Preston v	Wolves	-	2-0	1-2	0-2	-	2-2	01-02-0
Reading v	Stoke	1-0	3-3	1-0	1-1	0-0	1-0	08-04-0
Sheff Utd v	Leeds	-	-	-	-	-	2-0	02-02-0
Southampton v	Millwall	-	-	-	-	-	-	00-01-0
Watford v	Ipswich	-	-	-	0-2	1-2	2-2	02-03-0

COCA-COLA LEAGUE 1

Barnsley v	Southend	-	-	-	-	-	-	03-02-01
Brentford v	Blackpool	2-0	-	2-0	5-0	0-0	0-3	08-02-02
Bristol C v	Oldham	1-1	2-2	3-0	2-0	0-2	5-1	04-03-02
Colchester v	Tranmere	-	-	2-1	2-2	1-1	1-2	01-02-02
Doncaster v	Walsall	-	-	-	-	-	3-1	03-00-03
Gillingham v	Bradford	-	-	0-4	1-0	1-0	-	02-00-01
Huddersfield v	Chesterfield	-	-	0-0	4-0	-	0-0	01-03-00
Milton K v	Hartlepool	-	-	-	-	-	4-2	01-00-00
Nottm F v	Yeovil	-	-	-	-	-	-	00-00-00
Port Vale v	Bournemouth	-	2-1	0-0	-	2-1	2-1	05-02-00
Scunthorpe v	Swindon	-	-	-	-	-	-	00-00-00
Swansea v	Rotherham	2-0	0-0	-	-	-	-	05-05-00

COCA-COLA LEAGUE 2

Barnet v	Mansfield	0-0	3-3	-	-	-	-	01-06-01
Boston v	Oxford Utd	-	-	-	1-3	1-1	1-0	01-01-01
Bury v	Chester	-	-	-	-	-	1-1	03-03-01
Carlisle v	Notts Co	-	-	-	-	-	-	00-01-00
Cheltenham v	Darlington	0-0	1-0	0-0	-	2-1	0-2	02-02-02
Leyton O v	Grimsby	-	-	-	-	-	1-2	01-00-02
Macclesfield v	Torquay	1-2	2-1	0-2	3-3	1-1	-	02-02-02

234

Northampton	v	Stockport	-	-	-	0-3	-	-	01-00-01
Rochdale	v	Peterboro	1-2	-	-	-	-	-	00-01-05
Shrewsbury	v	Rushden & D	-	-	0-2	1-1	-	0-1	00-01-02
Wrexham	v	Bristol R	2-1	1-0	-	3-2	-	-	08-01-00
Wycombe	v	Lincoln	-	-	-	-	-	1-0	02-00-01

NATIONWIDE CONFERENCE

Accrington	v	Scarborough	-	-	-	-	1-0	2-1	02-00-00
Aldershot	v	Grays	-	6-0	0-1	2-1	-	-	02-00-01
Burton	v	Southport	-	-	-	1-0	-	-	01-00-00
Dagenham & R	v	Canvey Islnd	2-0	-	-	-	-	3-1	02-00-00
Forest G	v	Exeter	-	-	-	-	2-5	2-3	00-00-02
Gravesend	v	Woking	-	-	-	4-2	2-2	1-1	01-02-00
Hereford	v	Tamworth	-	-	-	-	0-1	2-1	01-00-01
Kidderminstr	v	Cambridge U	-	-	-	2-1	2-2	1-1	01-02-00
Morecambe	v	Altrincham	3-3	-	-	-	-	-	02-01-00
Stevenage	v	Crawley	-	-	-	-	-	1-0	01-00-00
York	v	Halifax	2-0	2-1	1-0	-	-	1-1	04-04-01

SATURDAY 22ND APRIL 2006

FA BARCLAYCARD PREMIER LEAGUE

Arsenal	v	Tottenham	2-1	2-0	2-1	3-0	2-1	1-0	10-06-01
Aston Villa	v	Man City	-	2-2	-	1-0	1-1	-	03-04-03
Blackburn	v	Chelsea	-	-	0-0	2-3	2-3	0-1	05-03-04
Bolton	v	Charlton	0-2	-	0-0	1-2	0-0	4-1	04-02-02
Everton	v	Birmingham	-	-	-	1-1	1-0	1-1	01-02-00
Fulham	v	Wigan	-	-	-	-	-	-	06-03-01
Man Utd	v	Middlesbro	1-0	2-1	0-1	1-0	2-3	1-1	06-02-03
Newcastle	v	WBA	-	-	-	2-1	-	3-1	03-01-00
Portsmouth	v	Sunderland	-	-	-	-	-	-	03-03-03
West Ham	v	Liverpool	1-0	1-1	1-1	0-3	-	-	04-04-04

COCA-COLA CHAMPIONSHIP

Cardiff	v	Norwich	-	-	-	-	2-1	-	01-00-00
Crystal Pal	v	Southampton	-	-	-	-	-	-	03-02-01
Hull	v	Preston	-	-	-	-	-	-	00-01-01
Ipswich	v	Derby	-	0-1	3-1	0-1	2-1	3-2	05-00-02
Leeds	v	Crewe	-	-	-	-	-	0-2	00-00-01
Leicester	v	Plymouth	-	-	-	-	-	2-1	04-01-00
Luton	v	Sheff Utd	-	-	-	-	-	-	02-00-02
Millwall	v	Burnley	1-1	-	0-2	1-1	2-0	-	03-02-03
QPR	v	Watford	-	1-1	-	-	-	3-1	01-01-01
Sheff Weds	v	Reading	-	-	-	3-2	-	-	01-00-00
Stoke	v	Coventry	-	-	-	1-2	1-0	1-0	02-00-01
Wolves	v	Brighton	-	-	-	1-1	-	1-1	01-02-02

COCA-COLA LEAGUE 1

Blackpool	v	Barnsley	-	-	-	1-2	0-2	-	00-00-02
Bournemouth	v	Colchester	4-0	2-2	0-1	-	1-1	1-3	02-02-02
Bradford	v	Port Vale	-	-	-	-	-	0-2	05-01-01
Chesterfield	v	Milton K	-	-	-	-	-	2-2	00-01-00
Hartlepool	v	Nottm F	-	-	-	-	-	-	00-00-00
Oldham	v	Swansea	-	1-1	-	-	-	-	00-01-00
Rotherham	v	Scunthorpe	-	-	-	-	-	-	01-02-01
Southend	v	Doncaster	-	-	-	-	0-2	-	01-00-01
Swindon	v	Brentford	-	2-3	2-0	2-1	2-1	3-0	04-01-02
Tranmere	v	Bristol C	-	-	1-0	1-1	1-0	0-1	05-04-01
Walsall	v	Huddersfield	2-0	-	-	-	-	4-3	02-00-01
Yeovil	v	Gillingham	-	-	-	-	-	-	00-00-00

COCA-COLA LEAGUE 2

Bristol R	v	Boston	-	-	-	1-1	2-0	1-1	01-02-00
Chester	v	Barnet	0-2	-	1-0	1-1	1-0	-	04-01-03
Darlington	v	Bury	-	-	-	3-1	1-3	1-2	03-01-04
Grimsby	v	Cheltenham	-	-	-	-	-	1-1	00-01-00
Lincoln	v	Leyton O	0-0	2-3	2-0	1-1	0-0	3-4	03-04-03
Mansfield	v	Carlisle	1-1	1-1	2-0	-	2-3	-	02-04-03
Notts Co	v	Rochdale	-	-	-	-	-	0-0	01-01-00
Oxford Utd	v	Northampton	-	3-1	-	-	3-0	1-2	02-00-01
Peterboro	v	Macclesfield	2-2	-	-	-	-	-	00-01-01
Rushden & D	v	Wycombe	-	-	-	-	2-0	1-2	01-00-01
Stockport	v	Shrewsbury	-	-	-	-	-	-	02-00-02
Torquay	v	Wrexham	-	-	-	2-1	-	1-0	03-02-01

BELL'S SCOTTISH FIRST DIVISION

Brechin	v	Queen of Sth	-	-	-	-	0-1/2-1	-	04-03-05
Dundee	v	Clyde	-	-	-	-	-	-	01-00-00
Ross County	v	Airdrie Utd	-	1-1/3-4	0-1/4-1	-	-	1-2/3-1	02-01-03
St Johnstone	v	Hamilton	-	-	-	-	-	3-0/0-2	05-01-01
Stranraer	v	St Mirren	-	-	-	-	-	-	00-01-03

BELL'S SCOTTISH SECOND DIVISION

Alloa	v	Dumbarton	-	-	-	-	1-2/3-0	3-2/4-2	06-00-04
Ayr	v	Forfar	-	-	-	-	-	3-3/1-0	04-05-01
Morton	v	Stirling	-	-	-	5-1/2-2	-	3-0/2-0	07-06-03
Gretna	v	Raith	-	-	-	-	-	-	00-00-00
Partick	v	Peterhead	-	-	-	-	-	-	00-00-00

BELL'S SCOTTISH THIRD DIVISION

Albion	v	Montrose	1-3/0-2	3-2/2-1	0-0/0-0	1-1/3-0	0-1/3-0	1-2/1-2	09-06-11
East Fife	v	Arbroath	-	-	-	-	0-1/1-2	-	04-02-07
E Stirling	v	Berwick	0-3/0-1	-	-	-	-	-	07-03-05
Elgin	v	Stenhsmuir	-	-	-	-	-	1-1	00-01-00
Queen's Park	v	Cowdenbeath	1-0/3-1	-	-	-	0-0/1-2	3-2/2-3	12-03-08

NATIONWIDE CONFERENCE

Accrington	v	Tamworth	-	-	-	-	3-0	2-3	01-00-01
Aldershot	v	Woking	-	-	-	-	2-1	4-0	02-00-00
Altrincham	v	Grays	-	-	-	-	-	-	00-00-00
Burton	v	Forest G	-	-	-	2-3	2-3	4-1	02-00-02
Canvey Islnd	v	Exeter	-	-	-	-	-	2-2	00-01-00
Crawley	v	Halifax	-	-	-	-	-	1-2	00-00-01
Dagenham & R	v	Kidderminstr	-	-	-	-	-	-	02-01-01
Hereford	v	Southport	2-1	0-0	0-0	0-2	-	-	01-04-01
Morecambe	v	Gravesend	-	-	-	2-0	2-2	1-3	01-01-01
Scarborough	v	Cambridge U	-	-	-	-	-	-	04-01-01
Stevenage	v	York	-	-	-	-	-	2-2	00-01-00

SATURDAY 29TH APRIL 2006
FA BARCLAYCARD PREMIER LEAGUE

Birmingham	v	Newcastle	-	-	-	0-2	1-1	2-2	00-02-02
Charlton	v	Blackburn	1-2	-	0-2	3-1	3-2	1-0	03-02-03
Chelsea	v	Man Utd	5-0	1-1	0-3	2-2	1-0	1-0	06-05-05
Liverpool	v	Aston Villa	0-0	3-1	1-3	1-1	1-0	-	09-04-03
Man City	v	Fulham	4-0	-	-	4-1	0-0	1-1	03-02-00
Middlesbro	v	Everton	2-1	1-2	1-0	1-1	1-0	1-1	04-04-03
Sunderland	v	Arsenal	0-0	1-0	1-1	0-4	-	-	02-03-01
Tottenham	v	Bolton	-	-	3-2	3-1	0-1	1-2	03-01-02
WBA	v	West Ham	-	-	-	1-2	1-1	-	00-02-02
Wigan	v	Portsmouth	-	-	-	-	-	-	00-00-00

236

COCA-COLA LEAGUE 1

Home		Away							Record
Barnsley	v	Bradford	-	-	3-3	-	-	2-2	02-03-01
Brentford	v	Hartlepool	-	-	-	-	2-1	2-1	05-00-00
Bristol C	v	Swindon	-	0-1	3-1	2-0	2-1	1-2	05-03-03
Colchester	v	Rotherham	-	0-1	-	-	-	-	01-01-01
Doncaster	v	Oldham	-	-	-	-	-	1-1	00-01-00
Gillingham	v	Walsall	-	-	2-0	0-1	3-0	-	06-01-04
Huddersfield	v	Yeovil	-	-	-	-	3-1	-	01-00-00
Milton K	v	Tranmere	-	0-0	-	-	-	-	00-01-00
Nottm F	v	Bournemouth	-	-	-	-	-	-	00-00-00
Port Vale	v	Chesterfield	-	-	4-1	5-2	1-1	1-0	04-01-00
Scunthorpe	v	Blackpool	1-0	1-0	-	-	-	-	04-00-00
Swansea	v	Southend	3-1	-	3-2	1-0	2-3	1-1	05-01-02

COCA-COLA LEAGUE 2

Home		Away							Record
Barnet	v	Stockport	-	-	-	-	-	-	00-01-00
Boston	v	Rushden & D	-	1-1	-	1-1	-	1-0	01-02-00
Bury	v	Mansfield	-	-	-	-	3-0	0-2	03-02-03
Carlisle	v	Torquay	0-0	1-0	2-0	1-2	2-0	-	09-02-02
Cheltenham	v	Notts Co	-	-	-	1-4	-	0-2	00-00-02
Leyton O	v	Peterboro	1-1	-	-	-	-	-	02-01-03
Macclesfield	v	Grimsby	-	-	-	-	-	3-1	01-00-00
Northampton	v	Chester	3-1	-	-	-	-	1-1	05-01-01
Rochdale	v	Bristol R	-	-	2-1	1-1	2-2	0-0	01-03-00
Shrewsbury	v	Lincoln	1-2	3-2	1-1	1-2	-	0-1	02-01-05
Wrexham	v	Oxford Utd	1-0	5-3	-	1-0	-	-	05-00-00
Wycombe	v	Darlington	-	-	-	-	-	1-1	01-01-01

BELL'S SCOTTISH FIRST DIVISION

Home		Away							Record
Airdrie Utd	v	Brechin	-	-	-	2-4/3-0	-	-	03-00-02
Clyde	v	Stranraer	0-0/1-1	-	-	-	-	-	03-06-02
Hamilton	v	Ross County	1-0/0-3	-	-	-	-	1-2/0-1	01-00-03
Queen of Sth	v	Dundee	-	-	-	-	-	-	00-00-00
St Mirren	v	St Johnstone	-	0-1/1-0	-	0-2/1-3	1-1/1-1	2-1/1-1	03-08-07

BELL'S SCOTTISH SECOND DIVISION

Home		Away							Record
Dumbarton	v	Partick	-	-	-	-	-	-	00-00-00
Forfar	v	Morton	-	-	2-1/2-1	-	2-3/2-1	2-0/0-0	05-03-05
Peterhead	v	Ayr	-	-	-	-	-	-	00-00-00
Raith	v	Alloa	-	1-2/2-1	-	-	-	-	01-01-01
Stirling	v	Gretna	-	-	-	0-1/1-0	0-1/0-1	-	01-00-03

BELL'S SCOTTISH THIRD DIVISION

Home		Away							Record
Arbroath	v	E Stirling	-	-	-	-	-	-	06-07-04
Berwick	v	Queen's Park	1-2/1-1	1-1/1-0	-	-	-	-	06-05-06
Cowdenb'th	v	Elgin	-	3-1/1-0	-	-	3-2/2-0	3-1/1-1	05-01-00
Montrose	v	East Fife	1-2/1-1	0-1/1-1	2-1/0-1	0-5/0-2	-	2-1	03-04-11
Stenhsmuir	v	Albion	-	-	-	-	-	3-0/1-1	06-03-03

NATIONWIDE CONFERENCE

Home		Away							Record
Cambridge U	v	Dagenham & R	-	-	-	-	-	-	00-00-00
Exeter	v	Scarborough	-	-	-	-	0-0	3-1	06-03-00
Forest G	v	Stevenage	3-2	2-3	0-0	0-3	3-1	1-1	02-02-03
Gravesend	v	Burton	-	-	-	3-2	1-2	0-2	02-01-06
Grays	v	Morecambe	-	-	-	-	-	-	00-00-00
Halifax	v	Canvey Islnd	-	-	-	-	-	4-1	01-00-00
Kidderminstr	v	Accrington	-	-	-	-	-	-	00-00-00
Southport	v	Aldershot	-	-	-	-	-	-	00-00-00
Tamworth	v	Crawley	3-0	0-2	2-0	1-1	-	1-0	05-01-01
Woking	v	Altrincham	0-1	-	-	-	-	-	03-01-02
York	v	Hereford	-	-	-	-	-	0-3	04-00-02

SUNDAY 30TH APRIL 2006
COCA-COLA CHAMPIONSHIP

Brighton	v	Stoke	-	-	1-0	1-2	-	0-1	01-02-03
Burnley	v	Luton	0-2	-	-	-	-	-	01-01-03
Coventry	v	Cardiff	-	-	-	-	1-3	1-1	00-01-01
Crewe	v	Millwall	-	-	1-0	-	1-2	2-1	02-01-01
Derby	v	Sheff Weds	3-3	-	-	2-2	-	-	04-03-00
Norwich	v	Wolves	1-0	1-0	2-0	0-3	-	-	04-01-03
Plymouth	v	Ipswich	-	-	-	-	-	1-2	02-01-02
Preston	v	Leeds	-	-	-	-	-	2-4	00-00-01
Reading	v	QPR	-	-	1-0	-	-	1-0	03-00-01
Sheff Utd	v	Crystal Pal	3-1	1-0	1-3	2-1	0-3	-	04-02-05
Southampton	v	Leicester	1-2	1-0	2-2	-	0-0	-	03-04-01
Watford	v	Hull	-	-	-	-	-	-	02-00-01

SATURDAY 6TH MAY 2006
COCA-COLA LEAGUE 1

Blackpool	v	Gillingham	1-1	-	-	-	-	-	05-02-00
Bournemouth	v	Brentford	4-1	2-0	0-2	-	1-0	3-2	07-02-03
Bradford	v	Nottm F	-	-	2-1	1-0	1-2	-	02-00-02
Chesterfield	v	Swansea	-	-	-	-	-	-	02-00-00
Hartlepool	v	Port Vale	-	-	-	-	2-0	1-0	02-01-01
Oldham	v	Scunthorpe	1-1	-	-	-	-	-	00-01-00
Rotherham	v	Milton K	-	-	3-2	2-1	3-1	-	03-00-00
Southend	v	Bristol C	-	-	-	-	-	-	01-02-03
Swindon	v	Huddersfield	2-0	-	0-1	0-1	-	1-2	03-01-03
Tranmere	v	Doncaster	-	-	-	-	-	2-4	00-01-01
Walsall	v	Barnsley	1-4	-	2-1	-	-	2-2	01-01-02
Yeovil	v	Colchester	-	-	-	-	-	-	01-00-01

COCA-COLA LEAGUE 2

Bristol R	v	Macclesfield	-	-	0-2	1-1	2-2	0-0	00-04-01
Chester	v	Shrewsbury	0-0	-	-	-	2-1	1-1	05-03-02
Darlington	v	Wrexham	-	-	-	0-1	-	-	02-01-01
Grimsby	v	Northampton	-	-	-	-	-	1-2	01-00-01
Lincoln	v	Rochdale	1-1	1-1	1-1	2-0	1-1	1-1	03-07-06
Mansfield	v	Cheltenham	0-1	2-1	2-1	0-2	4-0	1-2	03-00-03
Notts Co	v	Bury	2-2	1-0	1-2	-	-	-	02-01-03
Oxford Utd	v	Leyton O	-	-	1-1	0-2	2-1	2-2	02-02-01
Peterboro	v	Wycombe	-	3-2	2-1	1-2	1-1	-	04-01-02
Rushden & D	v	Barnet	-	-	-	-	-	-	00-00-00
Stockport	v	Carlisle	-	-	-	-	-	-	03-01-00
Torquay	v	Boston	-	-	-	1-1	2-0	-	01-01-00

SUNDAY 7TH MAY 2006
FA BARCLAYCARD PREMIER LEAGUE

Arsenal	v	Wigan	-	-	-	-	-	-	00-00-00
Aston Villa	v	Sunderland	1-1	0-0	0-0	1-0	-	-	03-03-00
Blackburn	v	Man City	1-4	-	-	1-0	2-3	0-0	05-01-03
Bolton	v	Birmingham	3-3	2-2	-	4-2	0-1	1-1	05-05-01
Everton	v	WBA	-	-	-	1-0	-	2-1	02-00-00
Fulham	v	Middlesbro	-	-	2-1	1-0	3-2	0-2	03-00-01
Man Utd	v	Charlton	-	2-1	0-0	4-1	2-0	2-0	07-01-00
Newcastle	v	Chelsea	0-1	0-0	1-2	2-1	2-1	-	06-02-03
Portsmouth	v	Liverpool	-	-	-	-	1-0	1-2	01-00-01
West Ham	v	Tottenham	1-0	0-0	0-1	2-0	-	-	06-02-04

Sponsored by Stan James